MW00630286

The Amazin' Mets,
1962–1969

ALSO BY WILLIAM J. RYCZEK
AND FROM MCFARLAND

The Yankees in the Early 1960s (2007)

*When Johnny Came Sliding Home:
The Post–Civil War Baseball Boom, 1865–1870*
(1998; softcover 2006)

*Blackguards and Red Stockings: A History of
Baseball's National Association, 1871–1875*
(1992; softcover 1999)

The Amazin' Mets, 1962–1969

William J. Ryczek

McFarland & Company, Inc., Publishers

Jefferson, North Carolina, and London

All of the photographs used in this book were provided by the
National Baseball Hall of Fame Library, Cooperstown, New York

LIBRARY OF CONGRESS CATALOGUING-IN-PUBLICATION DATA

Ryczek, William J., 1953–
The amazin' Mets, 1962–1969 / William J. Ryczek.
p.   cm.
Includes bibliographical references and index.

ISBN-13: 978-0-7864-3214-1
softcover : 50# alkaline paper ∞

1. New York Mets (Baseball team)   2. New York Mets (Baseball
team)—History.   I. Title.
GV875.N45R93   2008   796.357'64097471—dc22   2007027474

British Library cataloguing data are available

©2008 William J. Ryczek. All rights reserved

*No part of this book may be reproduced or transmitted in any form
or by any means, electronic or mechanical, including photocopying
or recording, or by any information storage and retrieval system,
without permission in writing from the publisher.*

On the cover: Marv Throneberry pretending to reach for a throw at first base
(National Baseball Hall of Fame Library, Cooperstown, New York)

Manufactured in the United States of America

*McFarland & Company, Inc., Publishers
Box 611, Jefferson, North Carolina 28640
www.mcfarlandpub.com*

To the memory of William F. Cotter, Sr.,
who for the first ten years of my life
gave me the unqualified love
only a grandfather can provide

Acknowledgments

First and foremost, I owe a huge debt to those who graciously agreed to be interviewed for this book. They include:

Craig Anderson	Shaun Fitzmaurice	Fred Kipp	Bobby Pfeil
George Altman	Larry Foss	Bobby Klaus	Jim Pisoni
Dennis Bennett	Bob Friend	Lou Klimchock	Dennis Ribant
Jim Bethke	Rob Gardner	Gary Kroll	Gordon Richardson
John Blanchard	Rod Gaspar	Clem Labine	Les Rohr
Len Boehmer	Jake Gibbs	Jack Lamabe	Don Rowe
Don Bosch	Joe Ginsberg	Frank Lary	Dick Rusteck
Ed Bressoud	Jim Gosger	Phil Linz	Dick Schofield
Hector Brown	Bill Graham	Ron Locke	Ted Schreiber
Bill Bryan	Eli Grba	Hector Lopez	Bob Shaw
Larry Burright	Joe Grzenda	Al Luplow	Norm Sherry
Don Cardwell	Bob Heise	Felix Mantilla	Tom Shopay
Duke Carmel	Bob Hendley	J.C. Martin	Billy Short
Harry Chiti	Bill Hepler	Jim McAndrew	Bobby Gene Smith
Joe Christopher	Rick Herrscher	Danny McDevitt	Tracy Stallard
Galen Cisco	Jim Hickman	Gil McDougald	John Stephenson
Billy Cowan	Joe Hicks	Tom Metcalf	John Sullivan
Bud Daley	Chuck Hiller	Bob Meyer	Darrell Sutherland
Joe DeMaestri	Dave Hillman	Pete Mikkelsen	Hawk Taylor
John DeMerit	Jerry Hinsley	Larry Miller	Ron Taylor
Bill Denehy	Jay Hook	Bob Miller	Sammy Taylor
Jack DiLauro	Ron Hunt	Herb Moford	Ralph Terry
Ryne Duren	Al Jackson	Bill Monbouquette	Frank Thomas
Doc Edwards	Johnny James	Joe Moock	Lee Thomas
Dave Eilers	Ken Johnson	Al Moran	Tom Tresh
John Ellis	Bob Johnson	Dennis Musgraves	Bill Wakefield
Chuck Estrada	Sherman Jones	Don Nottebart	Gordon White
Jack Fisher	Rod Kanehl	Nate Oliver	Nick Willhite

While all of the interview subjects shed a light on some aspect of the Met experience, many were especially helpful in developing certain areas of the book. Craig Anderson, Jay Hook and

Bob Miller made possible the chapter called "The Three Wise Men and the Two Bob Millers." I leaned heavily on the accounts of J.C. Martin, Bobby Pfeil, Rod Gaspar, Jim McAndrew and Jack DiLauro for the story of the 1969 pennant race. Each had terrific recall and a great sense of humor.

Donn Clendenon, who has since passed away, was too ill to be interviewed, but was kind enough to send a copy of his autobiography. Rod Kanehl who, unfortunately, like Clendenon, is no longer with us, was a revelation. I expected a carefree, happy-go-lucky sort, but instead encountered a thoughtful, introspective man who provided terrific insight into many personalities on the early Mets.

Others who provided particularly interesting interviews were Larry Miller, Shaun Fitzmaurice, Frank Thomas, Jack Fisher, Bill Wakefield, Joe Christopher, Bill Denehy and Galen Cisco. I'm certain I have omitted a few others, but the people listed above had interesting insights and stories that set them apart. Denehy has written his memoirs, and I wish him the best of luck with them.

Gordon White, a New York sportswriter for many years, was once again very generous in sharing his memories of covering New York baseball in the 1960s.

As this book was researched and written simultaneously with *The Yankees in the Early 1960s*, those who assisted in the research of that book also helped with this one. They include the research staffs of the Wallingford Public Library, the New York Public Library and the Central Connecticut State University Library.

I want to thank my colleague and friend Fred Dauch, who undertook the tedious chore of reading the entire manuscript in rough draft. Fred was once again the provider of sound, practical and sometimes blunt advice from the reader's perspective.

Finally, I want to thank my wife, Susan, who allowed me the freedom to spend thousands of hours researching and writing about a subject that gave me so much pleasure during my childhood and adolescence. From a wife's perspective, writing is better than gambling or philandering, but not as admirable as mowing the lawn or fixing the railing on the laundry room stairs. Thank you for looking the other way.

Table of Contents

Introduction

In the summer of 1963, when we were nine years old, my best friend Harold and I decided to write fan letters to major league baseball players. Our favorite teams were the Yankees and Mets, but we didn't think Mickey Mantle and Whitey Ford would have time to write to a couple of grammar school kids. So we picked the Mets, who were wallowing deep in the National League basement. Harold wrote to Duke Snider, the white-haired former Brooklyn star who was lumbering painfully around the Polo Grounds outfield on damaged knees. Harold wasn't a big fan, and Duke was one of the few players he knew. I decided to write to Tim Harkness, the Mets' semi-regular first baseman. I played first base and Harkness had just won a game with a grand slam home run, so he seemed a natural choice. I told him how much I liked the Mets, congratulated him on his home run, and asked if he could give me some tips on playing first base.

We sent the letters, and a couple of weeks later I was at Harold's house when the mail arrived. Stuffed into a large envelope addressed from the Polo Grounds was a big, glossy, autographed picture of the Duke. We were elated. Any day, I knew, I would receive an autographed picture of Harkness, along with some advice on scooping low throws out of the dirt, and maybe a couple of batting tips.

The weeks went by, however, with no word from New York. Maybe Tim was busy during the season and waited until the winter to answer his fan mail. The season ended, the autumn leaves fell, and the winter snow followed. Still no letter. In 1964, Harkness was sent to San Diego, leaving with a vicious broadside against Casey Stengel. He played a few more years in the minors, then retired. Even in retirement, Harkness didn't find the time to answer my letter.

The decades flew by. Harold went on to a long military career, retirement and teaching. I went into the finance business and began writing books on sports history, but never, after the Harkness episode, sent another fan letter to an athlete.

In 2001, when I began to conduct interviews for this book, I wrote to Harkness, now living in Ontario, Canada. In return, I received a long letter on the stationery of the San Diego Padres. Tim was scouting for the Padres and had drafted his memoirs. Was I interested in collaborating with him? I called Harkness, and found him to be a pleasant, down-to-earth fellow. I mentioned the long ago letter and he laughed. "The stars like Snider had other people answering their mail," he said. "Guys like me — they probably threw mine away." I laughed too, and told him I'd like to look at his manuscript. "One more thing," I said. Could he send that autographed picture I'd waited almost 40 years for? Of course he could.

A few days later, a large package arrived. I took out the manuscript, reached inside the envelope and felt around. I held it up and shook it. There was no picture.

Despite the missing Harkness picture, I plunged forward, interviewing countless players I'd watched as a young boy. I was once asked during a radio interview whether I thought the game of baseball had changed since we were young. I said that the game was certainly different, but the biggest reason we sense it has changed is that *we* are different. We will never see baseball in middle age as we saw it in our youth, when a ninth inning loss to the Pirates in May brought about the deepest despair, the kind we later experience only upon lost love, the loss of a job, or a publisher's unjust rejection. Occasionally, when my team suffers a particularly tough loss, I feel that youthful heartache again, but it is rare. For the most part, we turn off the television and get on with life.

Nearly all baseball fans remember the teams of their youth with far greater clarity than they recall the players on last year's club. Those were the days before we worried about careers, finances, families and other concerns of responsible adults. We studied *The Sporting News* each week, and fretted over the slump of that promising, power-hitting first baseman in Double A ball. He hadn't hit a home run in two weeks. Had they found his weakness?

The prevailing memories of the Mets during the 1960s are their comical first season of 1962 and the miraculous happenings of 1969. Real baseball fans recall much more about the decade. There were the center fielders: Jim Hickman, a shy, talented youngster from Tennessee, who struggled to realize his great potential in New York, and Don Bosch, a slim, nervous youngster unfairly billed as a superstar, who fought the curse of bloated expectations.

There are a number of delightful and seldom-told stories. In 1962, the Mets had a pitching staff that, while they finished last in the league in earned run average, could have defeated any National League staff in a round of *Jeopardy*. Jay Hook was a rocket scientist who sometimes surrendered home runs with jet propulsion. Ken MacKenzie was the self-proclaimed lowest paid member of the Yale class of 1956. Craig Anderson and Bob Miller now hold masters' degrees. The story of these men, who had high IQs and even higher ERAs, is told in Chapter 5, "The Three Wise Men and the Two Bob Millers."

Nearly all of the players I spoke with enjoyed the opportunity to reminisce. "This is the kind of stuff I never do anymore," said Hook. "I hardly talk baseball at all." Said Joe Christopher, "You're trying to bring me out of mothballs."

"Geez," said Dick Rusteck, "you really brought back some stuff." "Oh, gosh, this has been fun," said Rick Herrscher, who inquired about the whereabouts of former teammates and asked to be remembered to them.

I called Met reliever Sherman (Roadblock) Jones, who spent the first few weeks of the 1962 season in New York, and asked if he could spend a half hour or so talking about his Met career. "That won't take a half hour," he said, laughing. Several players began the interview with a disclaimer. "You're talking to someone who's seventy years old," said Ed Bressoud, "and we don't remember a lot of things." He then named players he followed in the Pacific Coast League during his youth and recounted detail after detail of his long career with amazing clarity.

I found the recollection of those who played only briefly in the major leagues to be extremely detailed, and discovered almost a direct inverse relationship between the length of major league tenure and the quality and detail of the interview. "That's what I would have expected," said Met pitcher Jim McAndrew, "because the shorter the tenure, the more impressionistic the time is upon the individual. If you're around for twenty years, a few moments might be no big deal. If you were around for three years, it might have been the focal point of your entire life. If you call Jack DiLauro or Bobby Pfeil from our '69 team, I'll bet they remember every minute." He was absolutely correct, for both DiLauro and Pfeil gave excellent, detailed accounts of the Mets' dramatic run to the World Series title.

During the course of many interviews, I learned more than I could have imagined about baseball of the 1960s. "I'm letting you in on some good stuff, here, boy," said ex–Dodger Nate

Oliver. I learned about hitting, I learned about managing, and I absorbed so much pitching knowledge that, had I been 30 years younger, I perhaps could have gone out and thrown a few innings myself. I'd gut it out for nine, like they did in the old days, and if anyone tried to lunge across the plate on me, I'd knock him on his kiester, just like Gibson and Drysdale.

This is a book of digressions, which seems appropriate for a story in which Casey Stengel plays such a major role. Although Dick Stuart, a certifiable character, spent only a short period with the Mets, his eccentricities were worth a brief diversion. Bob Shaw's adventures with the spitball led to a discussion of the wet delivery, and so on. I hope the reader will come with me as I wander across the landscape of a remarkable decade.

• 1 •

The Team Has Come
Along Slow but Fast

Even in 1962, when the Mets were the laughingstock of baseball, they had little difficulty drawing fans. People from Brooklyn and New York came not just to see the Mets, but to watch their old heroes from the Giants and Dodgers, only five years removed from the metropolis. They came to see Willie Mays and Duke Snider, and wound up falling in love with Rod Kanehl and Marv Throneberry.

Met fans adored their team, lived and died through the futile late inning rallies that were characteristic of the early clubs, and possessed a zaniness that had been characteristic of the old Brooklyn faithful. Still, during the first few years of the Mets' existence, the Giants and Dodgers were the big draws. In 1962, the Mets' attendance was 922,000, a remarkable figure for a team that lost 120 games. Forty percent came to see the two West Coast teams. When clubs like the Cubs, Phillies and Colts visited the Polo Grounds, attendance was meager. The Mets closed out their home season with their 116th loss of the season before just 3,744 fans. The day before, attendance had been 3,562.

By 1969, fans were coming to see the Mets, no matter who they played. Even Truman Capote knew who they were. "They're going to win a pennant or something," he said. "That's nice." In that final year of the decade, the year a man first landed on the moon, 400,000 people congregated at Woodstock to celebrate peace and love, and Richard Nixon was inaugurated as the President of the United States, the Mets landed in first place, perhaps the most astonishing happening of that incredible year. Young pitchers Tom Seaver, Jerry Koosman and Gary Gentry were nearly unhittable, and, at last, the team found miraculous ways to win games rather than lose them.

The Met tale in microcosm consists of two season ending games in Chicago. Prior to the Mets' first year, people kept asking Stengel where he thought his club would finish. "In Chicago," he would tell them, "on September 30th." Sure enough, on September 30, 1962, the maiden Met club closed the season by losing its 120th game at Wrigley Field, before 3,960 spectators. The Mets were buried deep in the cellar, and the Cubs were one rung above them in ninth place. Trailing 5–1 in the eighth inning, the Mets rallied. Sammy Drake led off with a pinch-hit single and Richie Ashburn followed with another hit. Catcher Joe Pignatano hit a broken bat, looping line drive into short right field, and Drake and Ashburn took off. So did Cubs second baseman Ken Hubbs, who made a fine catch and threw to Ernie Banks at first for a double play. Banks threw to shortstop Andre Rodgers, who stepped on second. Drake had already rounded third and the Cubs had an easy triple play. The game concluded with the score still 5–1, and with the end of the game came the end of Pignatano's major league career. In his final at bat, in true Met fashion, he had accounted for three outs.*

The veteran catcher played two seasons in the International League, then joined former teammate Gil Hodges as a coach with the Washington Senators. When Hodges became manager of the Mets in 1968, Pignatano came with him as bullpen coach. He was seated in the Met bullpen in the right field corner of Wrigley Field on October 2, 1969, as the Mets again finished the season against the Cubs. In 1962, the Mets had suffered their 120th defeat on the final day, but in 1969, they entered the last game with just 61 losses, against 100 victories. As they had in 1962, the Mets lost to the Cubs and, as in 1962, the result was meaningless, but for a different reason. Over the prior six weeks, New York had overcome a 9½ game Cub lead to win the first championship of the National League's Eastern Division.

In the Mets' first base coaching box stood Yogi Berra, who, as the first World Series of the decade ended, stood in his Yankee uniform against the left field wall at Forbes Field and watched Bill Mazeroski's home run sail over his head, bracing himself for a carom that never came. Now Berra was a Met. Not only had the Yankees lost their supremacy on the field, they had committed a number of public relations blunders that enabled the Mets to hire George Weiss, Berra, and most important of all, the man who created the Met image, Casey Stengel.

Two weeks after the regular season ended, the Mets stunned the baseball world by winning the World Series. The strength of the team was its pitching. Tom Seaver captured the Cy Young Award, and Jerry Koosman was not far behind, but the miracle of the Mets was accomplished by 25 players. There were no superstars on the offensive platoon, but manager Hodges displayed a nearly flawless knack for selecting the right pinch hitter or the perfect substitute off the bench. All season, one night after another, a new hero would appear at the crucial moment to pull a key game out of the fire. Rod Gaspar, J.C. Martin, Al Weis, Ed Charles and the much-maligned Ed Kranepool came through time and time again and made Hodges a genius.

How did it happen? How did a team that had never finished higher than ninth win the World Series? The outward manifestation of change came with remarkable suddenness. The Mets added Rookie of the Year Seaver in 1967, but still finished last. They added Koosman, plus manager Hodges, in 1968, and finished ninth. The following year, they won the World Series in five stunning games.

While the results had not been apparent, there had been forces which quietly gathered the momentum needed to achieve the sudden outward reversal of fortune. As Casey Stengel said in 1969, after the Mets had clinched the division title, "The team has come along slow but fast." The Mets, as they continued to lose, patiently assembled a formidable young pitching staff in an era when pitching dominated the game of baseball. Beginning in 1964, the Mets brought an unending wave of young pitching prospects to the major leagues. Some had arm trouble. Some simply couldn't win in the big leagues. But the Mets kept trying, and eventually found the right combination.

Still, virtually no one, even those intimately involved with the Mets' rise, predicted the dazzling accomplishments of 1969. After remarkable events, experts, with flawless hindsight, invariably put forth the reasons that logically explain the inexplicable. No one, however, could put their finger on what had enabled the Mets to change from patsies to champions. It was fate; it was a miracle; it was destiny. But was it foreseeable? Read on, and draw your own conclusions.

*That was also the final major league game for Ashburn and Drake.

◆ 2 ◆

The New York Beatniks
The Mets Are Born

Almost from the moment the Giants and Dodgers left town in 1957, New York began its quest to obtain another major league team. Mayor Robert Wagner assembled a committee consisting of former Postmaster General Jim Farley, retailer Bernard Gimbel, attorney William Shea and Clint Blume, with a mission to bring baseball back to New York. By 1959, the most promising opportunity was the Continental League, a circuit which, under legendary baseball executive Branch Rickey, was planning to compete with the two established major leagues. Bill Shea was to head the local Continental League franchise, under the majority ownership of Mrs. Joan Whitney Payson.

The Continental League, a product of the major leagues' continuing refusal to expand, tried to co-operate with the American and National Leagues. When organized baseball demanded outrageous indemnities to permit Continental League franchises in cities already occupied by professional clubs (including minor league franchises), the new league took the battle to Congress. With their encouragement, Senator Estes Kefauver of Tennessee introduced a bill which would have severely limited the reserve clause by restricting the number of players who could be under contract to any organization to one hundred. The bill would also have given the players more freedom of movement. It was the threat major league baseball had feared for 40 years. Commissioner Ford Frick said it would destroy the minor leagues.

In July, 1960, with Congress nipping at its heels, the National League voted to expand to ten teams, which practically assured New York a franchise and effectively doomed the Continental League, for the expansion would take two of the principal territories of the Continentals. In August, 1960, the Continentals held a monumental meeting with the two major leagues in Chicago, at which they agreed to suspend operations. In return, the existing leagues promised to expand in 1961 or 1962 to include four Continental League cities. Although the four cities were not identified, it was considered a near certainty that New York would be one of them. Minneapolis, Houston and Toronto were given the best chance to obtain the other three franchises. It was expected that the new clubs would not begin play until 1962, given the need to select cities, find suitable places to play and stock the teams with players.

New Yorkers always expected that, if they obtained a new franchise, it would be in the National League, since the American League already had the Yankees. On October 11, 1960, New York stockbroker Donald Grant made a formal application for a National League franchise on behalf of Mrs. Payson, a longtime Giant fan, a former Giant stockholder, and a great admirer of Willie Mays. "When the Giants moved to San Francisco," she once said, "it killed me." Grant, a Giant director, had cast the lone dissenting vote against the move to San Francisco.

7

The 57-year-old daughter of financier Payne Whitney, and sister of John Hay Whitney, Ambassador to Great Britain, Mrs. Payson was a member of the highest caste of New York society. Her brother owned *The New York Herald Tribune*. Her mother was Helen Hay Whitney, daughter of John Hay, secretary to Abraham Lincoln and Secretary of State under McKinley. Her paternal grandfather, William Whitney, was Grover Cleveland's Secretary of the Navy.

When Mrs. Payson's father died in 1927, he bequeathed her an estate valued at $239 million, which left the young heiress plenty of time for leisure activity. She was co-owner of a stable which produced a long line of thoroughbred race horses, and took part in virtually all of the activities popular with the rich and famous, including art collecting and assisting and contributing to a plethora of civic and charitable causes. Mrs. Payson was also a heavy contributor to the Republican Party.

Despite her aristocratic ancestry, Mrs. Payson's favorite sport was the plebian game of baseball. She saw her first game at the age of six, and attended regularly thereafter. She usually kept score, and saved the scorecards from memorable games. At the time Grant submitted her application to the National League, Mrs. Payson and her husband were in Pittsburgh, rooting against the Yankees. .

Mrs. Payson was one of the last of the old sportsmen/women breed of owners, never meddling, always rooting and always with checkbook at the ready. She followed the Mets religiously, even when she was in Europe. When the owner was in Maine in August, 1969, as the Mets chased the Cubs for the division title, she reportedly paid a local station $10,000 to carry eight Met games. Mrs. Payson's chauffeur attended every Met home game and kept a scorecard, which he presented to her on her return.

On October 17, 1960, just two days before the Yankees fired Casey Stengel, the National League approved Mrs. Payson's application and granted her the league franchise for the City of New York. It was the first time a woman had owned a major league club other than by inheritance. The Mets, along with an entry from Houston, would begin play in 1962, giving them a year to build an organization.

On October 26, the American League announced that its expansion would take place during the 1961 season, a year earlier than anticipated and a year before the National League. For one season, the two leagues would play an uneven number of games and have an unequal number of teams. Spring training for the two new American League teams, which had no players, owners or managers, would begin in just four months.

The American League announced the identity of only one of its two new teams. Calvin Griffith's Washington Senators would re-locate to Minneapolis and an expansion franchise would replace them in Washington. Although the second franchise wasn't identified, it was rumored that it would be in Los Angeles. Shea and Rickey were livid, for the American League had reneged on the agreement reached in Chicago. Minneapolis was a Continental League city, but the American League franchise would be operated by Griffith. Neither Washington nor Los Angeles had been a part of the Continental League. "It is the worst thing I ever heard of in United States sports," Shea fumed. He called the move "one of the lowest blows below the belt in the history of sports." "This is not expansion," Rickey echoed. "The dictionary definition of perfidy has now been confirmed." The American League responded that the committee that met in Chicago had recommended, not promised, that the Continental League franchises would be taken. "We considered them," said one owner, "and we didn't want them." All Shea and Rickey could do was fume, for the Continental League was history. Besides, Shea had done his job, which was to bring National League baseball back to New York.

Shea and Rickey were not the only persons disturbed by the American League announcement. Commissioner Frick inexplicably said that he believed that the League had lived up to its agreement, but was upset that the American League had acted without consulting the National

League owners. "I wish you boys had got together on this thing," he said. Under baseball's top-light structure, all a commissioner could do was wish.

Walter O'Malley of the Dodgers was upset that the American League planned to move into his territory without consulting or compensating him. Frick said that if O'Malley wasn't compensated, he would prevent the new Los Angeles franchise from operating, apparently by wishing really hard. O'Malley didn't need Frick, however, since under baseball rules, neither league could expand into a city occupied by the other league without unanimous consent. That meant, of course, obtaining the agreement of the owner already in residence, in this case O'Malley. Walter said he wouldn't consent unless he got what he wanted.

The American League scrambled for alternatives. Toronto was mentioned as a potential replacement. Yankee co-owner Dan Topping suggested that the National League's incursion into his territory was compensation for the American's move into Los Angeles. The American League proposed that, if there were no club in LA, each league could operate with nine teams and commence interleague play. The National League immediately declined. They were the stronger league and had no desire to share the wealth.

A few days later, with O'Malley apparently having gotten what he wanted, the National League agreed to allow the new Los Angeles franchise to operate. They would not follow the lead of the American League, however, and indicated that their new clubs would begin operations in 1962.

New York's new franchise was owned by the Metropolitan Baseball Club, a corporation owned principally by Mrs. Payson. In January, 1961, the club's office at 680 Fifth Avenue still had a sign on its door which read "The Continental League of Baseball Clubs." The name of the corporation was not necessarily the name of the new team, of course, and Mrs. Payson cautioned patience in the search for a nickname. "If you pick the wrong manager," she said, "you can correct that by paying him off. But when you pick a name, you're stuck with it and it better be a good one."

There was no shortage of possibilities, and suggestions began to arrive as soon as the franchise approval was announced. From the animal kingdom came the familiar Lions, Hawks, Eagles and Falcons. Other fans suggested Knights, Lancers, Spartans, Pioneers, Blue Sox, Gold Sox, Knicks, Bankers, Farmers, Troopers, Trojans, Legends and so on. Since the club would eventually occupy a new stadium in Flushing Meadows, one creative soul recommended calling the new team the Meadow Larks, or simply Larks. A pessimist submitted the name Moles, on the premise that the new club was likely to occupy a position at the bottom of the standings. In order to assuage Brooklynites, who would not receive a replacement for their beloved Dodgers, some suggested calling the new team the New-Brooks, or the Atlantics, in honor of the legendary 19th century Brooklyn club.

By early February, 1961, 1,500 fans had flooded the office of the un-named team with 468 different possibilities. Frivolous entries, many reflecting the seamy underside of the city, included (in alphabetical order): Addicts, Beatniks, Broads, Dancers, Juveniles, Leprechauns, Muggers, Queens, Slumlords, Toughs and Zorros. Many of the names would not have survived political correctness, including Dwarfs, Midgets, Mother-in-Laws, and a myriad of Native American appellations. Some were unwieldy, such as Knights of the Diamond, and others have since acquired different meanings, such as Brooklyn Queensboys and Dykes. Perhaps anticipating the arrival of Rod Kanehl, one writer suggested the team be called the Hot Rods. Some names reflected the franchise's ownership and management, including the Paysons, the Mahatmas, the Shea-Rickeys and the more melodic Rickey-Sheas.

From the multitude of suggestions, the club selected a list of ten finalists from among the serious entries. The finalists (again in alphabetical order) were: Avengers, Bees, Burros, Continentals, Jets, Metropolitans, NYBs (pronounced nibbies), Rebels, Skyliners and Skyscrapers.

Columnist Arthur Daley expressed a preference for Continentals, although he feared it might be shortened to Cons, or Con-artists, which would be little better than Muggers or Toughs. Someone else preferred Rebels, on the premise that a Yankee-Rebel World Series would create a unique sense of drama. Skyscrapers struck a chord with some, while others thought it a more appropriate name for a basketball team.

Time weighs heavily on the hands of baseball fans during the winter months, and suggestions continued to pour in to 680 Fifth Avenue. Some came appended to lengthy treatises, such as the one suggesting the name Castanets. "The name of the mayor of New York is Wagner," it began. "Wagner was the greatest player of the old Pittsburgh Pirates; Pirates recently captured the Santa Maria; Santa Maria was the flagship of Christopher Columbus; Columbus is the capital of Ohio; Ohio's official tree is the Buckeye; Buckeye is another name for horse chestnut; Chestnut in France is Castagnette; Castanets are so called because of their fancied resemblance to halves of chestnut shells. So why not call the New York team the Castanets? They should be able to cast a net over the pennant almost every year." "Ouch," replied Daley.

By the end of April, less than ten months before it was to open its first spring training camp, the new club had an owner, a chairman of the board (Grant), an office staff, and working agreements with three minor league teams, but still no name.

Finally, on May 8, the nickname was announced. In all, 9,613 letters had been received, suggesting a total of 644 different names. Fans had been asked to vote for one of the ten choices listed above. Mets was the leading vote-getter with 61, followed by Empires with 47 and Islanders with 45 (the last two were not on the top ten list, but the baseball world would soon learn that Met fans were not conformists). Mets it would be. This came as little surprise, since writers had already been referring to the club as the Mets, due to the franchise's corporate name.

The name New York Mets had an ancient and proud history, thanks to the club which played in the American Association from 1883 through 1887. Unlike their inept namesakes of the early 1960s, the original Mets were a successful team, appearing in the first World Series in 1884, although they did manage to lose to the National League's Providence Grays in three straight games. Grant cited the historical connection with the 19th century Mets, the relationship to the corporate name of the club, and the fact that the brevity of the name would please headline writers. Also, Mrs. Payson liked it. Skyliners, Continentals, Burros and Beatniks were consigned to oblivion. The new team had a name, and all that remained was to find a manager, 25 players and a place to play.

In March, the Mets hired George Weiss, who had resigned under pressure as Yankee general manager just five months earlier, as president. Branch Rickey had been Mrs. Payson's first choice to run the Mets, but Rickey wanted to operate from Pittsburgh, which Mrs. Payson found unacceptable. He also wanted a virtually unlimited operating budget, which even the owner of the massive Whitney fortune found unreasonable.

Over dinner at the Savoy Hotel, Don Grant asked Weiss if he was interested in returning to baseball. *Was he?* Weiss had no other life than baseball. He had been wise enough to turn down the opportunity to work for eccentric Charley Finley, but working for Joan Payson in New York was too good an offer to reject.

Weiss had been in professional baseball for more than fifty years. While attending Yale, he became involved with a semi-pro team called the New Haven Colonials. The Colonials were in competition with the Eastern League's New Haven franchise, which played in a much faster circuit. Weiss displayed a promotional genius that would have astonished those who knew him in his later years, and gave the professionals a run for their money. He lured Ty Cobb to New Haven for an exhibition game, and played against all-female and all–Chinese squads. After competing with Weiss for a few years, and generally emerging on the short end, the owners of the Eastern League franchise offered to sell their club to him. Weiss borrowed $5,000 and, in 1919, at the age of 25, became the owner of a professional ballclub.

After operating the New Haven franchise for a few years, Weiss moved to Baltimore, where he became general manager of the International League club. In 1932, he joined the Yankee organization, serving as general manager from 1947 through 1960, and was named major league executive of the year ten times. Only once in Weiss's 52 years in baseball had a club he operated finished out of the first division.

When the Mets announced Weiss's hiring, it was made very clear that he would not be general manager, for his Yankee consulting contract stated that it would be terminated if he accepted another general manager's post. It didn't say anything about becoming president, and Weiss began simultaneously collecting paychecks from both New York organizations. The change of affiliations put Weiss in a difficult spot. As Yankee GM, he had argued long and hard against the building of a new National League stadium. It was too expensive, Weiss said, impractical, and unfair to the tax-paying Yankees to subsidize their competition. "I have a different picture now," he said after joining the Mets. "With the additional information I have received, I think the new stadium is a good deal for both the city and the club."

A grand new stadium was planned for Flushing Meadows, but there was no chance it would be ready for the 1962 season. Topping said he wasn't interested in having the Mets as his tenants at Yankee Stadium, and reminded Weiss that he had been vehemently against the idea of any National League club sharing his facility when he was GM of the Yankees. Weiss couldn't possibly ask for the same deal now that he was on the other side of the table, could he? Topping suggested the Polo Grounds. Walter O'Malley offered to act as arbitrator between Weiss and Topping. "[W]e'd clear this matter up in no time," he said. "And besides, I haven't been in the middle of a good row in more than a week." The Mets decided on the Polo Grounds, presumably for just a year, while the new stadium in Flushing rose from the marshes.

Back in February, the new team had taken its first steps toward finding some players. The club announced affiliations with Mobile of the AA Southern Association, Raleigh of the Class B Carolina League and Lexington of the Class D Western Carolina League, each of which would employ New York prospects during the 1961 season. The Mets signed scouts, including recently-retired Yankee Gil McDougald, old Brooklyn hero Babe Herman, former Yankee relief star Johnny Murphy and Hall of Famer Rogers Hornsby. By June, the club had signed 65 players.

The final pieces of the Met puzzle were the major league players, who would be selected in a draft on October 10, and a manager. When Weiss became president of the Mets, many thought they knew the identity of the latter, for where Weiss went, they thought his old friend Casey Stengel wouldn't be far behind.

• 3 •

Marvelous Marv and Hot Rod
The 1962 Season
(Part I)

One of the common fallacies regarding the '62 Mets was that, in the expansion draft, George Weiss condemned the Mets to years of ineptitude by choosing old, washed-up veterans, while the Houston Colt .45s selected young players of great promise. That was simply not true. The Met draftees were actually, on the average, one year younger than the Colt selections, and among veterans like Gus Bell, Roger Craig and Gil Hodges were youngsters Jim Hickman (24), Craig Anderson (23), Jay Hook (25), Bob Miller (22), Al Jackson (25), Felix Mantilla (27), Joe Christopher (25) and Elio Chacon (24). The pitching selections, in particular, were principally youngsters with potential. Solly Hemus, one of the Met coaches, had managed the Cardinals from 1959 to 1961, and was instrumental in the selection of promising St. Louis prospects Anderson, Miller, Hickman and Chris Cannizzaro.

Met coaches and scouts spent the summer of 1961 scouring the major and minor leagues, but finding young or old talent among the players available in the expansion draft was a difficult proposition. Before the draft, National League owners vowed they would do better than their counterparts in the other league, who had left precious few serviceable players available for the Senators and Angels. Predictably, however, self interest prevailed and the Mets and Colts wound up with little to choose from. "The villains in this tragedy," wrote Arthur Daley, "are the eight club owners in the National League who permitted selfishness and greed to dictate their expansion policies."

Each of the existing eight teams made 15 players available to the two expansion clubs, including just seven from their 25 man roster of August 31, 1961. Further, the clubs had the opportunity to send promising young prospects to the minors prior to August 31 to protect them from the draft. Thus, the top player the new teams could draft was the 19th best on a major league roster. It would be difficult to beat the established teams with a lineup of players who weren't good enough to start for them.

A few days before the draft, after seeing the list of available players, the Mets and Colts asked the National League to change the process and put more talent on the table. Houston General Manager Paul Richards was much more vocal than Weiss in expressing his displeasure. "Gentlemen," Richards told reporters upon seeing the list, "we're fucked." Two days after Richards' initial complaint, following a meeting of National League general managers, Richards and Weiss proclaimed themselves satisfied. "I have said all I am going to say for a while," Richards remarked upon leaving the meeting. League President Warren Giles told him the process would remain the same and to keep his opinions to himself.

When Richards met reporters after the draft, he said, "Had I known the teams would be this good, I never would have said a word. We feel the National League lived up to the letter and the spirit of its pledge." Was he speaking with tongue in cheek, a reporter asked. "No," Richards replied solemnly.

Outwardly, everyone expressed satisfaction. Cardinal manager Johnny Keane even said, "Houston and New York could field clubs better than those already in the league." The presence of big name players past their prime made the list of potential draftees look better than it was.* The true quality was evidenced by the fact that by May, 1963, the Mets retained just six of the draftees and the Colts seven. Washington and Los Angeles, which had started a year earlier, had just three and eight draftees, respectively.

On October 10, 1961, at the Netherland-Hilton Hotel in New York, the Mets selected 22 players at a total cost of $1.8 million. The price was steep in relation to the quality of the merchandise. The pitchers drafted by the Mets had a combined total of 15 major league victories in 1961, and managed only three complete games among them. Former Dodger Roger Craig was the leader with five wins. Among the batters, Don Zimmer had the most home runs (13).

The theory that Weiss botched the draft selections is groundless. There was simply very little proven talent available. Weiss's only hope was to gamble on strong young arms like those of Jackson, Anderson, Hook and Miller and pray that one or two would develop into solid major league pitchers. "If three of them came through for us," Weiss said, "say with ten or fifteen victories each, we may surprise a lot of people."

The Mets may not have gotten great players, but with former Dodgers Gil Hodges, Don Zimmer and Roger Craig, they had some crowd pleasers. A few more ex–Giants and Dodgers nearly signed on. Former Brooklyn ace Don Newcombe asked for a tryout, but the Mets weren't interested. Three days after the expansion draft, Weiss purchased 31-year-old left handed pitcher Johnny Antonelli from the Braves. Antonelli, one of the first big bonus players, twice won 20 games for the Giants in the Polo Grounds, and was one of the heroes of 1954 Series. Antonelli's sun sank in the west, however, and when the Giants went to California, he lost his effectiveness. He made a few disparaging remarks about the conditions in San Francisco, which earned him the enmity of the local press. In 1960, Antonelli won just six games and blamed everyone else for his failure, including the press and his manager. He worked just 59 innings for the Indians and Braves in 1961, with terrible results. But if Antonelli could pitch at all, he would bring many of his old fans to the Polo Grounds.

In late January, however, Antonelli decided to retire. He had a growing tire business and a restaurant in Rochester, and was tired of traveling and being away from his family. "Basically," Antonelli said, "I didn't want to be out there. I'd lost all desire. Without desire, everything is worthless.... Returning to the Polo Grounds would have been a thrill and I was offered a nice salary. But money isn't everything." Scratch an old Giant hero.

Lefthanders are supposed to be flaky. One of the oddest pitchers of the 1950s, however, was right hander Billy Loes, who achieved notoriety by predicting before the 1953 Series that the Yankees would beat his Dodgers in six games. Loes also became the first pitcher in Series history to lose a ground ball in the sun. His post-baseball ambition was to be a mailman in Brooklyn. In 1956, when Mickey Mantle was threatening Ruth's record of 60 home runs in a season, Loes said that if he pitched against Mantle when he had 59 homers, he'd groove two for numbers 60 and 61. "That's the only way I'll get in the record book anyway," he said.

If the Mets were going to lose games, the presence of Loes would add excitement. He was

*The Phillies left a young infielder, Richie Allen, exposed to the draft, but neither the Mets nor Colts saw fit to select him.

a native New Yorker, an old Dodger, a favorite of local fans, and could always be counted on for a colorful quote. The Mets signed Loes, who had suffered from arm trouble for several years, three days after the signing of Antonelli. Like Antonelli, Loes was just 31 years old, and if his arm was sound, he would be as serviceable as some of the pitchers the Mets had chosen in the draft. Like Antonelli, however, Loes would never pitch for the Mets. A few days before the start of spring training, he informed the Mets that he would not play in 1962. "My arm hurts me even when I walk around the house," he said. Scratch an old Dodger hero.

Following the draft, Weiss took inventory and decided he didn't want to field a team comprised of the players he had selected. "I'll admit our roster isn't exactly what we would like it to be," he said, "but we still have a few deals and purchases pending. I feel certain we'll be in pretty good shape when we open the season at the Polo Grounds next April." Where would the players come from? Trade possibilities were limited. How could Weiss trade players back to teams that hadn't wanted them in the first place? Early in the season, Stengel addressed the Sales Executive Club. "We had to purchase these men from the demon salesmen in baseball," Casey said, "to get into business. And sometimes we put these men back up for sale. And those wonderful salesmen, those wonderful people in baseball, would you believe it, they don't want those men back."

When he was running the Yankees, Weiss dealt from a position of strength. He had plenty of young prospects that other teams wanted and needed. Now, holding a weak hand, he had only one option. Flush with Mrs. Payson's money, Weiss set out to buy what he could not draft or obtain by trade.

Spending money was a new experience for Weiss, who had parted with very little of it when operating the Yankees. Over the next three months, however, the old dog learned some new tricks. He purchased second baseman Charley Neal from the Dodgers, and outfielders Frank Thomas and Richie Ashburn from the Braves and Cubs, respectively. As with the young pitchers he'd drafted, Weiss was more hopeful than certain of success. Neal, a star for the '59 World Champion Dodgers, had faded dramatically during the next two seasons. Although only 30, he had gone from being one of the best second basemen in the game to expendable. Ashburn, a batting champion in 1955 and 1958, hit just .261 in 1961 and had lost most of his vaunted speed. In the vast center field of the Polo Grounds, a slower Ashburn was an alarming prospect for Casey Stengel.

Houston, which would play in a temporary facility while the Astrodome was constructed, was in an enviable position. First, Houston fans were so delighted to have big league baseball that Richards didn't need to acquire aging name players to draw crowds. The Mets, competing with the Yankees, did. Second, the temporary Houston stadium was not yet built. Richards could choose his team and then design the park around it. After drafting a number of singles hitters, the Colts constructed a spacious park with a right field fence that sprouted up somewhere near Galveston. Each foul pole was 360 feet from the plate and the "power" alleys were 427 feet away. The Mets had no such luxury, for their park had been in existence since 1911. Although they expected to spend just a single season in the Polo Grounds before moving to the new stadium in Flushing Meadows, the Mets built a team suited to their cozy ballpark.

Assembling a team to play in the Polo Grounds consisted of finding sluggers who could pull the ball toward the foul poles, which were just 279 feet and 258 feet in left and right field, respectively, and getting pitchers who could prevent the other teams' hitters from doing so. "Bobby Thomson and Dusty Rhodes pulled the ball all the time," said old Dodger pitcher Clem Labine. "If you could keep the ball down against those fellows, they couldn't get the ball in the air and you had a pretty good chance of getting them out." "You had to pitch them outside," said Met pitcher Dave Hillman. "You couldn't pitch them inside with that short line and that extended overhanging deck."

The outfielders deployed in unique fashion in the Polo Grounds. Because there was so little territory to guard down the lines and so much ground for the center fielder to cover, the left and right fielders always played far from the lines to give the center fielder assistance. "It was actually an easy defensive field to play on," said Met outfielder Duke Carmel, "because everything went to the middle. If you were playing center, you had the left fielder and right fielder right next to you. There was no use playing the lines, because anything hit down the line was a double off the wall."

At one time, Stengel had patrolled the Polo Grounds outfield. When the Mets first arrived in New York, John DeMerit was standing in the outfield when Casey came over to him. "Hey, kid," Stengel said. "He came over," DeMerit remembered, "and was pawing the dirt. 'When I played here in 1910,' he said, or 1912 or whenever, 'there used to be a stone out here somewhere and when I played against so-and-so I'd be 10 steps to the right of the stone and when I played against somebody else I was six steps in back of the stone.' He was amazing me."

Frank Thomas, a right-handed slugger, was a man made for the Polo Grounds, whose left field overhang jutted out over the field, a tempting 250 feet from home plate. He leaned over the plate and pulled everything right down the line, rarely hitting anything to the right of second base. "I was in South Carolina," Thomas said, "playing for Rip Sewell. Rip told me to move closer to the plate. By moving closer, I could be quick with my bat and quick with my hands. It made me a pull hitter." Thomas ranked second among all visiting active players with 22 Polo Ground home runs, and homered for the Pirates in the last game the Giants played in New York in 1957. From 1953 to 1957, no visiting player hit as many Polo Grounds home runs as Frank Thomas.

In addition to pulling home runs down the line, Thomas had other unique talents. He could catch anyone, he claimed, bare-handed, from sixty feet, six inches. "When I was a kid," Thomas said, "my mom and dad couldn't afford to buy me a glove." Playing fast pitch softball, he became accustomed to catching the ball bare-handed. When he was in the minor leagues in Waco, Texas, one of the pitchers was popping off in the outfield about how hard he could throw. Thomas tired of listening to him and said, "I'll catch your best fastball bare-handed." But first, Thomas told him, go down to the bullpen and warm up so you're good and loose. That was ridiculous, the pitcher told him; Thomas couldn't catch him even if he wasn't warmed up. They marked off the pitching distance and Thomas caught him not once, but three times. Unbelieving, the pitcher went down to the bullpen and warmed up. When he came back, Thomas caught five more. "It kind of deflated his ego," Thomas remembered. "That's why I did it."

One day in New York, Ashburn goaded Willie Mays, possessor of one of the finest throwing arms in baseball, to challenge Thomas. He offered Mays $100 if Thomas couldn't catch him. Mays came out cold, threw as hard as he could and Thomas caught it. He warmed up a little and Thomas caught him again.

Don Zimmer presented the biggest challenge. Zimmer stretched Thomas's rules to the limit. He would draw a line in the grass, sixty feet, six inches from Thomas, retreat about twenty feet, take a running start, wind up and fire on the run. Thomas caught him easily. "Anybody who could do that," said pitcher Don Rowe, "I'm not fooling around with."

In addition to catching bare-handed, another of Thomas's avocations was assisting stewardesses in serving meals to the players. He loved to work the aisles and see how fast he could get the food out. Thomas could remember the beverage orders better, he claimed, and pointed out that players were less likely to engage him in conversation, and thus delay the service, than they would an attractive young stewardess. Thus, when the Mets took to the air, their cleanup hitter took to the galley, bringing out the trays the stewardesses had prepared. "I enjoyed that very much," he said. "I had a lot of fun with that. We could serve a meal in half an hour." In the spring of 1963, Thomas abruptly retired as a flight attendant. The players had been referring to him as Mary. "I just feel I've had enough of everybody's kidding," he said. "They'll be sorry when they don't get fed as fast. They'll miss me. Oh, yes."

Thomas loved the New York fans. He loved all fans. "When I was a kid in Pittsburgh," he said, "most of the players would come out and push us aside. They wouldn't sign for you. The one that did was Rip Sewell. One day, he put his arm around me and walked all the way up the street with me. He asked me why my pants were torn and I told him I did it playing baseball. I played for Rip when he was managing Charleston in the Sally League and told him that story. It made him feel real good. I vowed that if I ever reached the big leagues, I would never refuse to sign an autograph for a kid. My card's not worth anything today, because I signed for everybody."

Thomas assembled an extensive collection of Topps trading cards, from 1952 to 1991, which were destroyed in a fire at his home. The fans he'd signed autographs for over the years came to his aid, sending him replacements. One fan from New York sent a batch of cards along with a message. "I remember when you were in the Polo Grounds," the man wrote, "and I stood in line for two and a half hours to get your autograph. You were friendly to all the kids." "You can't beat stuff like that," Thomas said.

Stengel didn't need a circus performer, a baseball card collector or a flight attendant. He sorely needed an outfielder who could reach the Polo Grounds seats, and Thomas, in 1962, filled the bill very nicely, smacking 34 home runs (the first seven of which were hit in the friendly confines of his home park, and driving in 94. His home run total was not surpassed by a Met until Dave Kingman hit 36 in 1975.

Like many free swingers, Thomas was a notorious streak hitter. He fell into deep slumps, but when he was hot, no one could stop him. Early in the 1962 season, Thomas had an 18 game hitting streak, and was batting over .300 in late May. Throughout June and July, he was cold. During the first few days of August, he hit four home runs in eight at bats, and had two homers in each of three consecutive games, tying a major league record. A streaky hitter is frustrating to a manager, but better than one who couldn't hit at all, which was the case with many Mets. Like most of his teammates, Thomas was a one-dimensional player. "He'd hit the ball out of the ballpark," said sportswriter Gordon White, "and then he'd drop a fly ball. He was not the greatest left fielder who ever played, but he was all right." Thomas was even worse at third base, where his scatter arm made him a danger to the spectators behind first base.

The Mets had another potential power hitter in first baseman Ed Bouchee, drafted from the Cubs. Bouchee, a big, 200 pound left handed hitter, had been *The Sporting News* Rookie Player of the Year for the Phillies in 1957, after posting a .293 average, 17 home runs and 76 RBI. His ability and willingness to attend charity and publicity events endeared him to the fans, and he was awarded the B'nai B'rith Outstanding Citizen Award.

During the winter of 1957, however, Bouchee's career took a precipitous nosedive. In February, while home in Spokane, Washington, he was arrested and charged with exposing himself to two young girls. Bouchee, who was married with one child and another on the way, admitted to the charge, was placed on probation for three years, and ordered to undergo psychiatric evaluation. Doctors concluded that he suffered from a condition known as "compulsive exhibitionism." Bouchee went to the Institute of Living in Hartford, Connecticut, underwent treatment, and waited to see if he would be allowed to continue his baseball career. The Outstanding Citizen awarders of B'nai B'rith kept their own counsel.

In early June, Bouchee left the Institute of Living, went to Philadelphia, began working out with the Phillies, and waited for a ruling from Commissioner Frick. He was chaperoned around the city by coach Benny Bengough, to re-acclimate him to social situations and gauge public reaction. Bouchee was accepted by the public and his teammates, and was re-instated on a probationary basis on July 1.

Bouchee returned dramatically with a home run in his first game, but his performance for the rest of the year didn't equal that of his fabulous rookie campaign. In 89 games, he hit .257 with 9 home runs. Bouchee played adequately in 1959, but was traded to the Cubs in 1960. He had a poor 1961 season, and with Ernie Banks slated to move to first base in 1962, Bouchee was expendable. He was selected by the Mets in the expansion draft. Although just 28 years old, and but five years removed from his rookie of the year season, Bouchee was a question mark.

When the Mets gathered for spring training in February, 1962, no one had any idea how bad they would be. Stengel was asked in January how he thought his club would fare. "I haven't the slightest idea," he said, "but the more I look at our roster, the better I like it." President Weiss was even more vague. He said at the end of the exhibition season that the Mets had "demonstrated we belong somewhere in the league." Prior to opening day, Stengel said he thought 70 wins were a distinct possibility, and that he was shooting for a .500 record. *Sports Illustrated* opined that the Mets might finish as high as sixth. Veteran reporter John Drebinger picked the club to finish seventh, ahead of the Colts, Phillies and Cubs. "No one can discount the amazing resourcefulness of Stengel," he wrote, "nor the overall sagacity of Weiss." Neither Stengel nor Weiss, Drebinger failed to note, would be playing.

Many of those who would be playing, however, were as optimistic as Drebinger. Hodges said he thought fifth place was possible. "To be honest with you," said Thomas recently, "I thought we had a good ballclub. If we had a closer and a long man like they have today, we probably would have been in the pennant race."

"I didn't think they were as bad as they wound up," said outfielder John DeMerit, who spent spring training and the first few weeks of the season with the Mets. "I don't think anyone had any thoughts other than competing reasonably well. But the people who were old got older." "The way we played in spring training was decent," said infielder Felix Mantilla. "I thought we were going to be better than we showed in the regular season, but I was wrong. I thought in the beginning we had a decent team, but we were kind of weak in the pitching staff."

Amid the wave of optimism, there were dissenting views, such as that of the perceptive Clem Labine, who had been signed as a free agent. "What I expected was what happened," he said. "I couldn't think any great things were going to happen to this club. We just didn't seem to have enough to even come close. All of us wanted to do it but we couldn't do it." "I came to spring training," said pitcher Sherman (Roadblock) Jones, "with the attitude that it would be great if this team could jell, but I knew it would not, because the ability to be aggressive was just not there. Some of the guys were over the hill and some hadn't made it yet." "We just had a very poor ballclub," said Al Jackson, "and there wasn't nothing great going to happen in 1962."

"Their team on paper looked pretty darn good," said former Pirate Dick Schofield. "The only thing was, you didn't realize that a lot of those guys were too old to be able to play a full season." Roger Angell, the poetic baseball writer, cut through the hopeful optimism. "The team is both too young and too old for sensible hopes," he wrote. "Its pitchers will absorb some fearful punishment this summer, and Chacon and Neal have yet to prove that they can manage the double play with any consistency." If Angell had stopped there, he would deserve plaudits for his perspicacity. When he predicted a lively fight for the cellar among the Mets, Colts and Phillies, he couldn't have been more wrong. It wasn't even close. The Mets seized the bottom rung early and clung to it tenaciously.

Opening night in St. Louis was a triumph of sorts, for the Mets didn't lose. They were rained out. The following night, there was no such luck, and the Mets were soundly beaten by the Cardinals 11–4. Larry Jackson of the Cardinals, who would beat the Mets 18 times before they beat him, threw the first pitch ever to a New York Met. Ashburn grounded it foul. On Jackson's second pitch, Richie flied to center field. Gus Bell got the first Met hit, a single to center field in the second inning. Ashburn scored the first run in the third, driven in by Neal's single. In the fourth, Hodges hit the first Met home run.

On the other side of the ledger, Craig committed the initial Met balk, which led to two Cardinal runs in the first. Neal committed the first Met error, which was followed by miscues of catcher Hobie Landrith and shortstop Mantilla. The Cardinals stole three bases against Landrith. Craig departed for a pinch hitter in the fourth and was followed to the mound by rookie Bob Moorhead, minor league veteran Herb Moford and Labine.

The opening day loss was followed by the Mets' grand entrance into New York, celebrated with a parade, watched by 40,000 people, down Broadway to City Hall. The parade was followed by eight more losses. During the fifth inning of defeat number three, the first "Let's Go Mets" chant started up spontaneously. Most of the losses were one-sided, but the Mets also found ways to lose the close ones. "Disaster showed up later than usual for its daily appointment with the New York Mets yesterday," wrote Robert Teague after an eleven inning Colt win on April 17. Early or late, disaster showed up regularly before Jay Hook beat the Pirates 9–1 on April 23 for the first Met win.

What were the Met weaknesses? Was it the hitting? The pitching? The fielding? All three? It was hard to judge the hitting. On April 30, seven Mets were batting above .300 and seven below .200. The fielding wasn't very good, but there was no question that pitching was the Mets' most glaring weakness. At the end of April, the team ERA was 6.30.

On April 28 came a ray of hope, as little lefthander Al Jackson threw the first Met shutout, against the Phillies, raising the club's record to 3–12. Jackson, a 26-year-old drafted from the Pirate organization, didn't have an overpowering fastball, but when he kept his good breaking stuff low, he was very effective. "The one who had the best stuff?" Labine said of the young Met pitchers. "Al Jackson. Absolutely. He had a sinking fastball and he was a thinker. He had a lot of good ideas about pitching." "He knew what he was doing," said Galen Cisco. "Mostly, he knew how to keep the ball down." In the Polo Grounds, keeping the ball down was a very useful talent, one Jackson worked very hard to perfect. "One day we were in spring training," recalled Joe Christopher, "and he went out early in the morning, got a big bag of baseballs, picked a spot on the wall of the dugout under the bench, and kept throwing sinkers against that wall."

"I wasn't a power pitcher," Jackson said. "About my third year in professional baseball, in A ball, I really learned how to pitch. Actually, I learned who Al Jackson was. I wasn't a power pitcher and I wasn't a curve ball pitcher. I had to find my niche, and came up with a two seam fastball and a slider. I spent the whole season trying to develop those pitches. That's who Al Jackson should have been, but nobody told me. I just learned through trial and error."

Jackson had been a victim of the limited number of opportunities in the sixteen team major league structure. In 1958, he won 18 games at Lincoln and posted the best ERA in the Western League. The next year he was 15–4 in the Triple A International League, but made only a few token appearances with the Pirates. It was not until expansion took place that Jackson finally got a chance to show what he could do in the big leagues.

Jackson was not just a pitcher, he was an athlete, quick as a cat getting off the mound. "You would think he was a player [non-pitcher]," said Stengel in the '62 camp, "if he wasn't left-handed." "They always said," Jackson recalled, "that if you can't find Al Jackson, he's probably in the batting cage. I wanted to hit .300. I wanted to win a Gold Glove. I really wanted to be an infielder, but being left-handed, that was out of the question." Jackson ran track and played football in high school, and was one of the fastest players on the squad. Stengel often used him as a pinch runner. Jackson was not a great hitter, but he battled the pitchers, and took advantage of his speed by learning how to drag bunt.

Jackson pitched three more shutouts in 1962, the only four whitewashes by Met hurlers. Three of his first five wins were shutouts, one of which was a one hitter against the Colts in June, easily the best performance of any Met pitcher. In August, he pitched 15 innings in a losing effort against the Phillies. At the end of the season, Jackson was named to the Topps All Rookie team, despite an 8–20 record.

Time after time, Jackson pitched gutty games, only to be undone by errors, a lack of runs, or some other undeserved quirk of fate. "The two teams that could hit," said pitcher Gary Kroll, "were the Reds and the Braves. You put Jackson on those teams, with the way he knew how to pitch, and he'd have been a big winner. If Jackson played on that Cincinnati ballclub, he'd win 20 games every year."

With the Mets, the odds always seemed to be against Jackson. "I didn't think that way," he said. "I just felt that I could win. I got that from Roger Craig, who was a big help to me. I could see that each and every time he went out there, he was prepared to win. That's the only way to be. If you have defeatist thoughts before you even go out there, there's no point in going out there."

The Mets gradually started to show signs of improvement and, a few wins later, people were starting to take them seriously. On May 9, the club put an end to that sentiment when they purchased first baseman/outfielder Marvin Throneberry from the Baltimore Orioles, a transaction that would affect the franchise in a way no one could possibly have imagined. *The New York Times* commented, "Throneberry's acquisition marks a radical departure from the Mets' previous practice of stocking the club with vintage talent of limited ability but crowd-drawing appeal." Never was the venerable journal so mistaken. By the end of the season, no one in New York—not Mickey Mantle, Roger Maris or Whitey Ford—had more fan appeal than Marvin Eugene Throneberry.

Throneberry was a product of the bountiful Yankee farm system of the '50s, a power-hitting left handed batter who received a $50,000 bonus at a time when the Yanks disdained big bonuses. They refused to meet the asking price of Carl Yastrzemski. They thought Sam McDowell wanted too much. But they paid $50,000 for the privilege of signing Marv Throneberry in 1952. Throneberry, whose older brother Faye was an outfielder/first baseman with the Red Sox and Senators, could use the money, for he was married and the father of an 18-month-old daughter by the time he graduated from Memphis South Side High School. At South Side, he lettered in baseball, football, basketball and track. "I was a sprinter," he later told a disbelieving interviewer. "I can still run."

The Yankees outbid the Phillies, Cardinals, Tigers, Browns and Red Sox to sign the youngster, who had hit .550 in American Legion ball. His Legion coach, Lew Chandler, dutifully noted that Throneberry was not a very good fielder. But boy, could he hit. "He's green," said Yankee coach Bill Dickey after watching the teenager work out at Yankee Stadium, "but Mickey Mantle is the only man on the Yankee club who can hit for greater distance."

Some athletes are remembered only for one incident or epoch in their career. Bill Buckner is known as the man who let the ball go through his legs in the 1986 World Series, not the player who had a 20 year major league career and once led the National League in batting average. Bobby Thomson is the man who hit the home run that beat the Dodgers. Likewise, Marvin Eugene Throneberry is known to a younger generation as the middle-aged, heavy-set, bald man in the Miller Lite commercials, and to a slightly older demographic as the clown who played first base for the Mets in 1962. Before he became a Met, however, Throneberry had another identity, that of one of the most promising prospects in the minor leagues.

During his first few years in the Yankee system, Throneberry looked like he might, as Dickey had suggested, be another Mantle. He hit 16 home runs in half a season at Quincy in 1952, then hit 30 the next year. In 1955, Throneberry jumped all the way from Class B to Triple A and led the American Association with 36 home runs and 117 RBI. He also struck out 150 times, however, and didn't dazzle anyone with his fielding.

The following year, Throneberry was named the league's most valuable player, after hitting 42 home runs and driving in 145. There were a number of other good prospects in the American Association that year, including Roger Maris of Indianapolis, but Throneberry was rated the most valuable of them all. A poll of major league farm directors in the spring of 1957 ranked Throneberry's potential well ahead of Maris's.

Throneberry took the task of being the next Mantle literally. Most Yankee minor leaguers of the '50s wanted to be like Mickey Mantle, but Throneberry really wanted to be like Mantle. "The first time I saw Marv," said Bob Johnson, who played with him at Kansas City, "I said, 'This guy's trying to emulate Mickey Mantle.'" Throneberry copied Mantle's batting stance. He even mimicked his appearance. "He wore his socks the exact same length as Mickey did," recalled former Yankee Johnny Blanchard. "If Mickey would go out there without a T-shirt, Marv would go out there sleeveless. He tried to run like Mickey, walk like Mickey, he'd pull his cap down like Mickey did. Nobody ever said anything to him about it, but we all knew. You couldn't help but notice." "He'd adjust his pants like Mantle, and he trotted like Mantle," remembered Rod Kanehl. "He did that in 1954. I thought, 'This guy's trying to run like Mantle, but he's only half as fast.'"

In the spring of 1957, with two outstanding seasons in Triple A behind him, Throneberry was given a good chance to win the Yankee first base job. Veteran Joe Collins, the left handed half of Casey Stengel's platoon, was 34, and Bill Skowron, the right handed half, was prone to injury. Stengel said that if Throneberry came through, he might try Skowron at third and play the youngster full time. The main reason Casey made that statement was to put the needle to third baseman Andy Carey, with whom he had a running feud, but with Throneberry's minor league record, it seemed as though Stengel needed to find a spot for him. That spot had to be first base, for Marv couldn't play any other position. It was first base or pinch hitting. Throneberry just hoped it wasn't back to Denver.

That spring, writer Dan Daniel authored a lengthy profile of the young rookie, who was already taking on the persona that would make him a lovable Met. "Marv," Daniel wrote, "who looks considerably older than 23, rarely is seen to laugh. He sits around the lobby of the Soreno, of an evening, reading and smoking a cigar. He already is balding." Bad luck plagued Throneberry in 1957, and he developed an infected tendon in his arm, which prevented him from playing often or well. Skowron looked terrible at third, and returned to first while Throneberry, who had one minor league option left, went back to Denver.

For the third season in a row, Marv tore up the American Association, with 40 homers and 124 RBI. In three years at the Triple A level, he had hit 118 home runs and driven home 386. Some said his success was due to playing half his games in Denver. The thin air of Denver was conducive to home runs, but the right field fence, which was 365 feet from home plate, was not. During the winter of 1957–58, Throneberry proved he could hit at lower altitudes when he set a Nicaraguan League home run record and led the league in batting.

By 1958, Throneberry was beginning to lose his patience, and said that if he didn't get a chance with the Yankees that year, he wanted to be traded. "Even the thought of being sent out again makes me shudder," he said in the spring. There was nothing more he could prove in the minors.

Throneberry, with no options remaining, finally made the Yankee squad in 1958. He didn't come close to equaling his Denver performances, batting just .227 in 60 games, with only seven home runs. The next year was more of the same, with a .240 average and eight homers in 80 games, and Daniel described him as a "bitter disappointment" to Weiss and Stengel. Throneberry was hospitalized with a bad case of the flu in May, 1959 and never was a contributor to a Yankee team that finished third. In December, he was sent to Kansas City in the trade that brought Roger Maris to New York.

Following one mediocre season in Kansas City and a second split between the Athletics and Orioles, Marv found himself back in New York. On May 11, 1962, Throneberry played his first game as a Met, starting at first base against the Milwaukee Braves, and the legend of Marvelous Marv began. In the second inning, Denis Menke lifted a high foul pop near the first base stands. Marv staggered unsteadily under it, and the ball fell untouched on the warning track. It would take Marv a while to get used to the unfamiliar park, Bob Murphy told his listeners.

Marv Throneberry pretending to reach for a throw at first base. All too often in 1962, he only pretended to catch them. One of the top prospects in the Yankees farm system during the 1950s, Throneberry achieved lasting notoriety as Marvelous Marv, a symbol of the Mets' ineptitude during their first season.

In his first at bat as a Met, Marv fouled out. In the third inning, Hank Aaron lifted a pop foul between first base and home plate. Catcher Sammy Taylor, having watched Throneberry maneuver tentatively under Menke's popup, was taking no chances. He sprinted as hard as he could toward the first base dugout. That was fortunate, for Throneberry was not going to get there. Taylor made the catch as Throneberry, arriving late on the scene, nearly ran him over. Three innings, three adventures, and the ball hadn't even gotten into fair territory. It was a sign of things to come.

Throneberry hadn't played very much with Baltimore, and his batting eye was rusty. When Marv arrived in New York, Stengel analyzed the first base situation. "I have one great first baseman, Hodges, when he can play, which is as much as he tells me he can play, and I got a left-hander [Ed Bouchee] who did me no harm and I also had this fellow [Throneberry] and I know he can maybe move around first base, but whether he can hit I don't know."

Throneberry got off to a slow start, but once he regained his timing, Marv began to hit with some of his old power. He became the first player to homer into the distant right field stands in Houston. Like his hero Mantle, however, Marv struck out a lot. Further, contrary to the assurances of Bob Murphy, Marv never became adjusted to fielding in the Polo Grounds, and it was as a fielder that he established his reputation. "Throneberry is a serious baseball player," Jimmy Breslin wrote in *Sports Illustrated*. "He tries, and he has some ability. It's just that things happen when he plays."

Indeed they did. Marv's specialty was the ground ball that went through his legs. He didn't make as many errors as people remember, but he made plenty of them, and it seemed that every one came in a key situation. Al Jackson pitched fifteen innings against the Phillies, only to be undone when a ground ball eluded Marv's stationary glove. With a chance to atone in the bottom half of the inning, he struck out with two runners on base.

Some of Throneberry's escapades became legend. His most famous blunder took place in a game against the Cubs, when he was guilty of interference in the first inning, igniting a big Chicago rally. Throneberry made up for it, however, in the last half of the inning by hitting a long blast to right center, but missed both first and second base and was called out.

One by one, the other first basemen fell by the wayside. Hodges was hampered by a knee injury. Jim Marshall was traded to the Pirates. Bouchee, who hit a few homers early in the season, slumped and was sent to Syracuse. Throneberry began getting most of the playing time. At first, the fans booed his failures. In late June, Robert Lipsyte wrote about, "Marvin Throneberry, whose less than graceful play around first base has subjected him to some cutting remarks from the box seats...." No matter how much the fans got on Marv, however, he never let it bother him. "So long as they pay me," he said, "they can say what they want." "A ballclub like ours needed a patsy," he said the following spring, "and I don't mind it. When they were on me, they laid off guys who couldn't take it." Writer Steve Jacobson summarized Marv's contributions to the Mets. "By accepting the razzing of the fans," he wrote, "and by kidding himself, he helped draw the attention of the fans and the press away from the artistically aromatic performance of the Metropolitan Baseball Club, Inc."

Slowly, the tide turned and the fans fell in love with the balding 29-year-old. They cheered every routine play that Marv executed successfully. The Marvelous Marv Throneberry Fan Club paraded through the stands wearing T shirts bearing his name and carrying banners extolling his virtues. Writer Leonard Schecter christened him Marvelous Marv, and Throneberry had Jay Hook, who he assumed could write neatly since Hook had a master's degree, print a sign that said "Marvelous Marv," and hung it above his locker, where the non-descript "Throneberry" had been. Clubhouse manager Herb Norman said that by the end of August, Throneberry was getting more fan mail that any other Met, including Stengel.

One of the things the fans loved about Marv was that, while he had a tendency to blunder, he often came through in the clutch. One day in August, Stengel sent Throneberry out to coach first base after Solly Hemus was ejected. With the Mets losing 4–3 to the Pirates in the ninth, Marv was called off the coaching lines to pinch hit with a runner on first. He slammed the ball into the right field stands for a home run and a most improbable 5–4 Met win, adding yet another chapter to his legend. He homered again a few days later, and a member of his fan club leapt atop the Met dugout and began dancing, before he was removed by the police.

Throneberry's popularity could have presented a problem, for Stengel liked being the center of attention, and resented players who tried to steal the spotlight. Throneberry had become a folk hero, however, not because of his own efforts, but in spite of an almost complete lack of charisma. Marv posed no threat to Stengel, for he was not a character by any stretch of the imagination. His aura was created by the writers, the fans, and Richie Ashburn, who acted as Marv's unofficial publicity man. "He was a big old farm boy from Tennessee," said pitcher Larry Foss. "He wasn't the life of the party," said John Blanchard. "He'd go the whole ballgame without saying a word. If you talked to him, he'd talk, but he didn't add a lot to any conversation."

Marv had a decent, if not marvelous, season in 1962, at least at the bat. He hit 16 home runs, second only to Thomas, and finished the season with an average of .244. "He was a good power hitter," said Joe Christopher, "but only on cripple pitches." The following spring, Marv made the mistake of holding out. He had brought many fans to the Polo Grounds, Throneberry reasoned, and should get some of the revenue they generated. Johnny Murphy, Weiss's assistant, pointed out that Throneberry's defensive play had also driven some fans away. Marv pointed out that he had taken a lot of abuse. Murphy countered that he deserved it. "You are confusing the Good Guy Award," said Weiss, "with the Most Valuable Player Trophy."

With five other first basemen in camp, the Mets weren't desperate to sign the Marvelous One. They offered him $15,000, but Marv wanted $17,000. As the impasse continued, outfielder Gene Woodling got into the act. Woodling had battled with Stengel when both were with the Yankees, and Gene's best friend in baseball was Ralph Houk. He was in the Met camp reluctantly as a player-coach, for what he really wanted to do was coach for his old buddy Houk. Apparently, there had been conversations during the winter, during which Houk offered Woodling a coaching job if he could obtain his release from the Mets. This was clearly tampering with a player under contract, which was illegal. Woodling denied discussing a job with Houk and, since the Mets wouldn't release him, reported to St. Petersburg for spring training.

Already angry with the Mets, the first thing Woodling did when he came to camp was gripe about the food. He complained when the Mets announced his signing as a player rather than player-coach. Then, Woodling took Throneberry's side in his dispute with Weiss. Marv had purchased a one way plane ticket and flown to St. Petersburg, but Weiss refused to meet with him, insisting that all discussions take place with Murphy. Woodling, who'd come in to the locker room to change his shirt in the middle of a workout, told Throneberry that, since he'd taken the first step, Weiss should meet personally with him. Murphy overheard the remark, which led to a heated discussion.

Weiss finally spoke directly with Throneberry, huddling with his recalcitrant first baseman in a car in a parking lot. A final meeting with Murphy was arranged, Marv signed a contract, and donned his Met uniform for the 1963 season. At the same time, Woodling turned in his uniform. He had so angered Murphy and Weiss by his interference that they had released him. "I'm a fired-up guy and I got fired," Woodling said. Complicating the situation was the fact that, by this time, the Yankee job was no longer open. Woodling called the Angels, looking for a job as a pinch hitter. They weren't interested. Finally, he became a coach for the Baltimore Orioles.

Throneberry was in uniform, but rarely played, for the Mets had acquired Tim Harkness from the Dodgers. Harkness, like Throneberry, had some power and, unlike Marv, could catch the ball. He'd been one of the top minor league prospects in the country when he was in the Dodger organization, and was the front runner for the starting job. Stengel wanted Throneberry to play the outfield, but Marv, who'd tried the outfield briefly and ineffectively in the minors, preferred first. He wound up playing neither. Throneberry lingered on the Met bench, appearing only occasionally to pinch hit. Every time he emerged from the dugout, his fan club erupted. On May 5, in what was to be his final appearance as a Met, Throneberry struck out as a pinch hitter. Four days later, when the Mets had to cut their squad to 25, he was optioned to Buffalo. "I may be back a lot sooner than people think," Throneberry said, sitting in his locker beneath the Marvelous Marv sign, puffing on his ever-present cigarette. The sign remained, but Marv and his cigarettes left for the International League.

At first, Throneberry's fans remained loyal, carting banners to the Polo Grounds demanding his return. The night after he was optioned, a banner was paraded through the stands that read, "We Miss Marv." The following night, another pleaded, "Bring Back Marv." The following year, 1964, there was an entry at Banner Day which read, "Marvelous Marv, We Love You." Throneberry's Buffalo home runs were reported on Met radio broadcasts. *The New York Post* printed a daily log of his performance. After his first home run, Stengel said, "Now he has only 24 or 49 to go. I told him that if he hit 25 or 50, I'd bring him back." In mid–May, after three home runs in three nights, it looked as though Marv might be back, but he soon went into a deep slump, going hitless in 32 at bats.

After a few weeks, the fans adopted new heroes, and Marv's exploits were noted only in Buffalo, which, in many cases, was fortunate. One day, the Bisons were at Jacksonville and Marv was playing first. The score was tied in the ninth inning, with a Jacksonville runner in scoring position, when the batter hit a slow ground ball to first. "You had to see this," said Buffalo team-mate Ted Schreiber, "because you wouldn't believe it. The ball just kept bouncing and bouncing and bouncing, it was hit so slow. You could almost measure each bounce. Marv had iron hands. If they were on the ground, they didn't come up. If they were up, they didn't go down. He saw the ball and put his hands down. The ball bounced over them and through his legs. Like a center who has just snapped the ball, he looked back between his legs. The ball was going so slow it stopped just a few feet behind him."

The winning run crossed the plate and Buffalo lost the game. Kerby Farrell, the Bison man-ager, began to weep. "Old Kerby took his losses hard," said Bison Joe Hicks. It was only an Inter-national League game, but Farrell had never, ever suffered such a frustrating defeat. "Kerby just went nuts," recalled Craig Anderson. "He slammed a chair in the shower stall and cried a lot."

What about Marv? "He just folded his glove under his arm and walked into the clubhouse," said Anderson. "Marv just sat there and never showed any emotion." As Farrell wept in his office, Throneberry sat in front of his locker, puffing on a cigarette. "Marv always had these dirty undershorts on," Anderson said. "He'd cross his legs and light up a cigarette. He'd inhale and when he took the cigarette away from his mouth, he'd flare it out. Then he'd bring it in, blow the smoke out and move his hand away. He'd always pose." Finally Marv spoke. "A lot of guys have said bad things about me," he said, "but that's the first time anybody cried."

Throneberry wound up back in Buffalo in 1964 and held out again. In mid-season, with-out any fanfare, the Bisons released the first Met folk hero. "The trainer came over," recalled shortstop Al Moran, "and said he had a message from New York. Marv was on the phone for a while and came back and said, 'You'll never believe what happened. I just got released.' He never changed his expression. He put his cigarette back in his mouth and said, 'I'll go home with my brother Faye and we'll do something.'"

Marv went back to Tennessee and became a salesman for the Sherwin Williams Paint Com-pany. The next time Moran and most of his teammates saw him was when he appeared many years later in the Miller Lite commercials, delivering his famous tag line, "I still don't know why they asked me to be in this commercial."

In May, 1962, despite the acquisition of Throneberry, the Mets began to play in the fash-ion many had thought they would. On May 12, they swept a doubleheader from the Braves. Eight days later, they took another doubleheader in Milwaukee to raise their record to 12–19. The Mets were in eighth place and, since losing their first nine games, had gone 12–10. Moreover, they were playing exciting ball, with late inning rallies, clutch hitting and heart-stopping finishes. Seventh place, which Drebinger had predicted before the start of the season, might be pes-simistic.

In the midst of the hot streak, long before the legend of Marvelous Marv was created, Met fans discovered another hero. He was not a home run hitter or a fireballing pitcher. The fans, who would soon become known as the New Breed, adopted a pinch runner as their icon.

At 28, Rod Kanehl was a year younger than Throneberry and, like him, a product of the Yankee organization. "I signed in 1954 with Tom Geenwade [the same scout who signed Man-tle]," Kanehl said. "He impressed me with the fact that the Yankees were the best and that I should sign with the best. He told me that someday I'd play with a winning team in Yankee

Stadium. He was right. In 1963, I played with the Mets in Yankee Stadium when we won the Mayor's Trophy Game."

Like Al Jackson, Kanehl was a fine all-around athlete. At Drury College, he finished second in the NAIA decathlon, clearing 6'2" in the high jump and 12'10" in the pole vault. Kanehl could long jump more than 21 feet and ran the hundred yard dash in 10.5 seconds.

Kanehl's progress through the Yankee farm system was slow. In 1954 and 1955, he went to the pre-spring training instructional camps for "special" prospects, but never came within hailing distance of the New York roster. In 1954, at McAlester of the Sooner State League, Kanehl had a 34 game hitting streak, and gave the first sign he might be a future Met when he hit an apparent inside the park home run only to be called out for missing third base.

Despite several good minor league seasons, it didn't appear as though Kanehl would ever be a Yankee. He was an outfielder with speed, but no power. "That ain't good for an outfielder," said Stengel, who advised Kanehl to try switch hitting. In order to take advantage of his quickness, the Yanks moved him from center field to shortstop. "They did that to everybody who played center field," Kanehl said, "because they were looking for a replacement for Rizzuto and Casey thought that anybody who could play center field could play shortstop. He moved Woodie Held and Tony Kubek from the outfield." Kubek wound up in New York, Held went to Kansas City and Kanehl went back to the minors.

"I had a family," Kanehl said. "I had children. I would go to Drury College in Springfield for one semester and then go to spring training. I did that for three years. I decided that 1958 was going to be my last camp. I'd go down and see what happened." What happened was that Kanehl, who had been loaned to the Reds' organization, reported to camp in Laredo, Texas and couldn't agree on a contract. He called his father, the track coach at Drury, told him he was coming home and asked him to see about getting him back into school or helping him find a job.

Before Kanehl left Laredo, Phil Seghi, an executive with the Reds, told him that the Dallas team would pay him what he wanted if he could make the squad. They were willing to give him a five day trial. "It's on your way home, Rod," Seghi said. Kanehl agreed to stop in Dallas, made the team and had a good year, leading the Texas League in stolen bases, which got him an invitation to the Yankee camp in 1959.

Kanehl didn't make the Yankee team in 1959, nor in either of the next two years. He played for Richmond, Dallas and Nashville, where he finished the 1961 season, batting .308. After eight years of professional baseball, he had yet to play a game in the major leagues.

In the minor league draft conducted in December, 1961, Kanehl was selected by Syracuse, an affiliate of the Minnesota Twins. Subsequent to the draft, the Twins dropped their affiliation with Syracuse and engaged Vancouver of the Pacific Coast League as its Triple A club. The Mets picked up Syracuse, which they would share with the Washington Senators.* What major league team owned the rights to Rod Kanehl? The Twins and Mets both laid claim to his services. In late January, Commissioner Frick ruled that, since Kanehl remained on the Syracuse roster after Minnesota had cancelled its agreement, he was the property of the Mets.

Kanehl was a non-roster invitee to the Met camp which, he discovered, bore great similarities to Yankee camps. In the Yankee system, each minor leaguer learned to do everything the same way — the Yankee way. They learned base running, bunting, relays and all of baseball's fundamental skills. For twelve years, Casey Stengel had conducted Yankee spring drills, and Kanehl knew exactly what Stengel wanted. On many occasions, when Stengel wanted someone to demonstrate the proper way of doing something, he called on Kanehl. Casey couldn't

---

*Both clubs said the reason they shared an affiliate was that neither had enough Triple A players to stock a complete roster. Actually, both clubs had plenty of Triple A players. The problem was that most of them were playing with the Mets and Senators.

remember the names of most of his players, but he knew who Kanehl was and that Kanehl knew how to do things the Yankee way. "I was the only one in camp who'd played for Stengel before," Rod recalled, "so he'd say, 'Kanehl, show them how to lead off first base.' He'd have me demonstrate the Yankee way of rounding the bases. All the other guys were asking, 'Who's Kanehl?'"

Many writers described an incident on the first day of camp, in which Stengel took his club on a tour of the bases, as if his players were so green that Casey needed to point out the location of each. Kanehl knew from his Yankee experience that this was not a joke. "He'd take us to home plate and say, 'Here's where you start, because the object of the game is to start at home and get back to home as soon as possible.' He'd show you how to take the signs, how to look and at what time to look. Then we'd go to first and he'd show us how to lead off first. We'd go to second and he'd show us how to turn the base and how to lead. Then we'd go to third and do the same thing. Every year, whether it was the major league camp or an advance camp, he'd do the same thing."

One of the reasons Stengel liked Kanehl was that the rookie was a throwback to the old days, who looked like Casey's idea of a ballplayer. He was a tobacco chewer who seemed to end up with stains all over the front of his uniform by the end of a game. In exhibition games, Kanehl played like a ballplayer as well. "I played in the intrasquad games and the B games and hit pretty good," he said. Kanehl was not a great hitter, and had little power, but he had speed and, most of all, versatility; he could play any position but pitcher and catcher. When training camp began, Ted Lepcio, a veteran American Leaguer, had the inside track on the utility infield job. "I beat him out," said Kanehl, "because I could do a little bit more than he could. He wasn't that fleet of foot and he couldn't play the outfield."

Kanehl was versatile, and he was hungry, believing the Mets were his best and perhaps last chance to reach the major leagues. "Rod Kanehl came to that camp," said Craig Anderson, "and showed more hustle and tried harder to make that team than anyone. Stengel noticed it and got to like him. He made the team on outright hustle. He was not that talented a player, but he was in the right place at the right time." "He was a little sergeant," said Al Jackson. "He was Casey's right hand man, and was almost like the bench coach. He kept the old man alive. To me, Rod didn't have enough ability to play in the big leagues, but he did the right thing at the right time."

"Rod would promote himself," said Ted Schreiber. "He was very verbal in the dugout. He'd yell and scream. Casey always knew Rod Kanehl was there. So if he needed somebody, he'd say, 'OK Rod, you go in there.' He wasn't the greatest ballplayer, but he could play a lot of positions. He was smart and very confident of his ability."

By the end of the exhibition schedule, Kanehl, who no one but Stengel knew when camp started, was one of just a few candidates for the final roster position. "I think I made the team on the first Met game that was ever televised back to New York," Kanehl said. "We were losing 3–1 to the Dodgers in the ninth inning when I came up against Koufax. I ducked away from a pitch and it hit my bat and wound up as a line drive down the right field line that tied the game. Felix Mantilla got a hit to drive me in to win it. George Weiss couldn't get rid of me after that." When the Mets came north, Kanehl was still with the team, but didn't have a major league contract. When Christopher was sent to Syracuse the day before the season opener, Kanehl was in.

During the first few weeks of the season, Kanehl's activity was limited principally to pinch-running. On April 28, he scored the winning run against the Phillies. On May 12, he scored the tying run in a game the Mets won. A week later, he scored the winning run, and a day later scored again, all as a pinch-runner. Six times in all, Kanehl scored the tying or winning run as a pinch runner, and one must remember that the Mets were not winning many games. "Lucky" Kanehl, or "my little scavenger." Stengel called him. Howard Tuckner described him as "'Runner Rod Kanehl,' whom Casey loves more than money."

To become a true Met folk hero, Kanehl needed a nickname, and he soon had one — Hot

Rod. Not only did he out-hustle everyone else, but Hot Rod, unlike Throneberry, had an ebullient, outgoing personality which endeared him to the Met fans. Rod reveled in his new-found fame. He was happy to talk with the press and, when the team went to the West Coast, hung out with Hollywood celebrities. "He was a wheeler-dealer," said Don Rowe. Stengel, who had loved Billy Martin like a son, developed a similar affection for Kanehl. "For some reason or another," remembered Met outfielder Duke Carmel, "he and Casey got along very well. He would kid Casey sometimes, wake him up in the dugout." "When I came to spring training in '63," said Al Moran, "I thought he was one of the coaches. In the dugout, he'd suggest stuff to Casey and Casey would do it. The coaches liked him and Casey liked him." "I understood Casey," said Kanehl. "I knew his next move and knew what he was thinking."*

As the season went on, Casey started playing Rod more and more. On June 30, he was batting .365, with 19 hits in 52 at bats. In early July, he hit the first grand slam in Met history. Pretty soon, Kanehl was starting frequently at both third base and second. With Charley Neal suffering from a nagging hand injury during the second half of the season, Kanehl became the regular second baseman. At the end of July, his average was .312, but

Twenty-eight-year-old Rod Kanehl won a job with the 1962 Mets due to his versatility, drive and sheer hustle. He played with the Mets for three years and became a favorite of Casey Stengel and the fans.

the more he played, the more his average plummeted and the more his defensive liabilities were exposed. Kanehl never mastered the art of avoiding the runner while making a double play pivot, and took a beating at the keystone. "I was getting tired in August," Kanehl said, "because I'd played a lot in July. Then I hurt my knee. I had a cartilage problem in my right leg. I'm not saying that had anything to do with my batting, because pitchers find things out. They started getting me out in August. I joke that they were talking me up for Rookie of the Year until I started reading about it." Once opposing pitchers found Kanehl's weaknesses, his average dropped, and he finished at .248. Still, it had been quite a season. The man who was not even expected to make the team in spring training wound up playing 133 games, including 62 at second, 30 at third, 20 in the outfield and a few at shortstop and first base. But in May, Kanehl was still a pinch runner, for a Met team that appeared to be headed for the first division.

*When Stengel died in 1975, Kanehl was the only former Met who attended his funeral.

◆ 4 ◆

Elio, Choo Choo and
a Lot of Losses
The 1962 Season
(Part II)

Following their doubleheader sweep in Milwaukee, which brought their record to 12–19, a jubilant eighth place Met club boarded a plane for Houston. The Colt 45s were in ninth place and dropping quickly after a fast start, while the Mets were coming on strong. Sixth place was only a game and a half away and the first division appeared reachable. The Mets couldn't wait to get to Houston.

Wait, however, was exactly what they did. First, mechanical trouble delayed the boarding. Then, for two hours, the players sat impatiently on the plane, waiting to take off. When they were finally airborne, they learned that Houston was blanketed in fog. The plane was diverted to Dallas, where it sat on the ground for another two hours. The club finally arrived in Houston at eight o'clock Monday morning, roughly twelve hours after leaving Milwaukee. They hadn't had a meal in almost 15 hours. "If any of the newspapermen asks for me," Stengel said, "tell 'em I'm bein' embalmed." Just twelve hours after they arrived, the Mets played the Colts. They didn't play very well and lost all three games in Houston.

From Houston, the Mets flew to Los Angeles, suffered from more delays, arrived at 5 A.M., and lost three to the Dodgers. Then it was on to San Francisco, where they arrived at 3 A.M., for three more games. The first game was won by the Giants on a tenth inning home run by Willie Mays off Jay Hook.

The following day, in the first game of a doubleheader, the Mets won a battle but lost the war. In the seventh inning, with New York trailing 3–1 and Willie Mays on second, Roger Craig hit Orlando Cepeda with a pitch. Cepeda, as he walked to first, yelled at Craig, then started to charge the mound. Fortunately, he was intercepted by Giant manager Alvin Dark and re-directed toward first base. As Craig prepared to pitch to Felipe Alou, Cepeda, still hot, led recklessly off the bag, daring Craig to try to pick him off.

Craig probably had the best pickoff move of any righthander in the National League, nabbing 13 base runners in 1962. He learned his move from Clem Labine, who in turn had learned it from Hoyt Wilhelm. "None of us could get away with it today," said Labine. "It was a balk," said Don Rowe. Craig's move consisted of putting his weight on his front foot and leaning forward while in the stretch position. Most of the time, he would lift the leg and throw home, but sometimes, with the same motion, Craig broke his knee, jumped, wheeled and threw to first.

Not only did Craig have a deceptive move, he had infinite patience. He would throw to first again and again, at varying speeds. "Once I counted 14 throws to first when Maury Wills was on," said Dodger catcher Norm Sherry. Even if Craig didn't pick his man off, he tired him out. After diving back to first 14 times, Wills would be a bit less fresh when he finally took off for second.

Craig decided to go to work on Cepeda. He had him upset and, like the crafty veteran he was, would take advantage of it. Craig wheeled and threw to first, where Cepeda was caught completely asleep. Craig's move was so quick, however, that he also fooled first baseman Ed Bouchee, who dropped the ball, and Cepeda was able to scramble back safely. That was all right, for Cepeda was still highly agitated. So was Mays, who Craig had knocked down twice earlier in the game.

What the Met pitcher didn't know was that his shortstop, Elio Chacon, was also upset. Chacon was a lightning-quick 5'9" Venezuelan, whose father had been an outstanding player in Cuba for many years. Elio was a flashy fielder with a strong arm. "Even if he doesn't do everything right," Stengel said during spring training, "he is always doing something."

Chacon was talented but erratic, both on and off the field. He spoke virtually no English, even after several years of playing in the United States, and was always smiling. "He certainly is a nice little fellow," broadcaster Ralph Kiner told his audience. "Elio was like a little teen-aged, happy-go-lucky kid," said Craig Anderson.

Chacon was quite a ladies' man. He supposedly owned 18 suits and 23 pairs of shoes, not counting the ones with spikes on the bottom. "He had a cousin in every town we went to," said Rob Gardner, who played with Chacon in the minors. "I could never figure out how he could have so many cousins. And they were all women. That was really weird. He had no male cousins."

Gardner recalled an incident that occurred in the spring of 1964, when he, Chacon and Ron Swoboda were with Buffalo. The three players were leaving the ballpark one day when they noticed a sporty MG convertible in the parking lot. "Man, that's a great looking car," Swoboda said. "You like that car?" Chacon asked in his heavily-accented English. "It's my car." Swoboda was impressed, and Chacon asked him if he wanted to take it for a drive. The keys were inside, and Swoboda got in and drove the car around Dunedin. Eventually, he stopped at a gas station, where the attendant noticed that the MG was very much like one owned by a friend of his. The two cars were so similar, in fact, that they had identical license plates. "To make a long story short," said Gardner, "It wasn't Elio's car. It belonged to a guy who worked in the front office. So when Swoboda brings it back to the ballpark, the cops were waiting for him. Of course, it got straightened out and no charges were filed."

"Elio used to do some goofy things, but he was a decent shortstop," said Felix Mantilla, Chacon's roommate. "He was a little different." Off the field, Chacon was friendly, but on the field, he was highly excitable. Earlier in the Giant game, Mays had slid hard into him, and Elio was determined to get even. Mays and Chacon had also been involved in an incident the previous season, when the Giant outfielder slid into Chacon and opened a cut that required ten stitches to close. "I told him, 'Cool it,'" said Mantilla, who was playing second, "but he said, 'No, I'm going to do something.'"

Craig set, then wheeled and tried to pick Mays off second. Willie went sliding back in and spiked Chacon, who jumped to his feet and took a swing at Mays. "All of sudden," said Mantilla, "he was throwing punches all over the place. I jumped on top of Willie and tried to separate him from my roommate. Somebody came up behind me and hit me on top of the head." Mays picked up the 160-pound Chacon and threw him to the ground. Meanwhile, Cepeda, sensing an opportunity, charged at Craig and the two began exchanging blows as both benches cleared. "The verdict on Cepeda," wrote Jack McDonald, "was that he was far more ferocious while he was being restrained by teammates than he was after he broke loose and took his first wild swing at Craig, after which he went into a protective crouch." Mantilla was still trying to get Mays off Chacon when Gil Hodges, one of the strongest men in baseball, threw himself into the pile and pried Chacon and Mays apart.

Others were acting more sensibly. Veteran pitcher Dave Hillman left the Met bench with everybody else. "We all headed for the infield," Hillman said. "I happened to know a boy on the Giants [Ernie Bowman] who was from Johnson City, 19 miles from me, so I hunted him up. I said, 'Ernie, go with me. We got no damn business in that place over there. Let them boys go at it.'" Hillman and Bowman squared off at a safe distance from the main event and shadow-boxed a bit until it was all over.

Chacon was ejected and later fined $100. Craig and Cepeda were sent to neutral corners to calm down, but both were allowed to remain in the game. When play was resumed, Cepeda again took a long lead off first. Craig whirled and threw, and had Cepeda easily, except that the ball once more eluded Bouchee, this time getting completely past him, allowing Mays to go to third and Cepeda to second. Both scored a moment later on Felipe Alou's single.

The Giants won both games of the doubleheader, taking the second on a four run rally in the last of the eighth off Craig Anderson. It was Anderson's second straight loss, a statistic forgotten in the excitement of the brawl. Anderson's losses would, by the end of the season, become another source of amazement.

On May 30, the Dodgers returned to New York to play their first regular season game since 1957. New Yorkers hated Walter O'Malley for whisking the Dodgers out of Brooklyn, but they still loved the players. A crowd of more than 53,000 had come to Yankee Stadium in 1960 to watch the Dodgers play the Yankees in an exhibition game. They cheered for Snider, Hodges and Gilliam and all the other guys they didn't recognize. What would happen when the Dodgers returned to play a game that counted?

In the Mets' first fifteen home dates, attendance had averaged just over 10,000 per game. For the first appearance of the Dodgers, a Memorial Day doubleheader, a crowd of over 55,000, including wheelchair bound ex–Dodger catcher Roy Campanella, packed the stands in a World Series atmosphere. It was the largest Polo Grounds crowd since 1942. The entire roster of each team was announced prior to the game, and each player came out to line up along the foul lines.

A few of the old heroes returned, but most of the Dodgers' stars had never played in Brooklyn. Campanella was paralyzed, Pee Wee Reese, Carl Furillo, and Carl Erskine had retired and Duke Snider was a pinch hitter and part time outfielder. Tommy Davis, Willie Davis, Frank Howard and Maury Wills had all joined the Dodgers in Los Angeles. Don Drysdale had played in Brooklyn, as had Sandy Koufax, but Koufax was just a wild young lefty when he pitched in Ebbetts Field. There were more old Brooklyn heroes in Met blue and orange than Dodger blue and gray. "When the Giants and Dodgers played there," said Mantilla, "those were the biggest crowds we had. They were usually pulling for us, but when the Dodgers and Giants were there, it seemed like they were pulling for them."

Reporter Gordon White disagreed. "They were definitely rooting for the Mets," he said. "The Dodgers and Giants were anathema. They were the bad guys because they had left us. St. Louis didn't get upset when the Browns went to Baltimore, because St. Louis couldn't have cared less about the Browns. But the Dodgers and Giants leaving New York was a blow to the city's pride. The Dodger and Giant fans who became the Met fans were very bitter. Nobody was rooting for the Giants and Dodgers when they came back with 'SF' or 'LA' on their hats."

The fans got what they came for, other than a Met win. Koufax won a lopsided first game, 13–6, but Hodges hit a home run. When the Mets staged their traditional last gasp rally, coming from 10–0 to 13–6, the "Let's go Mets" chants rang out. The second game was more exciting.

The Mets pulled off a triple play. Hodges hit two more homers, and the score was tied 5–5 in the ninth inning. Willie Davis homered off Anderson, dealing the Met bullpen ace his third straight loss and giving the Dodgers a sweep.

The Giants followed the Dodgers in for a Friday night game on June 1. "The Polo Grounds still feels like home," said Giant coach Whitey Lockman, a member of the '51 and '54 Giant pennant winners. All of the Giant coaches, in fact, had played for the club in the Polo Grounds. Mays was the last Giant to emerge from the locker room, and was besieged by his loyal New York fans. "I hear you're a fighter now," teased Johnny Antonelli, who had come out to pitch batting practice. Mays didn't want to talk about it.

San Francisco fans had never warmed to Mays as had the Giant faithful of the Polo Grounds. "For a while they seemed to expect me to hit a home run every time I got to bat," he said. Joe Dimaggio was the favorite center fielder in San Francisco, and Cepeda, who arrived in a big way in the Bay area, became more popular than Mays. To his fans in New York, however, neither Cepeda nor anyone else could compare to Wonderful Willie. "The center field turf in the Polo Grounds," wrote Arthur Daley, "looks normal this week-end for the first time in almost five years. Willie Mays has come home."

As they had been before the first game of the Dodger series, the rosters were announced to the crowd, which gave Mays a thundering ovation. "That was really exciting," said Rod Kanehl. "The crowds were fantastic. They were happy to see the Giants again, but they were rooting for the Mets." Chacon expected to be booed, but the crowd cheered him, too.

The game was typical of the Mets' season. Craig was knocked out of the box early after surrendering two home runs to Willie McCovey and one to Mays. Hodges' knee was bothering him too much to play so, with lefty Billy Pierce starting for the Giants, Stengel asked Kanehl if he could play first base. "I said sure," he recalled. "I'd only played first once or twice in the minor leagues, but Hodges let me borrow his glove and I went out and played first base." Kanehl hit his first major league home run in the sixth, but as the Mets went to bat in their half of the eighth inning, they trailed 9–1. Chacon led off by reaching on an error. Two singles and a double followed, then a home run by Mantilla. It was 9–6 and the fans were screaming. The Giants were changing pitchers. Stengel was up on the top step of the dugout.

Roger Angell, the urbane observer for *The New Yorker*, looked around him in amazement. "It seemed statistically unlikely," he wrote, "that there could be, even in New York, a forty- or fifty-thousand-man crowd made up exclusively of born losers.... What we were witnessing was precisely the opposite of the kind of rooting that goes on across the river [at Yankee Stadium]. This was the losing cheer, the gallant yell for a good try.... This was a new recognition that perfection is admirable but a trifle inhuman, and that a stumbling kind of semi-success can be much more warming."

The Met rally ended in stumbling semi-success when Throneberry fouled out as a pinch hitter. The Mets got two runners on in the ninth, but couldn't get over the hump, and went down to their 12th straight defeat. That was to be a Met pattern for their early years. They would get themselves into a seemingly hopeless position, only to rise up off the mat to stage a desperate rally, which invariably fell just short. In their 120 losses, the Mets brought the tying run to the plate in the last inning 56 times. Thirty-nine of their losses were by a single run. "He concedes defeat almost daily," Robert Teague wrote of the Met fan, "but only after the very last Met has been retired."

The following day, the Mets did it again. Trailing the Giants by two in the bottom of the ninth, they got two on with no outs, but couldn't get them home. Thus came consecutive loss number 13. The league had found the Met weakness—good teams. They lost 26 of their first 27 contests against first division clubs.

Finally, on June 8 in Chicago, the Mets snapped the horrendous losing streak at 17 games.

It was Jay Hook, who had broken the season-opening nine game skid, who came to the rescue. The Cubs also came to the rescue in their own way, allowing an unearned run in the ninth that proved to be the winner.

Although the Met streak had ended, the caliber of the club was now apparent. Weiss had long since realized that the veterans were not going to come through and began to look to the youngsters. Labine was released, as were Herb Moford and catcher Joe Ginsberg. Outfielder Gus Bell was sent to Milwaukee as partial payment for Frank Thomas and the Mets talked about building for the future. They traded Don Zimmer to the Reds for Bob (Lefty) Miller and third baseman Cliff Cook, the American Association's Most Valuable Player in 1961.

Cook, 25, had a history of hitting home runs in the minors, having poked 32 at Albuquerque in 1958, 31 at Savannah in 1959 and 32 at Indianapolis in 1961. In between, he'd had a brief trial with Cincinnati in 1960, batting just .208 with three home runs in 54 games. If he could realize the potential he'd shown in the minor leagues, Cook could be a threat at the Polo Grounds. Unfortunately, he reported overweight, struck out a lot, wasn't much of a fielder and also had a bad back, which required surgery at the end of the season.

By mid–June, the young players weren't doing any better than the veterans, so Stengel got another veteran, 39-year-old Gene Woodling, who'd had a running feud with Stengel when he played for the Yankees. The crux of the disagreement was the fact that Stengel platooned Woodling rather than play him every day. "Now he can play all he wants," Stengel said. Woodling was not the player he'd been, of course, when he was with the Yankees eight years earlier. After watching the old veteran struggle around the bases running out his only Met triple, one observer said, "If Woodling had been a horse, they would have shot him."

Young or old, it made no difference. The Mets kept losing. "When you pitched against them," said the Phillies' Dennis Bennett, "it was a win. You just marked down a W. They had some hitters that could hurt you, but they didn't have any who could beat you." No one was talking about the first division, seventh place, or even ninth place. The Mets' destiny was clear. They were going to be the most entertaining last place club in baseball history.

On June 29, the Mets earned their first victory in Los Angeles, beating the Dodgers in a pre-game egg throwing contest. They lost the baseball game, of course, and the next day found Sandy Koufax throwing another kind of egg, goose eggs, as he pitched the first no hitter of his career. After a 10–1 loss to the Giants a few days later, Robert Lipsyte wrote, "The San Francisco Giants today discovered the Mets only three weaknesses— pitching, fielding and batting." "The Mets are bad for many reasons,' wrote Jimmy Breslin, "one of which is they do not have good players." Later in the season, Lipsyte referred to "the dreaded Met disease, which turns fingers to butter and bats into licorice whips." Actually, Lipsyte was exaggerating. The pitching and fielding left a lot to be desired, but the hitting was actually rather good. Thomas, when he was hot, was hitting with considerable power, and Ashburn seemed to be on base all the time.

Ashburn, who was slowed by a series of nagging leg injuries early in the season, excelled as a pinch hitter. In his first twelve appearances, he had four hits and four walks, and wound up with a pinch hitting average of .419. The pipe-smoking Ashburn's specialty was an ability to hit foul ball after foul ball, prolonging an at bat and drawing walks. When he retired, Ashburn ranked 13th on the all-time walk list with 1198. He also discovered new-found power in the Polo Grounds, hitting seven homers for the season, more than he had ever hit in his previous 14 years in the big leagues. When he connected on June 10, it was his first home run since 1959, and only his fourth since 1956. The same month, Ashburn got the 2500th hit of his career. He finished the season with a .306 batting average, his best since he won the batting championship in 1958, and was the only Met to top the .300 mark.

On September 3, Ashburn had a most unusual evening in Pittsbugh. It was a memorable occasion of which Ashburn had no recollection whatsoever. In the fifth inning of the first game of a doubleheader, Bill Mazeroski of the Pirates hit a fly ball down the right field line. Ashburn raced into the corner after it. The ball bounced into the stands for a ground rule double and Ashburn bounced off the fence and collapsed in a heap. He sat on the ground for a few minutes, then got to his feet and resumed his position. Ashburn played the remainder of the first game and, while waiting for the second game to start, sat in front of his locker eating a popsicle. A visitor consoled him on the Mets' tough loss. "I don't remember," Ashburn replied. "I can't remember a thing. You mean we lost this game? We didn't win this game? What was the score? How did we lose it? We didn't lose it." Catcher Joe Pignatano overheard the conversation and summoned trainer Gus Mauch. Mauch called Pirate team physician Dr. Joseph Finegold, who hustled Ashburn off to the hospital for observation. "I'm good enough to play," Richie protested. "I just can't remember, that's all." "From the fifth on," Finegold told reporters, "this man's been playing on nothing but reflex."

At times during the 1962 season, Stengel probably wished he could suffer from a similar loss of memory. "The way we've been going," he said after learning of Ashburn's amnesia, "maybe it's too bad I didn't forget the whole year." "I'm shell-shocked," he said at one point. "I'm not used to gettin' any of these shocks at all, and now they come every three innings."

Despite all the misfortune, a number of good things happened to the Mets, mostly on offense. Thomas and Throneberry had some blistering hot streaks. Neal, Hickman, Mantilla and Kanehl also hit well. On the few occasions that Gil Hodges was healthy, he hit for power, smashing nine homers in only 127 at bats. Gil was bothered by a bad knee from spring training on, and then, at a Saturday night reception after the Old Timers Game on July 14, collapsed from a kidney stone attack. The subsequent operation and hospitalization essentially finished his season.

The Mets finished the year with a .240 team batting average, last in the league, but hit 139 home runs, better than four other clubs. The nearby fences of the Polo Grounds helped, as 93 of the 139 were hit at home. As far as pitching and fielding, however, Lipsyte was right on target. Arthur Daley, in his pre-season prognosis, was not. "The most pleasant surprise this spring," Daley wrote just before the start of the season, "has been in the pitching." If the pitching was surprising, it wasn't a pleasant surprise, nor was the team defense. The Mets' ERA of 5.04 was half a run higher than the next worst team, and their fielding average was the lowest in the NL. "Roger Craig should have been a reliever, but we had to use him as a starter," said Kanehl. "We expected more out of Miller and Hook. They had great stuff, but they just lit up the scoreboard. People just teed off on them."

Following the All Star break, the Mets started another losing streak, this one a mere 11 games.* As the losses and injuries mounted, Weiss looked to his Syracuse farm club for reinforcements. There wasn't a whole lot to look at, for Syracuse was destined to finish last in the International League, with a 53–101 record that was only slightly better than that of the parent club. The Mets recalled 26-year-old infielder Rick Herrscher, a former baseball and basketball star at Southern Methodist University, and catcher Clarence (Choo Choo) Coleman.

In his final Syracuse game, Herrscher, who'd played professional basketball with the Hawaii Chiefs of the American Basketball League, had been playing left field when he crashed into the fence and broke his thumb. When he reported to New York, he met with Johnny Murphy and told him of his injury. "Oh, my god," Murphy replied, "whatever you do, don't tell Casey. We've had injuries all year long, and now if I bring up a kid from the minors with a broken thumb! Just keep it quiet." "I ended up putting a pad over my thumb," Herrscher said, "sort of taped some sponge rubber over it and started hitting with my hands a little bit apart."

*During the year, the Mets had streaks of 9, 11, 13 and 17 losses, meaning that 50 of their defeats were part of long losing stretches. Fifty losses is slightly less than a pennant winner will have in an entire season.

Coleman, who was hitting just .195 at Syracuse when he was recalled, arrived a few days before Herrscher. Choo Choo, claimed from the Phillies in the expansion draft, had hit the first Met home run during the exhibition season, then was optioned to Syracuse in the final cut. He was a veteran of the Indianapolis Clowns, a barnstorming semi-pro club, and the Dodger and Phillie farm systems. Shortly after Coleman was recalled from Syracuse, Stengel told a reporter, "Do you know who my player of the year is? My player of the year is Choo Choo Coleman and I have him for only two days. He runs very good."

Coleman had some defensive skill—"my low ball catcher," Stengel called him, he could run, "my little runnin' fool," and he had left-handed power that might prove useful in the Polo Grounds. Anyone who could pull the ball was a threat in the Polo Grounds, and Coleman could pull. Lord, could he pull! His problem was that he couldn't keep the ball fair. "Choo Choo used to hit foul balls to right field," recalled Ted Schreiber, "not just foul balls, but very foul balls. He didn't want to change the way he hit, because then he couldn't hit his foul balls. He was using his shoulders to swing the bat. It was such a bizarre way to hit. I don't know how anyone could even entertain it."

"Hell," said Jim Hickman, "he would pull the ball into the first base dugout. I remember Casey saying that one of these days we're going to tape his wrists so he can't turn them over." "I used to call him Exit 16," said Al Jackson. "He'd hit them right over the dugout."

Choo Choo became another fan favorite, following in the footsteps of Throneberry and Kanehl. The three Met heroes had personalities that were as diverse as three personalities could be. Kanehl was outgoing and articulate, and helped create his own persona. Throneberry was a quiet, easygoing country boy. Choo Choo made Marvelous Marv seem a bubbling extrovert, for he rarely spoke at all. "He'd carry on a conversation with you," said infielder Larry Burright, "but to keep it going, you had to do most of the talking." Coleman was a man of few, but unusual words, Yogi Berra with about 350 fewer home runs. Stengel couldn't remember the names of most of his players, but he could at least recall his wife Edna's name. Coleman was once asked his wife's name by Ralph Kiner during a post game interview. "Mrs. Coleman," Choo Choo replied. He referred to all of his teammates as "Bub."

One day in 1963, Coleman was warming up in front of the dugout with Chris Cannizzaro, Don Rowe and Al Moran. He was throwing to Moran and Cannizzaro was playing catch with Rowe. "Watch this," Cannizzaro said to Rowe. He asked Coleman who he was playing catch with. "This was about July," said Rowe. "We'd been together since March." Coleman didn't say anything, just kept throwing the ball to Moran. Cannizzaro kept asking, "Who is he?" Finally, Coleman threw the ball in the dirt, so that Moran had to turn and run after it, showing Choo Choo his back. Coleman turned triumphantly to Cannizzaro. "He's number

Choo Choo Coleman couldn't remember the names of his teammates (or even his wife) but he knew the hitters in the National League. Coleman hustled and was adept at blocking low pitches, but he couldn't hit.

40," he said. "They always teased him for not knowing anybody's name," said Jackson, "but if you gave him a number and the team the guy played on, he would tell you what the guy hit and what he couldn't hit. He was one of the better catchers I've ever had."

Met fans appreciated Choo Choo's constant hustle. "Nobody could try any harder than this guy," said Clem Labine. Coleman wasn't the most skilled catcher in the world, but he crouched low and attacked balls in the dirt. "He was a boxer," said Labine, "someone who doesn't catch the ball most of the time, but he'd keep it in front of him." Writer Roger Angell said Coleman "caught as though he were fighting a swarm of bees." Joe Ginsberg, the 35-year-old veteran who spent spring training with the Mets, loved Coleman's enthusiasm. "Joe would be catching batting practice," said outfielder Bobby Gene Smith, "and he'd call Choo Choo over and tell him he had to go to the bathroom. Then Joe would disappear and Choo Choo would have to catch the rest of batting practice." With a nickname like Choo Choo and Stengel's endorsement as player of the year, all Coleman needed was a little panache and an occasional clutch hit to become a darling of the Met fans.

A tenth place team can salvage a sorry season by playing the role of spoiler for one of the pennant contenders. Nineteen sixty-two was a good year to play the spoiler, for the National League race was a tight one. The Mets favored neither of the top two teams, the Dodgers and Giants. They lost 14 of 18 to the Giants and 16 of 18 to the Dodgers. The third team in contention was the Cincinnati Reds. The Reds, defending champions of the National League, had gotten off to a slow start and fallen well off the pace. In early July, they were in fifth place. By Saturday, August 5, they had moved up to third, 8½ games behind the Dodgers. With two consecutive doubleheaders coming up with the Mets, the Reds seemed poised to move even closer.

On Saturday, the Mets won the first game easily, 9–1 behind Craig. They took the night-cap 3–2 on a home run by Thomas in the 14th inning. The first game on Sunday was scoreless in the third inning when Herrscher, who had batted six times in the major leagues without getting a hit, came to the plate with two runners on base. Stengel had taken him aside and told him to look for an outside pitch and hit it over the short right field fence. Sure enough, Red pitcher Jim O'Toole threw an outside pitch and Herrscher, just as Stengel had instructed him, hit it over the right field wall for his first major league hit. "When I came into the dugout," Herrscher recalled, "Casey gave me a big wink."

The Mets won the opener but lost the second game. Still, three losses to the Mets in two days were too much for Red manager Fred Hutchinson, who was not known as The Bear because he was cuddly. Although just 43, decades of heavy smoking had lined his face, and hundreds of temper tantrums darkened his features. Bobby Klaus played for Hutch in 1964. "One time after we'd lost a game," said Klaus, "He came in and tipped over one of those after-game chow tables and said, 'You sons of bitches, you just lost a goddam game and you're eating!' He was tough."

After the final game of the Met series, Hutch sat alone on the bench, stewing, for several minutes. Then he picked up the dugout phone and called the clubhouse, saying he was about to begin making the long walk to center field. He did not want anyone there when he arrived. Herrscher had just finished being interviewed on Ralph Kiner's post-game show and was walking from the television studio to the clubhouse. "Hutchinson had just thrown the water cooler on the field," Herrscher remembered, "and was starting his walk to the clubhouse. I was heading up there, too, when I saw all these players coming out half-naked, trying to put their clothes on. One of them said, 'Hutchinson's on his way up.'" When the Cincinnati manager finally reached the clubhouse, it was completely empty. The Reds finished the season three games out of first place, the three Met wins in August making the difference.

The Mets were beginning to set records. On August 7th, they were eliminated from the pennant race. On the 30th, they lost their 100th game, the first time a New York or Brooklyn team had done so since 1912, when the Yankees finished last in the American League with a 50–102 mark. The Giants, playing in New York from 1883 to 1957, had never lost as many as 100 games. The Mets had done it in their first year with a month to spare. On September 9, the Mets clinched last place. The American League had operated with 10 teams in 1961, but the Senators and Athletics had tied for 9th. The Mets were therefore the first team since 1900 to assure themselves of a tenth place finish. Edna Stengel said she considered her husband the manager of a 20th place club. After all, she pointed out, all of the other 19 teams in the majors had better records.

On Monday, September 10, Bob (Righty) Miller lost to the Braves, dropping to 0–12 and equaling the record of another R.L. Miller, Russ Lewis, who finished 0–12 for the 1928 Phillies.* In the process, Miller surrendered home runs to Eddie Mathews and Henry Aaron. Aaron's was the 185th home run allowed by the Met staff, tying the National League record held by the 1955 Cardinals. After the game with Milwaukee, which took place on Monday, the team headed home for what Howard Tuckner of the *Times* assured his readers would be "their most successful home week of the season. They're off until Friday night."

After three glorious days without suffering the pall of defeat, the Mets returned to action and watched Anderson give up a home run to Vada Pinson to break the league mark, in the same fashion that the Met reliever suffered so many indignities that year. Pinson's homer was an inside the park job, a line drive to centerfield that got by Jim Hickman. This game ended differently than most Met affairs, however, with a ninth inning rally that didn't fall short. With the score tied 9–9, Coleman hit a fly ball toward the foul pole in right. Most times Choo Choo did this, the ball curved foul. This time, it barely made it inside the pole, giving Roger Craig his eighth win of the year. He had lost 23, the most in the major leagues, and would lose one more before the season ended. Jackson had 20 losses and Hook 19, as the Mets narrowly missed having three 20 game losers. Not since the 1916 Athletics had a team had three pitchers reach the 20 loss mark in the same season.

One by one, records continued to fall. On September 18, rookie Larry Foss gave up a homer to Colt .45 catcher Merritt Ranew that broke the major league mark for home runs given up by a staff, surpassing the mark of the 1956 Athletics. On the 25th, Jay Hook threw the Mets' 71st wild pitch of the season, breaking the mark of the 1958 Dodgers. Hook gave up more runs than any pitcher in the league, closely followed by Craig. The Mets finished with the league's worst ERA, the most hits surrendered, the most runs, gave up the most home runs, hit the most batters and had the fewest strikeouts.

On September 20, the Mets lost a doubleheader to the Colts. The second loss, their 115th of the season, tied the National League mark set by the Boston Braves in 1935. Few witnessed the feat in person, for there were only 1,481 in attendance when the doubleheader began, and probably not more than 200 in the stands when it ended. The New Breed appeared much more often when the old breed of Dodgers and Giants were in town than they did when the infant Houston club played. In five dates against the Colts, a schedule condensed and truncated because of doubleheaders and rain, the Mets drew a total of just 26,251, an average of 5,250. In 1963, the average New York crowd for a Met-Colt encounter was just over six thousand.

In rapid succession came loss #116, setting the National League record, #118, breaking the major league (post–1900) mark of the 1916 Athletics, and #120, which broke the Mets' previous record of 119. The only record the Mets wouldn't set was for the lowest winning percentage in a season. The 1916 Athletics (.235) held off the Mets (.250) with a couple of losses to spare. Bill Veeck insisted the Mets were even worse than his old St. Louis Browns clubs. "You can say anything you want," he declared, "but don't you dare say my Brownies were this bad.... There are

---

*On the next-to-last day of the season, Miller beat the Cubs to win his first game of the year and avoid the ignominy of a winless season. It was his first complete game since 1959.

still a few Brownies in the major leagues and this is nine years later. How many Mets do you think are going to be around even two years from now? I'm being soft here. I haven't even mentioned my midget, Eddie Gaedel."

Not co-incidentally, the two teams whose loss records were broken, the Boston Braves and Philadelphia Athletics, were no longer in the same location. Failure and fan apathy had driven them westward to Milwaukee and Kansas City, respectively. The Mets were different. Despite a number of meager crowds, particularly when the weather turned cold, they didn't appear to be in danger of being run out of town, for small late season crowds were not unusual in the early '60s. On September 28, 1962, with their teams out of contention and a fall chill setting in, only 595 fans showed up in Chicago and just 588 in Detroit.

The Mets' attendance of 922,000 was unheard of for a last place team, and well in excess of the 800,000 estimated breakeven point. On August 5, the Mets surpassed the 1957 attendance of the Giants. It wasn't just the numbers that were astounding. The fans didn't merely show up, they participated, much like the old Dodger faithful who trooped to Ebbets Field. "The 'Let's Go Mets' chant would start in the first inning," recalled Joe Hicks, who played with the '63 club, and it would go on through the whole game." "It was awesome," said Felix Mantilla, "to see the way the people got behind that team, which was a pretty bad team. I used to take the subway, and the fans would follow me and ask me for my autograph. The Met fans were a little different.'

Less than two weeks into the season, when it wasn't quite clear how bad the Mets would be, Robert Lipsyte of the *Times* spoke with a psychologist about the implications of rooting for a team that had lost its first nine games. "Perhaps," the psychologist said, "rooting for the Mets and becoming emotionally involved with them is a kind of masochism. A kind of painless flagellation. Or maybe people absolve their guilt for being unkind to individual losers by becoming kind to this group champion of losers. I'll have to think about it."

Another psychologist said, "The Yankee symbol is a top hat. And just the name 'Yankees' brings up images of founding fathers and New England aristocracy.... And I've noticed on ads this year that [the Mets] have a picture of a baseball with a man's face superimposed, Mr. Met — kind of a John Q. Public caricature."

Policemen who worked at both Yankee Stadium and the Polo Grounds unanimously agreed that Mets fans were less patrician. "The Metophile," wrote Lipsyte, "is a dreamer. He believes that one day he will punch that arrogant foreman at the plant square on his fat nose; that he will get in the last word with his wife; that he will win the Irish Sweepstakes; that the Mets will start a winning streak.... To the Metophile, who is more internal, the Yankees represent that stuffed shirt at the bank who refused his loan application, the haughty maitre d' who seemed to sneer at everything he ordered."

In early June, when the Giants and Dodgers made their glorious return to New York, Lipsyte's colleague Robert Teague updated readers on the Met fan. They appreciated their Mets, Teague said, but they also remembered their departed heroes on the Dodgers and Giants. "[T]he Met fans' idea of a perfect game," Teague wrote, "is one in which Mays belts five home runs but the Mets win 6–5." Roger Angell dismissed notions of masochism, guilt and self-loathing in favor of a simpler theme. "The Mets are refreshing to every New York urbanite if only because they are unfinished." Stengel, who had been in New York since 1912, said the assemblage that watched the Mets and Dodgers was the most amazing crowd he'd ever seen. So did Duke Snider.

Being a Met meant low expectations and a high level of affection. "When the Dodgers or Giants came to town," said pitcher Galen Cisco, "if we won one game of a three or four game series, it was great. If somehow or another we could win two, you'd have thought we won the pennant." "If someone found out you were a Met," recalled Hawk Taylor, who joined the club in 1964, "it was like you were the mayor. Here I was, just the second string catcher, and people still looked up to me."

"If a pitcher won a ballgame," said Bob (Lefty) Miller, who won two, "he'd get a champagne dinner for two at fourteen of the best restaurants in New York. You'd get three cardigan sweaters from Jantzen sportswear, six shirts from Arrow, a suit from Hart, Shaffner and Marx, a sports coat and slacks from Howard Clothes. It was just unbelievable. How many blue suits can you wear? How many gray suits can you wear? Met Mania had taken effect and the sponsors wanted to get in on it."

"These Met fans are really something," said Gene Woodling. "You strike out with the bases full, and they cheer you when you go to the outfield. They whoop it up when you get a walk even though you're nine runs behind." The Met faithful never lost hope. In 1964, with his club buried deep in the National League basement, a fan paraded through the stands with a banner which read: "Predictions for 1965 — Mets, World Champions. [Ron] Hunt, the National League's Most Valuable Player. [Charley] Smith 62 Home Runs and [Jack] Fisher, a 32-game winner."

"My wife always said that was the most fun place we ever played," said Ed Bressoud, who spent only one of his twelve big league seasons in New York. "She described herself as a participant rather than a spectator. There was an awful lot of excitement in the ballpark all the time. We were being beaten by eight or nine runs in the seventh, eighth or ninth inning and the 'Let's Go Mets' chant would start up. You'd feel, 'Golly sakes, they're really with us' and you'd try a little harder."

When Hal Reniff was traded to the Mets in 1967, he commented, "The fans at Shea act like they're at a big party. The fans at Yankee Stadium come out to see only one man — the Smasher. That's Mickey Mantle. They don't seem to recognize anyone else."

Most of the time the Met fans, who tended to be younger than Yankee fans, had good, clean fun, but sometimes they turned ugly. In 1963, during a doubleheader against the Reds, they pelted Cincinnati right fielder Frank Robinson with debris of various sorts, and exploded firecrackers on the field and under the stands. The disturbances continued throughout the second game, to the point where the umpires threatened to forfeit the contest if the bombardment didn't stop. A public address announcement in the name of Stengel failed to quiet the crowd. Finally, after a beer can narrowly missed the septuagenarian manager, order was restored and the game was completed. It was the first time a Met crowd had become unruly, which alarmed everyone. Had the raucous mass become too disorderly?

When banners first appeared at the Polo Grounds, Weiss attempted to have them banned, saying they obscured the view of other fans. Fortunately, he was unsuccessful, and bedsheets, posterboard and cardboard messages became the trademark of the Met fan. Banner Day, which began at 1963 in the Polo Grounds, was one of the highlights of the season. By 1968, 2,406 banners were entered in the contest, including one that read, "Who needs LSD. We've got the Mets." The following year, following the moon landing, a banner read "One Small Step for Hodges, One Giant Leap for Met-kind."

On the 6th of June, 1962, in the wake of total attendance of more than 197,000 for the series with the Giants and Dodgers, the Mets took out a large ad in the *New York Times*, signed by all the club's directors, thanking the fans of New York for their patronage. "Never in sports history," it began immodestly, "has there been such a heartwarming demonstration of loyalty and affection as we have received from the Met fans, the New Breed. They are the new Miracle of Coogan's Bluff."

Weiss never understood the phenomenon which took place on his watch. "I'm grateful," he said, "but I don't understand it." Veteran writer Dan Daniel, who spent decades on the Yankee beat, was another who failed to appreciate the New Breed. "If some baseball fan had motored down here from the moon," Daniel wrote, "he would have gotten the impression that for the first time in the history of the city, it had fans who were loyal, and who came out in large numbers." Daniel was offended and puzzled by the fact that fans would back a losing team with such enthusiasm, and couldn't understand why other writers were so excited. Daniel was of the Old Breed and oblivious to the magic of the New. He was also intrigued by the fact that the Mets seemed to draw many more blacks and Hispanics than the Yankees.

After the season, Daniel wrote, "The fans of New York are willing to forget the 1962 season, as if it never had happened." Daniel was never more wrong. More than 40 years later, the fans' admiration for their heroes on the 1962 Mets continues. Many of the players spent a great deal of time in the major leagues with other clubs. Some never played in the big leagues before or after. For most, that year was the defining moment in their careers. When the Mets returned to New York to play their first game in the Polo Grounds, Stengel called catcher Joe Ginsburg into his office. Ginsburg was 35, a 13-year major league veteran who had caught nearly 700 games. "Son," Stengel told him, "I'm going to catch you today. You're going to bat sixth in the lineup and you're going to catch the ballgame and I'm going to tell you something. You'll get more recognition catching the first game the Mets ever played in the Polo Grounds than you ever did in your whole career." "Casey was just trying to get me jacked up," Ginsberg said, "and I didn't think too much about it, but, believe me, the old man was right. I did get more recognition for the first game I caught in the Polo Grounds than I did for my whole 13-year career. I thought he was nuts, but he was right." Ginsberg played only one more game in the majors after the Polo Grounds opener, but his place in history was secure.

"We had a reunion," said Bob "Lefty" Miller. "You couldn't believe the thousands of people who showed up for the autograph and photo sessions. I couldn't believe it. You'd think we had won the world championship. My wife and I just came back from Europe recently. We were gone 14 days and I had 10 letters from people around the country who wanted my autograph. I get them from all over. It was a very special time in baseball history and unless you were there, you could never appreciate or understand what happened. When you talk about it, people have a difficult time trying to appreciate the aura that was there at that time. Sportswriters like Dick Young and Phil Pepe wanted to cover the Mets rather than the Yankees, who were in first place."

"That year is indelible in my mind," said Craig Anderson. "It's become historical and people keep talking about it. The people in New York have remembered so much about it that it keeps coming back. I get one or two autograph requests a week. People who write say they're collecting the autographs of the '62 Mets. We're still getting them and I like getting them. I'm glad they still remember. Richie Ashburn told me he got more mail, more phone calls and more messages about his one year with the Mets than all his years with the Phillies."

"I'm out of baseball 35 years," said Frank Thomas, "and I still get 20–25 letters a week." Rick Herrscher, whose big league career consisted of just 35 Met games in the last two months of the 1962 season, receives about a letter a week from fans seeking his autograph. As Bob Miller said, it was a very special time in baseball history. Never before and not since has a team that lost so many games been so loved and so well remembered by its fans. Maybe it was because of Casey Stengel. Perhaps New Yorkers were so happy to see National League baseball back in New York that they would have embraced any team. Maybe it was the unique characters who played on that first Met club. Whatever the reason, the 1962 Mets will live forever in the memory of New York baseball fans.

• 5 •

The Three Wise Men and
the Two Bob Millers

The 1962 Met pitching staff was not the best in the National League. It might not have been the best in the International League. But in terms of education and intellect, no staff in any league (save perhaps the Ivy League) could match the 1962 New York hurlers. There were veterans with a good deal of baseball smarts, like Roger Craig and Clem Labine, and there were young pitchers who had graduated from some of the finest schools in the country. The Met staff included Jay Hook, possessor of a Master's Degree in Mechanical Engineering from Northwestern, Ken MacKenzie, a Yale grad, Craig Anderson, a Lehigh alumnus who would later earn a Master's Degree in Education, and Robert G. (Lefty) Miller, holder of a Master's Degree in Business Administration from Northwestern. Al Jackson attended college in Texas, and Galen Cisco was a former Ohio State fullback.*

A college educated player was not the norm in the 1960s. In 1964, *The Sporting News* estimated that roughly 100 major league players held college degrees (approximately 20 percent of the total), with another 160 or so having attended but not graduated. Unlike many veteran baseball men, Casey Stengel, who had little formal education, was never intimidated by players with degrees. "Casey liked college guys," said Bill Wakefield, a Stanford grad who pitched for the Mets in 1964. "It was a unique thing in his era."

Robert G. Miller, who arrived from the Reds in May, 1962, was known as Lefty Miller to distinguish him from Robert L. (Righty) Miller, the former Cardinal bonus player who was a $125,000 premium selection by the Mets in the expansion draft. Lefty's journey to New York was recounted in dramatic fashion by Jimmy Breslin in *Can't Anybody Here Play This Game*, which appeared shortly after the Mets' dismal 1962 season. According to Breslin, Miller had been out of baseball for two years, and was selling cars in Zanesville, Ohio. Met scout Wid Mathews walked into the dealership one afternoon in January, 1962, reminded Miller that he needed only eighteen days in the major leagues to qualify for a pension, and convinced him to sign a contract to pitch for the Mets.

That's a wonderful story, tainted only by fact that it was a complete fabrication. Miller had signed with the Detroit Tigers in 1953, at the age of 17, reportedly for a $100,000 bonus. "Actually," Miller said recently, "it was $65,000, and that included three years' salary." On June

*In 1969, Joe Durso wrote an article chronicling the sophisticated reading taste of the young Met players. "They are utterly unlike the early comic book Mets of 1962," Durso claimed. "They are totally removed from the ballplayers of Casey Stengel's day who spent their time rolling dice, dealing cards and bootlegging beer to the bullpen." Durso was not on the Met beat in 1962, and couldn't have been more wrong.

25, 1953, two Tigers made their major league debuts against the Philadelphia Athletics. One was Al Kaline, fresh off the Baltimore sandlots, and the other was Bob Miller, just weeks out of high school, who pitched a scoreless eighth inning. Due to the size of Miller's bonus, Detroit was required to keep him on the major league roster for at least two years. He pitched very little in his first season, but in 1954, Miller got into 32 games and finished 1–1 with a very respectable 2.45 ERA. By 1956, he had moved into the starting rotation, only to have his wrist broken in an early season game by a line drive off the bat of Washington pitcher Connie Grob.

Two operations later, Miller was pitching again, but without the steam on his once-mighty fastball. "I lost what they call the forward wrist pop in my fastball," he said. "I had to learn how to pitch." Miller went into military service, pitched in the Mexican Winter League, then went to the minor leagues to learn to become a finesse pitcher. In 1961, he was the best relief pitcher for Cincinnati's top farm club in Indianapolis.

The following spring, Miller showed Red manager Fred Hutchinson enough to make the varsity. Just before the start of the season, however, Cincinnati third baseman Gene Freese, a stalwart of the 1961 pennant winning club, suffered a broken ankle, a break that would have a dramatic impact upon the career of Bob Miller. Desperate for an experienced third baseman, the Reds coveted Don Zimmer, suffering through a horrendous 0–34 slump with the Mets. On May 6, Zimmer was traded to the Reds for Miller and young third baseman Cliff Cook. What about Wid Mathews and the auto dealership in Zanesville? "I had to look on a map to find out where the hell Zanesville, Ohio was," Miller said. "I'd never lived in Ohio."

Shortly after the trade, Miller was dispatched to Syracuse, and did not return to New York until mid–July. On his first pitch as a Met, he surrendered a 12th inning game winning home run to Del Crandall of the Braves.

Miller's return from Syracuse led to instant confusion. "At first," he said, "I roomed with Joe Pignatano, but I had to be switched to room with the other Bob Miller because any time a phone call came to the hotel, the caller would say, 'Let me talk to Bob Miller.' The operator would ask, 'Which one?' They'd say, 'The pitcher with the Mets.' It got to be a little crazy." Stengel helped ease the problem by calling Robert L. Miller "Nelson."

There was a positive consequence of the unusual situation. The two Bob Millers were asked to appear on the television game show *To Tell the Truth*, with host Bud Collier. At the beginning of the show, each of the three contestants stated, "My name is Bob Miller and I pitch for the New York Mets." A panel of celebrities then asked a series of questions designed to weed out the imposters. After the round of questions, Collier, as he did each week, asked, "Will the real Bob Miller please stand up?" "You do a fumble and stumble kind of thing," Miller recalled, and each of the three feinted and began to stand. Finally, both Righty and Lefty Miller stood up and said, "My name is Bob Miller and I pitch for the New York Mets." While the studio audience looked at each other in confusion, the third contestant rose and announced, "My name is Bob Miller and I pitched for the Philadelphia Phillies." This was Robert J. Miller, who had last pitched for the Phillies in 1958. He and Robert L. Miller had been teammates on the Cardinals in 1957. Fortunately, that Bob Miller had already qualified for a pension, and Wid Mathews had not discovered him selling cars or pitching for Cincinnati. Three Bob Millers would have been too much even for the Mets.

There was only one Jay Hook. In the mid–'50s, Hook was a car-loving engineering major at Northwestern University who expected to spend his life working for one of the Big Three automobile companies in Detroit. He took a series of summer jobs in Wisconsin during his college years and pitched semi-pro ball at night. One of his managers was the father of Jay's catcher at Northwestern, who took a liking to Hook and recommended him to a number of big league scouts. One of the scouts worked for the Reds, and invited the young pitcher to work out with the team in nearby Milwaukee when they played the Braves. Hook was impressive enough throwing on the sidelines to cause the Reds to ask him to come back to Cincinnati on the team charter and throw batting practice at Crosley Field. "Being a young kid," Hook recalled, "you can throw hard, and you're a little wild. I'm sure they hated hitting against me, and they didn't hit the ball very well off me that day."

Gabe Paul, the Reds' general manger, invited Hook and his father, who owned a drugstore in northern Illinois, to discuss a contract. "Neither one of us knew much about negotiating," Hook said. "After we agreed on the bonus, Paul said, 'That will also include your first two years' salary.' But I'd have played for an old glove." One of the negotiating points won by Hook and his father was the right to report late to spring training so that he could complete work on his degree.

Later that season (1957) Hook was called up to the Reds and started two games. In the second start, he faced the Braves, who had already clinched the National League pennant. Hook pitched a no-hitter for five innings before manager Birdie Tebbetts took him out of the game, saying, "Kid, you're too young to pitch a no-hitter."

In 1960, Hook became a regular member of the Reds' rotation and posted an inconsistent 11–18 record. Sometimes he was knocked out in the first inning. Other times he pitched shutouts. He tied for the league lead in home runs surrendered with 31, but at his young age, and with his live fastball and good curve, the Reds thought 1961 would be the season Hook became a big winner.

Nineteen sixty-one was a great year for the Reds, who went from sixth place, 20 games below .500, to first place. It was a frustrating year for Hook. "Whenever they wanted someone to speak at schools," he said, "that is, when they wanted someone who'd speak for free, they'd ask me." Hook spoke at a grammar school in California and contracted a sore throat. "I got on the plane to fly back to Cincinnati," he said, "and I just swelled up all over." The "sore throat" turned out to be the mumps, which ruined his year.

Hook finished the '61 season with a 1–3 record and a horrendous 7.76 ERA in 22 games. He gave up 14 home runs in just 63 innings, and was the only member of the Reds who did not appear in the World Series. After the Series, while driving home with his wife in their Austin Healy, Hook heard on the radio that he had been selected by the Mets in the National League expansion draft.

Despite his spotty record with the Reds, Hook, still only 25 years old, had a great arm, and was expected to be one of the Mets' top pitchers. "He had real good stuff," said catcher Joe Ginsberg. "He had a good curve ball, a good slider and he threw the ball pretty hard." Leaving a pennant contender for an expansion team didn't bother Hook. "I thought it would be fun to go to New York and play for Casey Stengel," he said. "When you're that age, you don't really look at the past. I just said, 'Well, that's the way it's going to be.'"

Hook started the Mets' first exhibition game, but was inconsistent throughout the spring. On March 26, against the Orioles in Miami, Stengel decided to test Hook's mettle. Baltimore scored three times in the first, three more in the third, once more in the fourth, and another in the fifth. Despite the fact that Hook had given up eight runs, Stengel left him in the game for the fateful sixth. In that frame, the Orioles pounded out nine hits and eight runs as Stengel sat in the dugout and watched. Even Marv Throneberry, playing for the Orioles, had a single and a triple in the sixth inning. "I wasn't mad at Hook," Stengel said after the game. "I left him in there only because I want to make him a starting pitcher, a nine inning pitcher. I don't think what happened hurt him one bit." In six innings, Hook had surrendered 17 hits, four walks and 16 runs.

"I'll never forget that game," Hook said recently. "I came in after the sixth inning and told Casey he could take the ball and put it wherever he wanted to." "He came off the field," said

Met outfielder John DeMerit, "and he was crying. I could never tell why they did that. It was terrible. Nobody should have to go through that."

Hook survived the ordeal, and went north as a member of the starting rotation. The first news he made in New York, however, had nothing to do with his performance on the mound. As an engineer, Hook had a terrific theoretical knowledge of the mechanics of pitching. "I know why a baseball curves," he said in spring training. "Now I have to work on the applied aspects." Stengel agreed. "We got some guys with wonderful educations," he said, "but the ball won't go where their mind is."

Is education a help or an impediment to major league success? Or is it irrelevant? If intelligence and education were the prime determinant of baseball success, scouts would be roaming the halls of the Harvard physics department. Clearly, the mental aspect of the game contributes to overall success. The question is to what degree. "There's nothing to say that an education wouldn't help you," said infielder Ed Bressoud, who was a teacher during the off-season, "but baseball is such a reaction type of game. The ball is hit. The ball is pitched. You respond

Jay Hook was one of the Three Wise Men on the Mets' 1962 staff. He had brains, looks and a good fastball, but never became a consistently good pitcher. After leaving baseball, he achieved great success in the business world.

to it. You don't have a chance to think about it. You can prepare at shortstop. You know what pitch is coming and you know there's a tendency to hit the ball one way or another. I'm not sure you need to have a bachelor's degree or a master's degree to learn that, but there is some innate intelligence required to play baseball or any sport."

"I don't think an education helps you that much in terms of baseball savvy," said pitcher Larry Miller. "I think the actual education isn't as important as your emotional stability in dealing with difficult situations. I think an education helps you in the minor league system when it's easy to get overwhelmed. You're away from home. I think that if you've been to college, you're a little more mature as far as being able to handle yourself off the field. On the field, I'm not sure education has any value. Take Choo Choo Coleman. Choo Choo probably had a grade school education and was probably borderline illiterate. But he was a smart catcher. He knew where to pitch guys and how to throw to their weakness, because he studied the game. I rarely shook him off. "

"I don't believe that athletes are much different from people in other occupations," said reporter Gordon White. "The intelligent person has an edge over the less intelligent person. I don't think there's any question whatsoever that the intelligent athlete has an edge. If all things are equal physically, the man with the brains is going to win. Even if things aren't equal physically, the man with the brains, who may be less qualified physically, may be able to use his brain to make up the difference." There is a distinction, of course, between academic achievement and the type of intelligence that applies to sports. "Whitey Ford," White continued, "was an absolute genius in pitching. He was brilliant." Likewise, Ted Williams, who, like Ford, had little formal education, was a genius of hitting.

One advantage of having an education is that it gives a player options. In 1964, Miller was at Albuquerque in the Double A Texas League and wasn't pitching at all. "I'd always promised my wife," he said, "that I'd never haul her around the country as a minor league ballplayer. I said that if there was no future in baseball, I had my engineering degree and I'd quit. I made two phone calls. I called Fresco Thompson, the Dodgers' farm director, and Clay Bryant, my manager, and told them both the same thing. I said if they didn't give me a chance to pitch in a week, I'd quit." Three days later, Miller got a start, and pitched a two hit shutout. Eight wins later, he was on his way to Los Angeles. If he hadn't had a backup plan, he might never have spoken up.

"Having earned my college degree," said former Yankee Tom Tresh, "'gave me confidence that I wasn't going to be stuck in some mediocre job after I was done playing. It kind of guaranteed me another career, and the security itself makes you feel good. I don't know if it makes you a better player, but I certainly felt more comfortable that I had it."

In mid–April, looking for a story on a day the Mets were rained out, *New York Times* reporter Robert Lipsyte asked Hook why a curve ball curved. A baseball curved, said mechanical engineer Hook, due to Bernoulli's Law, the same principal that causes an airplane to stay aloft. Jay, then a member of the American Rocket Society, explained, "The baseball is spinning counter-clockwise and moving this way." He drew a line on a piece of paper. "Because of the direction of the spin, there is more pressure on the left side of the ball. The air is moving faster than the ball on the right side and there is less pressure there. Thus, the ball will break to the right." Hook drew a series of diagrams in further explanation, replete with mathematical formulae.

Lipsyte had not heard of Bernoulli, an 18th century Swiss physicist, and consulted the head of the Columbia University physics department, who confirmed what Hook had said. Lipsyte wrote a lengthy article, illustrated with Hook's diagrams, a few days later. About two weeks after the article appeared, Hook started a game and was knocked out early. Afterward, he was sitting at his locker talking with a reporter when Stengel walked by. Casey paused, looked at Hook, then turned to the writer and said, "If Hook could only do what he knows." "That's a great line," said Hook. "I've probably used it in more speeches than I can remember. It applies to so many things—engineering, religion—if he could only do what he knows. It was such a great comment!"

Doing what he knew was frequently a problem for the handsome young pitcher. Each year, the New York writers held a banquet, at which they performed a number of skits, most of which involved making up their own words to popular songs. One winter, Harold Rosenthal sang, "If you asked me, I could write a book/About the laws that force a baseball to hook/.... But despite my knowledge, my PhD/They just knock the brains out of me."

Sometimes, Hook could do what he knew. By April 23, 1962, the Mets had lost their first nine games. During batting practice before game number ten, Frank Thomas passed Pirate pitcher Jack Lamabe and said, "We can't lose them all." That was not a particularly bold prediction, particularly with the expanded 162 game schedule, but the way the Mets had been playing, it was not a sure thing. "We had lost nine in a row," Hook remembered, "and the Pirates had won ten in a row. They would have set a record if they won one more game and we would have set a record if we lost one more, so there was a lot more pressure on them than there was on us."

Hook pitched a complete game five-hitter, beat the Pirates 9–1 and became the first winning pitcher in Met history. "It was a delightful game," Hook said. "Afterwards, Casey was touting me and the writers spent a lot of time with me. After I finished talking to the writers there was no hot water left. I took a bath in the whirlpool." "I'm gonna let Hook pitch every day," Stengel said. "The way we played tonight," he added, "I don't see how we ever lost a game."*

In addition to his pitching heroics, Hook had scored two runs and driven in two with a second inning single. A left-handed batter, he hit .203 for the Mets in '62 and .237 the following year, quite good for a pitcher. Like most pitchers, Hook savored his success at the plate. "Tell me one pitcher who doesn't like to hit," said Bob Miller.†

Most pitchers, even those who didn't hit very well, thought they could hit. Craig Anderson recalled an event from early in the '62 season. "We were playing Pittsburgh, and they brought Herb Moford in," said Anderson. Moford pitched two scoreless innings, a rare feat for a Met hurler at that time, and was scheduled to lead off the seventh inning. "Hemus and Cookie Lavagetto were asking Casey," Anderson continued, "'Who do you want to pinch hit?' He thought they were trying to tell him what to do. If you backed Casey into a corner, he would rebel. Casey went over to Moford and said, 'Herb, are you a good hitter?' You never ask a pitcher if he's a good hitter. He wants to stay in the game, so he'll say, 'Sure, I'm a good hitter.'" That's exactly what Moford (with his career average of .045) said. He told Stengel he was a terrific hitter. Casey told Moford to go up there and hit. "The coaches are shaking their heads," said Anderson, "taking their hats off and slapping their thighs. We were sitting in the dugout, laughing and nudging each other, thinking it was kind of funny. All of a sudden, bang, Herb lines a hit to left field. Now we're going nuts in the dugout, saying, 'Look at that, Herb got a hit!' Then we look up, and Stengel put in a pinch runner for him! He went to all that trouble to keep the guy in the game, and then puts in a pinch-runner."

Stengel had another divine inspiration in early June. "We were in Chicago," Hook recalled, "and I'd been getting some hits, so Casey told me to take batting practice with the extra men. We had a doubleheader against the Cubs, and I won the first game, and got a hit. Usually, if you pitched the whole game, you just sat in the stands and watched the second game. But between games Casey came up to me and said, 'Hook, get another uniform and get dressed.'"

Hook sat on the bench during the second game, waiting for the call. "It was about the eighth inning and it was getting dark," he said. In those days, there were no lights at Wrigley Field. "Don Elston was pitching and we had a runner on first. Casey had all these good hitters on the bench, like Gil Hodges, but he said, 'Hook, I want you to go up and pinch hit.' I fouled off a couple of pitches, and then Elston threw me an inside fastball. I thought it was about four inches inside, but the ump called me out. I went back to the bench, and I don't think I ever got chewed out so bad in my life as I was chewed out by Stengel. He was embarrassed because he'd sent me up there and I'd struck out. His final comment was," ... and you can forget about hitting with the extra men.'"

Stengel never forgot. Years later, the two men met at a World Series game. Casey asked Hook why he had retired from baseball. Jay explained that, while playing with Milwaukee's Triple A team at Denver in 1964, he had torn up his knee sliding into second base attempting to break up a double play. "How did you get to first?" Stengel asked.

Hook's principal job was pitching and, through the early stages of the '62 season, he was the Mets' best hurler. On May 8, he pitched the Mets out of the basement by beating the Cubs. By July 15, Hook was 7–9 on a team that was 24–63 and 34½ games out of first place. He had six complete games and owned the Mets' only victory over the first place Dodgers. He was the first Met pitcher to win two games in a row.

---

*Ironically, the site of Stengel's first Met win was also the place in which he had suffered his final, and most crushing, Yankee loss.

†Well, Joe Grzenda was one. "When I got up to the plate in the minor leagues," Grzenda said, "and you had some guy firing the ball, I thought, 'Holy Christ, how does a human being hit this thing? God, the ball looks so small. How the hell do they hit it?'"

Hook was still yielding too many home runs (25 in his first 118 innings), but he owned more than 25 percent of the Mets' victories. That was the high point of Jay's career, however, as he wound up losing 25 of his next 30 decisions over two years. In 1962, he allowed more runs than any other National League pitcher and more home runs per inning than anyone in the major leagues. Many thought he needed to be a little meaner, and move the hitters off the plate more often, but he rarely did. In high school, pitching in twilight, he'd fractured a batter's skull, and the tragedy had a lasting impact on him.

Hook turned in some fine performances, including a two hit victory over the Cubs in 1963, an effort that, with a little luck, could have been a no-hitter. Both Chicago safeties were scratch hits that second baseman Ron Hunt couldn't handle cleanly. It was the best game Hook pitched in the major leagues. In his next start, he was knocked out in the fourth inning of an 11–9 loss.

Inconsistency was Hook's curse. In 1962, he was knocked out in the first inning three times, and twice more in the second. Once in 1963, the Cardinals hit Hook so hard that the Mets insisted they must be stealing signs. "That was probably my demise," Hook said recently. "I couldn't achieve consistency, and I really don't know why I couldn't. My golf game is the same way. Some days I'll go out and play a decent round, and other days...."

"The funny thing is," Hook said, "that sometimes after warming up, I'd say to the catcher, 'Boy, I've really got good stuff today,' and I'd get knocked out in the second inning. There were other days when I'd say, 'I'll be lucky to get through the first inning,' and I'd pitch a complete game. Maybe when I didn't have good stuff, I concentrated more."

"He had good stuff," said Norm Sherry, "but he seemed to make that bad pitch when he shouldn't. That always hurt him. That's the difference between him and Roger Craig. In a tough spot, Craig made the good pitch. He wouldn't give in to the hitter. I don't think Jay wanted to, but he'd get the ball where he shouldn't. You get hit that way." "I thought he probably had stuff as good as anybody on the staff," said Galen Cisco, "but he never could find a way to win." "I want to be successful," Hook said in the midst of a 1962 slump. "But so far I'm not. I can't understand it."

Hook had a fine spring in 1963, but when the season started, he reverted to his old form, a few great efforts interspersed with a series of poor outings. He continued his disturbing tendency to give up home runs, surrendering 31 in 1962 and 21 in 1963. "The straightest fast ball this side of Watts," said teammate Don Rowe. "He could throw hard, but it was straight." That meant it often came back, hard, straight and far. In 1962, after Hook gave up four home runs in the first four innings of one game, Howard Tuckner wrote, "Until he was lifted in the fifth, Hook spaced his homers nicely."

In 1964, Hook lost his spot in the starting rotation and the Mets finally tired of waiting for him to achieve consistency. In desperate need of a reliable shortstop, Weiss traded Hook to the Braves in May for aging All-Star Roy McMillan. "Edna's going to be mad at me," Stengel told Hook as he delivered the news. The childless Stengels had taken a great liking to Hook's two young children, Wes and Marcie, then aged three and two. "My wife would dress them up," Hook said, "and we'd go out to dinner. They acted pretty well in restaurants. One night, Casey and Edna were there. Wes had a tie on and Marcie had a skirt or a little dress on. The Stengels asked them to come over to their table. The kids were very polite that night. I'm not sure why, because they weren't polite all the time. But they were then and Edna really took a liking to them. We went to a luncheon when Shea Stadium was being built, and Edna had the kids up on the podium with them." Edna was sorry to see the kids leave, and Casey lamented having to trade their father. "He was a lovely fella," Stengel said when Hook was traded, "who busted his butt for you and lived nice. You wish he coulda done better."

Casey needed a shortstop, however, and the Hooks, with Wes and Marcie in tow, departed for Milwaukee's Denver farm club, where, later in the season, Jay pitched a nine inning no hitter but managed to lose the game in the tenth. It was symbolic of his entire career.

In joining the Milwaukee organization, Hook could take solace in the fact that he would no longer have to face Braves' slugger Hank Aaron. "When Aaron hit his 715th home run," Hook recalled, "Wes, who was 14 or so, came home from school and said, 'Hey, Dad, how many did he hit off you?' I said, 'I don't know, but it was quite a few.' The next day, the newspaper listed every home run Aaron hit, three or four pages of them. Wes got the paper and counted. When I came home from work, he said, 'Hey, Dad, you were only in the league five years and you gave up nine home runs to Hank Aaron. If you could have pitched ten or eleven years you would have held the record.'"

"We were at Don Rowe's house a few years ago," said Craig Anderson. "I said, 'Don, did you give up a home run to Aaron?' He said, 'Yeah, number 299.' I said, 'I gave up 280.' We got the list out and started looking at it. I said, 'Here I am, 280 — Anderson. Look here. 183 — Hook, 190 — Hook, 203 — Hook, 210 — Hook, 299 — Rowe, 301— Hook.' There were a lot of Hooks in there."

"You know the dimensions of the Polo Grounds," said Hook, "and how far it was to center field (425 feet to the left center field fence). One day, I was pitching against the Braves and the bases were loaded with Aaron coming up. Casey came out to the mound and said, 'Hook, pitch him outside and make him hit to center field.' I threw a low outside fastball and he hit it 600 feet to center field." "It was the longest ball I ever saw hit as a spectator," said Anderson. Despite Hook's claim, the ball only went 460 feet, but it was only the second time a batter had ever hit a ball into the left center field bleachers.

"There's a book," said Hook, "by Leonard Koppett, called *The New York Mets, The Whole Story*. On the inside cover of that book is a picture of the Polo Grounds. There are three men on base, number 44 has just swung the bat and I've just thrown the pitch. That was the one."

Home run number 299, off Rowe, had an interesting sidelight. "We were in Milwaukee," Rowe recalled, "and Carl Willey, who'd played with Aaron, was in the bullpen with us. I asked him how to pitch to Henry. He said, 'Get ahead of him and then you can pitch him up and away.' I went in the game, got the first two guys out and Aaron came up. I threw him a slider inside and he pulled it like a rocket down the third base line —foul. I threw a slider farther inside and he pulled it more foul. He was right on it. Now, I said, I'm going to waste a fastball high and outside, because that's where Carl told me he'd chase them. He hit it over the center field wall. After the game, I said, 'Carl, you said up and away!' He said, 'I meant down and away.'"

By the time Rowe joined the Mets in 1963, Craig Anderson was pitching for Buffalo of the International League. Anderson holds a special place among those prodigious losers of 1962, for while he did not lose 20 games like Roger Craig and Al Jackson, or even match Hook's 19 losses, the final 16 of Anderson's 17 defeats came in succession. He added two more losses in '63 and another the following year for a grand total of 19 in a row. Anderson's mark stood as a Met record until Anthony Young left it far in the dust in the early '90s by losing 27 straight decisions. Since Anderson's consecutive losses were the last 19 decisions of his career, however, his streak is still intact. Should he choose to come out of retirement, he could take aim at Young's new record and, at nearly 70 years of age, the odds would be heavily in his favor.

Anderson felt that the achievements of the '62 staff merited some sort of lasting fame. "The five pitchers who did most of the starting: Jackson, Craig, Hook, myself and Bobby Miller, lost 92 games." He talked about Marv Throneberry's later fame in Miller Lite commercials, and mused, "I couldn't figure out why we didn't get a Miller Lite commercial, too."

In 1962, Anderson was a 24-year-old righthander with a good sinker and a resilient arm that allowed him to both start and relieve. As a Lehigh undergraduate, he pitched a no-hitter against Bucknell in true Met fashion, winning the game, but yielding a run on walks and a series of misplays. "I don't think my team even knew I had a no-hitter," he recalled. "It was a cold day and the game went so fast. We got the last out and ran to the locker room. I thought I had a no-hitter, but the other players on the team didn't know it."

Anderson signed with the Cardinals and had some good years pitching in relief in the minors. He was 6–4 with a 1.81 ERA at Tulsa in 1960, and made his major league debut in June, 1961. In his first game, he appeared in relief, hit a double ("my only extra base hit in the big leagues") and was the winning pitcher. Anderson was 4–3 in 25 games with a 3.23 ERA, and showed promise of being a good major league pitcher.

When he was drafted by the Mets, Anderson, like Hook, looked forward to playing in New York. "I'd had a good year with the Cardinals, and felt that wherever I went," he said, "I'd be okay. I didn't know the team was going to be that bad. I didn't have a clue they would be that bad a team."

During the early part of the season, Anderson was the Mets' bullpen ace. He peaked on May 12, when he won both games of a doubleheader against the Braves. In the bottom of the ninth inning of the first game, with the Mets down one run and a runner on base, Stengel sent left-handed hitter Hobie Landrith up to pinch hit against lefty Warren Spahn. It was an unorthodox move, but Stengel wanted to neutralize Spahn's vaunted screwball. All Landrith could manage was a weak fly ball, which carried only about 260 feet. Fortunately for Landrith, the right field fence at the Polo Grounds was so close that one almost needed to climb over it to get to first base. The ball dropped into the right field stands, and Anderson, who had pitched two scoreless innings in relief, was the winner.

In the nightcap, with the score tied 7–7, lightning struck a second time, again in the final inning, when Gil Hodges dropped a fly ball into the stands, just a few feet from where Landrith's had landed three hours earlier. The Braves had been swept by the Mets, which Brave manager Birdie Tebbetts called "an absolute disgrace." Anderson, who had pitched the top of the ninth, raised his record to 3–1. His earned run average declined to 2.25. The two wins were the last he would ever get in a major league uniform.

"The Polo Grounds was a tough place to pitch," Anderson recalled. "I made some great pitches there and gave up home runs. I'd say I gave up half a dozen home runs that were routine fly balls. I remember pitching against Harvey Kuenn of the Giants. I was ahead 1 and 2 and threw a slider about six inches outside. He just threw his bat out there and hit a little pop fly that fell into the right field bleachers." On May 12, 1962, however, no one was happier than Craig Anderson to see two weakly-hit fly balls drop into the right field seats.

Following his two wins, Anderson's long losing streak began. "I didn't pitch well every time I went out there," he said, "but when I did pitch well, other things would happen — errors — misplays. There were times when I didn't pitch well, but I should have been about .500. I hung in there, but I wasn't very happy. I had some trying moments."

Anderson was indeed the victim of non-support, leading the league by giving up 30 unearned runs. Yet, through 16 consecutive, sometimes agonizing losses, Anderson managed to keep his sanity. "If a guy had to have a losing streak," said Don Rowe, "he was the guy to have it." "It wasn't as tough as it would be today," Anderson said, "when they put you under the microscope as soon as you start a streak. The writers were sympathetic. I think the Mets bringing National League baseball back to New York was such a happy thing for so many people that they were sympathetic. It was a tough year, but I wouldn't trade it for anything. I loved the game. I still love the game. It's better to be a has-been than a never-was."

Anderson lost as a starter and lost in relief. He pitched poorly enough to keep losing, but well enough for Stengel to keep calling on him, for the Mets had no one better. "He'd be just about on the verge of winning," recalled Rick Herrscher, "and there'd be an error, a bloop hit or something that would keep his steak going. Every time he went out there, he kept feeling that this was the game he was going to win, but something would happen." On July 8, Anderson pitched a complete game against the Cardinals, but lost 3–2 on a home run by Stan Musial. On August 26, he lost 16–5 to the Dodgers as five Met errors let in eight unearned runs. That was

Craig Anderson (right), shown here with Casey Stengel, lost 19 consecutive decisions from 1962 through 1964. He was a sinker-balling reliever who managed to pitch well enough for Stengel to keep using him, but he always seemed to find a way to lose, often with the help of his teammates.

consecutive loss number 13. Number 14 came against the Cardinals in his next start. The score was tied 2–2 in the eighth when Anderson surrendered a two run homer to Charley James. Loss number 16 came in relief against the Colts on an unearned run in the ninth.

Hook, with his engineer's logic, put losing streaks in perspective. "Roger Craig [who lost 18 in a row in 1963] said 'It's difficult to set a record like that, because people usually give up on you long before you set that kind of record.' Craig [Anderson] lost a lot of games in relief. We lost games every way there was to lose them and I think we made up a few. But Craig kept his cool and he hung in there."

Anderson was sent to Buffalo at the end of spring training in 1963. "Let him pitch his way back," Stengel said. "He had his full share of chances." Anderson spent most of the season in Buffalo, but returned to New York in September (apparently against Stengel's wishes) for two more losses, including the final game ever played in the Polo Grounds. In the spring of 1964, he broke his hand and again was sent to Buffalo. Anderson was called up in mid-season, pitched briefly, lost once, and was dispatched to the perpetual oblivion of the International League. "I had my best year in 1964," Anderson said. "I was 13–7 and didn't get invited to spring training the next year. They kind of shut the door on me. As long as Stengel and Weiss were running the show, I wasn't going to get another chance." Anderson returned to Buffalo in 1965, and with a terrible Bison team, lost 10 of his first 11 decisions, including, for him, a mini-losing streak of a mere eight games. Convinced he would never return to the big leagues, Anderson retired after the 1966 season.

The third wise man on the Met staff was Ken MacKenzie, a Canadian who liked to refer to himself as "the lowest paid member of the Yale class of '56." MacKenzie was a studious looking, bespectacled, left-handed reliever known to his teammates as "Mr. Peepers." He pitched briefly for the Braves in '60 and '61, and was purchased by the Mets just after the expansion draft. MacKenzie had the distinction of being the only Met on the '62 staff with a record above .500 (5–4). He lived in Greenwich Village, where he enjoyed the bohemian atmosphere of the artsy community and the fact that he could walk around unnoticed. While Pete Seegar or Bob Dylan might attract attention, a baseball player would not. "We'd walk around," he said the next spring, "and see all the art shows, drop in the coffee shops or just watch the people. We liked the people down there. Everybody was open-minded. That's the way we like to operate."

MacKenzie lacked an overpowering fast ball but, as might be expected of a Yale graduate, was a smart pitcher. In the early stages of the '63 season, he won three games in relief, which, on the Mets, was worthy of notice. He had a two year record of 8–5 at a time the Mets had a cumulative mark of 74–196. In August, however, MacKenzie was traded to the Cardinals, and spent the next few years shuttling between Triple A and the major leagues, ending his active major league career in 1965.

MacKenzie became the baseball coach at his alma mater, but had one piece of unfinished business. When he left the Astros, his final big league stop, MacKenzie had served 661 days in the major leagues, one year and 27 days short of the five years needed to qualify for the pension plan. In 1969, the players staged a brief strike which resulted in a reduction in the required service time to four years. During the summer of '69, while the Mets battled for the Eastern Division crown, the old lefthander, now 35, pursued his own dream. He wrote letters to each of his former clubs, plus the newly-formed Montreal Expos, asking if there was any way he could get in his remaining time. John McHale, president of the Expos, had signed MacKenzie to his first contract with the Braves many years earlier. He now signed MacKenzie to another contract, with orders to report to the Expos on September 1, when the roster limits were expanded. MacKenzie pitched batting practice, sat in the dugout, and got his 27 days in the big leagues. It was the least baseball could do for the lowest paid member of the Yale class of '56.

How did the Mets intelligentsia blend in with the rest of the team, many of whom were high school graduates from rural areas? Hook believed that playing major league baseball gave relatively uneducated men a sophistication they would not have gained in other occupations. "They travel a lot," he said, "so they've got a knowledge of different cities. They probably read the paper a lot, so they're up on current events. They probably read the business page, and the stock quotes, because they've got investments. Back when I played, they probably dressed a little better when they traveled. You're on the road a lot, and you have time to read, to see movies. There's a lot of what I would call rounding that happens to people when they're put in that situation, and it was hard to tell who was educated and who was not. With the travel, current events, and the financial areas, whether they know thermodynamics or calculus doesn't make much difference."

Bob Miller, the Northwestern MBA, hung around with Jim Hickman, a Tennessee farm boy, and Joe Pignatano and Roger Craig, neither of whom was a college man. "We'd be in different towns," said Miller, "say, New York, and I'm taking them to museums and going to plays and Broadway musicals, and they're taking me to shoot pool with them."

For the most part, the less-educated players felt comfortable around the college men, as long as the latter did not flaunt their intellectual prowess. Anderson, who was gregarious and likeable, fit in easily. "We called him Mother Anderson," said Don Rowe, "because he was always organizing parties or picnics for all of us." "Baseball brings everyone together from all races and backgrounds," Anderson said. "I've always had a pretty good skill for blending in with anybody." Hook and MacKenzie were more reticent, and sometimes viewed as aloof.

The commonality of baseball enabled players to get along together while they played, but few kept in touch after their careers ended. "People on the team have a common interest in baseball," Hook said, "but the rest of their life is really so diverse. They come from different geographic areas. They come from different educational backgrounds, different family backgrounds. When they get out of baseball, some people go on to other careers. For some, baseball is the highlight of their life. Maybe there's not much commonality except for baseball."

Following their baseball careers, Anderson, Miller and Hook achieved the stardom that had eluded them on the playing field. When he retired from baseball, Anderson called the Lehigh placement bureau and asked them to put him in their job placement program. "I was going to go into the business world," he said. Anderson had begun to take interviews when he received a call from a Lehigh vice president, who asked if he'd be interested in working at his alma mater. Anderson and his wife had attended graduate school together at the University of Southern Illinois, where Craig earned a Master's Degree in Education, and both enjoyed the college atmosphere. Anderson accepted a job as a fund raiser at Lehigh, moved into the athletic department shortly thereafter, and remained at the school for 34 years, serving as pitching coach for the baseball team and retiring as associate athletic director.

Bob Miller retired as an active player following the 1962 season and accepted a job with General Motors. He became Vice President in charge of national sales for Chevway, the rental and leasing arm of Chevrolet, then left GM for a job as vice president of Barton Brands, the fourth largest marketer of distilled spirits in the world. Miller remained at Barton for 20 years, and served as co-chairman of the Executive Steering Committee of the National Alcoholic Beverage Control Board. Later, Miller became CEO of the Major League Alumni Association. He and his wife are very active in a number of charitable activities in the Chicago area, and have been extremely generous in sharing the fruits of their success.

When he was traded to Milwaukee in May, 1964, Hook needed only about 20 days to complete the five years needed to qualify for a major league pension. "I set an objective when I entered the major leagues that I wanted to last at least five years," he said. "I figured that at the end of five years, I'd know whether this was something I was going to make a lifelong career of, or, if I should say, it's been nice, but I'd better go on to engineering or business." Before he agreed to report to Milwaukee's Triple A team in Denver, Hook extracted a promise that he would be recalled after the roster expansion on September 1, to allow him to complete his five years. Despite the fact that he had seriously injured his ankle at Denver, and couldn't pitch, the Braves brought him up. Milwaukee finished fifth, which entitled them to a share of the World Series pool, from which they awarded Hook a partial share of $36.

Following the season, Hook, his pension assured, retired from baseball and went to work for the Chrysler Corporation. "I always liked to soup up cars and make them go fast," he said. Hook stayed with Chrysler for about four years, then moved to Rockwell, where he had a number of jobs, including the management of various divisions. One of those divisions was the casting division, which, among other products, made castings for the undercarriages of New York City subway cars. When Hook took over the division, he found there was a problem with the product; the castings were cracking. A number of trips to New York were required to resolve a series of product liability lawsuits, and during these trips Hook found himself working closely with James McDivitt, the astronaut who had flown around the moon on the Apollo 9 mission and was then an executive with Pullman-Standard. One day, Hook, McDivitt, and two of their colleagues took a cab together to the Federal courthouse in Brooklyn.

"Hey, cabbie," McDivitt said, "do you know that the guy sitting next to you in the front seat pitched the first game the Mets ever won?" The driver looked suspiciously at Hook, who said, "And do you know that the guy who just said that is an astronaut who's flown around the moon?" The cabbie said nothing, but as Hook was paying him, he leaned toward him. "Are you guys shitting me?" he asked.

After nine years at Rockwell, Hook moved on to Masco Corporation. "It was very entrepreneurial," he said. "They gave me six divisions to run. It was really a lot of fun, because it was as close as you could come to running your own business." Employment at Masco brought Hook the same type of excitement he had received from professional baseball. He was heavily involved in mergers and acquisitions, at one point had 20 companies reporting to him, and frequently criss-crossed the country by private jet. "It was really just a great existence," Hook related. "It was very similar to baseball. You're trying to achieve a certain objective and working together as a team, pulling a group of people together to achieve that objective." Hook believed that the time spent in professional sports served him well in the business world. "Determination, dedication, the willingness to work hard to achieve something. Those are all qualities that don't guarantee success, but they contribute to it." Finally, in the business world, Hook achieved the consistency he could never realize on the mound.

By the '90s, Masco had grown dramatically and split into two companies. Hook was set for life financially, and decided to embark on a third career. He returned to Northwestern, became a professor, and started a Master of Business Administration in Manufacturing Management program. Hook also became Chairman of the Board of a Methodist seminary and received an honorary doctorate. "We can't call you Doctor Jay [J]," his children told him, "because you can't jump any more."

Why does a curve ball curve? Why does someone like Henry Aaron hit it into the centerfield bleachers when it doesn't? Would the Three Wise Men have achieved such success after baseball had they made millions during their careers? How did such a collection of educated men come together on the 1962 New York Mets? Only the first question can be answered with certainty. The rest must be added to the many perplexing issues which surrounded the Mets in their first amazing season.

• 6 •

The Duke and the Balk Return
The 1963 Season

If the National League had permitted two platoon baseball in 1963, the Mets would have had a competitive team. They had defensive stalwarts who couldn't hit, like Al Moran, Norm Sherry and Chris Cannizzaro. They had strong offensive players like Frank Thomas, Jesse Gonder and Gil Hodges, who would have made fine designated hitters. It seemed like the last thing they needed was another one-dimensional ballplayer. Yet, the opportunity to acquire a splendid gate attraction like Duke Snider was too good to pass up.

The left-handed Snider hit 311 homers in nine full seasons in Brooklyn, exceeding 40 in each of his last five years. During the past five seasons in Los Angeles, however, Duke had connected for just 73 home runs. The decline was not the result of old age, for Duke was just 31 when he arrived in California. Snider's biggest problem was that he missed Ebbets Field. During their first four years on the West Coast, the Dodgers played in the Los Angeles Coliseum, which had been utilized almost exclusively as a football stadium prior to 1958. In order to adapt the configuration for baseball, a 40 foot screen was erected above the left field fence, a mere 252 feet from home plate. Pop flies dropped over the screen, line drives smashed against it, and right handed hitters salivated at the sight of it. In 1960, catcher Hal Smith of the Pirates hit 11 home runs for the season, seven of them at the Coliseum. Gene Freese and Frank Robinson of the Reds hit seven and six home runs, respectively, at the Coliseum in 1961.

There was no need for a screen to protect the right field barrier, which was a formidable 390 feet from home plate, jutting out to 440 feet in right center. In the Dodgers' first season in the Coliseum, 182 home runs were hit to left field, three to center and eight to right. In 1959, the distances were adjusted slightly, but still, during the four years the Dodgers played in the Coliseum, there were 743 home runs, 616 of which went over the left field screen. In his first year in Los Angeles, Snider, who'd hit 23 homers at Ebbets Field in each of his last five years, managed just six in his new home park. "Duke must have cried the first time he saw the Coliseum," said Clem Labine. "In our first game there, he hit a ball about 500 feet [sic] to center field and Willie Mays caught it. He came back to the dugout and said, 'Boy, am I going to have a good time in this ballpark.'" "Right center was a five dollar cab ride," said Dodger pitcher Fred Kipp. "Duke didn't hit many out there. Nobody did." "You're done, man. You're done," Mays chortled to Snider the first time he saw the park. In five years in Los Angeles, Snider hit just 39 home runs at home.

In addition to losing the advantageous contours of Ebbets Field, Snider missed the protection of the right handed batters who surrounded him in Brooklyn. Opposing teams had been afraid to pitch lefties against the Dodgers, who had right handed sluggers like Jackie Robinson, Gil Hodges, Roy Campanella and Carl Furillo; therefore, Duke saw mostly right handed pitching. Los Angeles had left handers Wally Moon, Willie Davis, Ron Fairly and John Roseboro, plus switch hitters Maury Wills and Jim Gilliam, and Snider found himself facing more lefties.

A third factor in Snider's decline was that Duke had been suffering for several years from a damaged knee, which was operated on the winter before the Dodgers arrived in Los Angeles. "When Duke got out here," Dodger team physician Dr. Robert Kerlan told *Sports Illustrated*, "he had this operated knee, and he was having this recurrent hydrathrosis, or water on the knee." Kerlan had to drain Snider's knee constantly, and gave him 20 cortisone shots in 1959 alone. Duke was in perpetual discomfort. "He'd play for a while and then his knee would swell," recalled Kipp. Young stars Tommy Davis, Willie Davis and Frank Howard came up from the Dodger farm system, and Duke became a sore-kneed fourth outfielder.

Prior to the 1961 season, there were rumors that the Duke would return to New York. The Yankees had often taken former stars and made them valuable bench players and pinch hitters. The rumored trade turned out to be one of the best the Yankees never made, for one of the players the Dodgers wanted in return was Elston Howard.

When the Mets set up shop in 1962, with ex–Dodgers Hodges, Craig, Neal and Zimmer, rumors again began to circulate that Snider was coming back. "If Walter [O'Malley] don't get that park [Chavez Ravine] done in time," Stengel said cryptically, "I'll get that man I want. He'll have to sell him to me. Got my eye on him already." The Polo Grounds, with its short fences, would be perfect for the aging slugger. The Dodgers left the Coliseum for a new park in Chavez Ravine in 1962, but Dodger Stadium, despite a more reachable right field fence, was not conducive to home runs. The Duke's bad knees and advancing age were not conducive to covering its vast outfield. The rumored sale to the Mets was never consummated, and Snider stayed in Los Angeles, playing a reserve role and growing a year older.

In December, 1962, Bavasi told Snider he was going to the Yankees. Duke then received a second call from Bavasi stating that the Yankees had roster problems and the deal was off. Still, it seemed apparent that the Duke was going somewhere. The Dodgers had two high salaried veteran outfielders, Snider and Wally Moon, on the bench, and one would have to go. Finally, just prior to opening day in 1963, the Mets purchased Snider from the Dodgers for an estimated $40,000. He was finally coming home.

The Met fans, many of whom were old Dodger rooters, cheered Duke's every move. On Opening Day, they carried banners reading "Bedford Avenue Duke" and "Welcome Back Duke. Your Loyal Fans." The Duke that returned, however, was a far different player than the one who had left six years earlier. His hair had begun to turn gray when he was 25, and by 1963 it was completely white. Although only 36, Duke, with a considerable paunch and his mane of white hair, looked almost grandfatherly. Yet, he could still hit the occasional long ball and, equally as important, would bring more fans to the Polo Grounds than Joe Christopher, who was sent to Buffalo to make room for him on the Met roster.

At no Met position was the split between offense and defense so clear as at catcher. Chris Cannizzaro was by far the Mets' best defensive catcher, but Cannizzaro was a weak hitter. "He worked so hard on his hitting," said Clem Labine. "I can't tell you how hard he worked." Eventually, Cannizzaro became a decent major league hitter, but not until long after he'd left the Mets. Although Chris first came to the major leagues in 1960, he didn't hit his first home run until 1968. In 1965, he somehow managed to drive in only seven runs in 251 at bats, and at one point went 110 at bats without an RBI. Cannizzaro's best hit of the year was a batting practice line drive that struck teammate Charley Smith in the face. Smith had to be carried from the field on a stretcher.

Stengel loved Cannizzaro's arm, however, for it kept the Mets from being embarrassed by teams like the Dodgers who, led by Maury Wills and Willie Davis, could run wild on the bases. In 1962, Wills stole three bases in a game against the Mets on three different occasions. The re-emergence of speed in the game was a new development, and many of the catchers from the '50s, a number of whom were acquired by the Mets, were big, slow, primarily offensive players. A strong arm wasn't essential, since few teams tried to run. In 1955, the Cardinals led the National League with 63 steals. The 1961 Yankees stole only 29 bases all season.

The Met catching staff was typical for the era. Hobie Landrith, the club's first pick in the expansion draft, could hit but couldn't throw. When the Mets chose him, Stengel pointed out the importance of a catcher, for if you didn't have one, Casey observed, you'd have a lot of passed balls. Even with Landrith, the Mets had passed balls, and runners took great liberties with his weak arm. Hobie's main accomplishment was to have his head cut open twice in the space of three weeks by a hitter's backswing. In June, 1962, he was sent to Baltimore as the player to be named later in the Throneberry trade.

In late April, New York acquired Harry Chiti, "not exactly a bullseye operator when it comes to throwing out runners," according to John Drebinger. Shortly thereafter, Sammy Taylor arrived from the Cubs. Taylor had suffered through a series of arm and shoulder injuries that made it difficult for him to throw. "Sammy could run the ball to second base a lot faster than he could throw it," said a former Cubs' pitcher.

Cannizzaro could always throw. In 1964, he gunned down three Dodgers in a game on one occasion and two on another. In 1965, Willie Davis stole 25 bases and was caught just nine times. On five of the nine occasions, he was thrown out by Cannizzaro. When he first came to the major leagues, however, Cannizzaro had trouble catching the ball, and also had difficulty staying healthy. He missed most of the '61 season after having an appendectomy, and broke a finger in '63. By 1964, he was healthy and had learned to catch the ball as well as he could throw it. "Chris was an excellent, excellent defensive catcher," said Jack Fisher. "I enjoyed pitching to Chris." "Chris was a good catcher," said Joe Ginsberg, "and he was a good kid. He had good hands, a good arm, and he worked at it. He worked at blocking the plate and he worked at blocking the low pitch."

"Chris was real proud of his arm," recalled Don Rowe. "In the bullpen, he'd catch a pitch, look at the ball, and then he'd throw it as hard as he could back to you — every goddamn time." The home team's bullpen in the Polo Grounds was located in deep right center, on the field of play, under a roof bearing the word "Listerine." The roof had been added during the 1950s. "People used to take little bottles," said Labine, "and drop them and try to hit us on the head. Finally they put up an overhang that didn't allow them to do that." "They served Rheingold beer in cans," said Rowe, "and one day some guy took a case of empty Rheingold cans and dropped it from the second deck. It landed on the overhang and scared the crap out of us. The upper stands were over the field. You'd be warming up and they'd spit on you."

One day, while Ken MacKenzie was warming up, a Pirate batter hit a long fly ball in the direction of the bullpen. "MacKenzie had just thrown a pitch to Cannizzaro," Rowe said. "Chris caught the ball, looked down at it, and got ready to launch it. Here comes the batted ball out toward the bullpen and the center fielder comes running after it. MacKenzie hears the commotion and looks over his shoulder. The center fielder and the ball arrive in the bullpen just as Cannizzaro drills MacKenzie right in the chest. Kenny was staggering around, two balls were rolling around, and they had to make a decision. Which ball do they take? Jimmy Piersall was in the bullpen screaming 'Take any one! Take any one!' Finally, our guy picked up one of the balls and threw it back in."

Jesse Gonder was the antithesis of Cannizzaro, a catcher who could hit but couldn't throw. In fact, Gonder couldn't catch very well either. He started his professional career in the Reds' organization, and was acquired by the Yankees in 1959. Gonder led the International League with a .327 average in 1960 and was called up to the Yankees in September. He batted nearly .400 the following spring, and .333 in 15 regular season games. With Elston Howard, Yogi Berra and Johnny Blanchard in front of Gonder, however, there was no room on the Yankees, and he was sent back to Richmond. After a poor season, in which Jesse batted just .226, he was traded to the Reds. In 1962, Gonder batted .342, was the Pacific Coast League's Most Valuable Player and also the Topps Minor League Player of the Year.

Gonder made the Reds' roster in 1963, but was used primarily as a pinch hitter. In mid–May, he started the second game of a doubleheader against the Mets, and showed why manager Fred Hutchinson had restricted him to pinch hitting. In the first inning, Ron Hunt, not a speedster, stole second. In the second, there was a wild pitch and passed ball on consecutive pitches. "Gonder has really been boxing the ball around," said Ralph Kiner. In the third, there was another passed ball. "Jesse Gonder does not stop *everything* that is thrown up there," said Lindsey Nelson, who had taken over for Kiner in the radio booth. The Mets, who stole only 41 bases all season, swiped two more in the fifth. A popup fell unmolested in the middle of the infield. Duke Snider's pop foul dropped on the warning track when Gonder couldn't locate it. Finally, after five innings, Jesse was taken out in favor of Johnny Edwards. Duly impressed, the Mets acquired Gonder in a trade just before the All-Star break.

With the Mets, Gonder hit well, batting .302 in 42 games. Stengel, desperate for offense, would have loved to play him every day, but he couldn't have a defensive liability behind the plate on a regular basis. The Mets brought former major league catcher Clyde McCullough to New York as a coach for the express purpose of working with Gonder on his defense. McCullough said he saw a number of flaws that could be easily corrected, but he wasn't any more successful than Gonder's previous coaches had been. "If he would work at it and listen to what our coaches tell him," Stengel said, "he could be a good catcher." Gonder never did. "I wish they would leave me alone and stop worrying about my catching," he said. His reputation for poor defense was overblown, he claimed. Continuing with his old ways, Gonder set a team record for passed balls in 1964.

Gonder couldn't catch and Cannizzaro, Sherry (.136) and Coleman (.178) couldn't hit. "If I could only get Coleman to hit some more," said Stengel, "he'd have five good points." Choo Choo managed to go 102 at bats without driving in run. Cannizzaro spent most of the season in Buffalo and got into only 16 games. Sammy Taylor was brought back for a few games. Taylor's arm was gone, and when he didn't hit that well, either, he was gone, traded to Cleveland.

The situation was much the same in the infield. Al Moran, acquired from the Red Sox organization as part of the trade that sent Felix Mantilla to Boston, played shortstop better than any Met had in 1962. Moran was steady and reliable and, unlike Elio Chacon, never punched Willie Mays. If he could have hit .230, he would have been a regular. He couldn't, however, ending up at .193 in 119 games. "[Y]ou can't be a .195 hitter and expect to hang on in this league," Stengel said.

What about Chacon, who'd batted .244 in 1962? After the season, Elio went to his native Venezuela to play in the winter league, but couldn't agree on contract terms. On opening day, he took part in pre-game drills with the Caracas Lions, but after being booed for his holdout, changed into civilian clothes and sat in the stands. During the game, he changed his mind, went down to the clubhouse, signed a contract and changed into his uniform. In the seventh inning, he entered the game and was booed even harder than before.

Chacon arrived late at the Met camp in 1963, explaining that the club had not sent him a plane ticket. Why had he waited two weeks to ask for one? Elio shrugged. Although he'd been the regular shortstop in '62, Chacon wasn't given much of a chance to win the job. "Where can I play him regularly?" Stengel said in February. "He can run and throw, but his shortstop is too deep and his RBIs too few." During the exhibition season, Chacon played very seldom, mostly in center field, as Moran got the lion's share of time at short. "What's a matter," Chacon complained, "I no play good short last year?" He went 0–17 in exhibition games and was sent to Buffalo.

Chacon had a good year at Buffalo, and was restored to the Met roster during the winter. Despite the fact that Moran had shown he couldn't hit big league pitching, Stengel still didn't think Chacon was the answer to the Met shortstop problem. "He can run," was Casey's response when asked about the little Venezuelan. Chacon went back to the minors in 1964 and stayed there, playing at the Triple A level through 1971. He was the International League's all star shortstop in 1965, but never received another chance to play in the major leagues.*

Larry Burright, acquired from the Dodgers during the winter, was tried at both second and short. In 1962, Burright was the surprise of the Dodger camp and the rookie sensation of the early season. He was the starting second baseman and found himself, in early June, among the league's top hitters with a .317 average. A hyperbolic *Sporting News* headline read, "Bulldog Burright Sinks His Teeth in Quivering Hurlers." "I just think I was going good," Bulldog Burright said recently, "and nobody could believe it. We were on the bus going to the ballpark in Philadelphia one day and one of the sportswriters said to me, 'Do you know you're in the top ten in the National League in hitting?' I said, 'No, I just go to the ballpark and try to get my hits every night. I let the averages be where they'll be.'"

The jinx was on and pitchers quivered no longer. "It seemed that from there I went 0 for 20 or something," Burright said. He actually went 38 consecutive times at bat without a hit, and his average bottomed out at .205 by the end of the season. He lost his regular job, and as the Dodger season collapsed in late September, was used mainly as a defensive replacement. In the ninth inning of the third and final playoff game against the Giants, Burright's error let in the final San Francisco run, sealing the Dodgers' fate.

In December, 1962, Burright, along with first baseman Tim Harkness, was traded to the Mets for Bob (Righty) Miller. Lefty Miller had been released in October, leaving the Mets Bob Miller–less for the 1963 campaign. Burright won the second base job in spring training, beating out Ted Schreiber, a former St. John's player selected from the Red Sox in the minor league draft. Johnny Murphy, who had known Schreiber from the Boston organization, was the one who wanted to draft him. "Casey didn't want me," Schreiber said recently. "He wanted a pitcher [former Giant Al Worthington]."

Burright started on opening day and had the only two Met hits. Schreiber spent most of his time on the bench before being sent to Buffalo in May. "I was very disappointed," he said. "I thought I had good ability, but I never got an opportunity to play. I said, 'Casey, I don't know why you're sending me down. I've already proved I can play in the minors. From where I've been sitting, I need an awfully long bat to get a hit. Play me for a week and if I don't do anything, send me down, bury me down there and I'll be happy. Just give me a chance for a week.'" Casey sent him down anyway. "I feel bad about it to this day," Schreiber said. "I never found out how much ability I had or didn't have. It's a very difficult thing. You go through life and know you were good enough to play in the minor leagues, but to this day I don't know how much ability I had. I was a local product, and there weren't many New Yorkers except Pepitone, Torre, Tommy Davis and a few others. There was a newspaper strike in 1963, and I didn't get any publicity. That hurt, because if there'd been some publicity, people would have said, 'What happened to Schreiber?,' and maybe they would have had to give me a chance."

Burright soon followed Schreiber to Buffalo. Charley Neal, who had been the regular second baseman in 1962 until he was injured, was moved to third and then traded to the Reds in

In 1968, while playing in Venezuela, Chacon became embroiled in a family dispute and was shot in the ankle, rendering him hors de combat for the Venezuelan League playoffs.

June. Rod Kanehl returned to a utility role. By the first of May, the Met second baseman was a brash 22-year-old who had spent the previous year playing in the Texas League.

Ron Hunt was the first Met to become a hero because of his playing ability, rather than lovable ineptitude or a charismatic personality. He had been conditionally purchased from the Braves organization in October, 1962, on the recommendation of Met coach Solly Hemus. The Mets had 30 days after the start of the season to decide whether to send Hunt back to the Braves or pay $25,000 and keep him.

"Hunt was the first guy I met in spring training in St. Petersburg," said Don Rowe. "We were in a bar, having a few beers, and I asked him where he played last year. He said, 'I played at Austin in the Texas League, but let me tell you something, I'm going to be the second baseman right now,' He just ran Larry Burright right out of there. He'd come to take ground balls and if somebody else was taking ground balls, he'd just push them out of there."

Hunt did not have great natural ability. He couldn't run. He didn't have much power. He didn't have a strong arm. He didn't have a lot of range. He was afflicted with a plethora of allergies. "I don't think he had a great deal of skill," said Ed Bressoud, "but, boy, he used 110 percent of what he had." "Hunt was a tough guy," added outfielder Al Luplow. "He was a throwback to the old-timers. He played awfully, awfully hard." "Ron was a very good teammate," said Galen Cisco, "and he was a bulldog. He wasn't healthy all the time, but he went out there every day and he was an inspiration. He was a gamer."

In 1960, his second year as a professional, Hunt batted .191 at Cedar Rapids of the I.I.I. League. Throughout his minor league career, the scrappy little infielder showed continual improvement, a tribute to his work ethic and dogged nature. By 1962, when he played for Austin, he had raised his batting average to .309. The increase in Hunt's batting average was mirrored by an improvement in his fielding. In his first year in the minors, he had a fielding average of .887. For two consecutive years, he led his league in errors at second base. At Austin, Hunt led Texas League second basemen in fielding percentage.

In the fall of 1962, Hunt played with the Met club in the Florida Instructional League. "That's when they got to know me," he said. "Solly Hemus was there. Paul Waner was there. Eddie Stanky was there. They were all guys I could relate to." Johnny Mize, the Braves' batting instructor, taught players to hit like he hit, which was fine if one were 6'2" and 215 pounds like Mize. Waner was small and taught Hunt to hit like he hit.

During the exhibition season, Hunt impressed Stengel with his hustle and eagerness and earned a job as a utility infielder. He made his presence known by arguing with umpires in intrasquad games, yelling at his teammates when they committed mental blunders, and generally making as much noise as possible. "Hunt had Solly Hemus pushing for him and Burright had Cookie Lavagetto," said Schreiber. "I didn't have anybody."

During the first week of the regular season, Burright played, while Hunt fidgeted on the bench. His 30 day clock was ticking and, if he couldn't get in a game, he would go back to the Braves and back to the minors. That spring, Marv Throneberry, during his salary dispute with Weiss, had popped off publicly. Stengel met with the team and told them that if they had a problem with anything, they should talk directly to him, not to the press. Hunt decided to take Stengel up on his offer and went to the manager's office. Stengel had said, Hunt reminded him, that any player with a problem should come to him. Hunt's problem was that he was not playing. Could Casey possibly get him some playing time or send him to another major league club where he could play? "You really want to play, don't you?" Stengel asked.

Casey put Hunt in the lineup, and on April 16, he marked his major league debut with two hits. Three days later, having lost their first eight games, the Mets trailed the Braves, Hunt's old organization, 4–3, as they entered the last of the ninth. The Met second baseman, an angry young man to start with, felt that the Braves had never given him a fair chance. He wanted revenge.

Hunt came to the plate with runners on second and third and slammed reliever Claude Raymond's high fastball into left field for a double that drove in the tying and winning runs. The Mets, at 1–8, were already ahead of their 1962 pace. Hunt was mobbed by his teammates as if he had just plated the World Series winner. His wife, Jackie, who had just arrived from St. Louis, received a bouquet of flowers from Mrs. Payson and her husband received a permanent place on the Met roster. After the game Stengel said, "[The Braves] are trying to get him back, but I won't give him back."

Hunt was soon playing every day and quickly became a favorite of the Met fans. "I think they liked me," he said, "because I didn't have a lot of talent, but I gave it all I had. We had blue collar fans. There weren't a lot of suits and ties in the Polo Grounds." Hunt dove after every ball within twenty feet of him. He slid headfirst into first base. "Ron never looked good doing anything he done," said pitcher Tracy Stallard, "but he always got it done." Hunt reminded everyone of Eddie Stanky, another scrappy second baseman who got the most of his limited ability. "He performs with such a fierce intensity," wrote Arthur Daley, "that every ballgame is a holy war with him ... the young man has feuds going throughout the league because of the violent way he slides." Since Hunt was a regular, and probably the Mets' best player, Stengel spoke with Weiss and got him a raise from the minimum salary of $7,000 to $8,000.

One of Hunt's talents was a knack for throwing his body in front of pitched balls to get to first base. "Gil Hodges once told me," he said, "that the outside two inches of the plate belong to the pitcher. The rest belongs to me. Then I realized that the pitcher had to be almost perfect with those two inches and that it didn't hurt that much to get hit." Hunt made a science of getting hit by pitches, setting the Met record of 13 in his rookie year. "He'd hug that plate," said teammate Bobby Klaus. "He didn't care who was pitching: Gibson, Drysdale, Koufax. 'If you're going to hit me, hit me,' he'd say. He wasn't afraid of anything."

Hunt was just getting started on his career as a human target, and eventually established a major league single season record of being hit 50 times in 1971 and a career mark of 243. He led the league his last seven years. "It seemed to me," said Galen Cisco, "that he liked to get hit. Late in the game, when the score was tied or we were one run down, they wouldn't pitch him inside because they knew he wouldn't move and he'd get on base."

By the middle of May, Hunt was batting over .300. He got the bat on the ball, and rarely struck out. Hunt had limited range in the field, tended to make routine plays look spectacular, and in his rookie year, led the league's second basemen in errors. But he could turn the double play reasonably well and, for the most part, got the job done. For the next four years, whenever he was healthy, Hunt was in the lineup. In 1963, he hit .272 in 143 games with 10 home runs, and finished second to Pete Rose in the Rookie of the Year balloting. At the end of the season, the fans voted him the Mets' most valuable player and awarded him an Amphicar, a small amphibious vehicle.

Hunt was, for the most part, a serious, intense individual. After a Met loss, which happened frequently, he didn't want to talk to reporters or anyone else. Hunt didn't have a lot of friends on the Met squad, which he said was intentional. He was competing with them for a job and, if trades were made, he'd be competing against them on the field. Only one of his former teammates had a story illustrating Hunt's rarely-shown lighter side. Bill Denehy, a rookie pitcher in the 1966 training camp, had gotten a date with a young lady in St. Petersburg. "Hunt had a big, black Cadillac, like the kind they drive in funeral processions," Denehy recalled. "I asked him if I could borrow the car to take my date out. He said he'd drive me. I thought he'd pick us up, drop us off and then pick us up again. But he came to my room with a chauffeur's hat and jacket on. He drove us around all night like he was my chauffeur."

In 1962, helped by the cozy dimensions of the Polo Grounds, the Met offense had not been all that bad. Pitching and defense had been the club's downfall. In 1963, while Stengel gushed about the improvement in his pitching staff, the offense became very inoffensive.

The Mets were not alone in their ineptitude. During the interlude between the '62 and '63 seasons, the upper limit of the strike zone was raised from the armpits to the top of the shoulders. The impact upon batting averages was immediate. In the first five days of the season, major league pitchers threw a one hitter, three two hitters, two three hitters and two four hitters. For the season, the composite National League batting average dropped from .261 to .245 and the American League average declined from .255 to .247. Only four American League hitters topped the .300 mark, compared with 11 in 1962.

Met hitters struggled right from the start. A few days before the season began, Stengel compared his club with the 1962 Mets. After noting improvement in the pitching, catching and infield, he asked rhetorically, "Does it need more hitting? I wonder." Casey didn't need to wonder long. On Opening Day, Ernie Broglio of the Cardinals shut his club out on two hits. This was a bad omen for Roger Craig, the Met starting pitcher.

Despite his 24 losses in 1962, Craig was in demand during the off season. With a pennant contender, Roger could have been a valuable spot pitcher. The Reds and Cardinals showed particular interest, and numerous possibilities were discussed, but on opening day, 1963, Craig was still a Met, doomed to a second season of agony.

In the second game of the year, the Mets were shut out 1–0 by Ray Washburn, who yielded only three singles. In their third game, the Mets not only exploded for six hits, they scored their first run of the season (a home run by Snider) while bowing to Milwaukee 6–1.

After three games, the Mets had been outscored 17–1, and the team batting average was .103. Two days later, in Craig's second start, he lost 1–0 to the Braves in ten innings, as his teammates managed just four hits. The winning run was unearned. The Mets had scored just three runs in 45 innings. In the team's first eight games, all losses, they were shut out four times.

With a hot streak in late April, the Mets pulled their batting average above .200, but still seemed incapable of scoring when Craig pitched. In his 31 starts, the Mets were shut out nine times. In his first 16 starts, the Mets averaged 1.8 runs per nine innings. In his first 20 losses, they scored only 38 runs. Craig lost five games by the score of 1–0 and another by a 2–0 score. He left a 1–1 game in the ninth inning without getting a decision. Once, coming off the mound during a scoreless tie, he said, "Fellows, I'll settle for half a run."

On the 4th of July, Craig lost 2–1 to the Cubs on two unearned runs. The score was tied in the bottom of the ninth, and Craig had allowed only one hit since the fourth inning. Ernie Banks led off for the Cubs and reached second on an error by shortstop Chico Fernandez. While pitching to Ken Hubbs, Craig threw a pitch in the dirt that eluded catcher Norm Sherry. Sherry retrieved the ball and threw to third, trying to get Banks. The ball flew into left field, Banks scored, and Craig had another loss. He walked slowly to the dugout and sat alone for ten minutes, pondering his fate. "I used to say, 'Roger,'" said Sherry, "'it' s like you send a guy to the plate five times and he hits five line drives right at somebody and goes 0 for 5. You've got to say, gosh, he's really swinging the bat good. He hit five line drives. You're pitching as good as you can pitch and you can't win. It's not your fault.'"

Between May 4 and August 8, Craig lost 18 consecutive decisions. "Roger was our best pitcher," said Al Moran. "It seemed as though every game he pitched, he was in the ballgame. We just didn't have the hitting, the speed or the defense." On July 19, Craig changed uniforms with Tracy Stallard, wearing Stallard's 36 rather than his usual 38. It didn't help. He entered the ninth inning with a 1–0 lead, only to surrender a two run homer to Roy Sievers of the Phillies, which saddled Craig with his 14th straight loss. Like Craig Anderson in 1962, Craig didn't always pitch well, but he didn't pitch poorly enough to lose 18 straight times. "Roger was a great competitor and a savvy pitcher," said Sherry. "He would pitch great games for us and we couldn't score runs and we'd make errors. But he could handle all that. That's why he was such a good manager."

"To lose 20 games," said reporter Gordon White, "you have to be as good as a pitcher who wins 20 games, otherwise you don't get sent out to the mound every four days. Craig was resigned to his fate. He wanted to win every time he went out, but he wasn't surprised if he didn't win. He was a very intelligent guy and very mature. I think he learned a lot from losing that most people don't get to learn. It's not the end of the world, and you can put it in the proper perspective. He didn't die from losing."

"You would never know he was in a losing streak," said Duke Carmel. "He just came out every day and did what he could." "He never looked back," said Galen Cisco, "and he never felt sorry for himself." "What should I complain about," Craig said in the midst of the streak, "I have a lovely wife and four wonderful children."

Craig always thought the next start would be the one that broke his streak. "One of the great things about baseball," said Jay Hook, "and one of the reasons I loved baseball, because I'm an optimistic kind of guy, is that no matter what happens today, there's always a game tomorrow. That's kind of a neat thing. It's so different from being in industry. In business, you come back the next day and the problems that you had yesterday, you've still got today. But in baseball, every day is a new start."

Friday night, August 9, was the start of a new day for Craig, who took the mound against the Cubs at the Polo Grounds. If he lost his 19th straight, he would tie the record of Jack Nabors of the 1916 Athletics. Craig's own number 38 had brought him no luck, nor had Stallard's number 36, so for the Cub game, he wore number 13. Craig was leading 3–2 in the eighth inning when Ron Santo drove in the tying run with a sacrifice fly. When Mets came to the plate in the bottom of the ninth, the score was still tied. With one out, Joe Hicks singled. With two outs, Al Moran doubled him to third. Stengel sent Tim Harkness up to hit for Craig. It was now or never. If the Mets didn't score in the ninth, Craig would be out of the game and couldn't win it. Cub reliever Lindy McDaniel walked Harkness, loading the bases for Jim Hickman. Hickman worked the count to 3–2, then hit a fly ball to left field. Cub outfielder Billy Williams camped under it and waited for the ball to come down. It never came down, hitting the overhang for a grand slam home run, a 7–3 Met win, and Roger Craig's first victory in 19 decisions, his first win since April 29. Hickman was mobbed at the plate like Bobby Thomson in 1951, and fans rushed onto the field. "It's about time you did something big," Craig told him.

The win started Craig on a mini-streak. After the Cub game, he was asked if he would change from number 13 if he lost. "I'm not going to lose any more," he replied. For a time, Craig was correct. He won three straight decisions before suffering another heartbreak in Philadelphia. The Mets had a 1–0 lead with two out in the ninth inning, when Craig surrendered a home run to the villain of July, Roy Sievers. He left the game without a decision and the conviction to walk Sievers the next time he came up in the ninth inning. The next time the Mets played the Phillies, Stengel said, "If Sievers comes up in the ninth, I'm leaving the park and taking Craig with me."

Fittingly, Craig lost his final two starts by 1–0 scores, becoming the first National League pitcher in nearly thirty years to lose 20 games two years in a row. His final record was 5–22, despite a very respectable 3.78 ERA. In the American League, Bill Monbouquette of the Red Sox finished with an almost equivalent ERA (3.81). Monbouquette won 20 games and lost 10.*

Nineteen sixty-three was a strange season. First, the offense disappeared. Then, for a few weeks, the focus of attention in the National League was on that rare baseball occurrence, the balk. The problem was that the balk was not very rare in 1963. In April, National League Pres-

*In 1967, the year after he retired, Craig pitched in his first old timers' game at Shea. He was the losing pitcher.

ident Warren Giles instructed his umpires to strictly enforce the balk rule, particularly the provision that required the pitcher, when throwing from the stretch position, to come to a full stop before delivering the ball to the plate. In 1962, only 48 balks had been called in 812 National League contests. In the first 20 games of the 1963 season, 20 balks were called. No balks were called by American League umps.

Why the drastic change in interpreting the rule, and what did Giles hope to accomplish? Many, including Phillie manager Gene Mauch and Braves' skipper Bobby Bragan, thought Walter Alston was the instigator. As Alston's Dodgers brought speed back into baseball, opponents did whatever they could to stop them, including ignoring the balk rule and delivering the ball to the plate with just a brief pause in the stretch position. "If the balk rule isn't going to be called," Alston told *Sports Illustrated*, "I want to know it. I want the same advantages for my pitchers that the others have — I was tired of this business of pitchers not stopping."

The issue was more important in the National League, where running was a much bigger part of the game. NL teams stole 798 bases in 1962, compared to just 560 in the American League. Not a single American League *team* stole as many bases as Maury Wills. National League superstars Mays, Aaron, Clemente and Frank Robinson could all run. American League stars like Killebrew and Colavito couldn't run, and Mantle and Maris rarely did.

With the umpiring staffs under league jurisdiction, there was no uniformity in the application of the new dictum. American League umps cracked down during exhibition games, then went back to their old ways when the regular season began. In the National League, things were different. In the Mets' opening game, Craig, whose deadly pickoff move was acknowledged to be a balk by everyone he taught it to, was called for two balks in the first three innings, equaling his total for all of 1962. Later in the game, Met reliever Don Rowe was called for another balk.

Two weeks later, in Philadelphia, Rowe made his first major league start, which he marked with three more balks. "The league had to make a special ruling for me," Rowe said. "When I went into my stretch I would lean forward off the rubber and then take the ball and pound it into my glove when I was on the rubber. If I missed the glove, it was a balk. They had to make a special ruling on whether that was legal. When I came up to hit one time, [veteran umpire] Al Barlick said, 'You'd better stop that or I'm going to call a balk on you.' I said, 'Wait a minute, they had a special meeting.' He said, 'I don't care about any special meeting. When I say I'm going to call a balk on you, I'm going to call a balk on you.' So I had to stop doing that."

After his three-balk start in Philadelphia, Rowe was returned to the bullpen, and brought in to face the Pirates about a week later. "When I started walking in from the bullpen," Rowe said, "Norm Sherry, who was warming me up, said, 'Make sure you stop.' I walk in toward the mound and pass Kranepool at first base. 'Make sure you stop now,' he said." When Rowe reached the mound, Coleman and Stengel were waiting for him. "Hey, Bub, make sure you stop," said Choo Choo. "Yeah, make sure you stop," Stengel added as he departed.

Rowe delivered his first warmup pitch without pausing for a tenth of a second, let alone the required full second. Coleman started sprinting to the mound almost before the ball hit his mitt. "I just wanted to see if you were paying attention," Rowe said. He got through his third of an inning without balking.

Although the rules only called for a pitcher to come to a full stop, and did not indicate what constituted a complete stop, National League umps decided that a one second pause was necessary. The Houston pitchers thereupon composed a poem to remind them of the rule:

> One full second must I wait
> Before I throw it to the plate
> One thousand one, one thousand two
> Here it comes, just for you.

Giles didn't feel that poetry was sufficient. He issued a letter telling managers and coaches that it was their responsibility to get their pitchers to obey the rule. "What do they expect us to do," asked an exasperated Stengel, "run out on the field and yell 'Stop!' every time a pitcher starts to pitch?" Craig and Cisco changed their pitching motions to make certain they paused. Theoretically, the balk rule would hurt each team equally, but it seldom benefited the Mets, who rarely put anyone on base.

Milwaukee manager Bobby Bragan took a more proactive approach than Stengel. After watching pitcher Bob Shaw balk five times in a single game, and his other pitchers commit five more during a three game series, Bragan announced a one hundred dollar fine for any pitcher who balked. Shaw was, according to Bragan, $250 poorer. Apparently he had been given a volume discount for his numerous transgressions.

Still, the madness continued. By April 26, 68 balks had been called against National League pitchers, while American League hurlers had been charged with only two. The most balks ever called in a full National League season was 76. Bob Friend of the Pirates had already set an individual record with six, in his first 17 innings. When a Houston game was rained out before it was official, Dick Young lamented, "Bob Aspromonte lost a home run and Al Barlick lost a balk call."

By May 6, the balk count was 96 for the National League to eight for the American. A new league record for balks had been established in less than a month. The situation became ridiculous. More attention was being paid to balks than to the action on the field. Finally, Commissioner Frick called a meeting of the league presidents on May 7th. Giles emerged from the session and indicated that his umpires would no longer insist on a one second stop, but only a discernible pause. Things quickly returned to normal.

With the balk controversy set aside, Met fans could get down to the serious business of watching their club take aim at ninth place. They would do so without Marvelous Marv, who left for Buffalo in May, his place at first base assumed by Harkness and 18-year-old Ed Kranepool, the first big bonus player the Mets had signed. They outbid virtually every other major league club and, in June, 1962, the day after his graduation from James Monroe High School in the Bronx, gave Kranepool $85,000 in return for his signature on a New York contract.

The youngster, whose father had been killed in World War II, had an outstanding scholastic career. He hit nine home runs in fifteen games during his senior season, breaking the school record held by Hank Greenberg, drove in 35 runs and batted .557. He also set a single season scoring record in basketball, averaging nearly 30 points a game. "There," said a Yankee scout, "stands the best 18-year-old hitter I've ever seen in my time in baseball." With his bonus money, Kranepool bought a house for his mother, and a new Thunderbird for himself, then departed for Auburn, New York of the New York-Penn League.

Kranepool was a Yankee fan, but signed with the Mets because he thought he would reach the big leagues faster. He was correct, for after playing with three different minor league teams in '62, he joined the Mets in September. Still just 17 years old, Kranepool played in three games and got his first major league hit. After the season, he went to Florida and played with the Mets' instructional league team.

In the spring of 1951, when Stengel was managing the Yankees, he saw Mickey Mantle play for the first time. George Weiss wanted to send Mantle to the minors, where he could play every day and gain confidence. No one could deny his tremendous ability, but he was only 19, and Weiss didn't think he was ready for big league competition. Stengel insisted, however, that Mantle could play every day with the Yankees. Casey had his way, and Mantle opened the season in New York.

In the spring of 1963, Stengel said many of the same things about Ed Kranepool. "To those who say Kranepool may not make it because of his youth," Louis Effrat wrote in the *Times*, "Stengel counters with, 'Why not? Mel Ott and Bob Feller made it when they were 18.'" The comparison with Ott was often repeated, for both played in the Polo Grounds, and Kranepool was a hitter, not a pitcher like Feller. One needed to have more in common with Ott than being 18, however, and it remained to be seen whether Kranepool had Ott's talent.

As he had with Mantle, Casey got his way and the youngster, with only 41 minor league games and three in the majors under his belt, went north with the Mets. A year earlier, Kranepool had skipped school, attended opening day in New York, and watched the Mets lose to the Pirates. In 1963, he started in right field and went hitless in four at bats, but over the next several weeks, the husky left-hander showed promise of fulfilling at least some of Stengel's expectations. On April 19, during the Mets' initial win of the season, he hit his first major league homer. Kranepool had 10 hits in his first 33 at bats, and after he hit a triple against the Reds in mid–May, Ralph Kiner told his radio audience, "I don't know how he can miss being one of the real great hitters in baseball." "If Kranepool keeps hitting for another week," added Kiner's cohort Bob Murphy, "he'll be compared to Mel Ott." "Ed Kranepool," wrote Joe King, "seems one of those natural players after just one year in pro baseball."

By early May, Kranepool's average had dropped, but was still hovering around the .260 mark. Since the Mets had a team average of .213, that made him a standout. Stengel played him at first and in the outfield, against both left and right handed pitching. Eventually, National League pitchers figured out how to get Kranepool out and, like Mantle in 1951, the rookie went into a prolonged slump. Kranepool went 26 times at bat without a hit. He became irritable, and annoyed his teammates with his immaturity.

By early July, Kranepool's average was down to .190, and he had only two home runs. Stengel was forced to take him out of the lineup, but stubbornly insisted that Kranepool would learn more sitting on the Met bench than he would by playing in Buffalo. Finally, good judgment prevailed and Kranepool was sent to Buffalo on July 7th. His attitude, which had been poor in New York, got no better in the International League. After he complained when Bison manager Kerby Farrell batted him eighth in the lineup, Farrell told him to show something and he'd move up. Umpires told him to improve his vocabulary.

After batting .310 in 53 International League games, Kranepool was recalled when the rosters expanded on September 1. Within a day of reporting, he refused to take a charter flight to St. Louis, paid his own fare for a later flight, and said he'd quit baseball if the Mets didn't reimburse him. The situation was resolved, but both off the field and on it, Kranepool had been a disappointment. In 86 games with the Mets, he batted just .210, with two home runs and 14 runs batted in.

Hitting was Kranepool's only skill, for he was no more than an adequate first baseman, and was painfully slow on the bases, even in his younger days. "Eddie had a great swing," said pitcher Bill Denehy, "and he had great hands. But he didn't have a great body. He didn't run very well, and he was old-looking at 19. I'm not talking about his face, I'm talking about his whole body. He was like a 19-year-old old man."

Kranepool's lack of power was surprising. "The boy has got major league power right now," Stengel said after watching him work out in 1962. A November, 1962 article in *The Sporting News* labeled Kranepool a "Met Muscleman." Yet, Kranepool never hit more than 16 homers in a season, and some years managed only three or four. He was a 6'3" 205-pound singles hitter. "When Kranepool tried out with us at the Polo Grounds," said Rod Kanehl, "he was hitting balls out of the park. He was pulling the ball and hitting it to center field. Then he came up to the big leagues and he was a Slapsy Maxie."

"He reminded me of Clint Hartung," said Gordon White, "the guy the Giants signed right after the war.* Every time Hartung came to bat, the world expected a home run hit farther than

---

*To those of White's generation, "The War" is World War II.

Babe Ruth had ever hit them. He had a very difficult time trying to live up to that. Terrible pressure was put on these guys. Kranepool was supposed to be the team's savior and it didn't work out. That's a crusher, putting so much pressure on one guy, especially a youngster. He just can't do it."

While an 18-year-old may possess great physical talent, teenage stardom is generally more indicative of great maturity. A young phenom must adapt to big league life and travel at a time when his friends are living in college dormitories, closely regulated and watched over by adults. A teenaged major leaguer must be able to interact socially with men in their 30s, and have the ability to play with confidence against men much older and more experienced, men he may have idolized as an adolescent.

Kranepool had an advantage in being a New Yorker. "Eddie had grown up in New York," said pitcher Bill Wakefield, "and was familiar with the city and its history. It might have been easier for him. It was a much bigger deal for somebody like [teenaged pitcher] Jerry Hinsley, who was from New Mexico. When Jerry and I arrived in New York, the first thing we did was run down to the Empire State Building with Larry Elliot. We were just walking around like tourists."

Kranepool was on familiar turf and didn't have to worry about the adjustment to city life. He also had no problem with self-confidence. "He was a brash young guy," said Rick Herrscher. "You had to rein him in a little bit. He was real cocky and thought he could handle anything." Stengel was impressed by the fact that the 18-year-old was ejected from a spring training game in 1963 for a vehement argument with the plate umpire over a called strike. He liked the fact that the youngster wasn't afraid to speak up. Casey was less impressed by an incident later that season.

"Every time Kranepool would play, they'd jam the heck out of him," recalled Norm Sherry. "He'd break all his bats. So in batting practice, he was telling all the pitchers to throw outside, because he couldn't hit the ball inside. Duke Snider came up to him and said, 'Why don't you have them pitch you inside? Then you'll learn to hit it.' Kranepool said, 'Who the hell are you to tell me how to hit?'"

When he was sent to Buffalo, Kranepool argued with umpires, sportswriters, and his manager, Kerby Farrell. "Eddie was a cocky kind of guy," said a Met pitcher. "He thought he could run the whole ballclub. If there was something wrong, he'd let you know about it." "He was aloof," said another teammate. "I don't think he got the most out of his ability," said a third. "He wasn't really friendly," said a '69 teammate, "but he wasn't a jerk either. He was one of those guys who would just come out and play the game, not say too much, go back in the clubhouse, and go home." In its preview of the 1965 season, *Sports Illustrated* said, "[W]hen things go bad, Kranepool has been known to sulk."

In 1963, Kranepool was one of a plethora of first basemen on the Met roster. In addition to Throneberry, and Harkness, the Mets still had Gil Hodges, who was attempting to come back after knee surgery and the removal of a kidney stone. In the spring, he said he had no idea what the season would bring. "Last year," Hodges said, "I predicted the Mets had a good shot at sixth place. I also predicted I'd have a good year — and I wound up twice in the hospital. What can I possibly say now that the people would believe?"

Hodges played very little in the early season and on May 9, the same day Throneberry was sent to Buffalo, was placed on the disabled list in order to reduce the squad to 25. Hodges had been slow to recover from his knee injury, and it was assumed that when his 30 days on the disabled list were up, he would be named a Met coach, and presumably Stengel's heir apparent.

Hodges was still inactive on May 22, when the Mets played in Los Angeles and lost to Don Drysdale, which was not news. The big story in Los Angeles that day was that the Mets had given Hodges his release so he could accept the job of manager of the Washington Senators, replacing Mickey Vernon.

Stengel said he anticipated that Hodges would eventually have been activated by the Mets. Gil had the right to play for the Senators if he wanted. Therefore, Casey expected to get a player from Washington in return for having granted Hodges his release. "I wouldn't be surprised if it's Piersall," Stengel said.

On May 24, the acquisition of Jimmy Piersall was officially announced. His arrival posed one immediate problem. Piersall had worn number 37 his entire career. Stengel also wore number 37. Someone suggested that Piersall be issued number 37A. Someone else suggested that both be allowed to wear the same number. "If our fans can't tell the difference between them," he said, "they don't deserve to be Met fans." Piersall temporarily took number 2, Marvelous Marv's old number, but switched to 34 when the Mets returned to New York.

Casey Stengel and Jimmy Piersall on the same team was a scenario for both anticipation and dread. Stengel, who once called Piersall the best outfielder he had ever seen, was hopeful that, if he still retained some of his former skills, he could cover the vast Polo Grounds outfield better than Rod Kanehl, the latest Met centerfielder. Piersall, always a volatile personality, had mellowed somewhat in recent years but, the day before his sale to the Mets, had been fined $100 for an argument with an umpire.

Most fans saw Piersall as an entertaining character, a showman and crowd pleaser. The press often portrayed him in a similar manner, a happy-go-lucky, younger version of veteran baseball clown Al Schacht. Piersall did pantomimes in the outfield. He clowned around in the infield before the game. "There is a joyous exuberance to Jimmy Piersall," wrote Arthur Daley. "[H]e is a bit of a screwball with an affinity for headlines." Piersall was often compared to Stengel, an analysis that couldn't have been farther from the mark. Stengel was an intelligent, calculating man who knew exactly what he was doing and slipped in and out of his comic character as he chose.

Piersall was also highly intelligent, but a deeply troubled man who suffered a nervous breakdown in 1952 and teetered on the brink of mental instability for years afterward. There was nothing premeditated or comical about his explosive episodes. "Probably the best thing that ever happened to me," Piersall wrote in his autobiography, "was going nuts. It brought people out to the ballpark to get a look at me, and they came to the places where I was invited to speak." That statement was disingenuous, for his mental state brought Piersall far more anguish than pleasure. He was involved in many fights, including a much publicized brawl with Billy Martin. He battled his own teammates and, in 1962, immediately after joining the Senators, was accused by teammate Gene Woodling of being a prima dona and demanding special privileges. Among other things, Woodling charged, Piersall had insisted on having a private room. He only had a single room, Piersall replied, because his psychiatrist recommended it. Senator GM Ed Doherty pointed out Piersall's high strung nature and suggested that perhaps Woodling would like to room with him.

Bench jockeying was cruel in those days, and nothing was out of bounds. Opponents tried to throw Piersall off his game by getting under his skin, which was paper-thin. Willard Nixon, Piersall's teammate, called him "Gooney." Dick Williams, playing with the Orioles, used to yell "Cuckoo, cuckoo, cuckoo," at him.

The 1961 season was perhaps Piersall's finest in the major leagues. He batted .322 and played centerfield as well as ever. "Other than Willie Mays," said teammate Al Luplow, "he was the best I'd ever seen at getting a jump on the ball." "He could really run the ball down," said Washington teammate Bob Johnson, "and he was the best outfielder for getting you a good relay throw. You could catch it bare-handed. It was always right up at your face where you could wheel and throw it. It was always right on target."

While Piersall was involved in some "incidents" in 1961, his behavior was nothing like the erratic, frightening conduct of the prior season, when he was ejected numerous times and staged some bizarre incidents. In June, 1961, he charged Tiger pitcher Jim Bunning, who had hit him on the wrist. Piersall took a wild swing at Bunning, then dropped to the ground and began kicking at him. Both benches cleared and Piersall was ejected.

On September 10, Piersall had a harrowing experience in center field at Yankee Stadium. In the seventh inning, he saw two young men running toward him. "You crazy bastard, Piersall," one of them shouted, "we're going to get you." Piersall waited until the first man was within striking range, then threw a left hand that dropped his would-be assailant. Piersall then turned on his friend, who decided discretion was the better part of valor, and tried to run away. Piersall started chasing him, and took a vicious kick at the man's backside, just missing. By that time, the stadium police had arrived, but not before Indian second baseman Johnny Temple and 6'7" outfielder Walt Bond arrived and landed a few punches.

Prior to the 1962 season, Piersall was traded to the Senators where, as the highest paid player in the history of the franchise, he had a disappointing year. Bothered by a series of injuries, he saw his average drop to .244 and his range in centerfield diminish dramatically. There were also a number of troubling episodes. On September 13, Piersall went into the stands at Baltimore's Memorial Stadium, trying to attack a 66-year-old heckler who shouted that not only was Piersall crazy, his mother was as well. Stadium police intercepted Piersall, arrested both men and charged them with disorderly conduct. The following day, at a Washington hotel, Piersall was knocked unconscious while going through a revolving door and had to have stitches taken in his head.

When Piersall was an All-Star, such episodes were more tolerable. For a fading 33-year-old on a last place team, they were not. The Senators tried to take a large slice out of Piersall's salary and, after a prolonged dispute, he settled for a small slice. In May of 1963, he was on the bench and available.

Met fans welcomed Piersall with open arms. Leonard Koppett wrote, "Casey Stengel is something new in Piersall's life. Together they might write the most entertaining chapter in it." Piersall had always wanted to play for Stengel and was eager to reach New York. He received a wonderful ovation before his first game at the Polo Grounds and posed for pictures on top of the tarpaulin with fans hoisting a "We Love Piersall" sign. "I just want to play for the Mets and avoid trouble," he said. "I get very excited and I don't always know what I'm going to do next, but I just hope that if I do something wrong, they'll tell me right away. I just want to play—to be myself, but not to cause any fuss."

Piersall's stay in New York was brief but uneventful. He hit the 100th home run of his career and ran the bases backwards. He took a few swings left-handed against the Cardinals. He served as home plate umpire during Old Timers' Day and ejected Al Schacht. When the Mets put on a rock 'n' roll show before one game, Piersall took the stage and did the Twist. He went on the Tonight Show when the Mets were in Los Angeles. He umpired again and played with his seven children on Family Day at the Polo Grounds. During an exhibition game against the Buffalo farm club, Piersall combed his hair at first base, batted left-handed, and spent the entire game entertaining the crowd.

During one game, catcher Sammy Taylor squatted down to give a sign to Roger Craig, then suddenly stood up and told Craig to wait. "What's the matter?" Craig asked. Taylor pointed out to second base, where center fielder Piersall was standing. "Go ahead," Piersall told Craig, "throw it. I'll be there." As Craig wound up and pitched, Piersall started sprinting toward the outfield.

Piersall got along well with his Met teammates. He and Frank Thomas, a great agitator, had lockers near each other, and the two traded barbs continuously. "He was a nice fellow," said Taylor. "I really enjoyed playing with him." Finally, at 34, Piersall had managed to channel his energy into entertainment rather than let it destroy him. "I roomed with him on a couple of trips," said Al Moran. "For all the things that had been written about him and all the things he did in the past, he was just a regular, average guy. I guess he'd matured. When you talked to him, you could tell he was a very intelligent person."

Unfortunately, good citizen Piersall did not play very well. In 40 Met games, he batted just .194, and was no longer the tremendous outfielder he had been in his prime. "He was struggling at the plate," said Joe Hicks, "and also in the field. He'd lost a step. Jimmy loved to play shallow, and balls that he would have caught earlier in his career were going over his head." On July 22, Piersall was placed on waivers and released.

Jobless in New York, Piersall went to Yankee Stadium to talk to Ralph Houk. Houk wasn't interested, so Piersall went to the visiting locker room and asked Angel manager Bill Rigney if he needed a center fielder. Rigney did and signed Piersall to a contract. Jimmy was named American League Comeback Player of the Year in 1964, and played for the Angels until 1967. He eventually went from being a controversial ballplayer to a controversial broadcaster, covering the games of the Chicago White Sox with enough candor to nearly cause a revolt among the players. He took lithium to quiet his demons, but never lost the fire that made him one of the most exciting players of his day.

Before the 1962 season, some expected the Mets to finish as high as seventh. After 120 losses, there were no rosy predictions for 1963. The Angels had performed a minor miracle by finishing third in their second season, but Los Angeles had not been as bad as the Mets in their first year. In spite of their 15–12 exhibition record, everyone predicted the Mets would finish last in the National League. The team didn't disappoint them. There were a number of changes from the '62 club, as 10 of the 14 who played in the previous opener were no longer with the team. Neal, Craig and Thomas were the only ones who started both the '62 and '63 openers.

Different was not better, however, despite some encouraging signs. In April, there was a spurt during which the Mets won six of seven, by far the best week in their history. In early May, they set a club mark with five straight wins and got as high as seventh place. At one point, the Met record was a nearly respectable 14–17.

The April spurt was a mirage, and by the middle of May the Mets had settled comfortably in the cellar. They played well at home, but horribly on the road, suffering through a 22 game road losing steak. Since they couldn't compete against the rest of the league, they began competing with the '62 Mets. The '63 club's longest losing streak was 15 games, shorter than the 17 game debacle of '62. On August 24, Carl Willey beat the Cubs for the Met's 41st win, breaking the all-time club record for victories in a season. They didn't lose for the 100th time until the 14th of September, compared to August 30 the previous year.

On September 11th, Al Jackson won his 11th game, besting the ten wins of Roger Craig in 1962. Jackson won two more to stretch the mark to 13, and was the only Met pitcher to win a game after September 10. He won seven of his last ten decisions to finish with a 13–17 mark.

The Mets' infield defense was far better than it had been in 1962. While Moran didn't hit, he covered shortstop better than any of the hands who were found wanting in 1962. Willey, acquired from the Braves just before the start of the season, became the first Met righthander, and the first Met other than Jackson, to pitch a shutout. He pitched three more later in the season, equaling Jackson's record of 1962, and finished with a 9–14 record and a fine 3.10 ERA. Willey also became the first Met pitcher to homer, hitting a grand slam for good measure.

Reliever Larry Bearnarth had an excellent rookie season. Bearnarth, a graduate of St. John's University, won 32 of 34 college decisions, and signed with the Mets in June, 1962, for a $25,000 bonus. The young pitcher was intelligent, articulate, likeable and a native New Yorker. A few years later, George Vecsey wrote of "Larry and Barbara Bearnarth, who could have been Tom and Nancy Seaver five years early with a little more hop on the fastball." Although he had gone 2–13 in a half season at Syracuse in 1962, Bearnarth reported to the Mets' camp in 1963 and had an excellent spring. He stayed with the Mets for the entire season, appeared in a club record 58 games, and was the club's first reliable relief pitcher.

There were disappointments. Frank Thomas, who'd been rewarded with a $3,000 raise for hitting 34 home runs in 1962, dropped to 15, and was dogged by injuries for most of the season. Snider got off to a strong start, with ten home runs by early June, and hit his 11th, the 400th of his career, on June 14. He was only the ninth player to reach the 400 plateau, and, as Lindsey Nelson pointed out, the first major leaguer to hit his 400th on color television. In his first at bat against his former Dodger teammates, in Los Angeles, Snider hit a home run off his old buddy Don Drysdale. In July, he was the only Met named to the All Star team.

With little to choose from, Stengel played Snider too often, and the white haired veteran faded in the second half. He finished with just 14 home runs, a .243 average and very sore legs. Still, in September, Duke said, "All in all, this has been a thrilling year. What made it so, I guess, are two factors—Casey Stengel and the fans." After so many years with the Dodgers, it had been tough to adjust to the losing, he said, but the fans had never given up.

As in 1962, there was a great deal of turnover on the roster. Stengel moved players in and out of the lineup as frequently as he had with the Yankees. In the Mets' first 75 games, he used 69 different lineups. In 1953, Casey devised 105 different lineups while leading the Yankees to a world championship, but these days he was rotating Larry Burright and Chico Fernandez rather than Hank Bauer and Gene Woodling. Burright, Schreiber and Moran all made visits to Buffalo, as did Christopher, Cannizzaro, Cliff Cook and Sammy Taylor.

Don Rowe went to Buffalo along with Moran and Burright. "Casey told us we were just going down there for ten days to give some other guys a shot," Moran said. "He told us to leave our families in New York. I came back, Larry came back and Rowe stayed. About three weeks later, we went to Buffalo for an exhibition game. We're in our dugout and Rowe hollers over to Stengel, 'Hey, Casey, how're my wife and kids. Have you seen them in New York?'" Rowe never returned to New York. "It took me nine years to get here," he said when he was demoted, "and only 56 innings [sic] to find out I'm not a big leaguer."

In July, the Mets recalled lefthander Grover Powell from Raleigh. Powell, 22, had pitched for the University of Pennsylvania before he was thrown off the team by Coach Jack McCloskey. One time, he asked McCloskey to take him out of a game because he was cold. When Powell missed a bus for a game at West Point, McCloskey reached the breaking point and booted him off the squad.

Powell had previously been offered $8,000 by a number of teams, but after his disciplinary problems, no one was interested. Finally, he persuaded the Mets, beginning their first season, to part with a $2,500 bonus in February, 1962. Powell was only 4–12 with Syracuse and Auburn in 1962, but when he struck out 87 batters in 83 innings at Raleigh in 1963, the Mets called him up to New York.

Powell spent his first few weeks with the Mets mopping up lost causes, of which there were many. On August 20, he made his first start, and pitched a four hit shutout against the Phillies. When reporters interviewed him after the game, they found that Powell was a genuine character. Was he nervous? Yes, Powell, replied, he always got nervous before his first big league start. What would he do for encore? He'd probably get bombed, he said. Stengel grabbed a pencil and pad and pretended to be a reporter. "Wuz you born in Poland?" he asked. "Not bad for a 14-year-old pitcher," Casey added. "Just imagine what he'll be like when he's 16."

Powell loved the attention, and tried to make everyone laugh. "Besides baseball," he once said, "comedy is my life." It was fortunate that he made the most of his fame, for it lasted only six days. In his second start, while shutting out Pittsburgh, Powell was hit in the face by a line drive off the bat of the Pirates' Donn Clendenon. The injury wasn't serious, but Powell, suffering from blurred vision and shock, had to leave the game.

Powell returned to action, and pitched fairly well, although he didn't win another game. He finished the season with a 1–1 record, having pitched 50 innings in 20 games. That winter, while pitching in Venezuela, Powell hurt his arm. He had altered his delivery after being hit in the face, and the change led to an elbow injury. Powell was diagnosed with tendonitis, which bothered him for the rest of his career. He went back to Penn for a while, then tried a come-back. After a couple of mediocre campaigns, Powell had a 16–6 record for Asheville manager Sparky Anderson in 1968, and led the Southern League in ERA. He pitched two more seasons in the minor leagues, but never got another chance to play in the big leagues. The glorious win in Philadelphia was his only major league victory. He died of leukemia in 1985 at the age of 44.

The Mets' final record of 51–111 was an improvement over the previous year, but still left the team deep in the basement, 48 games behind the pennant winning Dodgers and 15 behind the ninth place Colts. Thirty-two of the 111 losses were by a single run, and the Mets were shut out 30 times. In 1962, the team had been 18–62 on the road. They were even worse in 1963, post-ing a 17–64 record. The good news, therefore was that the club improved its record at home from 22–58 to 34–49. Just as the Mets were getting the hang of playing in the Polo Grounds, however, they were leaving.

At the end of the season, Snider was given a day at the old park, and the Mets said good-bye to the Polo Grounds for the second time. On September 23, 1962, the Mets had bid adieu for the first time, with all the nostalgia one would expect upon leaving a site with such a rich history. When the new park in Queens wasn't close to being ready in 1963, however, the Mets were forced to return for a second season beneath Coogan's Bluff.

On September 13, 1963, the Giants played in the Polo Grounds for the final time. Willie Mays hit a fly ball to center field in his last at bat. On September 18, the Mets' departure was final when, at 4:21 P.M., Ted Schreiber hit into a double play for the final outs of a 5–1 loss to the Phillies. Craig Anderson was the losing pitcher, his first loss of the year, but his 17th in a row over two seasons. It was a classic Anderson loss, in which he gave up three runs, all unearned. Only 1,752 fans witnessed the final game in the historic old park. The following spring, the wreck-ing ball delivered its fatal blows and the Polo Grounds ran out of lives.

As 1963 wound down, Stengel agreed to return for a third season. Casey was as popular as ever, and Met attendance was far higher than any last place club had a right to expect. By mid–August, attendance had surpassed the 1962 total. The million mark was reached on Sep-tember 1, and the final attendance was 1,080,104, a remarkable total for a ragtag outfit like the Mets, especially in an old park like the Polo Grounds.

It was great to have fans when the team was losing, but George Weiss wasn't accustomed to losing. He was looking toward the day when good players, not Casey Stengel, would be the Mets' main attraction.

♦ 7 ♦

Casey

The best thing about covering the Mets in their early years, said reporter Gordon White, was listening to Casey Stengel explain the tribulations of his sorry club. "This genius clown," said White, "was just a brilliant man who absorbed all the attention and took it away from his bumbling, incompetent, inept, over-the-hill gang. He was an absorbing character who just charmed you to death with bullshit. His talk was so wonderful and he was alive to everything that was going on. That was not some buffoon acting. Casey was a very dynamic and brilliant man who knew everything he was doing and everything he was saying. It was wonderful to listen to him because it sure made great copy."

"When we had a rainout," said Jay Hook, "the first thing Casey would do is get the press in and start regaling them with stories about the past. The writers really appreciated that, because if you've got a dozen inches of column to fill every day, it sure helped to have something to write about." "[H]e understood the functions and limitations of various newspapers," wrote reporter Jack Mann, "and the differences between them, which many high-priced public-relations pundits patently do not. A story that would call for a five-column headline in The *New York Post* would be virtually useless to the man from the *Times*, and Stengel knew that." He also knew the deadlines of the various journals, and delivered his interviews accordingly.

Casey's skillful handling of the press was a godsend not only for the reporters, but also for his team. Never have players who lost 120 games in a season departed in October with less criticism than the 1962 Mets. "I think Casey made a pact with the writers," said Rod Kanehl, "by saying that they could write anything they wanted about the team, but not to pick on individual players. Pick on us collectively, but not individually. They got on Throneberry, but in a jovial way. I can't recall them getting on any one player, but as far as the team was concerned, we took it collectively."

"I don't think there was another guy who could have handled it any better than Casey did," said Galen Cisco. "He took all the pressure off the players. He never bad-mouthed a player. All the writers wanted to talk to Casey. They didn't really care an awful lot about talking to the players. Casey would talk as long as the reporters wanted to talk."

"I didn't appreciate what Casey did until later," said Ron Hunt. "He kept the press from getting on the players by entertaining them." "There wasn't a lot to write about the team," said outfielder George Altman, "so they wrote about Casey and his antics."

Managing the New York writers wasn't an easy task, for they were probably the toughest in the major leagues. In Detroit, recalled Bob (Lefty) Miller, players could relax over a beer with a writer and be assured that whatever they might say wouldn't appear in the next day's paper. That was not necessarily the case in New York, as Jay Hook learned soon after joining the Mets. There had been rumors that Hook's 1961 Reds had stolen opposing catchers' signs from the center field scoreboard. The following spring, Hook was asked by reporter Barney Kremenko whether the rumors were true. Hook decided to play it coyly. "Gee, Barney," he said, "I don't want to get in the middle of this. I won't confirm it, but I won't deny it." "The next day," Hook said, "the headline read 'Hook Says Reds Stole Pennant.'"

Stengel loved the attention he received from the media. "He understood the market," said Hook, "and what was needed to sell the product. He knew that to get to the fans, he had to keep the sportswriters happy. He understood the communication link to his customers." The writers in turn loved Casey. He entertained them, gave them copy, and drank with them, even in his 70s. "Casey could drink," said White. "Holy Jesus, could he drink. Casey would drink everybody under the table and come back the next day sharp as a tack." "He killed a lot of sportswriters," said Tracy Stallard. "He'd stay up with 'em and you'd see 'em all the next morning. The writers looked like they'd been run over by a truck and Casey would be bouncing around on his crooked legs, spry as could be."

Former Yankee pitcher Ryne Duren, a substance abuse counselor for many years, said, "I don't think anybody could drink as much as Casey did, and not have it affect him. It was just a way of life that I don't think he could get out from under. He didn't know any better. I'm not saying it hurt his reputation, but I think it hurt him physically."

Stengel never did get out from under his drinking. Late one night in December, 1968, when Casey was 78, his car collided with another vehicle, bounced off, hit a third car and continued on for several blocks. When police arrived, they found Stengel walking around near the scene, and arrested him for driving under the influence. He pleaded no contest and paid a $322 fine.

Casey's stamina was legendary. "We'd be flying," said Sammy Taylor, "and if there was anybody awake, he'd sit down and start talking to them. He'd talk baseball all the time." "He was the ringleader of the circus," said Gary Kroll. "All the reporters used to follow him around. We'd fly from New York to L.A. and he'd sit in that round seat in the back of the plane. He'd still be talking when the plane landed in L.A. Some of the reporters would be asleep. He was funny and he was sharp. His mind was still there."

"On the airplane," recalled pitcher Dennis Musgraves, "his voice roared over the noise of the engines. He'd get the reporters around him and tell them stories about the Yankees. They'd be real attentive and laugh at all of his jokes. He was quite a guy. He never slept. I don't think that man ever slept."

Casey may not have slept at night, but daytime was another matter. "We were playing the Giants at Shea," Musgraves said, "and there was a disputed call at the plate. Casey was at the end of the bench and had kind of nodded off. He heard the commotion, woke up, stood up real quick and hit his head on the concrete top of the dugout. It kind of knocked him starry-eyed, and he sat down real quick. When he regained his composure, he ran up the steps and out to home plate. He was going round and round with the umpire when he never even saw the play."

"He used to fall asleep on the bench about the third or fourth inning," said Clem Labine. "Zimmer, who's an agitator, used to go right behind him, hit the wall and jump up as if somebody got a base hit. We weren't even at bat." "One day about the seventh inning," recalled Joe Ginsberg, "he fell asleep. All of a sudden he heard the crack of the bat. He woke up and started applauding. We said, 'Casey that's not us. It's the other team running around.' He said, 'That's all right. We'll get 'em next inning. We'll get 'em next inning.'"

Joe Hicks remembers a spring training game in Vero Beach against the Dodgers, when the sun was beating down mightily on the Met bench. About the third inning, Stengel fell asleep. He woke up, walked down to the end of the bench, sat down and nodded off again. Frank Thomas and Rod Kanehl decided to have a little fun, and went down and sat next to Stengel. Duke Snider swung mightily and missed for strike three. "Hot Rod and Frank jump up," Hicks recalled, "hollering, 'Way to go, Duke, way to hit it!' Casey woke up and yelled, 'Yeah, Duke, way to hit the ball.' I was thinking, 'Here I am trying to win a job and there's our manager sleeping on the bench.'"

"He was known for his night life," said Ted Schreiber, "and at two or three in the morning he'd be sitting in the lobby. One hot day at Al Lang Field he was nodding off in the corner of the dugout. The guy who always rooted was Rod Kanehl. He was loud and boisterous and active. Rod yelled, 'Hey, that was a bad pitch.' Casey woke up in a stupor and said, 'Yeah, it was high and inside,' You know, strangely enough, it was high and inside." "[Casey] could probably see more taking a nap," said Ralph Houk, "than most managers could see wide awake."

The stories of Stengel sleeping on the bench were first made public in 1962 by Howard Cosell. Cosell, who was born Howard William Cohen, had left the practice of law in the mid–1950s and was attempting to find fame and fortune as a reporter. "Howard was bucking hard trying to make a name in sports radio," recalled Gordon White. "He hadn't yet been touched by the magic wand of Roone Arledge." In 1954, Cosell began his broadcasting career by moderating a radio show in which youngsters asked questions of professional athletes. Two years later, ABC offered Cosell a steady job doing ten five minute sports reports each weekend.

With an ABC salary of $250 per week, Cosell quit his law practice to devote his full attention to building and promoting his broadcasting career. He thought sports journalism was too soft, and longed to make it a more serious profession. "Do you know how many really good sports announcers there are in America?" Cosell once lamented to fight promoter Harry Markson. "One less than you think," Markson replied.

Cosell was not a member of the media establishment and did not honor their code of looking the other way when sports figures transgressed. "If Howard Cosell were a sport," wrote veteran columnist Jimmy Cannon, "he would be the roller derby." Cosell was dogged, hard-working and unafraid of controversy. In fact, the more controversial the subject matter, the more he loved it. His unflagging goal, he insisted, was pursuit of the truth — except in regard to himself. Cosell had changed his name, wore a toupee to mask a rapidly receding hairline, and shaved three years off his age.

Cosell first roused Stengel's ire in 1958, when, after the Yankees lost the first two games of the World Series to the Braves, he asked Stengel if his team had "choked." "I haven't choked up," Casey virtually shouted at Cosell, "and none of my players choked up. Ball players don't choke up. But if anybody's gonna be choked up it's going to be somebody holding a microphone." Mickey Mantle had his own way of dealing with Cosell. When he didn't want to answer a question, Mantle just stared silently into the camera and ruined the tape.

By 1962, Cosell was handling both the pre-game and post-game shows for the Met broadcasts on WABC radio. "He used to set up shop in the clubhouse and try to interview people," recalled Johnny DeMerit. "Half the people wouldn't talk to him." When they did talk to him, they weren't always co-operative. "Do you think Shea Stadium will be ready by opening day," Cosell once asked Frank Thomas. "No," Thomas replied. "Why do you say that, Frank?" Cosell asked. "Because you told me to," Thomas replied.

Cosell used his podium to pound home his opinion that Stengel and George Weiss were old and incompetent and should be dismissed immediately. Years later, Cosell told Stengel's biographer, "he was a doddering old man and a racist who should have been retired twenty years before he was."

While the rest of the country adored the bumbling Mets, Cosell took umbrage at their ineptitude. "I'm suspicious of anything," he said, "that causes kids to fall in love with futility." Stengel developed an intense dislike for Cosell and refused to allow him access to the team. In 1963, Cosell claimed that Stengel (who he rarely referred to by name, calling him "the field leader") took credit for every win, while blaming the players for losses. The Mets had a record of 74–190, which, Cosell said, meant that Stengel was 74–0 and the players were 0–190. Cosell apparently knew what he was talking about, for he told his listeners he was "closer to the Met players than perhaps any newspaperman."

Cosell's original target was Stengel. With his characteristic megalomania, Cosell believed he had convinced Weiss to accept the wisdom of his opinion and dismiss Stengel. When he realized Weiss was not going to do that, he turned on the Met President. When Bing Devine, who Cosell described as a dear friend, joined the Mets, Cosell commenced a crusade to get rid of Weiss so that Devine could run the club.

Arthur Daley, who had pleaded with Stengel in his column not to retire in 1960, leapt to Casey's defense. "That is arrant nonsense," he wrote of Cosell's charges. "Stengel is doing a better job managing the Mets than he did during his glory years with the Yankees ... Casey comes closer than anyone else to being the indispensable man." If the last phrase had a familiar ring, it was because Daley had used almost identical words in the fall of 1960, just before Stengel was fired by the Yankees, referring to Casey as the closest thing to an irreplaceable man. His later column was penned in the summer of 1963, however, long after the Yankees, about to clinch their third straight pennant under Ralph Houk, had replaced Stengel quite nicely.

As the Mets experienced one sorry season after the next, many wondered whether Cosell or Daley was correct. Which Casey Stengel managed the Mets? Was it Stengel the genius clown or was it a tired old codger past his prime who dozed on the bench while the Mets lost game after game?

It was both. Part of Stengel's genius was adapting to the situation. He had been many different people in his life, starting as a talented young outfielder with Kankakee in 1910. Just two years after he began his professional career, Casey's ability brought him to Brooklyn, where he commenced his major league career with the Dodgers. Stengel was a very good ballplayer, a solid hitter and fielder who lasted 14 seasons in the big leagues, compiling a career average of .284. "I was such a dangerous hitter," he said years later, "that I even got intentional walks in batting practice."

In 1921, when Stengel was 31 years old and nearing the end of his playing career, he got what was perhaps the most fortunate break of his life. He was traded to the New York Giants and had the opportunity to play for John McGraw, then at the peak of his managerial career. Stengel played in two World Series under McGraw, winning the hero's laurels in a losing cause in 1923 when he hit two home runs, one of which won a game. He also learned the art of managing from a master. McGraw taught Stengel the value of platooning, which extended his career. He showed him that the manager had to be in complete control of the team, and schooled Stengel in the intricacies of strategy. Lefty Gomez, who tried out with Stengel's Braves after leaving the Yankees, observed Casey constantly invoking the name of McGraw. "McGraw did it this way," Gomez recalled Stengel saying, or "McGraw did it that way."

Stengel was an eager pupil. He soaked up the knowledge McGraw dispensed, and became the crusty old manager's devoted disciple. In the spring of 1923, McGraw asked Stengel to handle the Giants' second team in spring training, the first assignment of what was to be a legendary managerial career.

In 1924, Stengel was traded to the Braves, and the following spring, his playing career came to an end. In May, 1925, he was asked by Boston owner Emil Fuchs if he would like to try his hand at managing. Fuchs had acquired the Worcester team of the Eastern League and offered Stengel a job as player, manager and president. Casey accepted and began to build a resume. Thirty-one-year-old George Weiss was president of the rival New Haven club, and he and Stengel got to know each other well.

Stengel returned to the major leagues as a Dodger coach in 1932, and was named manager in 1934. He led terrible teams for three years in Brooklyn and six years with the Braves. None of his clubs was going to win a pennant, or even come close (his best finishes were fifth in 1935 and 1938) but Stengel livened things up with his antics and comic banter. When he was fired by the Braves in 1943, he returned to the minor leagues. After managing Oakland to 114 wins and the Pacific Coast League title in 1948, Stengel thought he might retire. He had accumulated a tidy fortune investing in oil with some of his old teammates, including Al Lopez, and his wife Edna's family businesses had prospered. Casey had a number of real estate investments, and was vice president of Valley Bank, which was owned by Edna's family. He didn't need the money baseball was bringing him, and he was 58 years old, too old to bounce around the bushes.

Then came a call from his old friend George Weiss. Weiss had become the general manager of the Yankees and had just fired manager Bucky Harris, who had committed three sins. First, he had not won the pennant in 1948, second, he had been too lax in enforcing discipline and third, he was drinking too much. Weiss wanted to hire Stengel, but had to convince co-owners Dan Topping and Del Webb that Casey was not the clown he had been while managing in the National League. The Yankees weren't in the business of hiring comedians. Weiss worked on Topping, and got Brick Laws, owner of the Oakland club, to lobby Webb. Stengel was not silly, Weiss told Topping, he was colorful. He knew as much baseball as anyone in the game. With a good team, Casey would win and bring fans to the park.

Weiss won his battle and Stengel was soon standing before a bank of microphones thanking Bob Topping for giving him a wonderful opportunity. "Bob" would not be sorry he had listened to Weiss, for Stengel, as Yankee manager, was a completely different man than Stengel the manager of hapless second division clubs. He made the right moves. He won pennants and World Series. Stengel entertained the press and brought fans to the park — until he turned 70 years old.

After leaving the Yankees, Stengel turned down an opportunity to manage the Tigers, and was under consideration for the Giants' job before Horace Stoneham hired Alvin Dark. He wisely rejected Charley Finley's offer to be his manager (and own 25 per cent of the franchise) when and if Finley acquired a club. As soon as Weiss was appointed president of the Mets, speculation began that he would bring his old friend Stengel along as manager. The other principal candidate for the Met job was Leo Durocher, a favorite of Joan Payson from her days as a Giant fan.

Durocher would have been a disaster with the Mets. Arthur Daley wrote, "[T]he private belief here is that Durocher is a superb manager of good teams and an indifferent manager of bad ones." Leo had a reputation for being good with veterans but not with young players. A manager of an expansion team had better be able to handle both youngsters and losing.

Gil Hodges was another candidate. Hodges, like Durocher, would have been the wrong man for the job. "Gil was the nicest guy in the world," said Gordon White, "but he would have been boring. Joe Torre would have been boring." Billy Martin might have hung himself by Memorial Day. "Or shot a few players," said White, "or drank himself into oblivion."

Throughout the summer of '61, Stengel would neither confirm nor deny that he was going to manage the Mets. He attended a number of Dodger and Angel games and threw out the first ball at one of the All Star games. Finally, Weiss told Stengel he needed a manager before the expansion draft. Don Grant called and made a formal offer, but Stengel declined. Finally, Mrs. Payson called Stengel in California and asked him to take the job. On September 29, just before the start of the World Series, the Mets announced that Stengel had signed a one year contract to manage the new club. At the press conference that took place when he was signed by the Yankees in 1949, he had referred to the Yankee owner as Bob Topping. At the Met conference, he referred to the club as the Knickerbockers.

In some ways, Casey was taking a risk. He was already a legend, and if he remained in retirement, would never lose another game. On the other hand, Stengel missed the limelight.

The longer he was out of the game, the less interest the public would have in Casey Stengel. Further, no one expected the Mets to win many games in their first few years and, in some ways, becoming their manager was a low-risk proposition. "You didn't have to be a great manager with either club," said Ryne Duren of the Yankees and Mets. "One was going to win and the other was going to lose."

Throughout his long career, Stengel had proven a master at adapting to the situation. He became a much different manager with the Mets than he had been with the Yankees. "I don't think anybody," said Rod Kanehl, "could have pulled off what Stengel did. When he was with the Yankees, he was really a hard-nosed guy to play for. But with us, he knew what he had and he didn't try to get any more from us than was possible. He wasn't tough on us at all. He knew how badly we wanted to win, but we just didn't have it."

"Casey didn't have much of a chance with the Mets," said Bill Wakefield, "because of the lack of talent, but he always made the right moves. We just weren't able to execute."

Sometimes, Stengel lost his patience with his struggling club. One day the Mets had the bases loaded with one out and Kanehl at the plate. When the count reached three and two, Stengel ordered a hit and run, an unusual call, to say the least. Kanehl struck out and the runner coming in from third was tagged out to end the inning. "That would have worked across the river," Stengel said as he paced the length of the dugout. "I thought, 'You don't have Bobby Richardson,'" said Norm Sherry. "What do you want from us, Casey?"

After the Mets finished the 1962 season in Chicago, Rick Herrscher, who'd come to the Mets in August, approached Stengel before leaving for the winter. He was assuming he'd be back with the club in '63, but wanted some assurance from Stengel. In the unlikely event that the Mets weren't planning on having him back, Herrscher said, he planned to go to dental school to become an orthodontist. "Well, Hershner," Stengel replied, "go back to dental school."

Overall, however, the Mets saw, for the most part, a kinder, gentler Stengel. "It was like working with your grandfather," said Jim Bethke, an 18-year-old pitcher for the 1965 Mets. When he was managing the Yankees, Casey was tough, especially when he thought he could get more out of a player than he was getting. "I saw Casey work on Mantle when Mickey wasn't feeling good," said former Yankee Joe DeMaestri. "He'd get Mickey so mad. He'd say, 'I guess you want to get out of the lineup.' Mickey would get all bent out of shape and say, 'No way. I want to play.' Casey would just turn Mickey's thoughts around." "He was tough to live with my first five years," said Gil McDougald, "and the last five years he was a dream. He knew his ballplayers. He knew which ones he could get on and which ones he couldn't."

While Stengel realized he wouldn't win often with the Mets, the games he really wanted to win were those against the Yankees, who'd sent him out to pasture. While the principal competition between the Yankees and Mets was at the box office, the two teams met on the field during the exhibition season. In 1962, when the Mets played the Yankees for the first time in Florida, Stengel threw his two best pitchers, Craig and Jackson, against the Bombers, started all his regulars, and managed like it was the seventh game of the World Series. When Richie Ashburn won the game in the bottom of the ninth with a pinch single, the Mets rushed out to home plate to greet Joe Christopher, who carried the winning run, as if they had just won the pennant. Weiss celebrated with a champagne victory party.

In 1963, the Mayor's Trophy Game, a staple when the Giants and Dodgers were in New York, was revived. The Yankees played the Mets, with the proceeds donated for the benefit of sandlot baseball in New York. "Every time we had the Mayor's Trophy Game," said Jim Hickman, "we were told that we needed to win and it would be a big thing for us if we won." The first attempt to play the game, on June 3, was rained out. The contest was rescheduled for June 19, despite the fact that the Yankees were playing the Washington Senators in the afternoon. In a unique doubleheader, the Yankees had the opportunity to lose to both last place clubs in a single day. They beat the Senators 3–2, and returned to Yankee Stadium to play the Mets at night.

It was just an exhibition to the Yankees, but the game meant everything to Stengel and the Mets. As he had the previous spring, Casey played his regulars, while Houk, who had already played one game that day, put his reserves on the field. It seemed as though about ninety percent of the crowd in Yankee Stadium was comprised of Met fans. They made the trek across the river and showed up with banners, bugles, cherry bombs and other implements of their trade. Such materials were contraband in staid Yankee Stadium, and ushers and guards spent a good part of the evening confiscating items from Met fans. Firecrackers are more easily concealed than bedsheet banners, and a number were detonated during the evening. Fights broke out in the stands. A group of Met fans tried to tear down the Yankees' 1962 championship banner. "It wasn't too bad," said World War Two vet Houk. "The Battle of the Bulge was worse." Met fans had a lot to cheer about, as their heroes launched a five run rally in the third inning and beat the world champions 6–2. Jay Hook won another big game.

When the Yankees encountered hard times in the mid–60s, the fun went out of beating them. It was no longer David versus Goliath. It was David versus David. As Leonard Koppett wrote dramatically, "Suddenly, the Mets found themselves in the position of so many peasant classes in so many societies after a revolution. The nobility, hated and envied for ages, has finally been pulled down from its pinnacle — but the peasants were still peasants, and little satisfaction could be gained from the further tribulations of former lords. By ceasing to be champions, the Yankees took all the fun out of the series." The Yankees, now the underdogs in New York, began to take the games more seriously than the Mets. By 1969, they'd won seven exhibitions in a row.

What made Stengel a great manager was not just his personality. Casey had studied every aspect of baseball so intently and for so long, he often saw things that were not apparent to others. "I learned so much from that man it was unreal," said Al Jackson. "I learned to make the other guy play my game. With runners on first and second, everybody is taught to bunt the ball to third. They never think that if a left hander is quick and can get over there, they shouldn't bunt there. Casey told me to throw a slider and take a little off it to give me time to get over there. 'Nobody will be able to sacrifice the guy to third,' he told me. 'Make them bunt the ball where they've been taught to bunt.' I went seven and half years without anyone sacrificing a runner from second to third. This man was so sharp it was unreal."

"One spring day when it rained," said Johnny James, who played for Stengel with the Yankees, "we were all in the locker room and Casey came out dragging a fungo bat. All he had on was a pair of shorts and shower shoes. He jumped up on the valuables trunk and gave a two and a half hour dissertation on how to hit a low, outside pitch with a fungo bat. If I'd taped that dissertation, I'd have made a lot of money off it."

"He was beautiful," said former Met Chuck Hiller. "I loved him. He was probably the most enjoyable man I've been around in all my years in baseball. He was dumb like a fox. He was the only manager I played for where you wanted to have a meeting because they were fun. He'd say 'Hiller' and then he'd go on for about half an hour and finally come back and give a reason why he called your name."

He might yell "Hitler" instead of Hiller; he might holler "Miller" or maybe "Larsen," for Stengel either couldn't or didn't care to remember his troops by name. Ginsberg recalled an incident from early in the '62 season. "About the ninth inning," Ginsberg said, "he looked around to one of the young guys and said, 'Goddamn it, can't anybody hit? Son, can you hit?' 'Yes, sir, Mr. Stengel, I can hit.' 'Well get a bat and get up there and show these guys what you can do.' He said, 'I would, Mr. Stengel, but I'm a pitcher and you took me out in the fourth inning.'" Stengel didn't miss a beat. "Goddamn it, go up there and take a shower. What are you doing sitting on the bench now? You're out of the game. Go take a shower."

"We were playing in the Polo Grounds one night," recalled Larry Burright. "Casey asked me to go in and play third base. I didn't want to tell him no, but I'd never played third base before. So I said OK." Burright went to third base and played an inning. "When I came back in, he said, 'Go pinch hit for Snider.'" Felix Mantilla recalled a similar incident in which he had been removed for a pinch runner during an extra inning game and then asked by Stengel to go up and pinch hit. Once Stengel decided to take Jackson out of the game between innings, but forgot to tell him. When Jackson went to the mound to warm up, he turned around and saw Ray Daviault walking in from the bullpen.

"I don't know to this day," said pitcher Larry Foss, "whether he was getting senile or just loved to play tricks. I always thought the latter. I think he was still pretty sharp. But one time we were sitting in the bullpen in the Polo Grounds and the phone rang. Red Ruffing (the pitching coach) answered. Casey asked Ruffing to send in Johnny Blanchard to pinch hit." If the Mets were home at the Polo Grounds, Blanchard was somewhere on the road with the Yankees. "Ruffing hung up the phone and said, 'You're not going to believe who the old man just asked for. I hope he doesn't call back.' He didn't."

Casey called Tracy Stallard "Larsen," apparently because Stallard reminded him of Don Larsen, who'd pitched for Stengel with the Yankees. "If I was relieving," said Stallard, "he'd call down to the bullpen and tell them to get Larsen warm. He'd come out to the mound and say, 'Larsen, what the hell are you doing?'"

"He called me Juan Pizarro, or something like that," said former Yankee Jim Pisoni. "If he called me anything that started with a P, I answered." Tim Harkness was Harshness. Charley Neal was O'Neal. "He'd call me 'that guy we got from Chicago,'" said Billy Cowan. "He'd call for guys who used to be on the Yankees. He'd say, 'Get me Bauer.'"

Don Rowe was "the other lefthander," the one who wasn't Ken MacKenzie, "my Yale man." Jay Hook was "Professor." Chris Cannizzaro was "Canzoneri." "Once he called me Cookie," said Sherman (Roadblock) Jones. "The only Cookie around was [coach] Cookie Lavagetto." The tall, lanky Stallard bore a general resemblance to Don Larsen but, Jones, an African American, was difficult to mistake for the middle-aged, Italian, Lavagetto.

"One time after a game he called me into his office," recalled Herrscher, "and said, 'Hershner, I like the way you run in from third base.' I said, 'Thank you.' He kind of hesitated and then said, 'That's all,' and waved me out of his office. I thought it was the strangest thing. I know he wanted to talk to me about something, but I'm not sure what it was. I guess he forgot it."

When he managed the Yankees, Stengel fell asleep on the bench from time to time, but he knew the games were to be taken seriously. With the Mets it was another matter. "We were in San Francisco one time," recalled Norm Sherry, "and a friend of his—I think it was Walter Mails [an old Dodger teammate]—came in. He started talking to Casey, even though the game was about to begin. Solly Hemus is at home plate and he's looking for the lineup cards. He has to send somebody to get them from Stengel. They get them and the game starts. It's about the seventh inning and Casey comes in from the clubhouse. He sits down in the dugout and looks at the scoreboard. We were losing about 11–2. He said, 'Hemus, you're doing a lousy job.' Then he said, 'Well, I'd better get out there. These people want to see me.' He walked out and doffed his hat. Everybody was screaming at him. He was a character."

There were many facets to Stengel's personality, including the kindly old codger who loved children, although he had none of his own. In 1974, when the Dodgers played the Athletics in the World Series, Larry Miller, who'd pitched for the Dodgers and Mets, brought his teenaged son to the Dodger offices to pick up tickets. When he walked in, he saw Stengel, then 84 years old. "I thought," said Miller, "'Oh, my gosh, here's a chance for my son to meet this great baseball icon,'" It had been nine years since Miller played for Stengel, and he assumed he wouldn't remember him, since he'd had a hard time identifying him in 1965. Still, he decided to introduce his son.

"Casey was the kind of guy who would meet total strangers," Miller said. "He was just nice to everybody." Miller went up and told Casey that while he probably didn't remember him, he was Larry Miller, who had pitched for him in 1965. "Why, hell yes, I remember you," Casey replied. "He started pumping my hand," Miller said, "and asking how the hell I was. Then he turned to my son and said, 'Is this your boy?' He reached over and grabbed his shoulders and said, 'By god, feel the shoulders and the arms on this kid. He's a ballplayer, isn't he? Man, this kid is strong. Feel these arms.' My son levitated for the entire weekend. He didn't care about the World Series. He couldn't wait to get home and tell his friends how he'd met Casey Stengel and Casey said he was going to be a ballplayer someday. I'm sure when Casey walked away, he thought, 'Who in the hell was that?' but he wouldn't show me up. That's the kind of guy he was. He wouldn't show me up."

The most enduring memory of Casey, of course, is the Stengelese that made him famous. "He was the only person I ever knew," said Miller, "who could speak for an hour without a comma, without a period, just one continuous flow of words, and never make a point." "I remember a discussion we had before a game in Milwaukee," said pitcher Darrell Sutherland. "I can't even remember what it was about, but it seemed like it was about some other team. I wasn't quite sure how it related to what we were going to do."

"At first I couldn't understand him," said Tug McGraw during his rookie year, "but after a few days I realized he spoke in parables, and from then on I could follow him fine. There was always a point in everything he tried to tell you."

"Casey was very quick-witted," said Hook. "Stengelese was something he could turn on and off when he wanted to. He'd be talking about one subject and thinking about the next one and then he'd jump to that subject. Then he'd remember he didn't finish talking about the last subject, so he'd jump back to that. He'd have two or three parallel thoughts going."

"I never knew what he was talking about," said catcher John Stephenson, "but he was great. I really liked him. He'd carry on three or four different conversations with you. He'd be talking about one thing and all of a sudden he'd jump to something else, then something else — and something else. But I really enjoyed being around him."

"Somebody," said Don Rowe, "I think it was Lou Boudreau, interviewed Casey in the clubhouse one day. He asked him a question and Casey just took off. Boudreau couldn't get him stopped. Finally they stopped him, but Boudreau forgot to turn the mike off. He said, 'What the hell did he say?'"

"In 1958," said Johnny James, "we were in Detroit to play the Tigers, and Casey held a clubhouse meeting to go over the pitchers. All he said was, 'The fellow from Detroit will throw us the soap ball and when he does, we slip him the Vaseline pot and then it's run, sheep, run.' I laughed, but everybody else knew what he meant. I asked Whitey or somebody about it, and he said, 'That fellow from Detroit was Frank Lary, who would throw the soap ball, which meant he would load it up, and we would slip him the Vaseline pot, which meant our pitcher would load it up and then it's run, sheep, run, which was his term for hitters just meeting the ball and not overswinging."

"I was in the dugout one day in the Polo Grounds," said Don Rowe, "and some guy kept sticking his head around the side of the dugout and yelling at us. Stengel looked at me and said, '10-80-10' I thought, 'What the hell does that mean?' After the game, we were walking to the center field clubhouse and I said, 'Mr. Stengel, there's one thing I want to ask you. What's 10-80-10?' He said, '10-80-10, son, is my philosophy of life. If you follow it, you'll be pretty successful. Today in this ballpark there were 55,000 people [that was wishful thinking, unless the Giants or Dodgers were in town]. Ten percent of the people in this stadium knew what was going on. Eighty percent think they knew what was going on but they don't. See those drunks out in centerfield who are beating on each other. That ten percent don't know and don't care. If you use that philosophy, the fans will never bother you because you'll be able to put them in whatever category you want.'"

Casey could talk for hours, but he was also a master of one liners, which were often delivered on the mound. Rather than send his pitching coach, Stengel generally visited his struggling pitchers personally. With the Mets, it was a full-time occupation. Larry Miller recalled one visit. "I knew he was going to tell me I was tired, so I said, 'Casey, I'm not tired.' He said, 'Well, Miller, you may not be tired, but the damned outfielders are exhausted,' and held out his hand for the ball." Stengel made the same remark to Gary Kroll. "I'm sure that was the line he had," said Miller, "for pitchers who said, 'Don't take me out, I'm not tired.'"

Stengel once visited Tug McGraw on the mound during McGraw's rookie season. "I can get this guy out," McGraw protested. "I did the last time I faced him." "Yeah, I know," Stengel replied, "but it was in this same inning."

When the Mets played at the Polo Grounds, Tracy Stallard rode to the park on an elevated train that started in Manhattan, went past the Polo Grounds, turned around in the Bronx and went back to Manhattan. Stallard got in trouble early in the game and Stengel came to take him out in the first inning. "He told me that if I hurried and took my shower I could go back home on the same train I came in on," Stallard said. On another occasion during that final season at the Polo Grounds, Stallard gave up two long home runs to the Phillies' Johnny Callison. "They went into the upper deck and really rattled around," Stallard recalled. Stengel came to the mound and asked how they were trying to pitch to Callison. "We're trying to pitch him inside," Stallard said. "Well, keep doing it," Casey replied. "That's one section they won't have to tear down."

Dave Hillman started a game for the Mets in 1962 against the Colt .45s. He gave up a few hits, which brought Stengel to the mound. "He said," Hillman recalled, "'You' re all right, young man. You're all right, young fella. You're all right.' I looked around and Casey was waving Vinegar Bend Mizell in from the bullpen."

Stengel was elected to the Hall of Fame in 1966, just months after he retired. There was normally a five year waiting period after retirement, but for Casey the rule was waived, on the petition of the Baseball Writers Association of America. The waiting period had been dispensed with just twice previously, for Lou Gehrig and Connie Mack. Do it again, urged Stengelphile Arthur Daley in a column titled "Phooey on the Rules." It was ridiculous, the writers said, to make a 75-year-old man wait five years; they wanted Casey to be honored while he was still alive. They also wanted to hear him make an acceptance speech.

The rules were amended to waive the waiting period for anyone over 65. A secret vote was taken early in 1966, and the result was announced on March 8 at the Met training camp in St. Petersburg. Commissioner Frick made the announcement and Stengel, who was present, was completely surprised. He had been asked to come to the game on the pretense of presenting awards to George Weiss and Wes Westrum. Casey hobbled onto the field, leaning heavily on his cane, and said, "They just put me in — if you don't know — the Hall of Fame."

The many stories about Casey Stengel follow several paths. The young Yankee players recall him as a cantankerous old man who demanded perfection. The Mets remember a funny old man who deflected attention from their horrendous performances and entertained them with his stories and catnaps on the bench. Writers remember him as a terrific source of material on slow news days. If Edna were alive, she would speak of a wise, loving, caring husband. There were many Casey Stengels, and he had the knack of calling up the right one on the proper occasion. He was a pillar of the Yankee dynasty and he was the comic symbol of the early Mets. Stengel was, above all, a larger than life figure who dominated New York baseball for the first half of the 1960s.

• 8 •

Vicarious Thrills
The 1964 Season

After two years spent deep in the National League basement, the Mets looked forward to 1964. The team didn't appear to be much stronger, but if they finished last again, they would do so in a gorgeous new ballpark. Shea Stadium, named after attorney William Shea, the man who was instrumental in bringing National League baseball back to New York, was a five tiered, state of the art facility, constructed by the City of New York at the then-astronomical cost of more than $20 million. "This stadium," Stengel told a group of Russian visitors later in the summer, "was built for us by the government, just like in your country."

The construction of Shea was a tortuous process beset by labor disputes, endless wrangling over the Mets' lease, weather delays and sizable cost overruns. When the Mets commenced operations in 1962, they expected to spend one season in the Polo Grounds, and move to Shea for the 1963 season. When continuing delays made the park unavailable for opening day, the Mets expected occupancy in July or August. By July, it became clear that the opener would be delayed until 1964.

The builders barely made the 1964 completion date. Just five days before the new stadium was to open, the landscaping remained unfinished, the scoreboard had yet to be installed, and the dining room wasn't furnished. When the first customers arrived at the stadium for the Mets' opener on April 17, workers were literally putting the finishing touches on the structure.

The atmosphere at Shea was decidedly different from the plebeian trappings of the Polo Grounds. Fans were escorted to their seats by 26 attractive young usherettes clad in stylish outfits designed by Saxony Clothes. Most of the women were college students who earned $13.25 per game ($15.50 for doubleheaders) for juggling the dual tasks of acting as hostesses and fending off the advances of the male portion of the New Breed.

The contours of the new stadium were more symmetrical than those of the Polo Grounds, which was discomforting to those who admired the unique shape of the old park. Met pitchers, on the other hand, were delighted. "I won't have to worry about a bloop homer beating me on every pitch," said Tracy Stallard. After yielding a few home runs in the new stadium, Stallard said, "The only way they can do me any good is by ripping the fences down altogether."

The Shea opener pitted the Mets against the Pirates, who sent Bob Friend to the mound. This was a bad omen for Met fans, for at that point, Friend boasted an 8–0 lifetime mark against New York, and had shut them out for 47 consecutive innings. Jack Fisher, making his Met debut, started for New York.

Opening day saw a number of firsts. At 2:12 P.M., Fisher threw the first pitch to Pirate leadoff hitter Dick Schofield, a strike on the outside corner. Schofield made the first out, popping up to second baseman Larry Burright. In the second inning, Willie Stargell got the first hit, which was also the first Shea Stadium home run. The first Met base runner was Jim Hickman, who walked in the second. The first Met hit did not come until the third, when Tim Harkness, who at that point had gone nearly a year without answering my fan letter, singled to right. Jesse Gonder drove in the initial Met run in the fourth, the first time the Mets had scored on Friend in 51 innings. Gonder's single scored Hunt, who barely beat Roberto Clemente's throw, precipitating the first Shea Stadium argument, and ultimately the first ejection, that of Pirate catcher Jim Pagliaroni.

The Mets' three run rally in the fourth gave them a 3–1 lead, but the Pirates scored once in the fifth and knocked out Fisher in the seventh. Reliever Ed Bauta yielded the tying run, and the Pirates won the game in the ninth on a single by that familiar New York villain, Bill Mazeroski.

The next memorable event at Shea took place on May 31, in the course of a doubleheader against the Giants. By the time the final out of the second game was recorded at 11:28 P.M., the two teams had played 32 innings in a single day. After Juan Marichal pitched a complete game victory in the opener, the second contest started at 4:05. Righthander Bob Bolin was on the mound for the Giants, opposing Bill Wakefield, a rookie reliever making a rare start. The Giants got to Wakefield early, scoring two runs in the first. Stengel pinch hit for his pitcher in the second, and sent Craig Anderson to the mound for the third. Anderson, recently recalled from Buffalo, was riding a three year, 19 game losing streak. He didn't lose his twentieth, but got only one out while yielding four runs on a flurry of singles.

In the seventh, the Mets trailed 6–3. Roy McMillan and Frank Thomas singled, bringing outfielder Joe Christopher to the plate. Christopher worked the count to 3–0, and got the hit sign from third base coach Don Heffner. Bolin grooved a fast ball and Christopher hit it deep to left center field. Willie Mays streaked back, timed his leap perfectly, and got his glove on the ball above the fence. When his hand hit the wall on the way down, however, the ball was dislodged and Christopher had a three run homer, tying the score.

Then the relief pitchers took control. Veteran Tom Sturdivant replaced Anderson in the third, and was followed by Frank Lary, who had just been acquired by the Mets and arrived in the middle of the first game. Lary was a former 20 game winner for the Tigers, who'd had arm trouble in 1962 and 1963. Since then, he'd pitched sparingly. Tiger skipper Charley Dressen removed him from the rotation in favor of a hard-throwing youngster named Dennis McLain, and decided it was time for Lary, a Tiger for ten years, to leave town.

Lary was informed of his sale to the Mets before the Tigers' Memorial Day game with the White Sox. During the second inning, with the White Sox at bat, he emerged from the Tiger dugout in street clothes, approached home plate and shook hands with Tiger catcher Mike Roarke and umpire Joe Paparella. Lary waved to the crowd, then continued across the field to the White Sox dugout, where he bid farewell to Manager Al Lopez and his club. The unannounced promenade was recorded by *Detroit News* photographer Scotty Kilpatrick, who had planned the episode with Lary. Dressen called the whole thing "bush." Lary in turn blasted Dressen, saying he had given up on him too soon, and that he had too many rules.

In his Met debut, Lary looked like the old Lary, retiring all six men he faced, striking out three of them. In the ninth inning, with the score still tied, Larry Bearnarth, who had pitched two innings in the first game, replaced Lary. Bearnarth pitched seven scoreless innings, surviving a close call in the 14th. Jesus Alou led off with a single, and Mays followed with a walk, bringing up slugger Orlando Cepeda. Cepeda ripped a solid liner up the middle as Alou raced for third and Mays for second. Shortstop Roy McMillan broke to his left, lunged, caught the ball, stepped on second base and fired to Ed Kranepool at first to complete the second triple play in Mets' history. "Roy could have had an unassisted triple play," said Rod Kanehl, "but he was just too tired to run over and tag the guy, so he threw to first."

Former Met Ken MacKenzie, Bob Shaw and Ron Herbel had succeeded Bolin for the Giants. In the 12th inning, 25-year-old Gaylord Perry took the mound for San Francisco. Perry was in his third season with the Giants but, shuttling between the starting rotation, the bullpen and Tacoma, had a career total of only six wins against eight defeats. Older brother Jim was the star of the family, having won over 60 games in the American League, including a league-leading 18 in 1960. One of Gaylord's six victories came on May 16 in San Francisco, a 15 inning win over the Mets, when he beat Galen Cisco.

In 1963, Perry had been 1–6 and was sent back to the minor leagues. Having received a $90,000 bonus from the Giants in 1958, he had been given numerous chances to prove himself. Now, he was running out of time.

Cisco replaced Bearnarth in the 15th and matched Perry zero for zero. "I wasn't expecting to pitch that night," Cisco said, for he had pitched seven innings three days earlier. "In the ninth inning I was sitting on the bench with my soft shoes on and I looked around and noticed we were running out of pitchers. Casey came up to me and said, 'Can you pitch?' I told him I wouldn't know until I warmed up."

Stengel told Cisco to put his spikes on and go down to the bullpen and see if he could get loose. "I guess it was about the 10th before I got down there and threw," said Cisco. "I had [pitching coach] Mel Harder call back and say I felt fine." Cisco came in and pitched a couple of scoreless innings. "Casey asked me how I was holding up and I told him I felt better than I expected. He asked me again after the 18th, after I'd pitched four innings. After the 21st, he said, 'Well, we're going to get you a run right here. You won't have to go back out.' But we didn't get a run, so Casey said, 'Look, I don't want to hurt you. You just go out and do the best you can and that'll be good enough for me.'" Cisco went to the mound in the 22nd and pitched his eighth scoreless relief inning, but the Mets couldn't score off Perry. "You're the only one I've got left," Stengel told Cisco when he arrived at the bench. "Just do the best you can."

Meanwhile, Wakefield and Bearnarth had showered and gone up into the stands. They moved from section to section, trying out as many vantage points as they could. Over 23 innings, they were able to sample quite a few. "Some fans recognized us," Wakefield said, "and some didn't. We sat down in one section where no one knew us, and the fans said, 'Where have you guys been? You missed a great game.'" As the evening rolled on, some of the fans grew restless. There were a couple of fights in the stands, and for a while a large group behind home plate threw wadded-up paper at each other. "People could leave the game," Ron Hunt said, "go to the World's Fair, come back and the game was still going on."

"It was a long day at the ballpark," recalled Hawk Taylor, who struck out as a pinch hitter in the 7th and then stayed around to warm up pitchers in the bullpen. After the 15th, his job was done, for the Mets had no more pitchers to warm up. Kanehl, who had been removed for a pinch hitter in the 2nd, spent the latter part of the game running hot soup from the clubhouse to the dugout. Both managers maneuvered their rosters until they had no one left. Willie Mays played a few innings at shortstop.

Finally, in the top of the 23rd, Cisco cracked. Jim Davenport led off with a triple into the right field corner. With Perry on deck, Cisco walked Cap Peterson intentionally. Alvin Dark summoned veteran catcher Del Crandall from the bullpen to bat for Perry, who had pitched ten scoreless innings. Crandall, the 39th player to appear in the game, bounced a ground rule double over the right field fence to score Davenport and finally break the deadlock. Later in the inning, the Giants added another run to make the score 8–6.

In the bottom of the 23rd, Bob Hendley came in to pitch. With two outs, John Stephenson, the 41st performer of the evening, batted for Cisco and struck out. Finally, at 11:28, with

10–15,000 of the original 57,037 fans still in the stands, the day was over. Perry was the winning pitcher and Cisco the loser, just as they had been on May 16. Perry's performance won him a place in the starting rotation, and he went on to win 12 games. Two years later, he won 21.*

"Well," read the headline in *The New York Post*, "You Don't Beat Our Guys in a Hurry." The 32 innings broke the one day record of 29 set by the Red Sox and Athletics in 1905. The combined total time of the two games (10:17) beat the record for a doubleheader by nearly two hours. The one game total of 23 innings was the fourth longest in history. No one had topped the 7 hours and 23 minutes it had taken to complete the second game. It was not, however, the longest game Casey Stengel had ever managed. In 1939, his Braves tied the Dodgers 2–2 in a game which also lasted 23 innings.

Seven Met starters played the entire game, including Ed Kranepool. In the spring of 1964, just one year after he had compared him with Mel Ott, Stengel became irritated when Kranepool reported overweight and pulled a muscle. "Who ever heard of a 19-year-old kid pulling a muscle," Stengel said disgustedly. In mid–May, with Kranepool batting just .139, Stengel sent him to Buffalo again. When Kranepool had been sent to Buffalo in 1963, he sulked. This time the demotion hit the youngster hard. He went down to Buffalo and, rather than pouting, earned a quick recall by hitting .352 in 15 games.

On Saturday, Kranepool had played a doubleheader for Buffalo that ended at 1 A.M. He caught a 6 A.M. flight and arrived in time to play all 32 innings, as did McMillan, Christopher, Jim Hickman and Charlie Smith. "We had an exhibition game in Williamsport the next day," said Wakefield, "and some of the guys just slept in the clubhouse. A bunch of them lived at the Manhattan Hotel and rather than take the subway home, they just pulled out some blankets and stayed in the clubhouse."

Each writer who covered the game received a "Certificate of Recognition and Admiration," which cited them for "Perseverance, tenacity, diligence, indefatigability, endurance, pertinacity, tireless doggedness and extraordinary devotion to duty in staying to a finale [sic] conclusion to report to the public on Baseball's Longest Day."

In Ferndale, California, a retired school teacher named Joe Oeschger listened to the entire game on the radio. On May 1, 1920, Oeschger pitched 26 innings for the Boston Braves in a 1–1 tie against the Brooklyn Dodgers. Opposing pitcher Leon Cadore also pitched a complete game. "I was more tired just from hearing those 23 innings," Oeschger said after listening to the Met-Giant contest, "than I was after I had pitched 26 — I was only 28 when I pitched that long one. I was right in my prime. I could have pitched in my regular turn, but the next day I pulled a leg muscle running around the park."

Oeschger noted a number of differences between the two games. The 1920 contest had taken only three hours and fifty minutes, compared to nearly seven and a half hours for the 1964 game. The Braves and Dodgers used a combined total of just 22 players, and Oeschger doubted that more than 25 baseballs were used in the entire game, compared to 264 used by the Mets and Giants.

The next momentous event at Shea Stadium took place on June 21, when Philadelphia's Jim Bunning took the mound to face the Mets in the first game of a Father's Day doubleheader. No one was better suited to pitch on Father's Day than Bunning, who at the time had seven children (he later added two more). The side-wheeling righthander was in his first year with the Phillies, after having pitched in the American League for the Tigers the previous nine years.

Bunning won 20 games for the Tigers in 1957, and 19 in 1962, but when he slumped to 12–13 in '63, Detroit swapped him to the Phillies along with catcher Gus Triandos, who was

---

Cisco lost a 14 inning game to the Giants later in the season, making him the losing pitcher in 15, 23 and 14 inning games to the same team in the same season.

behind the plate on June 21. The Tigers believed that, at 32, Bunning's best seasons were behind him. Bunning thought otherwise and, as of mid–June, appeared to be correct. In his first 100 innings of National League pitching, he posted a 6–2 record and an excellent 2.25 ERA.

Bunning set the Mets down in order in the first. He also retired them in order in the second, third and fourth. By the time the Phillies broke the game open with four runs in the sixth inning, building a 6–0 lead, Bunning had completed five perfect innings. "Nobody realized it was a perfect game until the fourth or fifth inning," recalled Phillie pitcher Dennis Bennett. "You know that it's taboo to talk about it, but Jim was talking about it." Unlike most pitchers pursuing perfection, Bunning was very vocal. "Nine more to go," he said when returning to the dugout after the sixth inning. Following the seventh, it was six more, then three. "Do something out there," he exhorted his teammates. "Dive for the balls." Triandos said he had never seen the pitcher so silly. "He was jabbering like a magpie," Triandos said.

"The further the game went," said Galen Cisco, "the more it looked like he had a shot at it because he just wasn't missing. Every time he tried to keep the ball away, it was away. When he got two strikes, he was throwing the ball off the plate, and we were swinging. We just weren't very patient."

According to Hawk Taylor, there was a good reason for the Mets' impatience. "He had pinpoint control," Taylor said, "but he also won over the umpire, who started widening the strike zone for him. On my last at bat, I got called out on a pitch that was probably six to eight inches outside. Not that he needed a lot of help, but I remember the strike zone being substantially enlarged." "When you're making good pitches and the umpire is in your corner," said Joe Christopher, "it's two against one."

After eight innings, the Mets still hadn't had a man reach base and Bunning was just three outs away from a perfect game. There had been only one difficult play. In the fifth, Jesse Gonder hit a line drive that appeared to be headed for right field. Second baseman Tony Taylor dove for the ball, knocked it down, and scrambled up to throw the plodding Gonder out at first.

In the ninth, Charlie Smith led off by fouling out to third baseman Cookie Rojas. With two outs left, Stengel sent George Altman up to pinch hit for Amado Samuel. Altman had arrived in New York amidst great expectations. He'd been an All Star for the Cubs in 1961 and 1962, batting over .300, with more than 20 home runs each season. At 29 years of age, he appeared to be in his prime. In 1963, Altman was traded to the Cardinals and got off to a strong start, hitting for a high average but without a lot of home runs. "We had that short right field porch in St. Louis," Altman recalled, "and someone told me they wanted me to pull the ball more. It was sort of an edict. I said, 'OK, I'll give it a shot.' So I'm pulling the ball, but I was really a line drive hitter. Now I'm trying to get the ball up in the air because the pavilion was really high. I started to uppercut and began to have problems." Altman's average dropped from .318 in 1962 to .274 in '63 and, despite his efforts to pull the ball, his home run production dropped from 22 to 9.

During the winters, Altman worked as a stockbroker. "I think that was part of my problem in St. Louis," he said. "I did a lot of studying, a lot of research, a lot of close work. When I went to spring training, I was having blurred vision. I even tried glasses for a while. I think there was a lot of tension behind the eyes, a lot of strain."

The decline in Altman's production brought him to New York in the deal that sent Roger Craig to the Cardinals. While a .274 average didn't cut it with the Cardinals, it was higher than that of any Met regular. If Altman could duplicate his '61 and '62 seasons, the Mets would have reaped a bonanza. Thus far, however, he had been a major disappointment.

"I wasn't too happy about going to the Mets," Altman said, "because everybody wants to win, and the Mets weren't likely to win the pennant." Altman injured his shoulder at the end of spring training, but Stengel asked him to play opening day, even though he wasn't ready. "He said, 'You're probably better than anybody else I've got at the moment,'" Altman recalled. "In those days, the philosophy was, when you're injured, throw some dirt on it and get out there anyway." Playing hurt much of the season, Altman wound up batting .230 with just nine home runs. "That was a terrible year and I just blocked it out of my mind," he said.

Despite his difficulties, and the way Bunning had been throwing that afternoon, Altman stepped up to the plate with confidence. "Bunning was sort of a sidearm pitcher," he said, "and lefthanders got a good look at him. He was the kind of pitcher you love to hit off, even though he had his best stuff that day. To me, it was a lot better than facing Koufax or someone like that. I felt I could handle him. Of course, on that particular day, he wound up handling all of us."

Altman scared Bunning with a long foul ball to right field, then struck out. That left only one man between Bunning and immortality. Two Met pitchers who had already come out of the game, Tracy Stallard and Bill Wakefield, sat in the Met dugout, watching to see if Bunning could consummate his masterpiece. As fellow pitchers, were they pulling for Bunning? "Hell, no!" said Stallard. Wakefield felt differently. He was secretly rooting for Bunning. "You always want to be professional," he said, "and you always want to root for your team, but it wasn't a situation that was going to cost us the pennant, or even a position in the standings." The Mets were 20–45, ten and a half games behind the ninth place Milwaukee Braves.

Stengel turned to rookie catcher John Stephenson and told him to hit for pitcher Tom Sturdivant. "Casey said, 'Johnny, go up there and get a base hit for us,'" Wakefield recalled. "John kind of looked at me and rolled his eyes, as if to say, 'I'm not sure what I'm supposed to do in this situation.'" At that point, Stephenson was 2 for 27 in his brief major league career and had already been a part of history by striking out to end the 23 inning game against the Giants.

"It was my first year in the big leagues," said Stephenson. "I was right out of college and had played about two months in the rookie league. I don't know why Casey saved me for the last one, but I went up there in front of 32,000 people and I was pretty nervous." "We all knew Stephenson couldn't hit a curve ball," said Dennis Bennett. "Bunning was a fastball, slider pitcher, but we knew if he could get three curve balls over the plate, he'd have his perfect game."

"He threw me all sliders," said Stephenson, "which were hard to pick up, the way he fell off the mound." They were curve balls, said Bennett, and most newspaper accounts agreed. Perhaps the fact that Stephenson couldn't recognize a curve was one of the reasons he couldn't hit them. With a 2–2 count, Stephenson took a curve ball for strike three and Bunning had the ninth perfect game in major league history, the first in the regular season since 1922 and the first in the National League since John Montgomery Ward pitched one for the Providence Grays against the Buffalo Bisons in 1880. Bunning also became the first man to throw a no hitter in both major leagues. He had thrown just 90 pitches, of which 69 were strikes.

Bunning's story wasn't over. On June 13, in his previous start against the Mets, he had retired the final four batters he faced. On August 9, the first time he faced them after the perfect game, he retired the first 14 New York batters, making a total of 45 New York Mets who went to the plate against Bunning without reaching base. Finally, Joe Christopher broke the string by bunting safely in the fifth inning.

Through mid–1966, Bunning made seven starts in Shea Stadium. He had seven wins, seven complete games and four shutouts. By early 1967, both at home and on the road, he had allowed just three runs to the Mets in 72 innings. He'd shut the Mets out six times at Shea.

Less than three weeks after Bunning's perfect game, on July 7th, Shea Stadium played host to the All Star Game, for which Hunt was the first Met ever voted to a starting position. "It was such a great thrill," he said, "to go into the locker room and meet the other players. In those days, you didn't fraternize with the opposition, so the All Star Game was the one chance you had to meet them."

Hunt got a single in his first at bat in the second inning, which brought a roar from the Shea crowd. The new $1.5 million scoreboard announced that the all-time Met batting average in All Star competition was now .667. Richie Ashburn had singled as pinch hitter in 1962 and Duke Snider had struck out in '63.

The first All-Star game at Shea was a thriller, won by the National League on a dramatic three run, two out home run in the bottom of the ninth by the Phillies' Johnny Callison. The only Met besides Hunt who made an appearance on the club's home field was Stengel, who served as first base coach for the National League squad. Ed Sudol was the home plate umpire. Sudol had also been behind home plate when the Mets and Giants played for 23 innings. He worked the plate when Bunning threw his perfect game. Apparently, when Ed Sudol worked behind the plate at Shea, great things happened.*

As the season wound down, the Mets showed little improvement over their first two campaigns. On September 1, their record stood at 44–86, and the team needed eight more wins in the final month to exceed 1963's total. Hunt and Christopher were hitting well, and both would finish with averages above .300. Hunt was as scrappy as ever, and had difficulty staying in the lineup, for he was forever banged and bruised from his combative style of play. He had an arthritic toe, a bad back and an assortment of allergies.

Christopher had seemingly come from nowhere. He grew up in St. Croix, working on mango plantations and in the sugar cane fields, and had been signed by the Pirates as a shortstop in 1954 for a bonus of $250. Christopher always hit well in the minor leagues, batting.327 at Salt Lake City in 1958 and .301 at Columbus the following year. In an era when stolen bases were rare, Christopher was a speed burner. He led the Mexican League in steals in 1957, and in 1959 at Columbus, stole 14 bases in his first 32 games. He was leading the league when he was recalled by the Pirates. From 1959 to 1961, Christopher filled a reserve role for the Pirates, and played sparingly.

Christopher was an exciting player, stealing bases with head first slides, diving around the outfield, and always hustling. *The Sporting News* said he was the most exciting Pirate since Clemente. Christopher went up and down between Pittsburgh and Columbus, playing just 141 games in three years, and was made available in the expansion draft. Having signed Christopher for just $250, the Pirates made a handsome profit when they sold him to the Mets for $75,000.

Christopher is a very complex, interesting man. He studied accounting in the Virgin Islands. He is a voracious reader, currently produces pre–Columbian art, and has a deep interest in the significance of numbers, believing that a man's destiny is controlled by the numbers contained in his date of birth. In his youth, he considered becoming a priest. "The laws of God are effortless," he told me. "The laws of man are a struggle. So therefore the glory of God is to hide things. The essence of man is to find them.... Man cannot find what is invisible to him because the invisibility of that visibility has already been ostracized. When a man wants something, what do you do? You question. But you can't question a question."

Unlike Hunt, Christopher was rarely injured, and, in contrast to Hunt's often irascible nature, was known for perhaps the broadest smile in baseball. "He loved to entertain the fans in right field," remembered Bill Wakefield. Christopher had the ability to manipulate his face in a way that would make his hat wiggle without him touching it. "He'd flash those pearly white teeth," said Wakefield, "and wiggle his hat and the fans loved him." "I'm a people person," Christopher said. "I really enjoyed the fans at Shea Stadium. The people in the right field section used to cheer me all the time. They gave me presents."

Sudol was also the home plate umpire at Shea when the Mets won their first National League pennant by beating Atlanta in the third game of the 1969 Championship Series.

Christopher's ability to wiggle his hat was, unfortunately, much more impressive than his ability to catch a batted ball. "Joe had a little trouble in the field," Wakefield admitted. "He got to a lot of them," said Bobby Klaus, "and a lot of them he didn't get to." Met pitchers cringed whenever a fly ball headed in Christopher's direction. "He was a good hitter," said Gary Kroll, "but he couldn't field worth a damn. One time I was pitching against the Braves in Milwaukee and there were two runners on base. Someone hit a ball to him in deep left field. He went back, jumped as high as he could, and the ball hit him in the belt buckle." "I think Joe was the kind of player who didn't care about playing the outfield," said Cowan, "so he didn't work at it that hard. He just wanted to hit."

In July, 1964, Tracy Stallard was on the mound when Cowan, then with the Cubs hit a fly ball in Christopher's direction. The action was described in the *Times*. "Joe Christopher ran a weaving course," the *Times* reported, "toward where he thought he and the ball would meet. They did, but only temporarily." The ball popped out of Christopher's glove, costing the Mets the game, and Stallard was furious. "Christopher is the only .300 hitter I have ever seen," he said, "who hurts a ball club. He improved his hitting this spring. He should have worked on his fielding, too." Stengel agreed the ball should have been caught. Christopher explained that he had had trouble with the wind. "It's not my fault if the ball drops safely," he said.

Christopher didn't share his teammates' opinion of his fielding. "Wherever I've gone," he said recently. "I've always been a tremendous fielder." Christopher was primarily, however, interested in hitting. "However I did," he said, "I used to take a bat back to my hotel room." "Joe wanted to be a .400 hitter," said Al Jackson. "He was a great student of hitting and if you see Joe today, I'd bet my life he's talking about hitting right now. [Jackson was absolutely correct. See Chapter 18.] He was my roommate for a couple of years and we used to sit up at night. He'd be hitting home runs off me and I'd be getting him out. We used to talk all night.'

For the first several years of his career, Christopher was a great student of hitting, but not a great hitter. After starting the 1962 season at Syracuse, Joe was recalled by the Mets in May and appeared in 119 games, batting .244. The following year, he also split the season between the Mets and their Triple A affiliate, and hit .221 in 64 games with New York. While at Buffalo, however, Christopher hit for power, something he had never done in the majors. He hit 19 home runs in just 85 International League games. "I haven't regretted coming down here at all," Christopher said early in the season. "I've had a chance to work on things down here."

During the winter following the 1963 season, Christopher read a pamphlet written by Hall of Famer Paul Waner, which stressed the importance of meeting the ball as early as possible. Christopher, who had always waited on the ball, decided to change his style of hitting. The results were immediate. With Altman and Thomas both injured, he became the Mets' regular right fielder, and hit for both average and power. In June, he was named the Most Popular Met by the Catholic Youth Organization. In July, he made amends to Stallard with a grand slam against the Braves that helped the righthander to a win. In August, Christopher batted .369 and was named the Mets' player of the month. For the season, he set Met records by scoring 78 runs and making 163 base hits. Admittedly, Met team records at this point were not Ruthian, but a .300 average, 16 home runs and 76 runs batted in made Christopher a valuable player despite his shaky fielding. He became the first man from the Virgin Islands to hit .300 and the 16 home runs were twice as many as he had hit in total during his previous five seasons.

His big season left Christopher anticipating a sizable raise. The Mets offered a 25 percent increase, which sounded good until one realized that it represented a boost from $10,000 to only $12,500, not all that impressive for a team's best hitter, even if that team was the Mets. Christopher responded to the offer with a lengthy missive explaining why he thought he deserved more. Letter-writing at contract time was a Christopher tradition, and this time he had some meaty subject matter. "Sometimes he writes as much as nine pages," said Johnny Murphy.

When training camp opened in 1965, Joe was still an author rather than a ballplayer, the first Met holdout since Marv Throneberry in 1963. He wanted to double his salary, and eventually got Murphy up to $17,500, the Mets' final offer, Murphy said. Christopher wasn't going for it. During Throneberry's holdout, Gene Woodling lost his job by insisting that President George Weiss talk to Throneberry. This time, Weiss got involved of his own volition. The Mets could do better than $17,500, he said. He was willing to go as high as $17,750. Christopher agreed and the impasse was ended. With his signature, another barrier fell. The total Met payroll now exceeded $500,000. Weiss's largesse must be noted with an asterisk, however, since the rolls included player-coaches Yogi Berra and Warren Spahn, who represented $100,000 of the total.

Christopher didn't forget Weiss's intervention, nor did his letter-writing cease. After the Mets traded him to Boston following the 1965 season, he sent Weiss a final missive, thanking him for the happiness Joe and his family experienced in New York:

Joe Christopher had the best season of his career in 1964, batting .300 with 16 home runs and 76 RBI. He remains a great student of hitting but was also known for highly adventurous work in the outfield.

Dear Mr. Weiss:

My wife, my kids and myself would like to thank you personally for all you have done for us. Because I know that without your decision to help us, we would have been in real trouble. I want to thank you from the bottom of our hearts, because we really appreciate it.I know, Mr. Weiss, *despite everything that has been said about you* [author's italics], that you are a kind, considerate, conscientious person. Also, thank you for the contract. It is the most money I have made anywhere.

Also, Mr. Weiss, thank you for the $1,000 you gave me in 1964 when Ron Hunt won the Mets' MVP award. Maybe I should have won, but I didn't; so thank you again for such a wonderful gesture. It surely built up my morale, and I also respect you for this. This is how I know that you are an honest and sincere man. The four years I did spend with the Mets' organization were the four most glorious years I ever did spend in baseball. I also want to thank you, Mr. Weiss, for having confidence in me. It made me have confidence within myself.

Yours very sincerely,

Joe Christopher

P.S. It still hurts not to be a Met.

True to form, Christopher was the last Boston player to sign a contract in 1966. Even though he was no longer a Met, Christopher's concern for the team never waned. In May, 1966, Joe was with the Red Sox in Anaheim, watching a Met-Giant game on television. He noticed that Cleon Jones' stance was all wrong, picked up the phone, called the Shea Stadium press box and had a message relayed to Jones in the dugout. "I told him, 'Your hands are too low,'" Christopher recalled. "'Bring them up about two inches.'" Cleon complied and got two hits.

Christopher liked to talk on the phone, in addition to writing letters. Late in 1966, when he was playing for Syracuse, he spent $168 in a single day talking to his family and friends in

Puerto Rico and the Virgin Islands. "Think nothing of it," said Syracuse manager Frank Carswell, "his monthly bills at the Hotel Syracuse go twice that."

Christopher played just a few games for Boston in 1966, and was sent to the minor leagues. His last professional season was spent with Reading of the Eastern League in 1968. "That was the worst mistake I made," Christopher said. He went to Reading with the understanding that the Phillies would bring him up the big leagues as soon as he got in shape, but he wound up spending the entire season in the Eastern League. Christopher continued to play winter ball in the Caribbean, and was again the property of the Mets between the 1968 and 1969 seasons. He chose to retire, however, rather than return to the United States for another year.

Christopher is now 70 years old. "If you look at me right now," he said, "you wouldn't think I'm 70 years old. I don't look it. I can go out and run 60 yards like I always did. Age has nothing to do with it. The cells are immortal. All man has to do is not let the fluid around the cell evaporate. Once the fluid around the cell evaporates, that sets off the aging process. Aging has to do with the structure of foods. If man understands the whole process of trilipids and triglycerides—you have to understand saturated and unsaturated. Then you have to go to the monosaccarides. You have to understand sugars."

Christopher and Hunt were not the only Mets who hit well in 1964. For the first time in the team's history, the club was generating offense from its catchers. Gonder batted .270 and, surprisingly, Cannizzaro hit .313 in 151 at bats. Third string catcher Hawk Taylor provided power off the bench. As a whole, however, the team had very little power. Away from the Polo Grounds and its short porches, the staff managed to keep the ball in the park, yielding only 130 home runs, but Met batters managed only 103, and only Houston had a lower team batting average. The pitching was little better than previous years, as the staff again posted the worst ERA in the National League.

The Mets lost their top right hander from 1963, Carl Willey, before the season even began. After leading the Mets in ERA the previous year, Willey had a terrific spring. He had not given up an earned run in 23 innings when he went out to pitch the seventh against the Tigers on April 3. Stengel planned to take him out after the end of the inning. With two out, Gates Brown came to bat, the last batter Willey would face. "Gates Brown hit a line drive," said Al Moran, "and damn near killed him. It was a heck of a scene." "He threw a low, outside fastball," recalled Bill Wakefield, "and Brown hit it right back through the middle." Willey threw his glove up in a futile attempt to protect his face, but the ball hit solidly off his right jaw and bounced toward first base. Dick Smith fielded the ball and stepped on the bag for the out, as Willey walked toward the dugout holding his jaw. "He knew he was in trouble," said Wakefield, "and he grabbed his jaw and just walked slowly off the field into the dugout." Willey had a compound fracture, and would be out indefinitely. His jaw was wired shut, and he learned to take his nourishment in liquid form through a straw.

Willey didn't pitch again until June, and shortly after his return, came down with tendonitis. Then he tore a muscle in his elbow. He pitched only 30 innings all year, and didn't win a game. The injury effectively ended Willey's career. He pitched at Buffalo most of the next two seasons, then retired.

Without Willey, New York's "big four"—Al Jackson, Jack Fisher, Tracy Stallard and Galen Cisco, finished with a combined record of 37–72. Stallard became the Mets fourth 20 game loser in three seasons, finishing 10–20. Today, 20 game losers are rare, due to the five man rotation and the fact that, should a pitcher be in danger of losing his 20th, managers often take them out of the rotation in order to avoid the stigma. Stallard had no such aversion. "Hell, no," he said. "That didn't mean anything to me. I just pitched when they told me to pitch. I told them the next year that 10–20 sounded like .500 to me. It didn't work."

Kranepool, Hunt, McMillan and Charley Smith gave the Mets an adequate infield, bolstered by the acquisition of Bobby Klaus from the Reds. "I was flabbergasted," Klaus said of his trade to the Mets. "How could they trade me? They had the choice of keeping me or Pete Rose. How could they do that?"

While the Mets were coasting to another last place finish, well beyond hailing distance of the ninth place Colts, affairs at the other end of the standings were much more congested. The Phillies, under the fiery leadership of Gene Mauch, had progressed steadily from last place and a 47–107 record in 1961 to an 87–75 mark in 1963. The following year, buoyed by the addition of Bunning and rookie third baseman Richie Allen, the Phillies took over first place on July 16 and stayed there. On September 20, with twelve games to play, they held a seemingly insurmountable 6½ game lead:

	W	L	Pct.	GB
Philadelphia	90	60	.600	—
St. Louis	83	66	.557	6½
Cincinnati	83	66	.557	6½
San Francisco	83	67	.553	7

The Mets, with a 50–99 mark, were 39½ games out. Despite the Phillies' commanding lead, Mauch was jittery, for his pitching staff was riddled with injuries, and he had little confidence in many pitchers who were healthy. Mauch believed he had only two reliable starters, Bunning and southpaw Chris Short. Early in the season, while the Phils were building their lead, Dennis Bennett, Art Mahaffey and Ray Culp pitched well, but all had succumbed to injury. Bennett's injury was perhaps the most serious. In late June, the young lefthander had an 8–4 record with an ERA of less than 3.00. After the All Star break, his shoulder began to bother him.

Bennett came to major leagues midway through the 1962 season as a 22-year-old with enormous potential. He was 9–9 on a mediocre Phillie team and seemed to have a very promising future. "They were comparing me with Koufax and everybody else," Bennett said, "If it hadn't been for that wreck down there, who knows?"

"That wreck" occurred in Puerto Rico, where Bennett was playing winter ball after the 1962 season. On the afternoon of January 7, 1963, he was a passenger in a car that was returning from a team outing, sitting in the front seat beside Jose Urdaz, a director of the Arecibo club. In the back seat were coach Al Widmar, Phillie farmhand Joel Gibson, and Gibson's wife. Urdaz was driving at a speed of about 30 miles per hour, when suddenly the car swerved and crashed into a stone culvert. "Urdaz had a heart attack and died while he was driving," Bennett recalled. "He just slumped over the wheel and was dead before we even hit the bridge." Bennett was thrown through the windshield and his ankle was snapped. An ambulance was dispatched to the scene, but while speeding toward the wreck, ran down two men on a motorcycle, killing both. Finally, another car arrived to take the unconscious Bennett to the hospital.

Fortunately, Widmar and the Gibsons suffered only minor injuries. Bennett was not so fortunate. "He'll be lucky to walk again," a Puerto Rican orthopedic surgeon told the Phillies. Bennett thought the prognosis was ridiculous, and said he expected to be ready to pitch in about two months. That was optimistic, but Bennett did return to the mound in '63 and posted a 9–5 record with a fine 2.64 ERA. When he got off to a good start the following year, everyone assumed that the effect of the accident was behind him.

When Bennett had been thrown through the windshield of Urbaz's car, the ankle fracture had been the most serious injury, but he had also sustained a hairline crack in his shoulder blade. A year of pitching had caused calcium to build up in the crack, and by mid–1964, Bennett's shoulder hurt. "I couldn't throw without pain," he said. Bennett lost 10 of his last 14 decisions, then, after the season, had surgery to remove a three-quarter inch piece of calcium that had been cutting into a tendon.

Other Phillies suffered from injuries. Danny Cater, a good looking rookie outfielder, broke his wrist in July. Frank Thomas, who had been acquired from the Mets in August and had been one of the team's hottest hitters, broke his thumb and was out for the year. Still, a 6½ game lead with only 12 to play seemed safe. The Phillies petitioned Commissioner Frick for the right to add box seats for the World Series, and made hotel accommodations for the press.

The Reds, Cardinals and Giants were still in the race, despite the Series tickets rolling off the presses in Philadelphia. The Reds were playing inspired ball. Their manager, Fred Hutchinson, had been diagnosed with cancer the previous winter, and was with the club only sporadically. By September, with Hutchinson too weak to manage any longer, Dick Sisler served as his interim replacement.

The Red players vowed to win for Hutch. On September 21, Cincinnati beat the Phils 1–0, when Chico Ruiz made an incredibly foolhardy attempt to steal home with Frank Robinson at bat — and made it. Mauch, still 5½ games ahead, acted as though he were 5½ behind, and staged a violent scene in the clubhouse. Gary Kroll, who played for Mauch in 1964, said, "He didn't like most of his players. He wanted 25 Johnny Callisons or 25 Richie Allens. Every pitcher can't be a Jim Bunning." (Author's note — Would *anyone* want a team of 25 Richie Allens?)

Don Bosch, who played for Mauch in Montreal, agreed with Kroll. "Gene played favorites," Bosch said. "With Gil Hodges everybody was equal, but Gene had his favorite players on the team. From my perspective, that's the main reason he never went to the World Series, because he never had a team."

Mauch was despised by many opposing players. He called them names, heckled them and did anything he could to get them upset. When Houston's Don Nottebart pitched a no hitter against the Phillies in 1963, he recalled that "Gene Mauch was all over my butt. Actually, he drove me to it. I loved a challenge." Once, when Mets' catcher Jerry Grote leaned into the Phillie dugout trying to catch a foul ball, Mauch shoved him and knocked the ball loose in a legal, but rarely seen, maneuver.

Mauch was disliked by many of his own players, and didn't care. "Everybody in the city knows he hates my guts," said pitcher Art Mahaffey, "and I hate his." Mauch didn't want to be loved; he just wanted to win. Like Leo Durocher a few years later, he would find that putting unbearable pressure on his players was not the best way to achieve that goal.

With Mauch leaning hard on the panic button, his Phillies lost to the Reds twice more, reducing the lead to 3½ games on September 24. "We got beat some tough games," said Bennett. "I think we always showed up at the ballpark with the attitude that we were going to break out of it. We were going to win." But the Philllies didn't win — and Cincinnati did. The Reds won three games from the Mets, extending their winning streak to nine and moving into first place:

	W	L	Pct.	GB
Cincinnati	91	66	.580	—
Philadelphia	90	67	.573	1
St. Louis	89	67	.571	1½

Mauch, now in a state of high anxiety, was consistently using Bunning and Short on two days rest. He did it six times, and on all six occasions, the Phillies lost. "Bunning would get knocked out," said Kroll, "and he'd pitch Short. Short would get knocked out and he'd pitch Bunning. He didn't have the confidence to go with Mahaffey or a number of other people he could have used. He thought that was the way to go, but they were tired and they were getting hit." Once, Mauch started rookie Rick Wise, but took him out after Wise faced just three batters. "Why he didn't use Ray Culp or Mahaffey, I'll never know," said Bennett. As early as August, Mauch had begun using his starters, including Bunning and Short, in relief. In St. Louis, Johnny

Keane faced the same shortage of pitching that confronted Mauch. He had only three reliable starters, Bob Gibson, Curt Simmons and Ray Sadecki. They volunteered to work with short rest, but Keane said no. It would hurt the club in the long run.

The Cardinals passed Cincinnati and moved into first place when the Reds lost a 16 inning game to the Pirates on a squeeze bunt by rookie catcher Jerry May. Like so many incidents that took place during the final days of the 1964 season, the appearance of May at the plate in the 16th inning had a sense of eeriness about it. May had recently arrived from Asheville in a series of maneuvers that *Sports Illustrated*'s Frank Deford described as similar to the events that led to the start of World War I. When the Pirates sold Smoky Burgess to the White Sox in mid–September, they needed a third catcher to finish the season. Ron Brand, the catcher for the Pirates Triple A team in Columbus, was their first choice, but Brand had already gone home to Los Angeles. Rather than bring him back, the Pirates decided to recall May from their Double A club. It didn't really matter who they brought up, because whoever it was would only pitch batting practice and wouldn't play except in a dire emergency.

While throwing batting practice, May hit Pirate first string catcher Jim Pagliaroni with a pitch and put him out for the season. That moved him up to second string. When the game against the Reds lasted 16 innings, he got into action. During the 15th inning, Danny Murtaugh asked him, "Son, can you bunt?" May said he could. "Okay, then," Murtaugh replied, "be ready." The next inning, May was batting with the winning run on third base, and dropped a perfect bunt toward third. Ruiz, the third baseman, rather than going for the ball, inexplicably retreated toward the bag, and the winning run scored. The loss knocked the Reds out of first place, and as the season entered its final weekend, the standings were as follows:

	W	L	Pct.	GB
St. Louis	92	67	.579	—
Cincinnati	92	68	.575	½
Philadelphia	90	70	.563	2½
New York	51	108	.321	41

On the final weekend, the Reds and Phillies played each other, while the Cardinals hosted the Mets, who they had beaten 10 times in 15 games. If the Cardinals swept the three game series, they would win the pennant. If they won two of three, the Reds would have to sweep the Phillies in their two game series in order to force a playoff. The Phillies, despite their horrendous collapse, still had a mathematical chance. They could force a playoff if they swept the Reds and the Mets swept the Cardinals in St. Louis. That seemed about as likely as Mauch converting to Zen Buddhism.

Cardinal success against the Mets seemed pre-ordained. St. Louis had been red-hot since finding themselves 11 games behind in late August. They had won their last eight games, and had Gibson (18–11), Sadecki (20–10) and Simmons (18–9) lined up to start the three games against the Mets. Gibson, due to start Friday night, had won nine of his last ten decisions. Johnny Keane rolled out all of the baseball clichés when asked about the Mets, but no one took him seriously. "We walk out there even," Keane said. "It doesn't make any difference what's on their uniforms—Milwaukee, Cincinnati, New York."

Keane was merely being polite, for it was not what was on the uniforms, it was who was in them. Not only were the Mets deep in tenth place, they were staggering to the finish line, having lost their last eight games, and were decimated by injuries, as they had been the entire season. Altman, who arrived with such fanfare, had his season ruined by a shoulder injury and a series of leg problems. Frank Thomas, before he was traded, suffered from a second injury-riddled campaign. Willey missed almost the entire season. When the club went to St. Louis for the year's final series, Hunt, Cannizzaro, Stallard and Bearnarth were all left behind in New

York tending various disabilities. The Mets tried to recall John Stephenson, but he was grounded in Hattiesburg, Mississippi by Hurricane Hilda.

While the Cardinals had everything at stake, however, the Mets had nothing to lose. "Back then," said Bobby Klaus, "we didn't have any money, so you wanted to do anything you could to cause some upheaval. When you're in last place playing a first place team, hell, what have you got to lose?" "We were playing very loose," recalled Hawk Taylor. "The Cardinals, fighting for the pennant, almost choked. They were dropping easy pop flies and booting routine ground balls. They were playing very tense. We really played good ball."

Bill Wakefield had been Tim McCarver's roommate one year in spring training. "I was talking to him before the first game," Wakefield recalled, "and I said, 'You guys must be really excited.' He said, 'I don't even want to talk about it. We're on pins and needles here.'"

On Friday night, Al Jackson beat Gibson. Again, mysterious events transpired. In the eighth inning, with the Mets clinging to a 1–0 lead, the Cardinals had runners on first and third with two out. Lou Brock hit a hard ground ball toward Roy McMillan at shortstop. Before the ball could reach McMillan, however, it struck umpire Ed Vargo and rolled into short left field. Since Vargo was standing in front of McMillan, the ball was dead and the runner from third, Dal Maxvill, had to return to his base. Brock was allowed to go to first to load the bases. The next batter, Dick Groat, hit a line drive to right field, where Groat's old Pirate teammate Joe Christopher was stationed. Jackson held his breath while Christopher chased the ball. "I told Al I was going to play Groat down the line," Christopher said, "because when we played at Forbes Field, and the game was on the line, he always tried to slice the ball down the right field line." Christopher caught the ball on the run and the threat was ended. "When Groat came around first base," Christopher recalled, "he threw his helmet down and said, 'Damn you, Joe Christopher.'" Tracy Stallard had said the same thing earlier in the season. The Mets held onto the lead and won 1–0. "When I see a team battle like the Mets did," Keane said, "I'm proud of baseball."

Meanwhile, the Phillies rose from the dead with a four run eighth inning rally to beat the Reds 4–3. Had the Reds won, they would have taken first place. Instead, they remained ½ game behind, while the Phils moved within a game and a half of the Cardinals. Due to some unusual scheduling, the Phillies and Reds had Saturday off while the Mets and Cardinals played a single game. The Cards were still confident. "After the first game," recalled St. Louis pitcher Gordon Richardson, "we said, 'All we need is one win. Surely we can win one out of two.'"

At Busch Stadium on Saturday, there was no repeat of Friday night's pitchers' duel, and the Cardinals did not appear as confident as Richardson claimed. Klaus, the Mets' leadoff batter, began the first inning by hitting a high pop foul near home plate. McCarver dropped it. Given a second life, Klaus hit a line drive to left field. Lou Brock dropped it. By the end of the game, the Cardinals had committed five errors, for a total of eight in the two games. Klaus, Altman, Smith, Christopher and Kranepool hit home runs, and the Mets had a 15–5 victory. Sadecki was knocked out in the second. As the Mets ran up the score, Jesse Gonder sat in the bullpen, located right next to the stands. "Get your Cincinnati World Series tickets right here," he shouted. "Get your Cincinnati World Series tickets right here." "If the season goes to Christmas," Stengel said at the hotel, "we'll win the pennant."

The pressure was now on the Cardinals. A St. Louis win coupled with a Philadelphia victory would give the Cardinals the pennant. A Cardinal win and a Cincinnati win would result in a playoff between the Reds and Cards. A Met win and a Cincinnati win would give the pennant to the Reds. A Met win coupled with a Philadelphia win was the most dreaded scenario for National League officials, for it would create a three way tie and a round robin playoff series, in which a team would be eliminated after two losses.

On Sunday, all eyes and ears were on St. Louis. Harry Caray called the Met-Cardinal game on KMOX, which sent reporter Roy May to Cincinnati to provide live updates for Cardinal fans.

The Yankees had clinched the American League pennant the previous day, and their announcers also kept an eye on the National League tussle. They had a small television in the booth, tuned to the Met game, and provided highlights to their radio listeners. Phil Rizzuto, who often had trouble keeping up with one game, was broadcasting two, frequently without segue. "Watching one game and doing another can get confusing," he told his audience.

If Rizzuto was befuddled, anyone listening was often at a complete loss as to which game he was describing. "That's ball one to Agee," Rizzuto said, "and Johnny Keane is coming out to the mound." He didn't bother to add that Agee was batting in Yankee Stadium and Keane was going to the mound in St. Louis. "The Indians have runners at first and third," Rizzuto said later, "and Keane is coming out again." Still later: "[Paul] Dicken gets a life as Bill White has just singled to right field."

To make things even more confusing, Rizzuto changed channels and checked in on the New York Giant–Detroit Lion football game from time to time. "The pitch is low to Lopez — and Tittle just had another pass intercepted by the Lions." "The ball is hit into deep right field." There was a long pause. "Johnny Blanchard caught it — but what a run someone on the Detroit Lions just made — 60 yards for a touchdown."

It was like a blind person watching ESPN Sportscenter. Finally, even Rizzuto couldn't take it any longer. Yankee broadcasters had a tradition in which the statistician would do play-by-play for an inning or two on the last day of the season. Rizzuto signed off with, "As Casey Stengel is signaling for a new pitcher, here's Bill Kane." Then, in the background, one could hear the Scooter, in a stage whisper off-mike. "What? The Phillies are leading the Reds 9–0?" A fourth game had been added to the simulcast.

Back in St. Louis, Caray was carrying a much lighter load, calling just a single game with periodic reports from May. Cisco, with a 6–18 record, started for the Mets against Simmons. For the Met pitcher, it was like being in a World Series. "It was very, very exciting," he said. "We almost pulled it off." The Cardinals scored a run in the second, but Charlie Smith tied the score in the fourth with his second home run in two days. The Cardinals took a 2–1 lead in the bottom of the fourth but the Mets scored twice in the fifth on a double by Roy McMillan. Simmons departed and Gibson, who had pitched a complete game Friday night, came in to relieve him. Gibson retired two straight Mets to end the rally.

Meanwhile, May's reports from Cincinnati caused the St. Louis crowd, holding their transistors to their ears, to roar at times when nothing was happening in St. Louis. Caray would shout, "Who's listening to their radios out there?" or "Are you all enjoying yourselves at the ballpark today?" and a crescendo would erupt from the stands. "You'd hear these roars," said Rod Kanehl. "If you were dozing on the bench, you'd jump up, wondering what the hell was going on. It was the people in the stands listening to the Cincinnati score." The news from Philadelphia was good. The Phillies were demolishing the Reds. If the Cardinals could come from behind, they would have their first pennant since 1946.

In the bottom of the fifth, the Cardinals knocked out Cisco and Wakefield, scoring three runs to take a 5–3 lead. Stengel, maneuvering as if it were the final game of the World Series, brought in Jack Fisher, who had started Saturday's game. In the top of the sixth, with one out, Hawk Taylor singled. With two outs and runners at second and third, Gonder, batting for Fisher, was intentionally walked to load the bases. Klaus was unintentionally walked, forcing in a run which closed the gap to 5–4. The bases remained loaded and Gibson, pitching on guts alone, appeared to be staggering. He managed to retire McMillan to end the threat.

By the ninth inning, Caray had a larger audience, for the Phillies had finished their game in Cincinnati and sat in the clubhouse, glued to the radio. "We couldn't leave Cincinnati until we saw who won the Met game," said Dennis Bennett. If the Mets won, the Phillies would fly to St. Louis for a playoff game. If the Cardinals won, there would be a somber trip back to Philadelphia.

Normally, a one-run lead was enough for Gibson, but the Cards went to work on the thin Met bullpen, hammering Willard Hunter and Dennis Ribant for six runs. When the Mets came to bat in the ninth, they trailed 11–4. Gibson, dead tired, had thrown 13 innings in less than 48 hours. After he walked two of the first three batters, Keane decided he was finished.

In from the Cardinal bullpen strolled Barney Schultz, a 38-year old knuckleballer who had been recalled in July from Jacksonville, where he was a player-coach. With the Cardinals seemingly out of contention, they had recalled a number of players from their Triple A club, including Schultz, Gordon Richardson, Mike Shannon, Mike Cuellar and Bob Humphreys. "I think the Cards had given up," said Richardson. "I was surprised when they called Barney to St. Louis, because I felt like he was through and was going to get into the coaching business."

Schultz had bounced around the minor leagues since 1944, tossing his knuckler in such cities as Wilmington, Schenectady, Rock Hill and Bradford, playing for 20 teams in all. He had thrown the knuckler since he was 13, and when he hurt his arm during his first few years in the minors, began to rely on it more and more. By the time he reached the majors, Schultz threw the knuckler almost exclusively.

For twenty years, Schultz pitched during the summer and worked as a carpenter and in a clothing store during the winter to supplement his meager minor league salaries. In 1954, he pitched at Columbus under manager Johnny Keane. Keane turned him into a reliever and instilled confidence in a struggling pitcher who, at the age of 28, had yet to pitch in the big leagues. After a brief stint with the Cardinals in 1955, Schultz returned to the minors and played for Keane at Omaha for three years.

Schultz pitched with the Tigers and Cubs with marginal success between 1958 and 1963, bouncing up and down between the majors and Triple A ball. His only claim to fame was that he could throw his knuckleball almost every day. In 1962, Schultz tied a major league record when he pitched in nine straight games. In the middle of the 1963 season, the Cubs placed Schultz on waivers. The Cardinals were the only team to put in a claim and Keane, Schultz's old manager, convinced Bing Devine to obtain the old knuckleballer in return for utility player Leo Burke.

All his traveling had taken its toll, and Schultz was a very grizzled 38. As the Cardinals made their late-season run, however, Barney Schultz became the key man in the St. Louis bullpen. In 30 games, he had 14 saves and a 1.64 ERA. Now he was in a position to nail down the pennant for the team that had banished him to the minor leagues in the spring.

Schultz fanned Charlie Smith for the second out, bringing up Kanehl as a pinch hitter. Rod, although he didn't know it, was making his last major league appearance. When he reached the plate, he congratulated McCarver on winning the pennant. "We haven't won it yet," McCarver said cautiously. "We haven't gotten you out." Kanehl singled to left, driving in a run and prolonging the Cardinals' agony. "[First baseman] Bill White was just as tense and nervous as McCarver was," Kanehl recalled. "These guys were really gagging."

Schultz got two quick strikes on Kranepool, and then got him to loft a high foul pop. McCarver made the catch and St. Louis had completed its miraculous run to the National League pennant. The Cardinals, who were 39–40 before the All Star game, had gone 54–29 after it. During the last two weeks of the season, their only three losses had been to the Mets. The Phillies heard the last out in their locker room at Crosley Field. "It's the first time," Dick Young reported, "that I ever covered two losing locker rooms."

There was mayhem in the Cardinal locker room. Branch Rickey, the Cardinals' 82-year-old consultant, grabbed Keane and said, "Johnny Keane, you are a gosh-dang [the most profane utterance that Rickey employed] fine manager."* Down below, in their quarters, the Mets, their season over, packed up quickly. After their bus left for the airport, there were only two

---

Two months earlier, Rickey had advised Cardinal owner Gussie Busch to fire Keane at the end of the season.

people left in the locker room. Kanehl lived in Missouri and was heading directly home. The second person in the locker room was former Cardinal general manager Bing Devine.

With the Cardinals struggling in August, Devine had been forced to resign. Shortly thereafter, he was hired by the Mets as an assistant and eventual successor to George Weiss. "You could hear the Cardinals popping corks and raising hell upstairs," said Kanehl. "I came out of the shower and it's just me and Bing Devine. It was eerie." "You belong upstairs," he told Devine. "You don't belong down here. You put that team together. It's your team. Go up there." "Thanks, Rod," Devine replied, "I think I will."

While the Cardinals thought about the Yankees, who they would meet three days hence, the Mets headed for home. It had been quite a season, but most of the exciting incidents that happened to the Mets in 1964 did not involve any significant accomplishments on their part. They lost the opener at Shea, lost to the Giants in the 23 inning game and lost a perfect game to Jim Bunning. Now they had lost to the Cardinals to send them to the World Series. The Mets' final record was 53–109, as the two victories in St. Louis had enabled the club to surpass the 51 wins of 1963. It was their best record yet, but such a pace would not get them to .500 until 1978. Casey was a year older. Ron Hunt was the only rising star on the horizon, and there was little to suggest that 1965 would be noticeably better than 1964.

• 9 •

Yogi and Spahnie

Warren Spahn was one of the greatest pitchers of the 20th century. He came to Milwaukee with the Braves in 1953 and fashioned nine 20-win seasons, including six in a row from 1956 to 1961. He led the league in complete games every year from 1957 to 1963. Spahn appeared to be an ageless wonder, for in 1960, at the age of 39, he won 20 games and pitched his first no hitter. "It's funny," he said after the no hitter, "but I thought it would be more exciting." Exciting or not, Spahn followed with another no hitter the next year. "This is ridiculous," he said. "A fellow my age shouldn't be pitching no hitters."

A few months later, in August, 1961, Spahn won his 300th major league game, becoming only the thirteenth pitcher to achieve that plateau, and just the sixth in the 20th century. In 1963, Spahn won 23 games, and completed 22 of 33 starts. His earned run average of 2.60 was the third best of his career.

Spahn's longevity was in large part due to his dedication and attention to technique. "His mechanics were flawless," said ex-teammate Bob Shaw, a great student of pitching. "He put very little strain on his elbow and shoulder." Spahn didn't have an overpowering fastball, and didn't throw a curve, but possessed an outstanding screwball that neutralized right hand batters, plus excellent control. "He had the best control you'd ever seen," said catcher Sammy Taylor. "You'd put your mitt up there and you wouldn't have to move it. He could throw the ball within inches of where he wanted to." Hawk Taylor caught Spahn in Milwaukee and New York. "I remember his pinpoint control," Taylor said. "He'd say, 'Put the glove on the outside corner,' or 'Put the glove on the inside corner' and you could just about close your eyes and catch him." "I spent my life throwing a baseball 60 feet 6 inches," Spahn once said. "Why shouldn't I be able to control it."

"Warren was very smart," said pitcher Bob Hendley. "He had great location and he was a great competitor. He loved the game. I'd put Spahn, Koufax and Gibson as the three greatest pitchers of my era. If you asked me which of the three was the better thinker and locator, it would be Spahn, because Spahn didn't just blow people away. The other two guys could." "Tom Glavine reminds me of Spahn," said infielder Chuck Hiller. "You couldn't wait to hit off him, but then you were always 0 for 4." "Every time he went out there," said Shaw, "he did a very good job. He didn't win all the time, but he was always in the ballgame."

"He had great mental capacity," said Hawk Taylor, "a marvelous body and a marvelous arm. When I got there, he was primarily a fastball pitcher. Then he lost a foot off his fastball, came up with a slider and wins 20 games for another two or three years. Each time he needed to, he made an adjustment that extended his career."

In the spring of 1964, Spahn was 43 years old and fresh from a 23 win season. "He throws with such effortless ease," said Brave manager Bobby Bragan, "he could last forever — or almost." No one could pitch forever, and when the end came for Spahn in 1964, it arrived suddenly. "[I]t's almost like the beautiful young gal in Lost Horizon," wrote Arthur Daley, "who steps beyond the pale into instant old age." In spring training, after Spahn held Charlie Dressen's Tigers to one hit in five innings, Dressen said Spahn was slipping. He'd never seen his control so bad, Dressen said.

For once, Dressen was right. From a 23–7 record in 1963, Spahn sunk to 6–13 the following season. His ERA more than doubled, soaring from 2.60 to 5.29, the second worst ERA of any National League pitcher. Spahn finished the season in the bullpen, for Bragan had decided that the great lefthander was finally finished. "I spoke to Spahn for two hours one day," Bragan said, "trying to explain our feeling that he shouldn't start games. We had to make room for young pitchers like Tony Cloninger and Denny Lemaster. They would've started five more games apiece if Spahn hadn't been in the rotation and they would have wound up winning 20 each." During the spring, Bragan had asked Spahn to teach the young left handers his pickoff move. "Hell, I'm not going to show them my move," Spahn replied. "These guys are trying to take my job."

Spahn, like so many proud, fading veterans, insisted he had just had a bad year. All he needed was steady work, which he hadn't gotten in Milwaukee. He said he had corrected some mechanical problems, but after that Bragan wouldn't let him pitch. "Physically, I'm sound," Spahn claimed. "You don't go from a middle-aged man to an old man in one year — at least I don't think so."

The Braves thought so and suggested he retire, offering him his choice of becoming a radio and television announcer, minor league pitching coach, or manager of Milwaukee's top farm club. Spahn wanted the job of starting pitcher, but the Braves had not included that among the options. Certain he could still win in the big leagues, Spahn asked the Braves to trade him to another organization. On November 23, he got his wish and was sold to the Mets, agreeing to a $65,000 contract as a player-coach (a reduction from the $85,000 he received in 1963). "Spahnie won't win six games for the Mets," Bragan said. Spahn thought he might win 20, which exhibited blind optimism not only in his own ability, but in the quality of the Met team.

Spahn's acquisition by the Mets brought about a reunion with Casey Stengel, who had been his first major league manager in 1942. Stengel was then a losing manager and Spahn a 21-year-old rookie. Now, 23 years later, Stengel had seven World Series titles and Spahn had 356 victories, and both were trying to prove they still had some life left. Spahn was fond of saying, "I played for Casey before and after he was a genius." Stengel might have retorted that he managed Spahn before and after he was a superstar.

The Mets had acquired the highest-paid coaching staff in baseball and created the oldest battery in major league history, for after being abruptly fired as Yankee manager in October, Yogi Berra had also signed with the Mets as a player-coach. On March 14, Berra caught Spahn for the first time. Would Stengel, with his flair for the dramatic, start the two of them on Opening Day against the Dodgers? "With Sandy Koufax pitching for them," Berra said, "nothing doing."

Yogi, 38, had worked out and taken batting practice with the Yankees in 1964, but batted only twice in games. In an Old Timers Game, Yogi hit into a double play. His other at bat was in the Mayor's Trophy Game, against Bill Wakefield of the Mets. "All of a sudden," Wakefield said, "I heard something that sounded like a subway. It was kind of a deep rumbling and it kept getting louder and louder. Then I saw Yogi coming out of the third base dugout." Wakefield threw Berra a slider and Yogi hit it to shortstop for a double play.

Ten years later, Berra saw Wakefield at a Mets Old Timers Day. "Hey, Dick," Yogi said. Dick Wakefield had played with the Yankees in the '40s and Berra always called Wakefield "Dick." "I'd quit correcting him by that time," said Wakefield. "I said, 'Yeah, Yogi?'" "You got me out in the Mayor's Trophy Game," Berra said. After thousands of major league at bats, and a World Series record number of hits, Berra remembered that Bill Wakefield had made him hit into a double play in an exhibition game.

At St. Petersburg in the spring of 1965, Yogi, as he had the previous year, took batting practice and caught batting practice. "We have a fake stop watch," said Stengel, "that clocks him going down to first base in very fast time." Berra played in a few exhibitions, but didn't seem too enthusiastic about getting behind the bat. On one occasion, he caught Wakefield. "All Yogi put down," Wakefield said, "was one finger, regardless of the situation. I pitched three innings and threw nothing but fastballs. With a guy on first base, he didn't want to handle anything other than a fastball." That was nothing new for Berra. Many Yankee pitchers had gotten upset with him because, with a runner on, he insisted on calling for one fastball after another. "Yogi was tough to pitch to," said Yankee pitcher Bud Daley. "He didn't like you to shake him off."

Yogi hit the ball fairly well in batting practice, but not as well in his limited game action. In eight at bats, he failed to connect safely. Spahn, pitching batting practice, once asked Yogi what pitch he wanted. Berra asked for a fastball, since he'd been having trouble catching up to fastballs. Spahn threw a fastball and Yogi took it. "Fastball with less on it," Berra said. At the end of the spring, Yogi elected to stick to coaching.

Two weeks into the season, each of the Met catchers, Cannizzaro, Gonder and Hawk Taylor, was batting under .200. Yogi couldn't do much worse, and agreed to go on the active list. On May 1st, Berra left the first base coach's box to pinch hit against the Reds, his first appearance in a regular season game in well over a year. He grounded out.

Three days later, Yogi started, got two singles in three at bats and scored the winning run against the Phillies. Two more appearances, however, convinced Berra that he could no longer play effectively at the major league level. He had just those two hits in nine at bats. Berra's back ached after he caught. His reflexes at the bat were gone. "After his last game," said Jack Fisher, "he said, 'Man, if I can't hit the fast ball, I ain't getting up there again.'" Yogi didn't want to be a sideshow, and asked to be released on May 11th, when the club had to cut down to 25 players.

Spahn, meanwhile, had become a solid member of the rotation, seemingly proving his assertion that he was far from washed up. At the time Berra returned to full time coaching duties, Spahn was tied for the team lead with two wins and had a 3.12 ERA. He pitched well every time he took the mound, a mound constructed to his specifications. "He had the grounds crew at Shea build the mound to suit his delivery," said pitcher Dennis Musgraves. "He liked a real tall mound."

Spahn had been encouragingly steady in the spring, and in his first regular season start against Houston on April 15, putting forth a solid eight inning effort which netted no decision. Warren's second start was against the Dodgers in Los Angeles. He was locked in a scoreless duel with Claude Osteen for seven innings before the Mets scored three runs in the eighth and ninth. In the bottom of the ninth, the Dodgers reached Spahn for two runs and had runners on first and third with no outs. Stengel came to mound, while youngsters Dennis Ribant and Tug McGraw warmed up in the Met bullpen.

Coach Spahn decided to let pitcher Spahn finish the game. It was a brilliant decision. Spahn struck out Jim Lefebvre, got Ron Fairly to hit a grounder back to the mound, then finished the game with a flourish by striking out John Kennedy. Spahn leapt as high in the air as a 43-year old could leap to celebrate his first complete game since the previous July. "I never saw Spahn any happier," said his catcher, Hawk Taylor. Taylor had been Spahn's teammate when he was in two World Series, but never did he see Spahn exhibit the joy he showed after the win in Los Angeles.

In his next start, two days after his 44th birthday, Spahn beat the Giants, retiring the first

17 batters he faced. Spahn had chosen to pitch the second game of a doubleheader, so that, he said, he could keep an eye on the bullpen during the first game. Coincidentally, that also enabled him to pitch against Bob Bolin, while during the first game he kept an eye on Juan Marichal shutting out the Mets.

On April 30, Spahn suffered his first loss, but broke Christy Mathewson's National League record for most strikeouts in a career when he fanned four Cincinnati Redlegs. On May 5, he pitched a four hit complete game against the Phillies, but lost 1–0 on opposing pitcher Jim Bunning's home run.

On May 20, Spahn returned to Milwaukee to face his old team and Wade Blasingame, who had replaced him in the Braves rotation. The Braves were lame ducks in Milwaukee, having already announced their intention to move to Atlanta, and attendance was predictably dismal. Only 2,335 came out the day before Spahn pitched and the Mets, as the visiting team, netted a mere $648 from the gate proceeds. The return of the old hero attracted a crowd of more than 17,000, the largest since opening day. The results vindicated the Braves' decision to jettison Spahn, as Blasingame pitched a one-hitter, while Spahn was driven from the mound during a seven run fifth inning.

Four days later, Spahn won his fourth game of the season, and the 360th of his career. The veteran lefthander was just 4–4, but he had pitched very well and his control seemed as good as ever, with just three walks in his first 41 innings. He led the staff in innings pitched and had kept the Mets in every game he started. Spahn's 360th win put him one game behind nineteenth century pitcher Jim Galvin for sixth place on the all-time list. Kid Nichols, another nineteenth century stalwart, was only one win beyond Galvin. Two more victories would make him the fifth winningest pitcher of all time.

The climb past Galvin and Nichols proved excruciating, for, by June, Spahn was having more bad starts than good. "I guess he just ran out of adjustments," said Taylor. "But he was such a competitor that he wouldn't acknowledge it. He wouldn't give in to anything, whether he was 25 winning his first game or 40-something, winning his last. He was just a competitor right to the very end."

"He wasn't the pitcher I'd seen in Milwaukee," said Galen Cisco. "You could tell he knew how to pitch, but he wasn't as consistent and didn't throw as hard. In his prime, he could make the ball sing. If he tried to pitch low and away, he either missed it or was right on the corner. As he got up there in age, he didn't have that command. He wasn't as consistent as he was in his prime. He knew how to do it, but his body just didn't let him it. He missed his spots." Spahn could no longer keep batters honest with his fastball, for they were all looking for the slow stuff. When it missed the plate, they took it. When it was over the plate, they hit it.

Spahn generally started out strong, but faded in the middle innings. Leonard Koppett wrote a column titled: Spahn's Problem: Spahn — What to do with a Pitcher, 44, Who Doesn't Finish What He Starts? Koppett pointed out with damning statistics Spahn's decline in effectiveness:

	First 4 Innings	5th–9th Innings
Innings	40	37.1
Runs	3	32
Earned Runs	3	28
ERA	0.68	6.75
Home Runs	2	8
Hits	23	57
Opponents' BA	.171	.333

Since Spahn appeared to have limited stamina, he might be more effective in the bullpen. That's where Bragan had tried to put him in 1964. Was coach Spahn being stubborn by keeping pitcher Spahn in the rotation? Part of the reason Spahn faded in the middle innings was that, with his fastball long gone, he needed to nibble and work patiently on each hitter. If he tried to challenge them, he was hit hard. Nibbling required a lot of pitches, and Spahn generally worked deep in the count, which took a toll on his 44-year-old arm. "The law of averages is simple," wrote Koppett. "The more pitches a man makes, the more likely he is to miss with some."

On June 25, Spahn lost for the sixth consecutive time, pitching four decent innings before being routed in the fifth by the Astros. Loss number seven came four days later, against his old club, when he gave up six runs in six innings. Spahn didn't lose his next start, but he couldn't last the five innings he needed to claim the win. After four innings of struggle, many pitches, eight hits and three walks, Stengel removed him from the game, even though he was leading 3–2.

Stengel wanted Spahn to go to the bullpen. As he had so often during his long career, Spahn was having difficulty with his manager. Early in the season, when the veteran lefty was winning, Stengel had been a terrific manager and the Mets were a wonderful organization. Now that Spahn was failing regularly, he said the Mets were poorly run and Stengel didn't know what he was doing. In early July, the two men had loud words behind the closed door of Stengel's office, after which Casey relented and gave Spahn one more chance. In his final start as a Met, on July 11th, Spahn lasted less than two innings and absorbed his eighth straight defeat. He had not won in his last ten starts.

By this time, everyone but Spahn realized he was no longer the pitcher he had been, or even one capable of helping the sorry Mets. "Too many great athletes acquire blind spots," wrote Arthur Daley, "when the end of the trail is clearly in view. They fail to see it even though everyone else recognizes the signposts that warn of the dead-end street.'

Spahn's troubles also affected his ability to serve as pitching coach. During spring training, he pitched more innings than anyone on the staff. The 126 innings he'd pitched thus far during the regular season led the staff. The young pitchers, who the Mets desperately needed to develop, were pushed aside to make room for him, and they were upset. Their coach clearly had a conflict of interest. "[H]is value as a coach," Daley wrote, "diminished along with his value as a pitcher."

The day after Spahn's latest loss, which dropped his record to 4–12, Stengel said he would probably move the veteran lefty to the bullpen, and try some of his young pitchers in starting roles. When Spahn re-iterated that he didn't want to pitch in relief, Stengel had no choice but to place him on waivers. For one dollar, any team could acquire the contract of a pitcher with 360 big league wins. If no team claimed Spahn within 72 hours, he would be released.

There were several interested parties at the price of one dollar, but none were major league baseball teams. The Mets received about a dozen inquiries, including an envelope that arrived from Minerva, New York, containing a folded dollar bill and the following letter:

> Dear sirs: Bunk 15 of Camp Baco would like to purchase Warren Spahn for the announced price of $1. May we please have him C.O.D. Our bunk has long been in need of a winning left-hander and we think Warren can turn the trick.
>
> Sincerely,
>
> Robert Cooper, The Baco Bombers

A second letter, filled with legalese, arrived from a Yale Law School student, making a similar offer, and with a Postal Money Order for a dollar. A caller asked about purchasing Spahn and wanted to know how he could sell him for two or three dollars, hoping perhaps to double or triple his investment.

Charley Finley, always looking for a gate attraction, wanted to sign Spahn, but Warren wanted to stay in the National League, and didn't want to leave one last place team for another. He could be valuable to a contender, starting occasionally and coming in from the bullpen on others. Spahn had refused to accept that role with the Mets, but perhaps he had learned a lesson, or maybe the opportunity to pitch in another World Series, even as a part-timer, would appeal to him.

On July 19, the San Francisco Giants signed Spahn for spot starting and middle relief duty. By waiting until the waiver period expired, they were not obligated to pay him the $65,000 salary he had received from the Mets. Under the pressure of a pennant race, Spahn pitched well for the Giants, who were locked in a tight battle with the Dodgers, Braves, and Reds. In early August, he moved into the starting rotation, and pitched one solid game after another. On the last day of the month, he had a mound duel with his old Milwaukee teammate Lew Burdette, then with the Phillies. Spahn pitched a one-hitter for 6⅔ innings, only to be beaten 2–0 on two late-inning home runs. On September 12th, he hurled a complete game win over the Cubs, his seventh win of the season and the 363rd and last of his big league career. The win gave the Giants a two game lead in the National League race.

Unfortunately, the Giants specialized in finishing second during the 1960s, achieving that feat in four consecutive years (1965–68). In 1965, they came up two lengths short of the Dodgers, but it was not the fault of their veteran left hander. In 16 games with the Giants, Spahn was 3–4 with a very respectable 3.38 ERA. His overall record for the season was 7–16.

In the middle of October, the Giants gave Spahn his unconditional release. He still believed he could pitch, and tried unsuccessfully to get a job with another major league club. The Giants offered to bring him to spring training on a conditional basis, but the proud Spahn refused. If he didn't have a contract, he wouldn't report. He threw all winter and worked on a knuckleball. In April, Spahn said he was considering an offer to pitch for El Paso in the Texas League. "I've been watching television," he said, "and I think I can do as well as some of those guys. I just might go there to show people I can still get them out."

Nineteen sixty-six was the first season of Warren Spahn's life that he hadn't played baseball, and while he raved about the newly-discovered beauty of the Oklahoma spring, he was still convinced he could pitch. "I did not retire," he said frequently. "Baseball retired me." In the middle of the season, Alejo Peralto, owner of the Mexico City Tigers, asked Spahn to spend four weeks with his team as a coach. He was an easy mark when Tigers GM Hector Barnetche asked if he would pitch a game. Barnetche's interest was the size of the crowd Spahn's appearance would generate, but all Spahn wanted was another chance to take the mound against professional hitters.

For five innings, Spahn set down the Jalisco Charros on just seven hits, but trailed 2–0 when he left the game. In the bottom of the fifth, as Spahn cheered them on from the dugout, the Tigers took the lead. If his relievers could hold on, Spahn would add one win in Mexico to his 363 in the United States. Alas, the bullpen was not up to the task and, although the Tigers rallied to win, Spahn was denied a victory in his final professional game. At the age of 45, he did what most ballplayers his age did. He became a manager and coach. The playing career of the winningest left-hander in the major leagues was finally over.

· 10 ·

A Thoroughbred Racer, a Young Colt and an Old Workhorse
The 1965 Season

Met hopes were modest in the spring of 1965. They weren't talking about a pennant, or even the first division. "Will this be the season the Mets finally bid adieu to the cellar that has been their home since they set up housekeeping in 1962?" asked *The New York Times*. "It could be." "Yes, I think we have a fine chance to get out of last place," Stengel said on the eve of the opener.

Despite the limited prospects of success on the diamond, there was no shortage of celebrities in St. Petersburg, even though none was in his baseball-playing prime. The main attraction, of course, was the 74-year-old Stengel, starting his fourth season at the Met helm. The two new coaches, Berra and Spahn, garnered almost as much attention as Stengel.

The Mets also added a non-baseball celebrity. Jesse Owens, the former Olympic sprint champion, was on hand to instruct the lead-footed Mets, who stole only 36 bases in 1964, in the art of base running. Owens was a showman and, like Stengel, favored a rambling style of discourse. "Face-to-face conversations between Stengel and Owens," Leonard Koppett wrote, "promise to be a highlight of the spring training season." Before each practice, Owens led the Mets on a lap around the field and a series of exercises.

Since winning his four Olympic medals in 1936, Jesse had been a barnstoming trackman and a businessman. His baseball experience consisted of a stint as part owner of the Pittsburgh Crawfords of the Negro Leagues, and running pre-game races against horses. The secret to beating horses, Owens said, was threefold. First, he liked to run against thoroughbreds, who were trained for long distances rather than the hundred yards he raced them. Second, he tried to get the owner of the horse, rather than the regular jockey, to ride. Finally, he got the loudest gun he could find to signal the start of the race. "When the shot was fired," Owens confided, "the horse became so startled he would jump. By the time he'd settle into stride, I was 25 yards ahead of him and that was ordinarily enough to win a race at 100 yards."

Owens' role in the Met camp was more for show than anything else, and the highlight of his tenure was a 30 yard dash by the reporters. Maury Allen of the *Post* led a field of seven. Dick Young fell face first after five yards and was last. As soon as the race was over, trainer Gus Mauch ran on the field with an oxygen tank and physician Peter LaMotte ran out carrying a stethoscope.

"Since most Met batters get thrown out by three steps rather than one," noted Koppett, "[Owens' training] in itself may not turn the Mets into pennant contenders overnight." The Mets also needed to beat a catcher's throw to second base, not a thoroughbred, but Owens believed he could work with the players to adjust their stride and gain a yard or two between bases. On the first day of camp, he led drills with enthusiasm. "Jesse was probably in his 50s [he was 51]," recalled pitcher Rob Gardner, "and the rest of us were just barely out of the cold weather, and he had us doing all these sprinters' exercises and sprinting to first base. He was doing them with us." Gardner laughed. "The next day," he said, "Jesse conducted calisthenics sitting on a chair on a raised platform. Of course, none of us could move either." Just before he left camp, Owens suffered a pinched sciatic nerve that had him doubled over in discomfort.

While elderly celebrities might create interest and generate a few newspaper articles, any success the Mets might achieve on the field would be result of their young players coming of age. In 1965, the Mets had the most youthful team in their brief history, and the youngest in the major leagues. In 1962, the average age of the club that reported to spring training was 29. The next year it dropped to 26, then to 25 in 1964. In the spring of 1965, the average Met was a beardless youth of 24. Only Hickman, Christopher, Jackson and Cannizzaro remained from the expansion draft.

One of the Met newcomers was Billy Cowan, a 26-year-old outfielder obtained from the Cubs. Cowan had speed, power and a strong arm, and had been the Most Valuable Player in the Pacific Coast League and *The Sporting News* minor league player of the year in 1963. "I understand he's faster than [Lou] Brock," said one of the Chicago coaches. Cowan had the potential to be a star if he could learn to make consistent contact, for his major weakness was the strikeout."*

"When I was traded to the Mets," Cowan said, "I was pretty disappointed, because I'd planned on having a good long career in Chicago. Even though I hardly played the last six weeks of the [1964] season, I hit 19 home runs. But I struck out a lot and they didn't like that. I got a call from Bing Devine, who said he was going to bring me to New York. I told him I didn't like New York and didn't want to go. I'm a small town guy. He told me that when he was with the Cardinals and had traded for Lou Brock, he'd wanted me instead, but the Cubs wouldn't let me go. I told him I still didn't want to go to New York. Bing told me, 'Look, you're going to come here and you're going to play every day. I don't care if you strike out 200 times. You're going to play every day.'"

Apparently, Devine hadn't advised Stengel of his plan. "I think Casey was one of the great old men of baseball," Cowan said recently, "but at that time he didn't really know that much about the team. The first intrasquad game he put me at shortstop. I'd been traded there to be the regular center fielder. I'll bet I didn't play more than 30 or 35 innings in spring training, and I wasn't ready. Opening day we played the Dodgers and Drysdale was pitching. He struck me out three times and the next day I was on the bench. It was the shortest starting assignment in the history of the game."

One of the reasons Cowan wasn't playing was that Stengel had again become enamored of a young phenom. Ron Swoboda, a husky Baltimorean, had been signed by the Mets, for a $35,000 bonus, after spending a year at the University of Maryland. He went to the major league training camp in 1964, before playing an inning of pro ball, and made such an impression on Stengel that he wanted to keep him. The youngster had a neck like Mantle's, Casey noted, although Mickey hit precious few home runs with his neck. Weiss recalled the Kranepool episode of the previous spring and insisted that the young outfielder go to the minors. Swoboda spent most

*"Cowan once struck out six times in a game against New York," reported Sports Illustrated," and you know the Mets couldn't resist having him." If Cowan could hit consistently, he could be the answer to the centerfield problem that had plagued the Mets since their inception.

of the 1964 season at Williamsport of the Eastern League, where he batted .276 with 14 home runs.

In the spring of '65, Swoboda was just 20 years old, but Stengel, as he had with Mantle and Kranepool, wanted him to stay in the big leagues. Stengel loved Swoboda and the affection was mutual. "Ron loved Stengel," said shortstop Ed Bressoud. "He told me he was starting to understand Casey and that bothered him. I think both of them were a little 'off the wall' at that particular time." "It becomes increasingly obvious," Arthur Daley wrote, "that Stengel wants to leave the Mets a monument in Swoboda, just as he left the Yankees one in Mantle."

Would Stengel leave the Mets a monument like Mantle or another one like Kranepool? In July of 1965, many were willing to bet on the Mantle comparison. On April 15, Swoboda got his first major league hit by blasting a pinch hit home run against the Astros. Four days later, in just his fourth major league at bat, he connected for home run number two. Koppett pointed out that Swoboda was five games ahead of Ruth's pace and eleven games in the van of Maris. On April 23, Swoboda hit another pinch hit homer. By May 18, he had eight homers and 17 RBI compared to Mantle's seven homers and 15 RBI. Reporters started asking Swoboda whether he could break Maris's home run record. In early July, he started his record breaking assault modestly by topping Jim Hickman's Met rookie home run mark with his 14th of the season. It was the only home run record Swoboda would ever shatter.

It was obvious that Swoboda had power. It was also obvious that he was not a polished major league player. His most glaring inadequacy was in the field. In spring training, when Stengel was given a cesta by Miami jai alai professionals, he gave it to Swoboda to use as a glove. "They called him 'Clang-Clang,'" recalled pitcher Gordon Richardson, for the sound the ball supposedly made when it hit Swoboda's glove.

During his first couple of years in the big leagues, it seemed as though Swoboda let in a run for every one he knocked in. In late April of Swoboda's rookie year, Jack Fisher lost a 2–1 pitching duel to Sandy Koufax when Swoboda and second baseman Bobby Klaus managed not to catch a popup to short right. In late May, the Mets blew a 7–0 lead when, with two outs in the ninth inning, Swoboda misplayed Cardinal shortstop Dal Maxvill's fly ball into a triple. In June, Spahn lost to Koufax 2–1 when Swoboda botched another ball in the outfield. His troubles continued all season, and with Swoboda and Christopher often in the same outfield, every fly ball or line drive was an adventure. But Swoboda was hitting home runs, and at the All Star break, Stengel said he "would play every day regardless of his faults in the field because of what he's doing for us."

Meanwhile, Cowan, a good fielder, languished on the Met bench. "I read something in the paper," he said, "about how Casey didn't want to expose the rookies to the better pitchers, so he was going to play me against the Gibsons, Drysdales and Koufaxes. How the hell are you going to hit if you're just playing against those guys?" Cowan didn't hit, ending up with an average of .179 in 82 games, many of them as a pinch hitter, and had just three home runs. Cowan's dream of a regular big league job had not materialized, and he told Devine, "Bing, I don't care where you send me, but I'm not going to sit here and waste away. I'll just go home to Bakersfield and climb on a tractor and go after it." In August, Cowan was sold to the Braves.

During the second half of the season, National League pitchers figured out how to get Swoboda out. They simply stopped throwing him strikes. Swoboda hit 15 homers before the All Star break and only four afterward, none after August 26. In one game, Bob Gibson struck him out four times. Swoboda finished the season a frustrated young man, one who often resorted to throwing helmets and stomping on them. "One time," said John Stephenson, "he stomped on a helmet in the dugout and got his foot stuck on it. He couldn't get it off his foot. It was hilarious." Stengel didn't find it hilarious and removed him from the game.

"It was unfortunate that a lot of pressure was put on Ron when he first came up," said Larry

Miller. "He was one of the few good things to write about, a guy who could occasionally hit a towering home run out of the ballpark. He was a pretty uptight individual in the clubhouse and he worked under a lot of pressure."

The media desperately wanted Swoboda to excel, for unlike many young athletes, he was articulate and quotable, an excellent after-dinner speaker who eventually became a broadcaster. Swoboda was, in many ways, the opposite of Roger Maris. Maris was at home on the field, and miserable off it. Swoboda often fought himself on the diamond, but off the field was very adept at dealing with the media, deflecting difficult questions with humor or a long, introspective discourse. During the winter following his rookie year, he delivered more than 50 speeches. Swoboda enjoyed living in New York and, if he could realize the potential he demonstrated during the first half of the 1965 season, the city would be his.

One of the most pleasant surprises of the 1965 season, at least during the early months, was the fine hitting of Kranepool. The big first baseman seemed as though he had been with the Mets forever, although he was still just 20 years old. During the first two months of 1965, it appeared as though the stardom many had predicted for Kranepool had arrived. On May 2, he led the National League with a .407 average and was among the leaders in RBI. At the end of May, he was still in the top ten with a .342 average. Kranepool's hot hitting continued through the first half of June, but then he fell into a deep slump. He went through an 0 for 31 drought, which dropped his average below .300. Still, he was the only Met named to the All Star team and, with a decent second half, could have a strong season. Kranepool didn't have a decent second half. He endured two more long dry spells (0–20 and 0–19), and went 46 games without a home run. From June 5 through the end of the year, Kranepool batted just .215. Like Swoboda, he was unproductive in August and September, and finished with a .253 average and only 10 home runs.

Many Met hitters had difficulties in 1965, as the team finished with a .221 average, by far the worst in the National League. They were shut out 22 times. Kranepool's .253 mark was the lowest average ever to lead the club and one of the lowest ever to lead any team. In September, the Mets got only one hit in each of two consecutive games against the Braves, the first time that had happened in 48 years. In June, they had a 23 game streak where they scored only 32 runs, had more strikeouts than hits, and batted just .181. They lost 20 of the 23 games.

Christopher's average dropped from .300 with 16 homers and 76 RBI in '64 to .249, five homers and 40 RBI, and his fielding was as shaky as ever. Just before the start of the season, Stengel observed, "He's learned to hit, but he's letting too many fly balls get away and his arm could be better. But I promised him the job so it's his." It was hardly a ringing endorsement. Finally, in June, after Christopher had started 159 consecutive games, Stengel put him on the bench. At the end of the season, he was traded to the Red Sox.

Cannizzaro, who had batted .311 in a part time role in '64, earned more playing time in '65, but hit just .183, driving in only seven runs all year. Hickman and third baseman Charlie Smith had decent years, with 15 and 16 homers, respectively, but no Met hit consistently all season. In addition to their weak offense, the Mets also lacked speed. After the spring sessions with Jesse Owens, the stolen base total dropped from 36 to 28, worst in the major leagues.

The Met defense was generally porous, with the exception of veteran shortstop Roy McMillan, who played 157 games at the age of 35. Roy had come to the Mets in a trade for Jay, Wes and Marcie Hook in 1964, and filled the club's pressing need for a capable major league shortstop. The thin, bespectacled veteran had played in the major leagues since 1951, and despite a frightening succession of injuries, rarely missed a game. He was with the Reds through 1960, winning the first three Gold Glove awards for National League shortstops in 1957–59, then played for the Milwaukee Braves from 1961 to 1963. By 1964, the Braves had a talented young player named Denis Menke, whose best position was shortstop, which made McMillan, nearing the end of the line at 33, expendable. In 1965, McMillan was the anchor of the Met infield and a steadying influence on the whole team. *Sports Illustrated* named him the Mets' MVP.

The greatest blow to the Mets' 1965 hopes came on May 11th, when Hunt, the only Met ever voted to an All Star team, and the club's best player, suffered a separated shoulder in a collision with the Cardinals' Phil Gagliano. Hunt was out of the lineup until mid–August, when he returned to action in an exhibition game against Williamsport. Most players returning from a serious injury would proceed gingerly, especially in a minor league exhibition. Not Hunt, who stole a base with a head first slide. Hunt's return to major league action came shortly afterward, but he played only 57 games and batted just .240, a precipitous decline from his .303 mark of the previous year.

The Mets' lack of hitting and speed, plus the leaky defense, put a tremendous strain on the pitching staff. Met pitchers didn't get many runs to work with, and the fielders behind them turned outs into runs with alarming frequency. Jack Fisher was the most aggrieved victim. When asked to describe Fisher, the word his former teammates use most often is "workhorse." "He wanted the ball and was ready to pitch any time," said Ed Bressoud. "Jack always wanted to pitch the big games for us," said outfielder Al Luplow. Not that the Mets had too many big games. "Jack was a real competitor," said catcher John Sullivan. "He went out there to beat you. He was a tough competitor and he knew how to pitch." For three straight years, 1964–66, Fisher led Met pitchers in innings pitched, and when he was traded after the 1967 season, held the Met career record for most innings.

"That's what I thought you should do," said Fisher. "Give me the ball and I'll go out and pitch. I had a fairly fluid delivery that didn't take a lot out of me. To pitch today would drive me absolutely batty. If they only gave me the ball every five days and told me to go out and pitch six or seven innings, I'd be bored stiff. You should relish the eighth and ninth innings. They're your chance to win. Casey was great to me. I was a guy who wanted the ball every four days and Casey gave me the ball every four days. If I wanted to relieve between starts, he let me do that, too."

Fisher always remembered something his Oriole teammate Robin Roberts said. "One day, after the pitchers and catchers had gone over the hitters," Fisher recalled, "[manager] Billy Hitchcock asked Robin if he had anything he wanted to say. Robbie said, 'Yeah, there is. I want to tell you guys that the greatest compliment anyone can give you is to hand you the baseball and tell you you're the starting pitcher. You should treasure that.' From that day on, I really did. It meant a hell of a lot to me for somebody to give me the baseball and say, 'It's your game to start.'"

Whenever Fisher pitched poorly, someone was sure to mention his weight, which ranged from 200 to 230 pounds. His nickname was Fat Jack, which he hated. "Call Jack Fisher anytime and almost anything," wrote Barney Kremenko, "but don't call him fat or portly." "Jack was a big guy," said Larry Miller. "He used to complain that when he was going good, nobody talked about his weight, but as soon as he lost a couple of games, everybody said he should shed twenty pounds."

"I didn't give a damn whether I weighed 200 or 220," Fisher said. "I always felt that I was in better shape than the guy I was pitching against. That's why I used to love the weather as hot as possible. I was in as good shape as probably 85 percent of the pitchers in the game. I could go nine anytime I walked out there, but that was the one thing the writers loved to get on me about, only, of course, when things weren't going so well. 'How much do you weigh, Jack?' they'd ask me. I'd gone out many a time weighing 220, went nine innings and pitched as good as I could pitch. I've also gone out there weighing 205 pounds and gotten my ass kicked. No one ever asked me about my weight then. That's kind of a sore spot with me."

Fisher began his major league career in 1959 as a member of Paul Richards' Baby Birds staff in Baltimore. He won 12 games in 1960, as the Orioles battled the Yankees into September, but his Oriole career was probably most notable for the surrender of two monumental home runs. In 1960, he gave up the final home run of Ted Williams' illustrious career. "My roommate, Steve Barber, got booted in the first inning," Fisher recalled, "and I wound up pitching until the ninth. I gave up Williams' home run in the eighth." The next year, Fisher surrendered #60 to Maris.

After a mediocre 1962 season in Baltimore, during which he suffered from shoulder miseries, Fisher was traded to the Giants, where he pitched poorly, posting a 6–10 record with a 4.58 ERA. In October of 1963, after the Mets and Colts had each endured a second dismal season, the National League decided to send some assistance their way. Each of the other eight teams put four players into a pool, from which the Mets and Colts could purchase up to eight each. It was a way for the expansion teams to acquire some much-needed talent, and a way for the other eight teams to get $30,000 each for their four worst players.

Jack Fisher was ready to pitch any time, as a starter, in long relief or in short relief. He suffered through consecutive 20-loss seasons with the bad Mets teams of the mid–'60s, but always gave one hundred percent on the mound.

Paul Richards said that when he saw the caliber of the available players, he asked to have the whole plan scrapped. Most of the potential draftees, Richards said, could either be obtained for the $20,000 waiver price or for $25,000 in the draft. Why should he pay $30,000?

The Mets made only two selections and the Colts one. New York chose Fisher from the Giants and 20-year-old first baseman Bill Haas from the Dodgers. Haas, signed by Dodger scout Tommy Lasorda, had a phenomenal batting record in the minors. In 1962, he hit .368 at Reno, with 33 home runs and 144 RBI. The following year, he batted over .300 with both Santa Barbara and Albuquerque, and many baseball executives were surprised he was available. "I admit our first thought was there must be something wrong with him," said George Weiss. There was nothing physically wrong with Haas, other than the fact that he couldn't field, but the Dodgers apparently knew something. Still, Weiss believed Haas could play in New York, which he did. He played in Buffalo, New York and Auburn, New York, plus Williamsport, Pennsylvania. He never, however, played a game in Flushing Meadows, or any other major league stadium.

Despite the fact that Haas hit over .300 in spring training, the Mets sent him to Buffalo to start the '64 season. He needed to learn to field, Stengel said. Haas didn't play well in Buffalo and was demoted to Williamsport. For a week, he refused to report, then went down and played the same mediocre brand of ball he had displayed in St. Petersburg and Buffalo. "Too bad about Bill Haas," Dick Young wrote after the 1964 season, "who has so much natural talent, and is so wasteful of it that the Mets have seen fit to outright him to Buffalo." The Mets had taken a $30,000 gamble and lost.

The Mets certainly got their money's worth from Fisher. During the winter of 1963, the Mets and Giants traded coaches, with Cookie Lavagetto, who had some health problems, going to the Giants so he could be closer to his Oakland home, and Wes Westrum coming to New

York. Westrum, an old catcher, was a shrewd judge of pitching talent, and when he recommended his old charge Fisher, Weiss selected him. Despite having five years in the big leagues, Fisher was only 25, and his arm was sound. The Mets could use any sound arm with major league ability, and Fisher quickly won a place in the starting rotation.

In 1964, his first year with the Mets, Fisher won 10 games and lost 17, starting 34 times and relieving in six other games. The ten wins tied Roger Craig's team record for most wins by a right handed pitcher. The following year, Fisher, who reduced from 230 to 215 pounds during the winter, was even busier, with 36 starts and seven relief appearances. On May 2, Fisher started the first game of a doubleheader against the Reds and was knocked out in the fourth inning, taking the loss. In the second game, with the Mets short of pitchers, he volunteered to relieve and lost again. During the first week of June, 1965, Fisher won his fifth game, and had a 5–4 mark, with a fine 3.14 ERA. He had won five of six decisions, had the most wins of any Met pitcher, and by far the best ERA of any starter. Fisher had a good chance of beating Al Jackson's Met mark of 13 wins, and of besting Carl Willey's team record 3.10 ERA.

By the end of the season, both Jackson and Willey's records were safe, but Fisher established Met standards for starts and innings pitched, and tied another mark, an unenviable one set by Roger Craig in 1962. In the first start after his fifth win, Fisher was locked in a tight duel with Gaylord Perry of the Giants in the eighth inning, when a couple of bloop hits and a weak throw by Swoboda saddled him with a 4–2 loss. It was the beginning of a string of unbelievably bad fortune. Fisher lost 2–1 to Juan Marichal. He lost 2–0 to the Cardinals and ex-teammate Tracy Stallard. He lost 3–2 to the Astros in the bottom of the ninth. He lost 3–2 to the Giants and 2–1 to the Reds. On September 10, Fisher lost his 20th game. He lost his last 8 and 20 of his last 23 decisions. By the time the season was over, he had a record of 8–24, tying Craig's Met record for most losses in a season. Like Craig, however, Fisher had a respectable 3.93 ERA, and allowed less than a hit per inning. "Every time I walked out there," Fisher said, "I thought I could win. I lost 44 games in two years, but there was never a time I walked out there when I thought I wasn't going to win." There were many times that Fisher should have won, had he been pitching for any team other than the Mets.

The following spring, when Fisher received the Mets' first contract offer, he realized that Weiss viewed him as a 24 game loser, rather than a dependable workhorse who had been the victim of a bad team and some horrible luck. "We're worlds apart," said Johnny Murphy. He pointed to Fisher's weight, which had ballooned to 230, and added, "He expected to receive a raise that would have been merited by a 15–8 won-lost record." With a halfway decent team behind him, Fisher might have been 15–8. "The way I stated it to them," the pitcher said, "was that I lost 24 ballgames, but, by god, I was there for you every time and I lost a lot of tough games, not only from lack of hitting support, but lack of defense."

Fisher had indeed always been there for Stengel and Westrum. He started every four days. He relieved when he wasn't starting, sometimes the day after a start. Fisher was also the man the Mets turned to when they needed a gutty performance. There were a number of "Met killers" in the early '60s, pitchers New York just couldn't seem to beat, and Fisher took on each one of them. Juan Marichal won 19 straight before Fisher beat him. Bob Friend bested the Mets 12 times before Fisher beat him, and Larry Jackson posted 18 straight wins before he lost to Fisher in 1967. Fisher beat Bob Gibson in 1967. When Tug McGraw finally beat Sandy Koufax for the first Met win over the Dodger lefty, Fisher picked up the save.

The 1966 contract talks dragged on into training camp. Weiss wouldn't give in, despite the fact that Fisher was the only bona fide major league pitcher on the Met staff. Fisher was just as stubborn. He'd been the Mets' best pitcher, despite all the losses, and wanted more than just a token raise. "Finally," Fisher said, "I was down in spring training and I wasn't signed. I think the whole dispute was over two or three thousand dollars. They wouldn't let me work out. Then

Dick Young wrote an article in *The Daily News* and really came out on my side. After the article came out I got a call from George Weiss asking me to meet him at the Mets' hotel. I went in and stood my ground and suddenly, I got what I asked for. I think it was a whopping $30,000. No, it wasn't even that much. It was in the 20s."

In 1965, the Mets had little pitching depth. Al Jackson, in his fourth year as a Met starter, joined Fisher in the circle of twenty game losers, matching his 1962 mark by finishing with a record of 8–20. The highlight of his season came on July 21st in Pittsburgh. No one had pitched a no hitter at Forbes Field since it opened in 1909. No Met had ever thrown one. Jackson came closer than anyone had ever been to either feat, losing his bid with one out in the eighth and finishing with a two hit shutout.

In addition to leading the Mets in losses, Jackson and Fisher were also the leading winners, as no other pitcher had more than six victories. Carl Willey, still suffering from arm problems, was virtually useless, and spent most of the season in Buffalo. He was just 2–9 in the International League, and would never return to the majors. Larry Bearnarth's performance had declined each year since 1963, and he also spent part of the year at Buffalo. Galen Cisco suffered from tendinitis in his shoulder and won just four games.

There were 43 roster moves during the season. Pitchers shuttled between New York and Buffalo all year long, with little improvement. Jim Bethke went down, and Dennis Musgraves came up. Willey and Bearnarth went down and Larry Miller came up. Even Bob Moorhead, an original Met who had developed a knuckleball after hurting his arm, was called up in August. When he made his first Met appearance, *The New York Times* observed that it was his first major league outing in 35 months, considerably longer than it took Mars to revolve around the sun.

None of the young pitchers, Bethke, Musgraves, Dennis Ribant, Tom Parsons, or McGraw, contributed much, although 20-year-old McGraw had a number of good games late in the season. He finished 2–7 with a fine 3.31 ERA and gave the impression that, after some much-needed minor league seasoning, he would be back in New York.

With Swoboda and Kranepool slumping, and Hunt injured, the Mets faded badly in the second half of the season. It is difficult for a team that is 29–56 at the All Star break to fade, but the Mets managed to do it. They suffered through a number of double-digit losing streaks, and were a miserable 21–56 after the break. For a month, from early July through early August, they lost 26 of 31 games. On August 20, with more than a month to go, the Mets tied a record by losing their 425th game in four years, matching the mark set by the Phillies in 1938–41. They reached their usual milestones, being eliminated from the pennant race on August 16, losing their 100th game on September 11th and clinching last place on September 14. The Mets finished the season 50–112, the first time they had failed to win more games than they had the previous season. They were 47 games out of first place and 15 games behind the ninth place Colts, while posting their worst record since the 40 win season of 1962. Wes Westrum, who'd taken over for the ailing Stengel in July, played his youngsters in the latter stages of the season but, other than Swoboda, none seemed on the verge of stardom, or even of becoming a solid major league regular.

There was little help forthcoming from the minors, since all of the young players were already with the Mets. Buffalo, the Mets' Triple A club, had the worst record in the International League and was probably the sorriest Triple A club in baseball. Virtually every player on the team was an ex–Met who had been sent down. Sammy Drake, Duke Carmel, Joe Hicks and Dick Smith played the outfield, Pumpsie Green, Amado Samuel and Larry Burright patrolled the infield, and Choo Choo Coleman, Hawk Taylor and John Stephenson were the catchers. The pitching staff was made up of former Met stalwarts Craig Anderson, Ed Bauta, Jerry Hinsley, Ron Locke, Bill Hunter, Dennis Ribant, Carl Willey, Bill Wakefield, Don Rowe and Darrell Sutherland.

Shortstop Bud Harrelson was the only young prospect at Buffalo who hadn't yet played in

New York. With the rules requiring the Mets to keep five first year men, it seemed as though the Buffalo club was playing in New York and vice versa. Buffalo performed as would be expected for a team made up of players discarded by the Mets. The 1965 Bisons lost 55 of their first 75 games, finished last with a 51–96 record, and were on the verge of bankruptcy all season. "In my opinion," said Larry Miller, "Buffalo, with War Memorial Stadium, was the armpit of the world as far as baseball was concerned. It was cold. I was the opening day pitcher, and they had to scrape snow off the field. It was twenty-seven degrees and I thought, 'Man, I've been sent to the Foreign Legion.'"

After the end of the season, Westrum was named manager of the Mets for 1966. If the new manager wanted to keep the job, he would need to find a way to bring the team closer to respectability, a difficult chore given the available talent. "It's a young club," Kranepool said in December, "with young pitchers, and I'm sure we'll scare a few people." One of them was certain to be Westrum.

⬥ 11 ⬥

The First Wave

After finishing last three years in a row with veteran clubs, Weiss and Stengel knew the Mets had to begin to develop young players, particularly pitchers. They would have preferred to see the youngsters spend their teenage years in the minor leagues, but under baseball's controversial "first year" rule, which took effect in December, 1961, all players who had spent a year in the minors had to be carried on the major league roster or be exposed to the draft, where they could be claimed for $8,000.

For the Mets and Astros, who needed to develop more young players than the established clubs, the rule exacted a disproportionate penalty. They were punished at the minor league level by the inability to gain experience for their young prospects, and at the major league level by being forced to carry players who were clearly not ready for the big leagues. Paul Richards suggested that the expansion clubs be allowed to option two first year players without counting them against the roster. If the Dodgers carried two first year men, Richards reasoned, his Colts (he made his comments in the pre–Astro year of 1963) with their greater need to develop young players, had to carry six in order to catch up, and were thus playing 19 versus 23. For the 1964 season, the rule was amended and the expansion clubs were allowed to option four players, plus one designated player, who could be sent to the minors but counted against the major league roster.

The Mets' 1965 opening day roster, the youngest in the majors, was loaded with players who had just one year of professional experience. They included pitchers Tug McGraw (20) and Jim Bethke (18), infielder Kevin Collins (18) and outfielders Danny Napoleon (23) and Ron Swoboda (20), each of whom was on the club solely in order to avoid losing them in the draft.*

In addition to the five rookies on their roster, the Mets optioned pitcher Dennis Musgraves to Buffalo as the designated first year player, which meant that he counted against the major league 25 man roster. Thus, the Mets, who had finished last while operating at "full strength," were going to take on the National League with 24 men, five of whom were the rawest of rookies. In order to keep the youngsters, the Mets were forced to cut some players who might have helped them, most notably pitcher Bill Wakefield, who set a Met record in 1964 by making 62 appearances.†

Bethke, the least experienced rookie, was the first to prove his worth. Although his entire professional career to that point consisted of 29 innings in the low minors, Stengel brought

*The youth movement brought some unanticipated problems. During spring training in 1964, 20-year-old left hander Steve Dillon, while putting some tonic in his hair, threw his head back and sprained his neck. The injury wasn't serious.

†Wakefield also set a record for most appearances by any pitcher who spent only one season in the major leagues, for he never returned to the big leagues.

Bethke in on opening day against the Dodgers. "I threw three ground ball outs," Bethke said, "and from then on Casey called me his ground ball pitcher." Three days later, in the third game of the season, Bethke got his first major league victory when Bobby Klaus hit a 10th inning home run to beat the Astros. It was the earliest win in Met history, coming after only two losses.

Playing in the major leagues was a heady experience for the 18-year-old. "Everything was like a big vacation," Bethke said. "We went to Los Angeles. I'd never been to Los Angeles. I'd never been to San Francisco. That was the first year they played in the Astrodome. It was like a free vacation for a young kid."

Bethke continued to pitch well in relief, despite his youth and nearly complete lack of experience. "I had no fear," he said recently. "Casey had a quote somewhere that said I had the guts of a burglar. I just felt that was where I belonged or I wouldn't have been there. The longer I was there, the more I felt I belonged." In early July, despite a 2–0 record in 17 games and a relatively low ERA, Bethke was optioned to Buffalo. "I had a clause in my contract," he said, "that I was to get a $7,500 bonus if I stayed 90 days. It was about the 88th or 89th day that they shipped me back."

When the Mets sent Bethke to Buffalo, they recalled Musgraves, a 6'4", 185 pound right hander who had been signed the previous summer for a $100,000 bonus, the largest ever given to a Met player. Musgraves attended the University of Missouri, but had not pitched very much. Freshmen were not allowed to play varsity ball at that time, and the Missouri frosh played just two games, a doubleheader against Warrensburg State College. Musgraves pitched in one of those games, and hurled a no-hitter. As a sophomore, his only varsity season, Musgraves pitched another no-hitter, finished the season with six wins and one loss and led the Tigers to second place in the NCAA tournament.

Despite his limited collegiate experience, Musgraves received offers from the Cardinals, Astros and Mets. His father handled the negotiations, and Musgraves wasn't all that interested until he heard the Mets had offered $100,000, far more than any other club. "That's more money than I had ever dreamed about," he said. "It was hard to believe they would do that. The Mets were a young team, and I guess they were looking for a few pitchers to help them out of the dungeon." Musgraves lost no time putting his name on a contract, and was assigned to the Mets' Triple A Buffalo team, pretty fast company for someone with his meager experience. He was 0–1 at Buffalo and 3–6 at Williamsport of the Eastern League during the second half of the 1964 season. "I felt they were expecting a lot of me just out of college," Musgraves said. "I was just a green kid. I didn't know anything and I put a lot of pressure on myself." After the season, Musgraves played winter ball, where he had the opportunity to pitch against major league hitters. After another half season in Buffalo, the Mets felt he was ready for the majors, despite his 2–5 record. Bethke's 90 days were almost up, and, in order to option him without subjecting him to the draft, the Mets had to call up Musgraves, the designated player.

On July 9, Musgraves made his major league debut at Shea Stadium, relieving against the Astros in front of 30,000 people, by far the largest crowd he had ever pitched before. "I was beginning to wonder if I was going to make it to the mound," he recalled, "my knees were wobbling so bad coming out of the bullpen." Musgraves made it to the mound and pitched three innings of one hit shutout ball. Three more strong relief efforts earned the bonus boy a start against the Cubs at Wrigley Field. Musgraves pitched very well, lasting seven innings, giving up only one run, but was not involved in the decision.

"The next day," Musgraves recalled, "my elbow had swollen up and was locked at a ninety degree angle." He had bursitis, and figured it would go away. It didn't. A few days later in Philadelphia, he was asked to warm up in the bullpen, but couldn't even reach the catcher. Musgraves was placed on the disabled list in mid–August and pitched no more that season. He was operated on during the winter, but still had pain throughout 1966 and pitched only 26 innings, all in the minor leagues.

A second operation, in which a bone was removed from his elbow, seemed to work, and Musgraves went back to the minors and attempted to build up his arm. He was put in the bullpen and, his fastball nothing more than a fond memory, relied on curve balls and change-ups. "I wasn't the same type of pitcher I was earlier," Musgraves said. "I relied more on control. I still had good movement on my fastball and felt that I was pitching well and getting people out." He was praised for his work ethic, his fine attitude and the fact that he hadn't just taken his $100,000 and gone home when the going got tough.

Musgraves had some success in the bullpen. While Tom Seaver, Jerry Koosman and Tug McGraw led the Mets to the world championship in 1969, he was 7–1 in Tidewater. There was a limited major league market, however, for a veteran reliever who relied on finesse, and Musgraves was eventually released by the Kansas City Royals, ending his professional career. For their $100,000, the Mets received five appearances, sixteen innings and a 0.56 ERA.

When the Mets placed Musgraves on the disabled list, they recalled Bethke from Buffalo. He finished the year with the Mets and, from that point on, his career paralleled that of Musgraves. Pitching in the minor leagues in 1966, he hurt his arm. "When you're young," he said, "sometimes you throw and you don't even know you've hurt yourself." Bethke became aware his arm wasn't right when he tried to warm up for the start of an inning and was so tight he had to come out of the game. After that, he could never cut loose again. "It's a fear factor," he said. "You're afraid to cut loose. I felt something snap and that was the beginning of the end. I still felt I was a decent pitcher, but I just never had the speed I had when I was young."

Like Musgraves, Bethke continued to pitch in the minors for several years. "I learned real quick," he said of his time with the Mets, "what it took to get there and stay there. The hardest part was being able to get back, which I never did." Like Musgraves, Bethke wound up with the Royals, believing that he would have a better chance to return to the majors with an expansion club. In 1971, he was still in the minors, and had acquired a wife and daughter. More importantly, Bethke saw baseball differently that he had as an 18-year-old in Shea Stadium, when anything seemed possible. "It just wasn't the same game to me anymore," he said recently. Pitching in the California League, Bethke caught his spikes on the mound and seriously injured his knee. The knee was placed in a cast for several weeks, and Bethke decided to retire. Exit a second Met prospect. "I think that I probably threw better in New York than anywhere else," Bethke said recently. "I'm not sure why. Maybe it was concentration."

On the last day of August, 1965, the Mets purchased another youngster, 20-year-old left-hander Rob Gardner, from their Buffalo farm club. Originally signed by the Twins, Gardner made a spectacular debut in organized ball. In 1963, with Orlando of the Florida State League, he was 16–11, with a 2.22 ERA and a league leading 213 strikeouts. The Twins elected to gamble and not protect Gardner on their major league roster. The Mets, desperate for young talent, drafted him in December, 1963. "I was disappointed," Gardner said. "I liked the Twins, and knew their pitching staff wasn't terribly strong. I thought I might have a chance there after starting my career on such a high note. I was probably dreaming a bit, but I was disappointed. Then I thought about the Mets' staff, and believed there was no reason I shouldn't be able to make that club. By the time I went to spring training, I was very enthusiastic."

Gardner didn't make the Met staff in '64, and began the season at Buffalo. After only three appearances, he was demoted to Salinas of the California League. "I won a game and lost a game," he recalled, "and then I made the manager mad. Back then, if you were a teenage rookie, like I was, you were supposed to hold to the party line and shut your mouth. I kind of annoyed [manager] Whitey Kurowski with a couple of things I said, and wound up in Salinas."

The demotion should have been a lesson to Gardner, but it wasn't. "I hated Salinas," he said. "We would get 'fogged out.' About the sixth inning a fog would roll in and they'd have someone hit a few pop flies. If the infielders could see them and catch them, the game continued.

If they hit them on the head they would call the game." When a local reporter asked Gardner what he thought of the city, Gardner, believing he was off the record, replied, "It's a great place to be if you're a head of lettuce." The writer published the quote and, rather than take the remark as a compliment to the city's tremendous agricultural output, fans deluged the youngster with letters defending Salinas and asking how he could say such terrible things about their home town.

Throughout his career, Gardner continued to court controversy. Speaking the party line was simply not in his makeup. When he was with the Mets, he once received a derogatory letter from a Yankee fan, which said something to the effect that while the fans at Shea Stadium were carrying around Mom's bedsheet and drinking beer, he'd rather be at Yankee Stadium drinking champagne. He also mentioned that he was a mechanic for American Airlines. Rather than ignore the letter, Gardner replied. The way the Yankees were playing (this was the mid-'60s, when Yankee fortunes had begun to decline), he said, they were lucky to even have beer over at Yankee Stadium. This prompted another letter from the fan telling Gardner how bad he and the Mets were. "I foolishly — very foolishly — wrote back again," Gardner said, "saying, 'I see why there are so many planes going down these days with you as a mechanic.' It was a pissing contest that didn't need to be. I was a wise ass."

Sometimes it wasn't Gardner's fault. Willie Mays was normally a terror against left handed pitchers, but for some reason, Gardner seemed to have his number. Dick Young of *The Daily News* asked him about it. "Well," Gardner replied, "if either he dies or I die, he'll never get a hit off me." The next day, Young wrote something to the effect that Gardner hoped that Mays died. "Do you think I got any hate mail over that?" he asked. "Oh, my God. And this was from New York fans, not San Francisco fans."

After pitching poorly at Salinas in 1964, Garner was sent briefly to Williamsport of the Eastern League, then to Auburn of the New York-Penn League, where he finally salvaged his season with a 9–1 record. He split the next year between Williamsport and Buffalo, pitching well enough to merit a September recall by the Mets.

Gardner made his major league debut the day after he arrived. "When I was called up from Buffalo," he recalled, "they had me go straight to the hotel rather than the ballpark because I got in late. I was watching the game on TV and saw my name up on the scoreboard as tomorrow's starter. That's how I found out I was pitching. Naturally, I got a good night's sleep after that."

Gardner faced the Astros in the second game of a doubleheader at Shea. "I was extremely nervous," he said. "There were 50,000 people there [there were actually 13,880 but to a rookie accustomed to pitching in Buffalo's cavernous War Memorial Stadium it must have seemed like 50,000. Moreover, 13,000 Met fans could sound like 50,000, and I couldn't hear anything but that yelling and screaming. I couldn't hear my catcher. I couldn't hear my infielders. I couldn't hear anything."

The first hitter for the Astros was light-hitting shortstop Bob Lillis. He hit a lazy pop up to short left field. "I'm thinking," said Gardner, "my first out in the big leagues. That wasn't too tough. Then I looked out to left field. Ron Swoboda did two pirouettes and fell down. It went for a double." Two batters later, Swoboda butchered another fly ball. Third baseman Charley Smith booted a grounder. Rusty Staub hit a three run homer and, before the first inning was over, the Astros had five runs. In the third inning, Jim Gentile hit a two run homer, a monstrous blast that hit halfway up the scoreboard. Gardner left the game, having surrendered six hits and seven runs.

Fortunately, Gardner's next four starts were good ones. In his final outing, on the next-to-last day of the season, the young lefty made his case for 1966. Pitching against the Phillies in Connie Mack Stadium, he worked 15 scoreless innings in a game that lasted eighteen. "I was almost out of that game in the fourth inning." Gardner recalled. The bases were loaded with two out and there was a 3–2 count on powerful Phillie first baseman Dick Stuart. "I thought, I'm not going to walk this guy," Gardner said. "I don't care if he hits it out or not. I just threw the ball as hard as I could and he swung right through it. As I walked off the mound, he looked at me and shook his head. I shrugged my shoulders as if to say, 'I don't know why you didn't hit it, either.'"

Later in the game, Richie Allen hit a fly ball that Cleon Jones caught near the center field fence, which was 447 feet from home plate. Inning after inning went by, and Gardner matched Philadelphia left hander Chris Short zero for zero. The season was nearly over, hitters were swinging freely, and Gardner had several easy innings. His arm felt fine. It was, by far, the longest a Met pitcher had ever shut out the opposition in one game.

"I think that record's going to last a long time," Gardner said. "In the year 2250, they'll say 'The modern day record is eight scoreless innings in a row, but way back in 1965, some guy named Rob Gardner pitched 15 scoreless innings.' It will be a trivia question and that's pretty cool."

In 1966, bolstered by his 1965 performance and a strong spring, Gardner made the Met opening day roster. He started out well, and pitched two consecutive four-hitters in May. "I had a lot of confidence at that point," he recalled. Then, Gordon Richardson, the Mets' only left-handed reliever, got hurt, and Manager Westrum told Gardner he needed him in the bullpen. Gardner had been a starter his entire career, and couldn't adapt to the bullpen duty. "I was not a power pitcher," he said. "I always threw the ball on the outside part of the plate with some movement, hoping to get a ground ball. The first thing to go when you don't pitch a lot is control of your breaking ball. Going to the bullpen did not help me at all." Gardner's season began to deteriorate, and he finished with a 4–8 record and a 5.10 ERA in 41 games.

The following spring, Gardner was sent to the minor leagues. "When Westrum was giving me the bad news," Gardner said, "He told me, 'I should have started you every four days last year, but I can't use you this year.' I never did quite understand that." Gardner pitched at Jacksonville for a while and was traded to the Cubs in June.

The year before Bethke, Musgraves and Gardner debuted, Jerry Hinsley had been the Mets' first beardless wonder. Hinsley was a high school phenom in New Mexico, racking up a 35–0 record, with three no-hitters. He was pursued by many teams, including the Mets. The Pirates signed him and sent him to Kingsport of the Appalachian League, where they tried to avoid the consequences of the first year rule by hiding him, which was a common ploy that rarely seemed to work. Whenever a highly touted prospect didn't play at all during his first year in the minors, the assumption was that he was being hidden, and therefore he was likely to be drafted.

Hinsley was on the Kingsport roster all year, but didn't pitch a single inning. In order to scare away any teams that might be interested in drafting him, the Pirates told everyone he had a bad arm. "There were four of us," Hinsley recalled. "We were all injured. One had a bad leg. I had a bad shoulder." Three of the four eventually made it to the major leagues. In addition to Hinsley, the other two were pitchers Bill Rohr, who nearly threw a no-hitter against the Yankees in his first major league start, and Dick Bosman, who went on to a fine career with the Washington Senators and led the American League in earned run average in 1969. None of the three ever pitched for the Pirate organization that tried so hard to protect them.

The Met scout who had pursued Hinsley in high school was not thrown off the trail by the sore arm story. He met Hinsley in Kingsport, told him that the Mets would have signed him if he'd just waited a few days, and asked him about his arm. "They told me to say I have a bad shoulder," Hinsley told him, "so that's what I'm saying." That winter, the Mets drafted Hinsley off the Pirate minor league roster.

In 1964, Hinsley arrived at the Met spring training camp even greener than Bethke. At least

Bethke threw 29 innings in the low minors. Hinsley had not faced a single professional hitter, and was a year younger than the Mets' batboy. "One year I was in high school," he recalled, "and the next year I was pitching in the big leagues." With no point of reference, Hinsley threw like he did as a schoolboy. "That's really all I could do," he said. "I had a fastball, a curve and a changeup and that's all I could throw. They put down a fastball sign and I threw it."

Like Bethke, Hinsley showed no fear of major league hitters. He didn't really expect to make the team but, throwing smoothly, he had several good exhibition performances. Stengel, who loved youngsters, championed Hinsley's cause and convinced Weiss to take him north on the Met roster.

In addition to pitching, Hinsley had another job — newspaper columnist. Barney Kremenko of the *Journal-American* decided to publish, in diary form, the observations of a Met rookie. It was a difficult decision for Kremenko, who had to choose early in the spring which rookie he thought might make the team, for if the player was cut, the column would come to an abrupt end. From Ron Swoboda, Dick Selma and Hinsley, he chose the latter. Each day in the *Journal-American*, Hinsley shared his thoughts with New York baseball fans. "I was supposedly keeping a diary and writing down my thoughts every night," Hinsley recalled. "Actually, I didn't do it. Barney did."

After a few good relief appearances, Hinsley got his first major league start on May 10 against the Cardinals at Shea. He had a splendid beginning. In the first inning, he set the Cardinals down 1-2-3. He did the same in the second. In the third, he set them down 1–2. There was no three. The Cardinals got five hits in a row and Stengel came to the mound. "Casey would say something like, 'That's all right, kid,' Hinsley recalled, "'We'll get 'em next time. We're going to get you right back in there. Don't you worry about it. See that gal right above our dugout — that blonde — I wonder how she'd be with a man on.'" A few seconds later, Hinsley departed with a man on and his first big league loss.

Later there was a second start in San Francisco, another three inning stint enlivened by an encounter with Willie Mays. In the clubhouse meeting before the game, the pitchers and catchers were going over the Giant hitters. "It usually doesn't matter who the hitter is," said Hinsley. "In those meetings it's always — fastball in, slider low and away. Well, if you can do that, you're going to get everybody out." But in this meeting, someone said, "When Mays comes up, just knock him on his tail. That's the best way to handle him." "Who am I to knock down Willie Mays?" Hinsley thought. But there was a fine of $25 for failing to honor a knockdown sign, and Hinsley didn't want to pay the $25. Therefore, Willie must go down.

Mays came up in the first inning and Hinsley sent him flying. "His bat and helmet went one way and he went the other," Hinsley recalled. "I just put him on his back." Mays was so intimidated he was barely able to struggle to his feet and hit a triple.

The next day, Mays beckoned Hinsley during batting practice. "Hey, kid," he said, "come here." Mays asked Hinsley if he had been throwing at him the night before. Of course Hinsley said he wasn't. The ball had just gotten away from him. Mays, long a favorite target of National League pitchers, had heard that one before. "Kid," Mays said, "you've got to get a couple more years in this league before you're entitled to throw at me." "Yes, sir," Hinsley replied, "I realize that." "But let me give you a pointer," Mays continued. "If you want to hit somebody, throw behind their back. If you just want to knock them down, throw at their head." "I said, 'Thank you, Mr. Mays,'" Hinsley recalled. "I'll remember that."

While Hinsley was not intimidated by pitching in the big leagues, the adjustment to living alone in New York City was difficult for a youngster who had just turned 19. If a teenager were far from home, like Hinsley, he generally had little companionship. He couldn't go out drinking with his teammates, since he was underage, which ruled out the primary form of major league social life. "I felt very much out of place," recalled Lou Klimchock, who joined the Kansas City Athletics as a teenager. "Although the guys treated me very well, I was pretty much of a loner, hanging out by myself."

"After the game was over," said Bill Denehy, a 21-year-old rookie in 1967, "all the wives went home with their husbands and I was left to myself. It was kind of tough, because there was no one to hang around with. There was really no one my age. Everybody else was older. After every game, I went back to my apartment by myself. Tommy Davis was great. The first day of every road trip, he would take me, Seaver and Don Shaw and show us a place to eat, a steakhouse or someplace like that. That way, at least we knew one place we could go after the game."

A native of New Mexico, Hinsley was intimidated by New York, and he was lonely. "I was in an old hotel with no TV," he recalled. "I was really down, and called my dad and told him I was thinking of coming home. He said, 'Son, you've got to do what you've got to do, but you worked awfully hard to get there. That's all I'm going to say.'" Hinsley decided to stay.

At the end of May, the Mets solved Hinsley's social dilemma by sending him to Buffalo. They maintained high hopes for him, and thought he might win a starting job in '65. Hinsley wound up being sent to the minors, however, and while pitching in the Eastern League, had his jaw broken by a line drive off the bat of Reggie Smith. "You heard the crack," said teammate Shaun Fitzmaurice. "God, it was the most sickening thing I ever remember." Hinsley returned to spring training the following year and claimed the injury never affected his pitching, but despite hurling in the minors until 1974, the former 19-year-old phenom pitched in only two more major league games.

Did coming up to the majors at such a young age have a detrimental impact on Hinsley's career? "Looking back," he said, "I think I would have been better off going to Double A ball. I didn't realize it at the time, and maybe I don't even realize it now, but I'm sure it did something to my confidence. There was no way I was ready for the big leagues. It probably hurt me more than it helped me."

The parade of young Met pitchers seemed endless. In December, 1965, the club drafted 20-year-old left hander Bill Hepler from the Washington Senators organization. The Mets either had to keep Hepler in 1966, or send him back to the Senators, and decided to keep him. Hepler pitched well in relief, and got a start against the Phillies in early July. He went into the sixth inning with a 1–0 lead and a one hitter. Unfortunately, Hepler had walked seven, and, having not pitched more than a couple of innings at a stretch, was tiring rapidly. "In those days," he said, "you expected nine innings and throw as many pitches as it took to get a win. Nowadays, they probably would have cut me off at about 90 pitches, but I was throwing good, really fluid." Hepler gave up three runs in the sixth, lost the game and started only twice more the rest of the year. "In my third start," he said, "I went seven innings against Houston and then didn't start again. I was very surprised. In those days, you didn't converse too much with your managers and coaches about how you were doing. I just went with the flow and pitched in relief, but I never got another start."

Overall, Hepler had a good year, finishing 3–3 for a last place team, with a good 3.52 ERA. "The guys were telling me I was going to be in the major leagues for ten or fifteen years," Hepler said. "'You've got the stuff,' they said. 'You can do it.'" Hepler went to the Dominican Republic and pitched during the winter, and read in the paper that he had been sent to the minors. "They never called me," he said. In 1967, Hepler started the year in Double A ball and was demoted to A ball. "I went from A ball to the major leagues back to A ball in less than two years," he said. Hepler bounced around the minors for a couple of years, hurt his arm, and retired. Another Met pitching prospect had appeared and disappeared with barely a trace. "I think I would have done well if I'd gone through the farm system like I should have," Hepler said recently. "The draft really hurt me. If I'd pitched in Double A or Triple A the second year, I think I would have been a major leaguer for quite some time."

One of the brightest Met pitching prospects of the mid-'60s was righthander Dick Selma, who first appearing in the Met camp as a 20-year-old in 1964. Selma was a Californian who attended the same high school that produced major league pitchers Dick Ellsworth and Jim Maloney, and many thought he threw as hard as the fireballing Maloney. Selma led the California League in strikeouts in 1963, fanning 224 in 185 innings, and showed exceptional poise for a 20-year-old. Stengel said he had a chance to make the team.

Selma didn't make the team that year, nor did he stick the following spring. After striking out 164 in 136 minor league innings, he was called up from Buffalo in September, 1965, and made an immediate impression. In his second start, Selma set a Met record with 13 strikeouts against the Braves. "He's the best pitcher the Mets ever put out there on the mound," said Brave manager Bobby Bragan.

Selma made the Met squad in 1966, and early in May was named the number one Met reliever. He didn't set the world on fire, and shortly thereafter was supplanted as the bullpen ace by Jack Hamilton. Westrum said Selma needed to learn another pitch to complement his fastball, and sent him to the minors. Selma spent part of the season at Jacksonville as a starter, and appeared in 30 Met games, posting a 4–6 record.

In August, 1964, the Mets acquired 6'6" 230 pound right hander Gary Kroll from the Phillies. Kroll, 23, could throw exceptionally hard, and, in 1960, struck out 309 men in the California League, including 19 in one game, while posting a 17-11 record.

Unlike Hinsley, Kroll had not been a star pitcher in high school. "When the Phillies signed me," he said, "I'd never pitched. I was working out at a park in LA, and one of the scouts came out and said, 'Hey, do you want to sign?' I said, 'Sure.' He said he was gong to sign me as a pitcher. I said I'd never pitched before, and he said they'd send me down to the instructional league and see what I could do. If I couldn't do any good, they'd send me back home."

Kroll did good. "I finished third in strikeouts," he said, "third in ERA and pitched a no hitter. The next year I threw another no hitter and had over 300 strikeouts." In 1962, Kroll won 12 straight games at Williamsport. "He throws aspirins," said Frank Lucchesi, his manager at Arkansas in 1963. The Phillies brought Kroll to the big leagues in 1964, but when they needed a veteran hitter for the stretch run, sent him to the Mets for Frank Thomas. Kroll didn't pitch much for the Mets in '64, appearing in only eight games, but he went to spring training the next year with a good chance to make the starting rotation.

"Everyone says there's never been a no hitter by a Met pitcher," Kroll said. "The only one who picked up on that was Don Sutton, when he was announcing for the Braves. He named the pitchers. It was against the Pirates in spring training. I pitched the first six innings and Gordon Richardson pitched the last three."

Kroll made the team in 1965, and pitched both as a starter and in relief. In August, with a 6–6 record for a last place club, he was sent to Buffalo. "Dick Schapp wrote a funny article about it," Kroll recalled. "He said that Gary Kroll got sent to Buffalo because he was too good. He had a 6–6 record and it was embarrassing the team."

Kroll refused to report to Buffalo. He wrote to the Mets and said that if he couldn't pitch in the major leagues, he would finish his education (he was a student at Brigham Young University) and find another occupation. Kroll eventually relented, and worked his way back to the major leagues, pitching for the Astros and Indians. He had arm surgery, and wound up his career pitching only 160 big league innings. Another Met phenom bit the dust.

In 1965, during baseball's first free agent draft, the Mets made a 6'5" left handed pitcher from Montana named Leslie Norvin Rohr their first pick. Based upon their last place finish in 1964, the Mets had the second selection, and after the Athletics tabbed Arizona State outfielder Rick Monday, the Mets chose Rohr. The new Met was born in Lowestoft, England in 1946, son of an American GI and an English war bride, and came to the United States at the age of four months. In the anonymity of rural Montana, he became an overpowering pitcher who dominated the local competition. "My last year of Legion ball," he said, "I won 23 games, lost none and my ERA was 0.64 or something like that." After having seen fellow Montanan Dave McNally receive a bonus estimated at $80,000, Rohr was a bit disappointed to get only $50,000 after being the second player drafted. The owners' plan was working. McNally had 16 teams bidding for him. Rohr had one.

After he signed, Rohr spent a few days with the Mets before reporting to the minor leagues. Pitching coach Warren Spahn said Rohr reminded him of former Yankee pitcher Rollie Sheldon, an odd comparison for the nation's second draft choice. Spahn also said Rohr had major league stuff but needed to learn control.

Rohr didn't pitch like a first round draft choice in the minor leagues. In his first two years, he was wild, and posted a record of 8–19. Rohr spent part of 1967 in the service, then made his first Met appearance in September, getting three starts at the end of the season. He beat the Dodgers twice, besting Don Drysdale with a shutout on the last day of the season. Like Musgraves and Dick Rusteck (see below), Rohr began his Met career in spectacular fashion, and like them, he was destined to fizzle out just as quickly.

In 1968, Rohr hurt his elbow, and, after starting the season in the major leagues, moved in rapid succession through Triple A and Double A all the way down to A ball, finishing the year with Raleigh-Durham of the Carolina League. In the meantime, the Mets were developing young pitchers like Tom Seaver, Jerry Koosman, Nolan Ryan, Jim McAndrew and Gary Gentry, and opportunities were becoming scarce. The wide open staff of 1967 had become a very exclusive fraternity. Rohr was called up to the Mets for the last few weeks of the 1969 season, but pitched just one inning in his final major league appearance. He ruptured a disk in his back, bounced around the minors for a while and retired. His big league career consisted of just 24 innings in six games. The two wins against the Dodgers were the only victories of his career.

"I wish I could have stayed around another year or two," Rohr said recently. "I just wish I could have gotten comfortable on the mound like when I pitched Legion ball. That's all I needed and you probably would have seen a left handed Nolan Ryan. If I hadn't gotten hurt ... but that's life. I guess you just have to take what comes."

Like so many youngsters from small towns, Rohr had difficulty adjusting to big league life. "I was young and dumb back then," he said. "You think you know everything, but you don't. I wish I would've done things a little differently. When you're a hick from Montana and you go to New York City, you have to grow up in a hurry. There isn't anything like it. It was a neat experience and I learned a lot, but I wish I'd have done things a little differently. I'm 57 years old and I would like to be 18 again and know what I know now." He laughed. We both knew he would never be 18 again, and that he would never be a left handed Nolan Ryan.

In June of 1966, the right handed Ryan was setting strikeout marks in the South Atlantic League, Hinsley, Bethke and Musgraves were in the minor leagues, and Kroll was pitching for the Astros. The Mets, with a hole in their rotation, recalled lefthander Dick Rusteck from Jacksonville. Rusteck was not a teenager like Bethke and Hinsley. He had a degree in economics from Notre Dame and had pitched in the minors since 1963. Rusteck had been 6–1 in Triple A ball when he was called up, completing seven games in eight starts and compiling an excellent ERA of 1.57.

On June 10, Rusteck made his major league debut against the hard-hitting Cincinnati Reds, who featured Pete Rose, Tony Perez, Vada Pinson and Deron Johnson, who had led the National League in RBI the previous season. "I was kind of nervous," Rusteck said, "just wondering if I would have really good stuff. I constantly tried to remind myself to just pitch the way I'd been pitching. I was just too nervous, too much of a rookie, to realize what I was about to undertake."

In his first big league start, Rusteck threw a four hit shutout. "I had really, really good stuff in that game," he recalled. "My fastball was moving all over the place. The ball was moving real late. It would come up to the plate and the last few feet it would just take off somewhere. That was a fun night. It was the most fun I've ever had."

It appeared that, after years of searching, after watching Jay Hook and Craig Anderson fail, and seeing Hinsley, Bethke and Musgraves struggle and depart, the Mets had finally found a dominating young pitcher. It was not just the fact that Rusteck won, or that he pitched a shutout. His stuff had been overpowering. He made Pete Rose look helpless. "I got Pete Rose out four times just on fastballs. I pitched him up and in, low and away, up and away and low and in," Rusteck said. "He didn't do much with any of those fastballs."

Westrum could hardly wait for Rusteck to make his next start. "Four days later," Rusteck recalled, "I tried to pick up a ball and I could hardly lift my arm. I had a real sharp pain in my shoulder. They pleaded with me to start, because after pitching a shutout, how could you possibly not come out for your next turn?"

"Things are looking up," Westrum said before the game, but Rusteck's second start was as bad as the first one had been good. He never got out of the second inning, as the Cardinals hammered him for five runs in a 9–2 loss.

Rusteck made a few more appearances before going on the disabled list in mid–July. He was sent back to Jacksonville in August with a 1–2 record in 24 innings. Like Bethke and Musgraves, Rusteck never pitched in the majors again. His shoulder finally felt better the next spring, but then he hurt his elbow and never regained his velocity. "If I could throw the way I did in that game," he said of his debut, "I could have stayed up there a long time. But I never threw like that again. I had to realize that I could no longer overpower somebody. I had to learn to pitch a little smarter and not just have the feeling of knowing that I was going to get somebody out."

Rusteck had an elbow operation after the 1967 season, and bounced around in the minors for several years, haunted by ill fortune. In 1968, he was walking down a Rochester street when a piece of glass from a building fell on him, opening a cut that required seventeen stitches in his right shoulder. Rusteck won 17 games in Double A ball in the Twins organization in 1971, was drafted by the Phillies and promoted to Triple A the following year. "By that time," he said, "I was already 30 years old and I knew that if I didn't knock somebody's socks off I was pretty much done." He was right. The Phillies released him in 1972 and his career was over, save for a brief stint with the independent Portland Mavericks in 1975.

The most effective of the first wave of young Met pitchers was righthander Dennis Ribant, a hyperactive 165 pound ball of fire who was acquired from the Braves in 1964 for veteran pitcher Frank Lary. The trade was a typical mid-season transaction. The Braves, fighting for a pennant, got a seasoned veteran in return for a youngster who could not help them immediately. The Mets lost a veteran who was not going to be around by the time they were ready to contend for a pennant, and obtained a youngster who might be.

Ribant certainly had potential. He'd posted a combined record of 21–4 for Quad Cities and Austin in 1961, completing 17 of his 19 starts at Quad Cities, with an earned run average well below 2.00. After pitching more than 200 innings that year, Ribant went to the instructional league and threw another thirty or forty. By the time he got to spring training, his arm was dead. Ribant began the season in Triple A ball, but was hit hard and sent back to Austin.

During the winter between the 1963 and 1964 seasons, Ribant pitched in the Caribbean and returned with a sore elbow. The Milwaukee team doctor suggested he sit out the entire season to allow his arm to heal, but Ribant would have none of that. He wanted to pitch. The Braves assumed he would not pitch very well, and dropped him from the 40-man roster. When he started the season 9–1 at Denver of the Triple A Pacific Coast League, the Braves knew they would lose him in the major league draft at the end of the season. By trading him to the Mets, they were able salvage some value for him.

Ribant was ecstatic when he heard about the trade. Not only was he going to the major leagues, but with the last place Mets, he thought he would get a chance to start regularly. It was not to be, however, and for two years, Ribant shuttled between Buffalo and New York, and the starting rotation and the bullpen. By the end of the '65 season, he had compiled a major league record of just 2–8. His finest moment came in one of his first starts in 1964, when he pitched a four-hit shutout against the Pirates and struck out 10, tying the Met single game record that was later broken by Selma.

Ribant's work in early 1965 was spotty, and he was sent to Buffalo, where he had a losing record. When he was called up at the end of the season, Ribant threw eleven shutout innings against the Pirates in one game. While he did not get the decision, he convinced Westrum that he was ready for the major leagues in 1966.

In the early part of the '66 season, Ribant pitched primarily in relief. On May 8, just a few days before the roster had to be cut to 25, he finally got a chance to start, in the second game of a doubleheader against the Cubs. Ribant saved his job by pitching a complete game 5–1 victory, his first decision of the year.

It was a great performance under pressure, but Ribant was not the type to be intimidated. The big crowds at Shea pumped him up. "I'm cocky as hell," he said recently. "If I've got my good stuff and I'm throwing well, c'mon! I loved pitching in front of a lot of people. I'm very, very cocky and very confident if I've got my good fastball and slider."

"He was kind of a character," said Bethke. "He was feisty and had an air about him. They used to call him a little banty rooster. Everything about him was fast. He walked around real fast. He was a real go-getter." "Oh, boy, he was hyper," said Gordon Richardson. "After every pitch, he'd walk halfway to home plate to catch the ball. He was really, really hyper. He might not have had the best ability in the world, but he gave it all he had."

"Dennis was ADHD before it was discovered," said Gardner. "He was as hyper a guy as I've ever met in my life. I think it served him well because he was able to control that hyperactivity on the mound and focus it on what he wanted to do. It made him a pretty good pitcher." Ribant sometimes seemed to get hitters out with sheer determination. "He was a bulldog," said Bob Friend. "He was a fighter. He had good stuff, but not great stuff, and did it with a lot of fight and desire." "He went a long way on a big heart," said Al Luplow.

By mid–June, Ribant was still on the team, but had just his one win against the Cubs. On June 11th, in the first game of a twi-night doubleheader, he got another start and followed Rusteck's blanking of the Reds with a shutout, only the second time Met pitchers had ever done that in consecutive games.

Gardner started the second game of the doubleheader and, for a while, it appeared that no one would ever score another run against the Mets. With two out in the ninth inning, the Mets held a 2–0 lead and Gardner was mowing down the powerful Reds' lineup. He walked catcher Jim Coker and gave up a pinch-hit single to Tommy Helms. Westrum came to the mound. "Wes said 'How do you feel?'" Gardner recalled. "I said I felt fine. He turned to [catcher] Hawk Taylor and said, 'How's he throwing?' Hawk says, 'He's throwing good.' Then Wes said, 'OK, I'll get somebody else in here.' I was so mad. I have never been so upset. I don't think I have ever gotten over that."

Larry Bearnarth entered the game to a chorus of boos from the Met fans. Bearnarth immediately gave up singles to Tommy Harper and Vada Pinson to tie the game, and the Mets lost 5–2 in the 11th. The aura of invincibility was shattered.

Although Rusteck soon disappeared with arm trouble and Gardner was exiled to the bullpen, Ribant remained in the starting rotation and, as the Mets posted the best month in their history in July, became the team's hottest pitcher. By the end of the month he was 7–4, had won five of his last six decisions and led the staff in complete games with six. "I finally got a chance to start every five days," he said. "That was the key to my success."

For the rest of the season, Ribant was the ace of the staff. He became the first Met starter to finish a season with a record above .500, compiling an 11–9 mark. Ten of those wins had come after the middle of June. His ERA was a fine 3.21, and he walked just 40 men in 188 innings. Finally, it appeared, the Mets had found a young starting pitcher with potential for the future.

Met GM Bing Devine, however, thought the Mets needed a regular center fielder more than they needed a starting pitcher. In 1966, the Mets had used Cleon Jones in center, but Cleon was better suited to left or right. Rookie Billy Murphy, a draftee from the Yankees, could play center field, but wasn't ready to handle big league pitching. Al Luplow was a journeyman. The Mets needed a young center fielder they could build their team around. Devine believed the Pirates had such a player in Don Bosch, who had been the International League's All Star center fielder in 1966. In December, Ribant and a minor league player were traded to the Pirates for Bosch and veteran pitcher Don Cardwell. Ribant left unhappily. "It killed me," he said. "It broke my heart when I was traded to the Pirates. It took a while to get used to it because I loved New York. I was the first Met pitcher to have a winning record. It was a big disappointment."

From the group of young pitching prospects the Mets had brought to Shea Stadium, all they had left were sore arms and minor leaguers. In exchange for Ribant, who had been the best of the lot, they had a centerfielder who could supposedly field like Willie Mays. The Mets did have a former USC pitcher named Tom Seaver at Jacksonville, but Seaver had been just 12–12 in his first professional season. They also had a lefthander named Jerry Koosman, who was 12–7 at Auburn of the New York Penn League, and led the league in ERA, but the New York Penn League was a long way from the majors.

• 12 •

The Man in the Middle
Wes Westrum

At the beginning of the 1965 season, Casey Stengel was 74, and the years were starting to show just a bit more. Casey was unusual, but not immortal, and there would come a time when he would need to step down. It was clear that the Mets would never become a contending team under Stengel. He was a terrific public relations ambassador, but the Mets were in their fourth year and not really improving. The time for entertaining had passed and the luster of a new stadium wouldn't last forever. If the Mets were going to continue to draw fans in record numbers, they would eventually need to put a better product on the field. It was obvious that Stengel was not the long-term solution, but who was going to tell him to leave?

The 1964 season saw Stengel the target of more criticism than ever before in his Met career. Casey had been taking cat-naps on the bench since his days with the Yankees but, other than Howard Cosell, no one had made an issue of it. Most of the players found it amusing, at least until Stengel released or demoted them. In August, when the Mets released Tim Harkness, he lashed out at the Met manager. "Casey has been a great man for baseball as far as publicity is concerned," Harkness told an interviewer, "but the game has passed him by. Some players he likes and some he doesn't like. The players feel it and it isn't too inspiring when the manager goes to sleep on the bench during a game."

Three months earlier, Jackie Robinson had said, "One of the problems of the Mets is Stengel." Casey was too old, Robinson said, to direct a team. Dick Young disagreed. Casey may have been 74 years old, Young admitted, and he might have fallen asleep on the bench once or twice, Young said, but Stengel, when he was awake, exhibited the energy of a much younger man.

Rob Gardner remembered an incident from the 1964 spring camp. "The first day," Gardner said, "Casey gathered all of the rookie pitchers on the mound and was going to show them how to execute a pickoff move to first base. Here's this 73-year-old man, he had a wishbone leg; his leg was all bent and he looked like Quasimodo by that time, all bent over. He gets up on the mound and he jumps up in the air like he's making a motion to throw to first base. I was amazed. Of course, he was talking away. 'You do—and then—and then you JUMP!' and he jumps up in the air. Then he got a right hander in to try it. The kid was nervous. He was trying to jump up and make the same move Casey made, but his spike catches on the rubber and he almost falls down. Casey just turned and walked away, mumbling, 'Goddamn rookies, ya can't teach 'em nothing.'"

Casey was healthy, and still had his biting wit. Too many of Stengel's jokes, however, were at the expense of his team. When the All Star Game came to Shea Stadium, Casey remarked how unusual it was to have great players in Shea. In a 1965 game against the Braves, with the Mets losing 4–1, Stengel brought lefthander Larry Miller in to face the right-handed Henry Aaron. Aaron hit a three run homer, and Casey was asked after the game why he had brought in a lefty to pitch to Aaron. "You don't bring in the best surgeon," he said, "when the patient is already dead." Those kinds of jokes had been funny in 1962, but the Mets were trying to build a team, and Casey's frequent deprecation of his players was beginning to wear thin. His behavior was reminiscent of his last years with the Yankees, when he frequently belittled his young players to the media.

The day before Harkness unleashed his broadside, there were rumors that Stengel was going to leave the Mets at the end of the season and accept a front office position with the Angels. The Angels were based close to Stengel's Glendale home, and a front office position would lessen the travel demands that were becoming increasingly difficult for the septuagenarian. The rumors also hinted that the decision to leave New York was not Stengel's; Weiss and Mrs. Payson decided they needed a younger man, and Alvin Dark, manager of the Giants and an old Payson favorite in his playing days, was that man.

The Giant manager was expected to be available at the end of the season, for he had gotten himself in deep trouble for some remarks he made to a reporter. Dark, who was from Louisiana, was quoted as saying that one of the Giants' problems was that they had too many black and Latin ballplayers, who didn't possess the mental alertness or team spirit of the white players. Dark, who thought he had been speaking to a friend off the record, didn't specifically deny having made the remarks attributed to him, but asserted that he was not a racist. Jackie Robinson, who had played against Dark for many years, came to his defense. The day after the incident became public, Horace Stoneham, owner of the Giants, denied that he had any intention of dismissing Dark. It was the proverbial kiss of death, and Dark was fired as soon as the season ended. He was available if the Mets forced Stengel to step down.

Stengel responded testily to the rumors of his impending departure. He had not made up his mind what he was going to do in 1965, he said, and would let the Associated Press know when he did. Weiss, mindful of the storm that had been unleashed when the Yankees fired Casey, tread softly. "It has always been up to Casey whether or not he comes back," Weiss said. Weiss spoke in the past tense, and a careful reading of the quote did not necessarily indicate that the decision would be up to Casey this time.

Dark did not become manager of the Mets. On September 29, the Mets announced that Stengel would return for the 1965 season, with an increase in pay. The decision had been Casey's all along, insisted Donald Grant, and when Stengel gave the word that he wanted to return, that was it. Stengel talked of the improvement the Mets had made during the season, although at that point, with just five games left, they had yet to surpass 1963's win total.

Casey returned to the Mets and, in April, won his 3000th game as a professional manager. In May, at West Point for an exhibition game, he was rendered *hors de combat*. Stengel was walking up a steep concrete ramp in the gymnasium when his spikes slipped and he fell heavily, landing on his right arm. The arm was broken and placed in a cast extending from the top of his hand to his elbow. Casey was back in the dugout, with his arm in a sling, the next night.

On July 22, eight days before his birthday, Stengel was honored at City Hall by Mayor Wagner. During his speech, he said, "When I leave this here ball club in the fall, at least I'll know I've left some young players who are improved and who will have some future." Did that mean, Casey was asked, that this was his last year? "It should be," he said.

After the ceremony, as Stengel was en route to Buffalo, where the Mets were scheduled to play an exhibition game, Weiss frantically tried to reach him to ask him to clarify his remarks. What he had meant, Casey said later, was that he would be leaving in the fall to go home to Glendale, as he had at the end of every season. He hadn't meant to say he was retiring. "Right now," he said, "I have no intention of retiring. But six months from now, how can I say? After all, I am 75 years old."

Four days later, in the early morning hours, Stengel's decision was made for him. Following the Mets' annual Old Timers' Game on the 25th, Casey attended a party at Toots Shor's. When he went to the men's room, he slipped on the wet floor and felt a twinge in his hip. He thought nothing of it, and returned to the party, where he remained until a friend of his drove him to his home at two o'clock in the morning. When Casey got out of the car, he landed awkwardly, and his hip was twisted again.

Stengel spent an uncomfortable night, and by morning the pain was almost unbearable. His friend called Met trainer Gus Mauch, who immediately knew Casey was seriously hurt. "I'd never seen Casey in such pain," Mauch said, "in all the years I'd been with him. I knew it was more than just a muscle spasm." Mauch called team physician Dr. Peter Lamotte, who immediately brought Stengel to Roosevelt Hospital and began to operate. Casey, who had defied old age for so long, had fallen victim to a common peril of advanced years, a broken hip.

In the hospital, Casey was as lively as ever. He held a press conference, at which he displayed his scars and described how a plastic ball had been inserted in his hip. "I don't know if it's a National League ball or an American League ball," he said. The most important question he was asked was whether he'd be back. He didn't know, he said, and would decide after the season.

Stengel had returned to the Mets the day after his broken wrist was set, but there was no question of him being in the dugout after hip surgery. Who would take his place while he recovered? "Wes is the fella," Casey said. "He's alongside me in the dugout every day, helps me decide the lineups, and knows what my thinking is." Thus anointed, Wesley Noreen Westrum, 42, became the interim manager of the Mets, their first manager who was not named Casey Stengel.

Stengel was the first manager of the Mets and Gil Hodges was the third. Each was a legend in New York. Westrum was not even a legend in his hometown of Clearbrook, Minnesota. He was fairly well-known in New York, for he'd been a catcher for the Giants for eleven years and a coach for the Mets since 1964. Westrum was not a character like Casey Stengel or a great player like Gil Hodges. Who was Wes Westrum?

During his playing days, Westrum was known as an excellent defensive catcher with power at the plate. In his best year as a Giant, 1950, he hit 23 home runs, and connected for 20 the following year, as the Giants won the pennant. Westrum had a career average of just .217, but his defensive ability kept him in the Giant lineup, and he averaged nearly 100 games a year. He was also renowned as one of baseball's great sign stealers.

After he retired as a player, Westrum served as a coach with San Francisco from 1958 to 1963. In the latter year, Giant manager Alvin Dark skippered the National League All Stars, and brought Westrum with him as bullpen coach. The night before the game, Westrum was sitting at a Cleveland bar, drinking a beer, when Casey Stengel and reporter Jack Mann sat down near him. Stengel bought Westrum a drink and asked him to join them. The three men talked at length and Stengel was impressed with Westrum's knowledge of baseball.

Met coach Cookie Lavagetto had lung surgery later that year, and wanted to be closer to his California home. Giant owner Horace Stoneham worked out a deal with the Mets which enabled Lavagetto to join the Giant coaching staff and Westrum to become a Met coach.

No one quote can pinpoint the personality of Wes Westrum, and no descriptions given by the men who played for him are particularly insightful, but the congruence of the observations is striking.

LOU KLIMCHOCK: "He was very low key."

ED BRESSOUD: "He kind of let the players do their thing. He wasn't a rah-rah kind of guy. He was not the kind of guy who would give you fire and brimstone. He was a very genuine man — a good person."

BOB JOHNSON: "Wes was just the nicest guy."

JIM HICKMAN: "He was a lot different than Casey. He didn't have a whole lot to say. Wes was all right."

DAVE EILERS: "Wes was all right. I liked him.'

GORDON RICHARDSON: "He was a quiet person, like Johnny Keane. He was very, very quiet. I think he did a lot of thinking. He didn't do a lot of talking."

DENNIS MUSGRAVES: "I thought he was a really nice fellow."

GORDON WHITE (former reporter): "Westrum was a very good baseball man. In any field, you see guys who were just made for what they're doing. Westrum was made for baseball."

DENNIS RIBANT: "He was a decent manager. I can't say he was outstanding."

JOHN STEPHENSON: "He was quiet. He didn't have any problems with anybody."

BOB HENDLEY: "He was a quiet person. He didn't have much to say."

BILL DENEHY: "Quiet. It was almost at times as if he had lockjaw. He kind of stayed in the background."

JIM SCHAFFER: "Westrum was the acting manager and all I can say is he was acting."

DENNIS BENNETT: "A nice guy in the wrong job. I don't think he could handle the ballclub. He couldn't motivate the players."

ROB GARDNER: "I think he was the most ambivalent manager I ever played for. I saw him turn to guys on the bench and say, 'Do you think I ought to take him out?'"

CHUCK HILLER: "Wes was a wonderful man. I think Wes was too nice a guy to be a manager."

BOB SHAW: "Wes was a nice guy. Nothing sticks in my mind. He was just a nice guy. Was he a motivator? We were a tenth place ballclub. I don't know what you're going to motivate. But he was a nice guy."

The quotes have a common thread. Wes was a good baseball man. Wes was a nice guy. Wes was quiet. Anyone who played for either Stengel or Hodges has a few thousand well-chosen words about them. Most loved them, a few disliked them, but no one dismissed Hodges or Stengel with a phrase or two. Most players struggled to describe Westrum, hemmed and hawed a bit, and settled for "nice guy" or "quiet." "[H]e is quiet," wrote Arthur Daley, "colorless and not particularly quotable."

Since Wes had little personality of his own, the press tried to invent one for him. "The Norman Vincent Peale of baseball," they called him, an incurable optimist. In December, 1965, Westrum said he was aiming for fifth place in 1966. Since the Mets had never finished as high as ninth, that statement alone qualified him a cockeyed optimist. "I'm going to tell the players that baseball is a serious game," Westrum said at the start of spring training in 1966. "We're going to aim for the first division. Kentucky windage they call it on the rifle range — aim higher." While the press wrote enthusiastically about the motivational clippings he posted in the Met clubhouse, however, none of the players remember any of them. Positive thinking couldn't win ball games without talent, and Wes and his optimistic sayings did not produce any miracles.

Wes Westrum served as manager of the Mets between the terms of Casey Stengel and Gil Hodges. Decent, quiet and totally lacking charisma, he resigned when the Mets returned to the basement in 1967.

For the remainder of 1965, he bore the title of interim manager, as Stengel still harbored dreams of recovering and returning to the bench. "We didn't miss a beat," said infielder Bobby Klaus. "We continued to lose under Wes just as we had under Casey." Even more so, in fact. Under Stengel, the Mets were 31–64 (.326). For Westrum, they were 19–48 (.284). By September, when it was clear the Mets would finish tenth again, Westrum turned to youth. "We've looked at the older players for four years," he said. "We've got nothing to lose giving some of the kids a chance."

Ron Swoboda (21), Ed Kranepool (still only 20), Cleon Jones (23), John Stephenson (24), Greg Goossen (19), Bud Harrelson (21) and Danny Napoleon (23) appeared frequently in September lineups. Westrum began pitching youngsters like Dick Selma, Tug McGraw, Tom Parsons and Rob Gardner. Although he was auditioning for a permanent job, Westrum looked to the future, a future which might not, given his 1965 record, include him as manager.

It soon became apparent that the Mets' future would not include Casey Stengel as manager. Stengel's recovery was steady but slow, and he would still be walking with a cane the following spring. A man who had survived decades of heavy drinking, thousands of cigarettes* and late hours had been undone stepping out of a car. On August 30, the Mets announced Stengel's retirement from baseball. He would remain with the club and take charge of their California operations (whatever they might be), including scouting. Casey thanked Weiss and Donald Grant for allowing him to manage without interference, and expressed disappointment that the Mets had not progressed more rapidly.

On September 2, Casey appeared at Shea Stadium, hobbling and leaning on a cane, to bid farewell to the team. He spoke with the players in the locker room before the game, and player representative Galen Cisco delivered a farewell address to Stengel on behalf of the players. Casey became the first Met to have his uniform number retired. After a brief reception, Stengel ascended to the club box to watch the Mets lose to the Astros in a manner which brought back memories of his days on the bench. Trailing 4–1 in the ninth inning, the Mets got two runs and had runners on first and second with none out. As they had so many times under Stengel, they failed to get the tying run across and lost the game 4–3.

Casey returned to Glendale and George Weiss continued his search for a new manager. He didn't intend to look very far. There was Westrum, of course, and in the first base coaching box was Casey's "assistant manager" from his Yankee days, Yogi Berra. "Yogi is the lovable Met image," wrote Dick Young, "and as long as he remains in the coaching box for the people to gape at, and kid with, he will retain that lovable image. Make him a manager, and they will boo him, because when the team loses, they boo the manger, and the Mets do lose." There was former Cardinal manager Eddie Stanky, the Mets' Director of Player Development, and Gil Hodges, the former Met who was under contract with the Senators through 1966.

Don Grant and Weiss decided on Westrum. "Is this the new manager of the New York Mets?" Grant asked when he reached Westrum by telephone. It was when Wes signed a one year contract on November 18. "This is the most happy day in my baseball career," said the man whose career included such happy moments as the Giants' 1951 playoff win over the Dodgers and the 1954 World Series sweep of the Cleveland Indians.

In 1966, Westrum, who had been enraptured with youth in September, 1965, turned to veterans. Youth had won less than 30 percent of their games, and Wes, with a one year contract, wanted to return in 1967. "Wes Westrum was one of the nicest guys in shoe leather," said pitcher Larry Miller, "but he was fighting for a job. A manager who wasn't fighting for his job would have given me another opportunity. He didn't have a lot of confidence in his position and that feeling was transferred to the players."

---

*In 1965, he was fined $200 for smoking in the dugout.

If 1965 had been a free ride with the team inherited from Stengel, 1966 was the year Westrum had to prove himself. He couldn't afford another 50-win season while he tried to develop young players. The Met club that first climbed out of the cellar was led by veterans like Ken Boyer, Bob Shaw, Bob Friend, Ed Bressoud, Al Luplow and Chuck Hiller.

After the Mets' first ninth place finish, *The New York Daily News* opined that Westrum should be named Manager of the Year. He wasn't, but Wes was rewarded with another one year contract, and a $10,000 raise which put his salary at $45,000.

In 1967, however, Westrum's luck ran out. Before the year began, he announced his goals as a modest 70 wins and eighth place. He didn't achieve either, as the Mets posted just 61 wins and returned to the basement. Even worse, attendance dropped from 1,932,693 to 1,565,492. Westrum was booed when he came to the mound to make pitching changes. At least when Casey was losing, he had been entertaining. Westrum was just plain losing.

As the season wound down, Westrum was kept guessing as to his fate. On August 27, Bing Devine, who had succeeded Weiss as general manager, was asked about Westrum's future and answered evasively, saying he would make a decision after the season. "I haven't heard a thing," was Westrum's only comment. Alvin Dark had just been fired by the Athletics and was available. Devine told Westrum not to worry about Dark, but gave him no clue as to his own future.

On September 21, 1967, convinced he was about to be fired, Westrum resigned. "I couldn't sleep," he said. "I was getting up three or four times a night. I think I know now that managing isn't the best thing personally for me or my family."*

Losing so frequently had been difficult for Westrum. "You could see it in his face," said reliever Gordon Richardson. "You could see the anguish in his eyes. You could tell he was hurting. He really wanted to win, but we just couldn't do it." "I think it was starting to get to him real bad," said John Sullivan. "We just weren't doing things properly and he was almost getting sick."

Arthur Daley wrote, "[Westrum] was swept by an unkind fate into the tormenting task of managing the New York Mets, an appalling assignment for even the world's greatest manager. And no baseball man ever accused Wes of being the world's greatest manager." Wes was a small man, Daley concluded, in a big job. He had been hired because he was expendable. Could the Mets have fired Hodges or Berra if the Mets continued to lose? "He was the stopgap," Daley continued, "that was an absolute necessity after Stengel. No baseball man alive could have followed the fantastic act that Casey had been putting on." Westrum was expendable because "he had no reputation and no following."

Westrum was offered another job with the Mets, but chose to return to the Giants as a coach. The Mets began looking for a manager who could win, inspire and, equally as important, bring fans back to Shea Stadium. "We're looking for a man who can win the pennant for us," said Don Grant. "That may sound facetious, but we're looking for a man who will move us up in the standings."

Berra was again a candidate. So was Harry Walker, the antithesis of Westrum. Wes was quiet, they said, and no one had ever accused Harry Walker of being quiet. Wes was also a nice guy, a term rarely used to describe Walker. Hank Bauer, whose Orioles had fallen from World Series champs in 1966 to also-rans in 1967, was an old New York favorite with a strong personality. He might soon be available. The most appealing candidate was Hodges, but Hodges was under contract to the Washington Senators. Since taking over the hapless Senators in 1963, he had gradually brought them from tenth place to sixth, and from 56 wins to 76. Hodges was a natural for the Met job, but couldn't even be approached, much less hired, without getting permission from Washington. Grant and Devine set out to get permission.

Westrum eventually returned to managing, leading the Giants in 1974 and 1975.

• 13 •

Dr. Strangeglove and
Prepare, Pucker and Pop
The 1966 Season

Throughout the spring of 1966, Wes Westrum preached positive thinking and vowed that the Mets would shed their comic image and begin to play serious baseball. Yet, on February 22, they acquired Dick Stuart, known to baseball fans as Dr. Strangeglove, a transaction that seemed to bring them back to the days of Casey Stengel and 1962. There were very few first basemen who were worse fielders than Marv Throneberry, but Stuart was one of them.

Old timers have always believed the game of baseball was better in their day, and in the early '60s, one of the areas in which they thought the sport was lacking was color. In December, 1961 *The Sporting News* published an article by veteran writer Fred Lieb decrying the absence of "color" in the game. Where were the Rabbit Maranvilles, Rube Waddells, Frenchie Bordagarays and Pepper Martins?, Lieb lamented. Current stars Roger Maris, Frank Robinson, and Harmon Killebrew were as bland as Richard Nixon. Lieb was very selective in his roster of current heroes, and omitted several unchallenged characters from his list. Admittedly, Throneberry's fame was a year away, but what about Stuart? What about Jimmy Piersall? They might not be stars, but they were certainly colorful. Lieb allowed that Piersall and Casey Stengel qualified as "colorful" but insisted that players with crowd appeal were few and far between.

With the exception of Piersall, the common attribute of many of the characters of the '60s seemed to be a sans souci attitude toward catching a batted ball, and no one had more disdain for a batted ball than Dick Stuart, a designated hitter born twenty years too soon. Felix Mantilla played for the Red Sox when Stuart played first. "All the infielders," recalled Mantilla, "Malzone, Bressoud and me, got really pissed off at the guy because it seemed as if he didn't give a damn about his fielding. He just wanted to hit. He was a good guy, but seemed as if he just didn't give a damn." "He was not the most elegant fielder," Bressoud added. "If you played shortstop," said Dick Schofield, a Pittsburgh teammate of Stuart, "you let go of it and then looked back at the scoreboard to see if it was E-6 or E-3. He could make some routine throws pretty exciting."

One day in spring training with the Mets, Stuart was fielding grounders next to Lou Klimchock. "Look at that photographer over there," Stuart said. "He's just waiting for me to boot one so he can take a picture." "He'll probably stay there all day if he has to," said Klimchock. "It's not going to take that long," Stuart replied.

"He could field," said Klimchock. "He just didn't want to. He thought that playing the infield was something you did while you were waiting to hit." Stuart poked fun at his lack of defensive skills. One day, when he saw a player accidentally step on his glove, he said, "Well, there goes the pennant."

One day when Stuart was playing for the Pirates, the public address announcer made his customary announcement, "Anyone who interferes with the ball in play will be ejected from the ballpark." "I hope," said Pittsburgh manager Danny Murtaugh, "Stuart doesn't think he means him." Murtaugh didn't usually think Stuart's fielding was funny, however. During his five years in Pittsburgh, Stuart set a record by either leading or tying for the league lead in errors by a first baseman each year. He also struck out a lot, but when he connected, Stuart had tremendous power. In 1955, he hit 52 home runs in the minor leagues. The next year, at Lincoln, Nebraska, he hit 66 homers and drove in 158 runs, a season he commemorated by writing "66"under his autograph for years afterward. In 1957, Stuart hit 45 homers with three minor league teams, and had 31 homers in 80 games at Salt Lake City when he was recalled by the Pirates in 1958.

Stuart had his best season in Pittsburgh in '61, when he slugged 35 homers, while batting .301 and driving in 117 runs. The following year, he slumped horribly, to a .228 average and just 16 home runs. For someone who fielded like Dr. Strangeglove, 16 home runs were not enough, and when he stopped hitting, the Forbes Field fans let him have it. After outfielder Bob Skinner was booed for dropping a fly ball, Stuart met him when he reached the dugout and shook his hand. "Thanks for taking my customers!" he said. Later, when he was booed in Philadelphia, Stuart said, "Ah, these Philadelphia fans are still amateurs in the booing department, compared to those in Pittsburgh." By the end of the 1962 season, Dr. Strangeglove had worn out his welcome in Pittsburgh. The Pirates, with young Donn Clendenon available to play first base, traded him to the Boston Red Sox.

The trade was the best thing that ever happened to Stuart. "In Pittsburgh they were 75–25 against me," he said. "In Boston, they're only 60–40 against me." Freed from cavernous Forbes Field and given the opportunity to take aim at Fenway Park's inviting left field fence, Stuart was named Comeback Player of the Year in 1963. He hit 42 home runs, led the league with 118 RBI and broke Jimmie Foxx's Red Sox record for strikeouts. "I knew I would break one of Foxxie's records," he said. Stuart also committed a league-leading 29 errors at first base.

In addition to the Green Monster, a second benefit of being in Boston was the increase in media exposure. Most fans loved him for his hitting, some blasted him for his fielding but, to Stuart's delight, no one ignored him. While Pirate fans, in his last years, had booed him unmercifully, Boston fans took to him immediately. "Dick Stuart is the most fun Boston has had," wrote Robert Creamer, "since the last time Ted Williams spit." Stuart had his own television show, *Stuart on Sports*, which had the highest rating of any televised sports show in the city. He was awkward at times in front of the camera, but knew how to attract attention, making headlines by tearing up Ralph Houk's picture on the air after Houk left him off the All Star team. Houk, said Stuart, was "a third-string catcher who couldn't know how important it is to be on an All-Star team because he couldn't make one." "Stuart has had no equal as a first baseman since Zeke Bonura," Houk replied, drawing a comparison to the legendarily inept fielder of the 1930s.

Other than his horrendous fielding, Stuart was most remarkable for his casual attitude. "Stuart's appearance," Creamer continued, "[on] the field is one of nonchalance bordering on insolence. He wears his cap rather forward on his head. He appears startled when a ground ball is hit in his direction. [P]aradoxically, his awful fielding is part of the charm he holds for Boston fans. This may trace back to Ted Williams, a Boston hero who wasn't much of a fielder either." Once, in late August, Stuart flinched on a hard shot hit toward him by Lu Clinton, then made

Dick Stuart at the bat rack. If there'd been a glove rack, Stuart wouldn't have known where it was. The worst-fielding first baseman of his era, Stuart could hit home runs — until he came to the Mets. He was also a charismatic, entertaining ballplayer whose fielding lapses earned him the name Doctor Strangeglove.

a fine stop and the putout at first. "You can tell it's getting late in season," he said to Clinton at the bag. "In the spring, I'd have been able to get out of the way of that one."

Stuart's fielding was not charming to Boston manager Johnny Pesky. When Stuart arrived at his first Red Sox training camp, Pesky expressed admiration for his improved attitude. "Don't ask me why," Pesky said, "but I like the guy. There isn't a mean bone in his body." After just a few weeks, however, Pesky said, "I wish he had a little more get up and go." After Stuart worked with infield coach Billy Herman on his fielding, Herman gave him a qualified endorsement. "I'm positive he's not the worst fielding first baseman we've had in Boston," he said. Maybe the hard Forbes infield had been the cause of his problems, surmised shortstop Bressoud. It was wishful thinking, and despite another excellent offensive season in 1964, when he hit .279 with 33 homers and 114 RBI, Stuart's act had once again played out with his manager.

Pesky benched Stuart for not running balls out and said he nearly quit in mid-season after one of his many arguments with his stubborn first baseman. Boston had a four run lead in the seventh inning and two runners on base. When Stuart came to bat, Pesky gave him the bunt sign. Stuart couldn't believe it. He made a half-hearted effort to bunt, then took three straight balls. Pesky gave him the take sign. Stuart swung away and popped up, for which Pesky fined him $50.

If the Red Sox had traded Stuart after the '63 season, Pesky surmised, things might have been different in '64, which was not a good year for Boston. Their record was 72–90 and Pesky was fired at the end of the year. Stuart was traded to Philadelphia for pitcher Dennis Bennett. "All I can say about Pesky," Stuart said when he heard about his former manager's derogatory comments about him, "is that when the Red Sox got rid of me, at least they got something for me." The next season, Stuart saw Pesky, coaching for the Pirates. "I made you what you are," Stuart told him, "a coach." When a reporter for *The Sporting News* called for an interview, he answered the phone "Johnny Pesky's residence."

Stuart did not get along much better with Philllie manager Gene Mauch. He had a decent year, with 28 home runs, but his batting average was low and he seethed when Mauch benched him against right handers, or dropped him to the sixth spot in the batting order. "I wasn't accustomed to sixth," Dick said. "I asked Gene to bat me fourth more." Once, when a reporter asked Mauch why he had benched Stuart, he replied, "I told Stu to sit here and help me manage." In addition to Stuart wanting to fill out the lineup card, Mauch had other problems. While Lieb mourned the dearth of characters, Mauch had at least two more than he needed. The Phils acquired eccentric lefthander Bo Belinsky at approximately the same time they got Stuart, and there were a number of jokes regarding the odds of the intense Mauch surviving the season with two of baseball's biggest flakes on his team.

Stuart was not a significant contributor to a team that, after leading the National League for most of the previous season, finished a disappointing sixth. His proudest accomplishment was the fact that, thanks in part to Mauch's platooning, he did not lead National League first basemen in errors. That title was assumed by Donn Clendenon, the man who had replaced him in Pittsburgh to strengthen the Pirate defense.

When the Phillies acquired All Star first baseman Bill White from the Cardinals, Stuart became expendable. "Stu would be perfect for New York," wrote Dick Young in January, 1966, "He's colorful copy and would help fill the publicity void left by Casey Stengel, or at least part of it. He also can hit a ball over a few fences." When the Mets acquired Stuart in late February for three minor leaguers (an indication of how far Dr. Strangeglove had slipped in just one year) *The New York Times* predicted, "He is expected to give the Mets their most wayward first base protection since Marv Throneberry and their most colorful antics since Casey Stengel." "As long as Stuart produces," said Westrum, "he can pop off. We need his bat."

Had the Mets still played in the Polo Grounds, Stuart would have been a threat to break Frank Thomas's Met record of 34 home rums, and might have taken a run at Maris's 61. But the Mets had moved to Shea Stadium, whose left field fence was less inviting than that at either the Polo Grounds or Fenway Park. A further complication was the fact that Stuart's arrival necessitated the move of Kranepool, who had shown sparks of life in 1965, to left field. Kranepool agreed to move, but was not happy.

Stuart's presence at first base also required a second baseman with sufficient range to flag down the ground balls that Stuart couldn't, or didn't care to, reach. Ron Hunt was a hustler, but had limited range, and Westrum envisioned balls bouncing through the right side of the infield with troubling regularity. Should the Mets leave Kranepool at first and try Stuart in left? "I wouldn't want to be the guy that was pitching that night," Stuart commented.

Westrum informed Stuart when he arrived that he would be platooned, and told him of the great value he would have as a pinch hitter. Stuart wanted no part of pinch hitting. "I can pinch hit when I'm 37," he said. "Now I need action." It was a situation that seemed destined for disaster.

Stuart had aged, but he hadn't changed. When he made a backhanded catch of a line drive in an intrasquad game, he acknowledged the cheers of the crowd by doffing his cap, turning to the stands and taking a deep bow. For the most part, however, his fielding didn't disappoint those who had come to see Dr. Strangeglove. More ominously, he wasn't hitting with the authority he had shown in Boston.

On April 18, during batting practice, Stuart pulled a muscle in his rib cage. The following day, while swinging and missing a pitch in a game against the Cardinals, he dropped to the ground holding his side. He had torn a muscle under his 12th rib. Stuart went on the disabled list and Kranepool returned to first base.

When Stuart returned to action, he played irregularly. On the 15th of June, he was released, with a .218 average and just four home runs in 31 games. New York had not had a chance to love or hate Big Stu. They barely had a chance to boo him. "Stuart, with his power," said Westrum, "could have been valuable to us as a pinch hitter. But he had it in his head that he couldn't hit unless he played regularly. So there was no use in keeping him on our roster."

Stuart was signed by the Dodgers and played in the 1966 World Series. In December, he attended a Shea Stadium game between the Jets and Patriots. "I'm just revisiting my favorite ballpark," Stuart said. "I still live in Greenwich, Connecticut. In fact, I live in a swankier neighborhood than George Weiss. I wouldn't be surprised if that was the reason he fired me. A great ballplayer like me a victim of envy!" The following spring, Stuart signed a contract to play in Japan, where he spent two seasons, hitting 37 home runs one year. He returned to the States and was signed by the California Angels, with whom he finished his big league career in 1969.

Stuart, a 33-year-old veteran, fit right in with the '66 Mets. After finishing last with a rookie-laden roster in '65, the Mets sent many of the youngsters to the minors for much-needed seasoning, and acquired a stable of steady veterans. The most prominent addition was third baseman Ken Boyer, who just two years earlier had been the Most Valuable Player in the National League. At the age of almost 35, after a mediocre 1965 season during which he was hampered by a back injury, the Cardinals thought Boyer's best years were behind him. He was part of the Devine-Keane family, and new GM Bob Howsam was clearing the decks of the old regime. He traded Boyer to the Mets for Al Jackson, New York's all-time winningest pitcher, and starting third baseman Charlie Smith.

Boyer provided something the Mets had been lacking: a steady veteran leader on the field. Frank Thomas had been the Mets' first slugger, but Thomas did not have the personality of a leader. Ron Hunt was scrappy and talented, but he was young. Boyer was accomplished, still capable of playing decent ball, and possessed leadership qualities that eventually made him a big league manager. He'd won four straight Gold Glove awards as a third baseman. During the 1966 season, Boyer was dogged by the kind of injuries that affect 35-year-old ballplayers, but managed to appear in 136 games, batting .266 and leading the club with 61 RBI.

Thirty-seven year old Roy McMillan, another steadying influence, returned at shortstop, backed up by 34-year-old Ed Bressoud, acquired from the Red Sox for Joe Christopher. Bressoud, the first player chosen in the 1962 expansion draft, when he was selected by the

Colts, had been the Red Sox's regular shortstop for three years before losing his job to Rico Petrocelli.

Bressoud had an interesting habit. After every pitch, as the catcher returned the ball to the pitcher, Bressoud ran behind the pitcher to back up the throw. When he was with the Giants, catcher Hobie Landrith had thrown the ball over the pitcher's head and San Francisco lost a game. "That made quite an impression on me," Bressoud said. "I said, 'Hell, there's only one thing for me to do. So I started doing it.'"

Another veteran on the '66 squad, at least for a few weeks, was Choo Choo Coleman, who had played at Buffalo the past two seasons. Choo Choo emerged from his exile and made the Met team, but was sold to Jacksonville, the Mets new Triple A farm club, on cutdown day.

Prior to the season, *The New York Times* commented that the Mets had "a pitching staff that includes only one accredited major leaguer." What was the Mets' biggest problem, Westrum was asked on the eve of the opener. "Pitching," he replied.

Westrum was correct. Jack Fisher, the Mets' one solid hurler, stretched his losing streak, which carried over from 1965, to 12 games before finally winning in mid–May. In early June, the staff broke down completely, and Weiss realized a change was necessary. In place of the young pitchers who had struggled in '65 and the first half of 1966, he brought in a veteran staff. The most notable addition was Bob Shaw, a 32-year-old who had been in the major leagues since 1957, with five different clubs. Shaw's best year was 1959, when he was 18–6 for the pennant-winning White Sox, and he had been 16–9 for the Giants in 1965.

In 1966, Shaw held out, incurring the displeasure of San Francisco management. Nineteen sixty-six was the year that Sandy Koufax and Don Drysdale decided to negotiate as a twosome, a tactic that threw a mighty scare into the baseball establishment. To the north, the Giants' two best pitchers, Shaw and Juan Marichal, were holding out individually, and with far less publicity that the Dodger tandem.

Marichal, who won 22 games in 1965, ended a 23 day holdout by signing for $70,000 on March 22. Shaw remained out of camp, not signing until the end of the month, for a salary of about $45,000. It was not the first time Shaw had been a holdout. After pitching just seven games in his rookie year with Detroit in 1957, he stayed out of camp the following spring. When he was sent to the minors in June, Shaw refused to go, and told the Tigers to trade him to another team. When the deal was made, he said, they should call him. He'd be home in Long Island.

The Tigers traded Shaw to the White Sox, where, under the tutelage of manager Al Lopez and pitching coach Ray Berres, he had an excellent season for the 1959 pennant winners. Two years later, Shaw angered the White Sox by holding out until April, and was traded to Kansas City. When the White Sox traded him, White Sox GM Hank Greenberg didn't pay Shaw $2500 in expense reimbursements accumulated while working for the club during the winter. He complained to AL President Joe Cronin and got his money.

A year later, Shaw moved on to the Braves, and in 1964, found himself in San Francisco. "I doubt that more than six pitchers in the majors are making more money than I am," he said upon his arrival. Shaw was reportedly making close to $40,000. After his 16–9 record in 1965, Shaw thought he deserved a sizable raise. "In those days," he said recently, "we didn't have agents and we didn't have attorneys, so I did all the negotiating myself. I won't use the word stubborn, but I had a good year for the Giants and held out to get what I thought was a fair salary."*

After finally reporting to the Giants, Shaw sealed his fate by irritating pitching coach Larry

*When Shaw signed with the Mets in 1967, Joe Durso described him as a man "who has harassed batters and executives in both major leagues for ten years."

Jansen. Shaw was a great student of pitching who later wrote a book on the subject. He was knowledgeable and opinionated and more than willing to help younger pitchers. "He preached and believed in good mechanics," said Rob Gardner. "That was all he talked about. He told one of the young pitchers that if he kept throwing a certain way, he'd wind up throwing mail into the slots at the post office. Bob wanted his arm to be in the right place at the right time, so he wouldn't throw across his body. He tried to make it easy on his arm by using his back and his legs. He preached that consistently."

When he was with the Giants, Shaw asked manager Alvin Dark if Dark minded him giving instruction to the young pitchers. Dark said he didn't, but when Bob Bolin asked for Shaw's assistance, Jansen took exception, and Shaw was asked to stop talking to Bolin.

Gaylord Perry, who struggled in his early years with the Giants, also came to Shaw for advice. "Gaylord would ask me about keeping his hands vertical, the position of his knee, the path of his arm and why you should do certain things," Shaw said. He gave Perry some advice, and Gaylord began to pitch better. "Gaylord listened to me," Shaw related, "and he got better and better. He was 1–6 the year before [1963] and they were going to send him down, so Jansen didn't really care if I talked to him. Then he had the best spring of any of us and makes the team and was doing real well. Alvin asked me to stop talking to him because the pitching coach wasn't very happy about it."

In May, 1964, after Perry pitched nine innings in the marathon game against the Mets, he gave Shaw credit for his improvement. Jansen was furious. "That's one of the reasons the Giants traded me," Shaw said. "I think they got a little fed up. Ron Herbel wanted some help and I helped him. He went out and pitched a shutout and gave me credit for it. I was getting myself in trouble by helping other pitchers. That's probably why I got traded to the Mets."

On one occasion, Perry asked Shaw for a very specific kind of help. In 1964, Shaw pitched in relief for the Giants and appeared in 70 games. "Toward the end," he said, "I couldn't get anybody out. Jansen gave me some emery paper and Doc Bowman, our trainer, gave me some slippery elm. I said, 'I think these guys are trying to tell me something.'"

During the winter, Shaw diligently practiced throwing a spitball. The basic concept of the pitch, which was reportedly discovered by outfielder George Hildebrand of the Eastern League's Providence club in 1902, is that a little lubrication on the pitcher's fingers will reduce the spin on the ball and cause it to drop as it approaches the plate. Unlike the knuckle ball, which flutters homeward, the spitter is thrown hard, and drops abruptly. When major league baseball outlawed the delivery in 1920, it allowed pitchers who were using it to continue to do so for the remainder of their career. Non-spitballers could not adopt the pitch and no one who came to the big leagues in the future could throw a legal spitball.

Frank Shellenback, a talented minor league pitcher, was caught in an unfortunate predicament. The spitball was his primary pitch, but since he was not in the major leagues in 1920, he could only throw the spitter in the minors. Shellenback, doomed to the life of a permanent minor leaguer, won 295 games in the Pacific Coast League and was one of the last to throw a legal spitball in professional ball. In the spring of '65, Shellenback became Shaw's tutor. "He taught me about slippery elm lozenges," said Shaw. "His theory was 'Prepare, Pucker and Pop.' You prepare the leather. Every time you get the ball, you rub it into one spot. You have to pucker and then you really have to pop your wrist."

Former Met pitcher Bill Denehy talked of the strategy of preparation. "What some guys did," said Denehy, "was use two different kinds of soap. They would use white soap when they were home and had white uniforms and gray soap when they were wearing the gray road uniforms. They would turn their pants inside out, wet the crotch and really rub the soap on the inside of the pants. As they'd sweat, the soap would seep through. Anytime they wanted to get something slippery, they could get some sweat on their hands and then go to the soap. If an umpire comes out there, he may feel the back of your neck or your hands or hair or glove, but he's certainly not going to grab your crotch." Particularly if it's damp.

By the spring of 1965, Shaw had quite a spitball, which helped him to his best season since 1959. "That kind of got me over the hump for two or three years," he said. "In those days, the umpires never said anything. If I had the ball loaded and they asked to see it, I would wipe it on the side of my pants and throw it in."

"He had a good one," said Met pitcher Bill Hepler. "He showed me how he threw it. He kept slippery elm in his mouth, loaded up the ball with his fingers and then he would act like he was rubbing the ball, but he wouldn't touch it with his fingers. If the umpire asked for the ball, he would scrape it off on his leg and throw it underhanded to the umpire, way up in the air. It would be dry by the time it came down. He showed us how to do it."

During the 1965 season, Perry, who was not pitching well, came to Shaw for advice, but Shaw, mindful of Jansen's suspicion, turned him away. "I said, 'Look, Alvin asked me not to help you anymore.' But one night we were out having a drink and he asked me if I would teach him the spitball. I said, 'I'll teach you the spitball if you don't tell anybody I taught you. He kept it a secret for many, many years and I never said anything to anybody. Then he admitted it in his book [*The Spitter and Me*]. When he was elected to the Hall of Fame, he remarked to somebody that he wouldn't be there if it wasn't for Bob Shaw."

Many pitchers learned to Prepare, Pucker and Pop during the 1960s, most by design, but some without malevolent intent. "I threw one by accident," said Oriole hurler Chuck Estrada. "I used to tinker with the ball all the time, and one day I was pitching against the Washington Senators. I had a left handed hitter up and knew I couldn't throw my fastball past him. I also knew that if I wiped the bill of my cap and got a little moisture on my fingers, the ball would go down. Gus Triandos called for a fastball. I wiped my forehead and struck the guy out. Gus almost botched the ball and the next day the hitter came up to me and said, 'Hey, Chuck, you don't need to throw that thing.' I didn't even know what the heck I did. It was a spitter."

After the 1961 season, Commissioner Ford Frick advocated legalizing the spitball. He thought it might cut down on home runs. Frick had an ally in Casey Stengel, about to begin his first season as Met manager. "Certainly, my pitchers will need all the help they can get," he said. Frick's proposal was not enacted, but it didn't seem to make any difference. In 1963, *Sports Illustrated* reported that widespread use of the spitball and other illegal pitches was an open secret. Phillie manager Gene Mauch estimated that twenty-five percent of major league pitchers threw a spitter. The article identified some of the most blatant practitioners as Jim Bunning, Ron Kline and Orlando Pena. Duke Snider said Don Drysdale had the best spitter in the National League. Mauch agreed. "Drysdale's is the best," Mauch said, "because he throws it the hardest."

Spit was not the only element involved. "I remember pitching against Bunning when I was with Baltimore and he was with Detroit," said Jack Fisher. "I was getting the balls at the beginning of the inning and there were slices in them. Now I'm not going to call time out and say, 'This ball's sliced,' so I pitched with them. Detroit had a catcher named Dick Brown who sharpened the end of his belt buckle and was slicing the balls for Bunning. As far as nicking the ball and scuffing it," Fisher continued, "I'm not going to say I didn't try it." He could prepare and pucker, but couldn't pop. "I tried spitters in the bullpen," he said. "I tried everything I could, but I couldn't get them to be consistent. If you can only throw one good one out of five, that's not a very good average. I liked the idea that I had the reputation for throwing it, though. It gave the hitters something else to think about."

Whitey Ford was frequently accused of doctoring the ball. The Orioles and Tigers said that Ford's name should appear in the box score with an asterisk next to it, such as the *Daily Racing Form* used to designate "mud marks" to thoroughbreds. Did Ford throw a spitter? "No, no, oh, no," said catcher John Blanchard. "When Whitey got two strikes on a hitter, he'd throw his mud pitch. He would reach down with his wet fingers and grab some clay. If you put a chunk of clay on the ball, no matter how you throw it, it's going to pull it down. If you put clay on the inside, it was down and away — if it's on the outside, down and in. He wouldn't do it every pitch or every other pitch, just when he needed it."

John Wyatt, star reliever of the Kansas City Athletics, was another suspect, whose specialty was believed to be the Vaseline ball. Wyatt called the pitch his Puerto Rican forkball. "Wyatt has Vaseline in his hair, on his uniform — just all over," complained White Sox manager Al Lopez. "If you tackled Wyatt around the waist," Joe Pepitone once said, "you'd slide off." Rusty Staub insisted that a Dodger pitcher used toothpaste to doctor the ball.

The Mets' Cal Koonce actually admitted that he threw a spitter. In 1967, when someone asked him about it, Koonce said he threw about six per game. He had been throwing wet deliveries ever since he started playing professional ball. "What was the point of all the hypocrisy," Koonce said later. "It was getting ridiculous, so I admitted it." He also said that many other pitchers did the same thing.

In 1962, Dick Farrell of the Colts admitted throwing a spitter to Stan Musial, just for kicks. It didn't do anything, Farrell said, and Musial got a single. The Colts tried to cover up Farrell's admission by claiming that the pitcher had said, "slipper" rather than spitter, but Farrell didn't have a slipper pitch in his repertoire.

The Senators' Dave Stenhouse, who made the 1962 All Star squad, confided to All Star manager Ralph Houk that he used pine tar to get a better grip on the ball. Houk nodded, and the next time Stenhouse pitched against the Yankees, ran out to the umpire, who made Stenhouse wash his hands.

Athletic pitcher Dave Wickersham, a devoutly religious man, claimed to have an excellent spitter, "but I won't throw it," he said, "because winning illegally is contrary to my Christian principles."

Everyone knew that illegal pitches were being thrown. Phillie catcher Clay Dalrymple once went on a postgame television show and talked about the sign he gave for Lew Burdette's spitter. In 1963, during an interview after a rare win, Bo Belinsky turned to veteran pitcher Bob Turley and handed him a small tube. "Hey, thanks for that stuff, Bob," Belinsky said. "It worked good." When a reporter asked what Belinsky was talking about, he explained that Turley had given him some sticky stuff to put on his hands. "Give me that stuff and keep your mouth shut," said Turley. "How dumb can you get?"

In 1965, after watching Shaw beat his Braves, manager Bobby Bragan said his pitchers had thrown 75 to 80 spitballs, to demonstrate that the umpires wouldn't do anything to stop them. He told them not to even try to hide the fact that they were doctoring the ball. Since the Brave pitchers gave up nine runs to the Giants, it does not appear that Bragan's hurlers had mastered the wet delivery as well as Shaw had.

In 1969, Bragan's successor, Luman Harris, became so frustrated at what he believed to be the widespread use of illegal pitches that he announced that every Atlanta pitcher would be taught to throw the spitball and would use it regularly. In preparation for facing the Dodgers' Bill Singer, a prime Vaseline ball suspect, Harris had his batting practice pitchers throw Vaseline balls to the Brave hitters. The league ignored Harris and the slippery life went on.

Throwing a spitter, however, was no guarantee of success, and Shaw fell on hard times. In 1966, after he ended his lengthy holdout, he had a difficult time getting untracked. Shaw's poor performance, combined with the Giants' disaffection with his negotiating and coaching, made him persona non grata in San Francisco. On June 10, with a 1–4 record and a 6.19 ERA, he was sold to the Mets.

Shaw was an interesting individual. It was not just his contentious negotiating style or his penchant for teaching young pitchers that made him unique. In an era when training consisted of jumping jacks and running a few desultory sprints across the outfield, Shaw had some advanced ideas about diet and conditioning. His father, who lived to the age of 95, was a Ph.D and a director of physical education who passed on many of his ideas to his son. "Way, way back," said Shaw, "he learned about flexibility and strength. This was back in the 1920s, so he was way ahead of everybody. He believed in dumbbells and light weights and wanted you to go through the full range of motion. Because of my dad, I did a lot of those things and it helped. I didn't use static weights, but I would use Indian clubs with lead in them or use light dumbbells or pulleys on the wall. I did a lot of pushups and pull-ups."

"My dad was also involved with health foods—vitamin and mineral supplements. I was very, very fortunate to be on Vitamin A back in the '50s and '60s. They would laugh at me. They'd look at me like I was crazy, but the diet of most athletes was terrible.

Bob Shaw was a pitching guru, a businessman, a pilot, a tough negotiator and possessor of one of the most effective spitballs in the National League. He joined the Mets early in the 1966 and became the best pitcher on the club that escaped the cellar for the first time.

You'd get on an airplane and the food would be cooked and put on a tray for two or three hours, so that there wasn't a lot of nutritional value in it. Once again, I thank my dad. He tried to educate me on nutrition. I'd eat some French fries and spaghetti, which I love — but I listened and took the vitamin supplements and it paid off."

Shaw always seemed to be doing something unusual. "Bob was always working on things," said John Stephenson. "In spring training, he'd put the catching gear on and go out and pitch to you. You were supposed to try to hit the ball by him. He was working on his fielding, and he had the mask, shin guards and chest protector on so he wouldn't get hurt."

Shaw was a man of many and varied interests. He was an accomplished businessman, owning a citrus grove and several real estate properties and, midway through his career, earned his pilot's license. "In 1957," he recalled, "I was playing for the Charleston Senators. We were flying through the Midwest and hit a thunderhead. Another plane actually went down. I was in the jump seat and I could hear them on the radio saying 'Mayday! Mayday!' We had three or four guys injured. Charley Lau was one of them. The cabin wasn't pressurized and water was coming in. The duffel bags had not been strapped in and were flying around the cabin. It was the most violent thing I've ever seen in my life."

The experience had a lasting effect on Shaw. "I've flown millions and millions of miles," he said, "but whenever we hit gray clouds, I automatically perspire. I thought that if I got my pilot's license I could beat it. When I flew, I could do a 180 degree turn and not go through any clouds, so I didn't perspire when I flew, but to this day I'm still affected by it. It's an unbelievable thing. I get mad at myself, but I still can't control it. You can sit there and watch the perspiration come out. I know better, but that's the way it is."*

While Shaw may not have perspired when he was flying the plane, he sometimes caused others to sweat profusely. "We were in St. Petersburg for spring training," recalled Rob Gardner, "and Bob offered to take me up in a small plane. I said, 'Sure, why not.' He took me up and let me do a couple of figure eights and then he said, 'Now, flying is very safe if you just don't panic. I'll show you what I mean.' He shut the engine off. I was trying to be cool and not say *'Jesus Christ, Bob, turn the engine on!'* so I was just sitting there. He was saying, 'As long as you don't pull back on the stick and lose all your lift you can glide. You could land over here. You could land over there.' He was pointing at different places. In the meantime, the engine still isn't turning. Finally, after about a minute — it seemed like five minutes— he started it back up. That's the kind of guy he was, very confident. But he scared the shit out of me."

Shaw started out fabulously in New York. In his initial four starts, he became the first Met starter ever to post four consecutive victories. The fourth win came against the Cubs, whose third base coach was Whitey Lockman, a Giant coach the previous year. Lockman led the harassment of Shaw, continually complaining to umpire Ken Burkhart that the Met pitcher was putting something on the ball.

Five days after Shaw arrived, the Mets acquired a second veteran pitcher, 35-year-old Bob Friend, who had been a reliable pitcher for the Pirates from 1951 to 1965 and a huge disappointment to the Yankees in 1966. The acquisition of Friend was a plus even if it did nothing other than keep him out of the hands of another National League club. During the first four years of the Mets' existence, few pitchers had been tougher on them than Bob Friend. He won his first twelve decisions against the Mets and, at one point, had a scoreless streak of 50 innings. "I had good luck against them," he said modestly. "They weren't a strong team, but I pitched pretty well against them and won a lot of games I shouldn't have. It's just one of those things. You gain confidence and they lose confidence. Once you get to 6–0 or 7–0, they feel they can't hit you." By the time he left the Pirates, Friend had a 14–2 mark against the Mets. When the Yankees acquired him in the winter of 1965, someone asked Ralph Houk if he planned to start Friend in the Mayor's Trophy Game. "One main reason we made the deal," Houk said with a straight face, "was to help the Mets out. You know, we New York clubs like to cooperate."

Like Shaw, Friend proved to be of immediate assistance to the Mets. On June 24, he beat the Cubs for his first win, equaling his Yankee victory total. While the Yankees were floundering, the Mets were on a hot streak, breaking club records for victories in a month and victories on a road trip. As Leonard Koppett pointed out, "all [Friend] needed was a better team behind him." Four days later, in his next start, Friend lost a heartbreaking 1–0 game in which he allowed only two hits. On July 23, he shut out the Dodgers in Los Angeles and on the 27th, beat the Astros in the Dome. His arm was fine, Friend claimed, and his confidence, severely damaged by his Yankee debacle, was back. Friend was 4–1, Shaw was 7–5, and the Mets had a solid rotation for the first time in their five years. By the end of the season, Shaw had 11 Met wins and 10 losses. Westrum called him the best pitcher in Met history and said that the Giants would have won the pennant if they'd kept him.

Like Shaw, Friend was reputed to load the ball. "Evidently he wet the ball up," said outfielder Shaun Fitzmaurice, "which I did not know. I caught a fly ball for the final out of an inning, and the umpire put up his hand for me to throw him the ball. I did. When I came into the dugout,

*In 1964, Washington pitcher Jim Duckworth was placed on the disabled list and put under psychiatric care because of his fear of flying. He returned to the active roster just in time for a harrowing trip to Cleveland, during which the pilot had to abort his takeoff because of a plane directly in his path.

they jumped all over me. Evidently, there was something on the ball and they thought I should have rolled it to him."

A third veteran on the 1966 Mets and, according to many, the most flagrant spitballer of them all, was big, six foot, two hundred pound righthander Jack Hamilton. Hamilton was 27, a hard thrower who had first come to the majors with the Phillies in 1962. He was 9–12 that year, was among the league leaders in walks and uncorked 22 wild pitches. For the next three years, Hamilton spent most of his time in the International League, with infrequent and ineffective appearances for the Phillies and Tigers. He had some shoulder trouble, but recovered and led the International League in ERA in 1965. The Mets purchased his contract from the Tigers after the season and sent him to Florida to pitch in the Instructional League. Hamilton was 5–0 in Florida and so impressed Westrum that he was named a regular starter.

Hamilton made his Met debut on April 17, in the second game of the season. He gave an excellent performance, beating the Braves 3–1 and, most important for a pitcher who struggled with his control his entire career, walked just one man. The win brought the Mets to a pinnacle they had never reached in their five years in the National League. With a 1–1 record, they were a .500 team. It was the earliest the club had ever achieved its first win, the initial milestone in what was to become a season of many milestones.

The game also marked the first time as a Met that Hamilton was accused of throwing a spitter. Bobby Bragan came out on three separate occasions to complain. Bragan's protests, of course, were futile, but the controversy continued throughout the year and for the rest of Hamilton's career. Usually, complaints were only made when he was pitching well. After he was hit hard by the Giants, Frank Litsky wrote, "The Giants kept charging last night that Jack Hamilton of the New York Mets was putting spit on the ball. The accusation apparently was not true. Hamilton appeared to be putting nothing on the ball." The fact that a Met pitcher was accused of throwing an illegal pitch was another unmistakable sign of progress. In 1962, someone asked Stengel whether any of his pitchers threw a spitball. "Spitters?" Casey replied. "I can't get them to throw regular pitches good."

"Jack was a good old farm boy from Iowa," said Jack Fisher, "who could just throw the hell out of the ball. He was a tough dude and he had a hell of a spitter." When Hamilton pitched in the American League, Gil Hodges, managing the Senators, called it "the most flagrant spitter I ever saw." Hodges admitted that many pitchers threw illegal pitches, but said "none continues to break the rule like Hamilton. He made a farce of the game." Hodges was so incensed he wrote a five page letter to American League President Joe Cronin, who expressed his sympathy but evinced little hope that anything could be done.

Hamilton got off to a flying start in 1966. On May 4, he became only the second Met to pitch a one-hitter. It was nearly a no hitter. In the third inning, Cardinal pitcher Ray Sadecki beat out a bunt down the third base line for the only St. Louis hit. Hamilton dominated the Cardinals, walking only one and raising his record to 3–1. He estimated that, of his 96 pitches, at least 85 were fastballs. He didn't provide an estimate of the number of spitters. In his next start, although it was a losing effort, Hamilton allowed only two hits in seven innings.

That was the high point of Hamilton's career as a Met starter. He lost six of his next seven decisions and, with the arrival of Shaw and Friend, found himself in the bullpen. It was a good move, for Hamilton proved to be the best relief pitcher the Mets had ever had. He threw very hard, and if his control was good, he could be overpowering in short bursts. Unlike many former starters, Hamilton was able to warm up quickly and pitch two or three days in a row. On a highly successful Mets' road trip in June, Hamilton saved four games. On one occasion in July, he saved both games of a doubleheader. By the end of the season he had saved a Met record 13 games, despite not going to the bullpen until June. Hamilton achieved the record partly because of his clutch pitching, and partly because 1966 was the first season the Mets had many leads to protect.

Hamilton's eventual undoing was his lack of control. He was simply too wild to be trusted in clutch, late-inning situations. In 1966, Hamilton had 88 walks and 93 strikeouts, a very poor ratio. The 88 walks, and his 18 wild pitches, were both Met records. Nearly every relief appearance was a high-wire act, getting into and out of trouble, or sometimes just into trouble. Part of the problem was that, particularly under pressure, Hamilton had a tendency to overthrow. "When he had that ball in his hand," recalled pitcher Jack Lamabe, "he put 120 percent into every pitch he threw. He threw his fastball hard and he threw his curve as hard as he could throw it." "He had great movement on the ball," added Ed Bressoud. "Maybe that's why he was a little bit wild."

Perhaps Westrum shifted Hamilton to the bullpen because he could stand an inning or two of stress much better than an entire game of agony. In early September, Barney Kremenko wrote, "Jack Hamilton is still pretty much in the picture, but Jolly Jack has been scaring Westrum too often with his steaks of wildness." "He made Westrum a top step manager," Lamabe said. "He'd be on the top step ready to take him out and then he'd strike somebody out. Wes would go and sit down. Then he'd walk somebody and Wes would be back on the top step."

Hamilton had just one season as the Met bullpen ace. He started the '67 season in New York, but was traded to the Angels in June. Dick Young commented sarcastically that maybe Angel pitcher Lew Burdette could teach Hamilton how to throw a spitter. It was in California that Hamilton achieved his greatest, and most unfortunate, notoriety. On August 18, pitching for the Angels against the Red Sox, he threw a high, inside pitch to Tony Conigliaro. Conigliaro froze, and the pitch shattered the left side of his face. "I think I was one of the first people he called," said Jack Fisher. "He told me, 'Man, I hit a guy tonight, Jack, and he's really hurt.' I said, 'Hell, you don't throw hard enough to hurt anybody.'" Unfortunately, Hamilton did throw hard enough to cause the injury that eventually ended Conigliaro's career.

As the 1962 season had seen the Mets set negative records nearly every day, 1966 marked the first year they could point to positive achievements. They were 14-10-1 in exhibition games, and the winning spirit continued into the regular season. The Mets avoided their usual opening day slump by being rained out the first three games of the season in Cincinnati.*

The Mets won their opening home game, and for the first time in their history, had a record better than .500, at 2–1. They were not over .500 for long, but neither were they in their accustomed spot in last place. Thanks to a number of rainouts, the Mets played only 11 games in April, and won five of them. At the end of the month, they were in seventh place, ahead of the Cardinals, Reds and Cubs. The Cardinals and Reds were bound to improve, but the Cubs showed promise of giving the Mets a tussle for the cellar.

By May 11th, the Mets had moved ahead of the Braves into sixth place, the highest standing ever for a Met squad, with a 9–10 record. They stumbled in the second half of the month, but on the 31st, were still 4½ games ahead of Chicago. Youngsters were blending with the veterans to produce what proved to be the best team, to that point, in Met history. Hunt, who'd taken diet pills during the winter to slim down, was off to an excellent start.† He made the All Star team, the first Met to be named twice, and sacrificed the winning run into scoring position in the tenth inning. He also became the Mets' all time leader in hits.

Cleon Jones was at last realizing the great potential the Mets always believed he possessed. Jones, the unusual specimen who batted right handed and threw left handed, first came up to the Mets late in the 1963 season, playing in a handful of games in September.§ The following

*When Mayor Lindsay threw out the first ball at the Met opener, Joe Durso noted that the Mayor, who had also thrown out the first pitch at the Yankee opener, had tossed two more pitches than any Met hurler.

†One can just imagine the hyper-active Hunt on amphetamines.

§Jones was a natural left hander who began batting right handed as a boy because his favorite players, Joe Dimaggio, Willie Mays and Roy Campanella, batted right handed.

spring, despite having played only 63 games in the low minors, he came to spring training and was given a chance to win a major league job. Jones was green, but had a quick bat and, most of all, tremendous speed. In high school, he had run the 100 yard dash in 9.7 seconds.

Cleon was selected to accompany the team on its 1964 trip to Mexico City and, along with his teammates, given a series of shots. He had a bad reaction, spent a week in bed, and never regained his strength sufficiently to challenge for a roster spot. "He looked ludicrously clumsy in the field," reported *The New York Times*, "looked bad at bat even in practice games, seldom displayed his speed and appeared to be either uninspired or terrified." Jones was sent to Buffalo for a year of Triple A experience.

After a solid season at Buffalo in '64, Jones came to camp the following year hoping to fill the Mets' continuing void in center field. That March an infected tooth caused more medical problems. This time, however, the Mets kept the youngster on the squad until cutdown day in mid–May, when he departed for Buffalo with a bruised ego and a .156 average. Jones looked unsure both at bat and in the field, and a trip to Buffalo was probably the best thing for him. "He may yet come back to be an outstanding player," wrote Leonard Koppett, "but the feeling of failure he carries with him today is something only other players who have been cut can really appreciate."

"It's tough," said former Yankee Bob Meyer, "when they send you out because at that age you're not able to see yourself as a person on one hand and a ballplayer on the other. It's all intertwined. When they send you down, you're worthless as a person in your own mind. You have this idea, especially since playing ball is the only thing you've done since you were a little kid, that your worth is centered on what you're doing as a player. When they send you out, you're a failure."

Jones was able to bounce back and had another good season at Buffalo, but was no better when he was called up to the Mets in September than he had been in April. With the Mets solidly entrenched in the cellar, Westrum played Jones frequently, but he finished the year with a .149 average in 30 games. He had demonstrated in the minor leagues that he had ability, but did he have the mental toughness to make it in the majors?

During the off-season, the Mets decided to send Jones to Latin America with instructions to learn to switch hit, to allow him to take better advantage of his speed and help with his inadequacy against right hand pitchers. The switch hitting experiment was abandoned nearly as soon as it began, but Jones, with the help of some advice from teammate Joe Christopher, had a fine winter season. He showed up in St. Petersburg with more confidence that ever before, and began to hit like he had in the minor leagues. He was also fielding better. Jones led the club with a .451 mark in exhibition games, and continued his strong batting when the regular season began.

Perhaps most encouraging to the Mets was Cleon's remarkably improved mental state. Coach Sheriff Robinson had seen Jones in Buffalo and in New York and marveled at the difference. "In Buffalo," said Robinson, "it didn't look like he had enough desire —[H]e had his head down and seemed uncomfortable when you had anything to say to him. But now you can talk to him." Jones agreed. "I didn't feel like a major leaguer before," he said.*

By the end of May, 1966, Jones was being touted as a candidate for Rookie of the Year honors. He was batting over .280, fielding well and doing something no Met had ever done before, stealing bases. Despite Stengel's famous "run, sheep, run" cry, the Mets had not run very often. The 1962 club, with 59 stolen bases, was the speediest Met team of the first four. The following year, they stole only 41 times, and in 1964 and 1965, just 36 and 28 times, respectively. In 1965,

*As Jones continued to improve, his personality blossomed. After the Mets won the World Series in 1969, one agent said Jones could become a "black Joe Garagiola."

they were dead last in the National league. Elio Chacon and Richie Ashburn shared the club record with 12 steals each in 1962. Since then, no Met had stolen more than six.

Jones broke Chacon and Ashburn's record on September 12th. By the end of the season, he had established a new mark of 16 steals. It wasn't a Wills-like pace, but it was a step up from the plodders of the Mets' first four years. With Bud Harrelson, who was called up in September, stealing successfully in his first seven tries, the Mets had 55 steals, their best mark since 1962.

In early June, before the acquisition of Shaw and Friend, the Met pitching was showing signs of strain. Hamilton, still in the starting rotation, was being hit hard, and Rob Gardner, who started strong, had a series of bad outings. Despite their fast start, the Mets were falling back toward the cellar. On June 9, they had exactly the same record as they had on that date in 1963 and 1965.

Suddenly, without warning, it all came together. Dick Rusteck came up from Jacksonville and pitched a shutout. Dennis Ribant followed with another shutout. Along came Shaw and Friend and suddenly pitching was carrying the club. On June 17, the club posted their first doubleheader sweep of the season, as Shaw and Fisher beat the Reds. Like Maris stalking Ruth in 1961, the Mets' record was being compared to that of previous Met clubs. Could this be the winningest team of all? After the doubleheader sweep, they were five games ahead of their previous best mark. On June 24, the Mets won their twelfth game of the month, tying the team record. They had their best road trip ever with eight wins. The Mets were eight games ahead of the Cubs, the greatest distance they had ever been from the cellar.

July was an even better month than June had been. On the 21st, the Mets tied their high for road wins with their 21st of the season. They won seven games in a row (another record) and broke the mark set in June by posting 18 wins in a month. At one point, Westrum's club won 12 of 15 games. In early July, the Mets had the same record as the struggling Yankees (35–44). From June 10 through July 25, they won 25 of 50 games, not a pennant-winning pace, but compared to prior teams, the 1966 edition was a veritable juggernaut. At the end of July, the Mets were 47–55, just a percentage point behind the eighth place Braves and just 2½ games behind the sixth place Reds. They led the Cubs by 15½ and the rarified air of ninth place seemed all but certain. They needed only seven wins in the last two months to break their all time high for victories.

Individual marks were falling as well. By hitting a pair of home runs in a game on June 10, Ed Bressoud tied the mark for most homers in a season by a Met shortstop, held by Elio Chacon with two. Bressoud broke the record shortly thereafter. Chuck Hiller, acquired from the Giants in 1965 after Hunt separated his shoulder, set a record in mid–August when he got his 14th pinch hit of the season, breaking the mark established by Richie Ashburn in 1962. For the season, Hiller was 16 for 46 (.348) as a pinch hitter. Swoboda set a record with the fourth pinch hit home run of his career. In August, Hawk Taylor hit the first pinch hit grand slam in Met history. Batting against big, hard throwing Pirate lefty Bob Veale, Taylor connected for a long blast over the left centerfield fence. "I hit it good," Taylor recalled. "I remember thinking, 'I've done my job.' I was feeling really good, just kind of floating on air. Then I got to thinking. I'd just won ten thousand King Korn trading stamps for hitting a grand slam home run. That did my Christmas shopping for me."

Success couldn't last, and the Mets skidded to 9–20 in August. Still, they broke the all-time team record with their 54th win on August 21st. The team staggered in September, but won their 63rd game on the 20th, assuring themselves that, for the first time in their history, they would not lose 100 games. Finally, on the 24th, the Mets achieved the ultimate goal, clinching a tie for ninth place. When the season ended, Westrum had led the club to 66 wins, thirteen more than ever before, and the first ninth place finish in their brief history. On the last day of the season, Wes treated his team to champagne in the locker room. The Mets hadn't won the pennant, but for them, ninth place was an achievement worthy of celebration. What was next? Eighth place?

• 14 •

Reluctant Heroes
The Search for a Center Fielder

The Mets began their existence with a perennial All-Star center fielder. Unfortunately, Richie Ashburn was a Met several years after being a member of the National League squad in 1948, 1951, 1953 and 1958. In his prime, Ashburn was perhaps the best leadoff hitter in the game and had the greatest range of any NL center fielder other than Willie Mays. On nine occasions, he had more than 400 putouts, the most times any major leaguer had surpassed that level. Ashburn was also the league's leading hitter in 1955 and 1958, led in on base percentage in 1960, and was one of the National League's top base stealers. In 1958, at the age of 32, he stole 30 bases, just one behind league leader Mays. When Ashburn joined the Mets, after 14 seasons in the big leagues, he had a career average of .308.

Ashburn was an All Star again in 1962, the only Met named to the squad, but he was chosen mainly due to the rule that each team must have at least one representative. Richie was still a very good player, one who could pinch hit, draw walks, slap the ball around, and play solid if no longer spectacular defense. Ashburn batted .306, the only Met to bat .300 in their first season, and hit a career-high seven homers, after having hit a total of just three in the six previous seasons. Richie had always liked hitting in the Polo Grounds. Even though it had never been his home park, Ashburn, prior to the 1962 season, had hit 9 of his 22 career home runs there.

Ashburn would have been a valuable role player on a contending team. During the first part of the year, he was hampered by leg problems and appeared mostly as a pinch hitter, with remarkable success. At the age of 36, however, he wasn't able to stand up to the rigors of everyday action. Stengel, with little to choose from, didn't have the luxury of using Ashburn for spot duty. When the Mets continued to lose, Stengel put him in center field. Center field in the Polo Grounds, which was over 450 feet deep, was simply too vast for him. Ashburn had never had a strong arm, and it was no better at 36. By the end of the season he was in right field. Stengel tried Joe Christopher in center, but Joe had difficulties in left and right, let alone the spacious middle pasture at the Polo Grounds. In fact, Christopher had trouble anywhere in fair territory.

Jim Hickman played center, but wasn't comfortable in the Polo Grounds. "I'd get out there in center field," he said, "and it was so big it scared me. Then when you played left and right, you had that wall right there. You were always afraid the ball was going to bounce off the wrong way and get away from you." By the end of the 1962 season, the Mets still hadn't found a regular center fielder.

Ashburn retired after the season to take a job in the Phillies' broadcast booth, and the following year Stengel acquired another great defensive outfielder who, like Ashburn, was in the twilight of his career. Jimmy Piersall had, at least outwardly, conquered his numerous personal demons, but Stengel would have preferred the unbalanced, hard-hitting, defensive wizard who roamed American League outfields in the '50s. When Piersall proved incapable of playing on a regular basis, the Mets tried Rod Kanehl, Duke Carmel, and Joe Hicks, none of whom was able to win the job.

For the Mets' first five years, their great hope was that Hickman would become the regular center fielder. He appeared to have all the tools. Hickman was 25 years old when he was chosen from the Cardinals in the expansion draft, an athletic 6'3", 195 pounds, with power, speed and a very strong arm. "He had an ideal physique," said Bobby Klaus. "Jimmy had great physical ability."

Signed by the Cardinals in 1956, Hickman spent six years in the St. Louis farm system, leading the Georgia-Florida League in home runs and RBI in 1957. Despite his obvious talent, the Cardinals hesitated to bring him to the big leagues, for they had received a scouting report stating that Hickman lacked the aggressiveness to be a major league ballplayer. He had all the tools to be a big leaguer, except confidence. "Jim was a very quiet, unassuming guy," observed Al Luplow. "I always liked Jim," said Rick Herrscher. "He was humble. Humility is a characteristic that is admirable in any human being, but for some reason, in baseball, they like cockiness. They like the guys who think they belong."

Hickman was (and is) an extremely humble man. He was too shy to ask teammate Duke Snider for advice. Duke, he explained, was very helpful when asked, but wasn't the type to volunteer information. "Heck," Hickman said, "I wasn't smart enough to ask him what I needed to ask him. At that point, I didn't know how to hit. I didn't know how to take advantage of the Polo Grounds."

When discussing his career today, Hickman gives the impression that he was a marginal player who spent a couple of years riding a major league bench, rather than a man who spent thirteen years in the big leagues and made the 1970 National League All Star team. Even in 1969, in the midst of a hot streak with the Cubs, Hickman didn't believe in himself. "I'll just have to do the best with what I've got," he said. "I guess that's why I get down on myself. I look and see what I've got and I ain't got too much."

Hickman, from the small town of Henning, Tennessee, was intimidated by New York City. "I was 25 when I came to Mets," he recalled, "and these kids out of the cities were 18 going on 30. It was a hard place to adjust to. I think if I had been a little tougher mentally, I might have been a better player. I'd get in a traffic jam on the way to the ballpark and somebody would cuss me out and, heck, I'd feel bad about it the rest of the day. But that was just a way of life there."

New York was a tough place for anyone to play, but especially so for country boys. Mickey Mantle was completely lost during his rookie season, spending most of his time alone in his room. Larry Foss, from Castleton, Kansas, felt the same as Hickman. "Getting to the Big Apple was a whole different deal," he said. "I was kind of a duck out of water up there. Marv Throneberry and I were walking down to The Stage Delicatessen. I was stopping, letting people go by, not wanting to bump into them or anything, and Marv said, 'When you're in New York, you've got to do what they do.' He just waded in there and if he bumped into somebody, nobody seemed to take offense."

Even city boys were intimidated. "I'm from Chicago," said former Yankee pitcher Eli Grba, "which is a big city, but I got to New York and I was completely overwhelmed. Everybody knew you there. I don't give a rat's ass what kind of player you were. They knew you. I could walk through the middle of Manhattan and somebody would say, 'Grba, hey, Grba you bum.'"

Hickman made the Met squad in 1962, but played very little in the first few weeks. Hoping for seventh or eighth place, Stengel went with his veterans, Thomas, Bell and Ashburn. When Bell was sold to the Braves, and Ashburn proved incapable of playing center field every day, Hickman saw more action. In June, *The Sporting News* ranked him with Lou Brock as the top rookie outfielders in the league. The Yankees expressed an interest in acquiring him to strengthen their bench. Hickman did well in the middle stages of the season, and was hitting .281 in late July. He tailed off in August and September, finishing at .245, with 13 home runs. He also led the Mets in strikeouts with 96, despite batting less than 400 times. Making contact had always been a problem for Jim, who led the Texas League with 107 whiffs in 1959.

"Jim Hickman has a beautiful swing," said *Sports Illustrated* in the spring of '63, "and maybe the top Met prospect, but he can be pitched to." Hickman's biggest problem, according to Stengel, was that he didn't employ that beautiful swing often enough. He took too many pitches, and far too often was called out with the bat on his shoulder. Other times, Hickman swung at bad pitches. "He hasn't mastered the strikeout yet," Stengel said. "They keep fooling him with the outside pitch. If this fellow can learn to cut down on his strikeouts, he could be one of the best hitters around. He has all the power he needs, but by now he should know that you can't hit a ball with the bat on your shoulder. You have to swing."

With the Yankees, Stengel often coaxed results from under-performing ballplayers by giving them the needle. "Casey would always make sure," said Frank Thomas, "that when he was talking to a writer about a ballplayer that the player was close enough to hear him. Casey always thought that Jim could have been a better ballplayer than he was. He wanted to light a fire under him." With a brash, confident player like Billy Martin or Gene Woodling, that was the perfect strategy. Stengel had mixed results with Mantle, and failed completely with Hickman. "I used to tell Jim," said Thomas, "that Casey was trying to use reverse psychology on him so he'd say, 'I'll prove to that son-of-a-gun that I'm a better ballplayer than he thinks I am.' But with Jim it had the opposite effect. When he left New York and went to Chicago he had a great year. He had all the tools, but he got down on himself because of Casey picking on him." Rather than make him angry and determined, Stengel's chiding reinforced Hickman's opinion that he was not worthy. "That was Casey's way," said Joe Christopher, "but it was not the other player's way."

In the spring of '63, the Mets expected Hickman, with a year of experience, to blossom. "Jim is a different ballplayer this spring," gushed broadcaster Ralph Kiner. "He sure is ripping into the ball. He's a take-charge man at the plate. If he can get real aggressive, he could be one of the stars of the league. He has all the tools." "He could be the player to lead us out of the wilderness," said coach Cookie Lavagetto. "I just think he was over his head in the Big Time. By that I mean he seemed to be awed by the whole thing."

Lavagetto had hit the nail on the head, for Hickman, by his own admission, didn't think he belonged. "In my first few years with the Mets," he said recently, "I probably should have been in the minor leagues." That was a very unusual statement, one I'd heard only from players rushed to the major leagues as teenagers, never from 25-year-olds with six years of minor league experience. Many players who were in the minor leagues thought they should be playing in the majors, but very few in the majors thought they should be in the minors.

In 1963, Hickman's early season performance was encouraging. At the end of April, he was batting .315 and was tied for the team lead in home runs. On April 21st, as the Mets swept a doubleheader from the Braves and climbed out of the cellar for the first time in nearly a year, Hickman hit a grand slam in the first game, and a two-run homer and a 450 foot double in the nightcap. He was the star of the day in New York, and was told that if he could reach the CBS studio by 8 o'clock, he could appear on the Ed Sullivan Show and receive a fee of $250. Unfortunately, the second game ended at 8:10, and Hickman left for Philadelphia without the $250.

As the year went on, Hickman's strikeout total climbed, and his average dropped. In midseason, Stengel decided that, with his great arm, Hickman might fill the Mets' gaping hole at third base, though he had been an outfielder all his life. "They just stuck me over there and it was tough," Hickman recalled. "Heck, I was half scared to death. I wasn't a natural third base-man and I just didn't know what to do over there. The game speeds up a lot from the outfield and I didn't speed up with it, which made it tough." Now, Hickman had something else to worry about. His fielding average was the lowest among National League third basemen and his hitting suffered. Hickman wound up with a .229 average, although he led a feeble Met offense with 17 home runs, including the last homer ever hit in the Polo Grounds. His strikeout total increased to 120, breaking the Met record he set the previous season. At the end of the year, discouraged, he said he wanted to become a pitcher.

The next spring, Stengel decided to find out whether, with a full training camp behind him, Hickman could play third base. He couldn't. After a miserable exhibition season in the field, Hickman returned to the outfield, where he played on a semi-regular basis. After a slow first half, Stengel was almost ready to give up on him. Twice, in a loss to the Cubs, Hickman was called out on strikes, once with the tying runs on second and third and none out. After the game, Stengel called Hickman into his office and told him, bluntly, to get the bat off his shoulder. "He better start swinging," Casey told reporters, "or I'll swing him out of the lineup."

Hickman started swinging. Platooned with left-handed Larry Elliot, he batted .304 from July 9 through the end of the season, lifting his overall mark to .257, his best average in three years with the Mets. Finally, Stengel thought he had found the answer. Batting mostly against left-handers, Casey believed, would allow Hickman to show his ability at last. He decided that in 1965, he would alternate Hickman in right field with left handed Johnny Lewis, who had been acquired in a trade from the Cardinals. Lewis was like Hickman in some ways. He was a product of the Cardinal farm system, he had power, he had speed and, like Hickman, a very strong arm. Like Hickman, he had felt pressure in St. Louis, which he believed hurt his play. In New York, far from a pennant race, Lewis expected less stress and better performance.

Bing Devine had also arrived from St. Louis, and knew Hickman from his years in the Cardinal farm system. He was as puzzled as Stengel about Jim's inability to hit consistently. "Jim Hickman, in center field," Devine said, "always looks like he should be good, but somehow or other doesn't quite get there. Or at least, he hasn't yet."

In 1965, it looked like Hickman might never get there. Lewis took the regular job in right by getting off to a sizzling start. Hickman saw some time at first base, but his average was below .100. Meanwhile, center field continued to be a problem. Cleon Jones got a chance to win the job, but was intimidated by major league pitching and sent back to Buffalo. Ron Swoboda had trouble in all fields, and was quickly moved out of center. Billy Cowan got a trial, but was another Hickman, with great potential and natural ability but prone to the strikeout. With his batting average well below .200, Cowan took a seat on the bench.

Finally, in early June, Casey turned to Lewis. "At long last," Barney Kremenko wrote, "Casey Stengel has come up with a bona fide, honest-to-goodness, regular, competent, every-day center fielder for his Mets.... Thus ended a four-season search that saw countless center fielders patrolling the area." Hickman was reduced to pinch-hitting duty and replacing Christopher for defensive purposes.

The very next week, Kremenko reported that the four-season search was on again. Hickman was going to be the regular center fielder, with Lewis returning to right. "This man [Hickman] has had too much criticism from the fans in New York," Stengel said, "He's the best center fielder I've got."

In July, when Wes Westrum replaced Stengel, he proclaimed his faith in Hickman and declared his intention to play him as often as possible. On September 3, Hickman justified Westrum's faith. In a game against the Cardinals at Shea, batting against St. Louis lefty Ray Sadecki in the second inning, he drove an outside fastball more than 400 feet into the right center field stands. In the fourth, he pulled a home run over the left field fence. In the sixth, he hit a third homer. It was the first time any Met had hit three home runs in a single game.

Afterwards, Hickman was asked about the frustrations of his Met career. Had Stengel been the problem? "I'm not going to say anything," he stated. "Maybe I've said too much already. No, Casey Stengel had nothing to do with it. Casey was a nice old fellow." In a recent interview, Hickman also spoke well of Stengel. "There's no question that Casey was past his prime." he said, "but, heck, he had a handle on things. Casey was good to me. I had a hard time trying to understand what he was trying to say for a good while, but in the end, Casey treated me pretty good. I've got nothing but good things to say about him. I think at times he was trying to protect me against certain types of pitchers."

Despite his September heroics, Hickman ended the 1965 season with an average of just .236, but with 15 home runs. "He maintained his inconsistency," said Devine. As in 1964, however, Hickman's late surge produced optimism for the following year. During spring training, Westrum predicted he would hit 30 home runs. Even Stengel, visiting the Mets in Florida, was impressed. "Jim Hickman is the only one who is going to play every day and he can hit over buildings," Casey said. "He has learned to lean over the plate to protect himself against the outside pitch. I would say he has become braver at the plate."

The Mets had another center field candidate in 1966, Shaun Fitzmaurice, a former Notre Dame star. Fitzmaurice was fast, having run the 60 yard dash on the Irish track team, he could field, and he could hit, having earned the MVP Award in the Basin League, a summer program for college players. In the Fall of 1964, just prior to signing with the Mets, Fitzmaurice played in the Tokyo Olympics. Baseball was not a medal event but, along with sumo wrestling, was presented as a demonstration sport.

By the time he reported to the Met camp the following spring, Fitzmaurice was perhaps better suited for sumo wrestling than baseball. "I wasn't big into weights," he said, "and I wanted to get bigger and stronger, so I thought I'd do it through excess eating." He got bigger, but not much stronger, and definitely slower. "During my sophomore year in college," he said, "I was in the best shape of my life. I would hit a routine ground ball to shortstop and beat it out." With the added weight, Fitzmaurice was no longer beating out infield hits.

Fitzmaurice eventually slimmed down, and regained most of his speed, but didn't make the team in the spring of '65 or '66. He came up at the end of the 1966 season and played in nine games, but had to serve time in the reserves and missed spring training the following year. He wasn't in shape when he returned, tore his hamstring and missed most of the year. "I was traded to the Pirate organization," he said, "because the Mets thought I was more interested in going to college than playing ball." Fitzmaurice eventually ended up playing for Richmond, Atlanta's top minor league affiliate. He had some good seasons, but the other Richmond outfielders were Dusty Baker and Ralph Garr. Fitzmaurice was nearly 30, and the other two were in their early 20s. He didn't have a prayer of getting to Atlanta. Following the 1973 season, Fitzmaurice retired. "I played Little League baseball with a team called the Braves," he said, "and I finished my career with the Richmond Braves. That's a full cycle there." Fitzmaurice looks back without malice on his career, and what might have been. "You can always blame your failures on somebody else," he said, "but sometimes you've got to step up and say, 'Hey, I was the one holding the bat.'"

Following the departure of Cannizzaro at the end of training camp in 1966, Hickman was the last remaining original Met, the only remnant of the club that had started the 1962 season. He beat out Fitzmaurice for the center field job, but didn't match Westrum's prediction of 30 home runs. In fact, he hit just four. On May 13th (Friday the 13th), in a game against the Giants, Hickman dove for a looping fly ball off the bat of Ollie Brown. He missed, and landed awkwardly on his left wrist, dislocating it. Hickman was placed on the disabled list, went home to Tennessee to recuperate, and didn't return to the Met lineup until the second week of August.

Before the season, Hickman confided, he had been considering retirement. When he returned to the lineup in August, however, it was with renewed desire. The injured wrist was still sensitive, which limited his swing and forced him to just try and meet the ball. He began hitting to all fields, rather than swinging for the fences, and was pleasantly surprised by the results. The high point of his season was a home run which enabled the Mets to win their 54th game, setting an all-time high.

Hickman was encouraged, both by the Mets' ninth place finish and by his own comeback, and looked forward to the 1967 season. "The way it looks now," he said in September, "they may have to tear the uniform off me." The Mets did just that. During the winter, they traded him, along with Hunt, to the Dodgers for Tommy Davis.

Hickman had had a difficult run in New York, and continued to be a target of abuse even after he left. In the spring of 1967, Davis asked the Dodgers to send films of him batting. He joked that Dodger executive Red Patterson had only sent pictures of him when he was in a slump. "The Mets promised to return the favor," wrote Jack Lang, "by sending Patterson pictures of Jim Hickman taking a third strike." Three years later, when he made the All Star team, Hickman had the last laugh, but for the gentleman from Henning, Tennessee, revenge was the last thing on his mind.

In 1967, Davis, two time NL batting champ, would play left field. The Met center fielder of 1967 and the future was switch-hitting Don Bosch, who had a lot in common with Hickman. While Hickman spent six years in the minor leagues, Bosch had spent seven. Most of all, like Hickman, Bosch was a modest man who was often filled with self-doubt. "There aren't a lot of real good memories for me," he said recently, "because I was never very confident. I was always running scared — trying to belong in the big leagues but never really feeling like I did."

When the Mets obtained Bosch from the Pirates, they believed he would be the solution to the center field woes that had plagued the club since 1962. "He is built like Curt Flood," Devine said, "and, in fact, plays like Curt in many ways." Devine also compared Bosch's defensive skills favorably to those of Mays. "He is as good as any center fielder in baseball defensively," said Larry Shepard, who managed him at Columbus in 1966. Dick Williams, the new Red Sox manager, who played 13 years in the major leagues against Mantle, Mays, Piersall et al, called Bosch the greatest defensive center fielder he'd ever seen.

Bosch read all the quotes. "You're 24 years old," he said recently, "and you hear that you're ready, but you're not really prepared for the change. I didn't realize what I was getting into in terms of going to the big leagues. There was a dramatic change in terms of media pressure, especially in New York. They made a big deal of me. They tried to imply that I was the next Willie Mays or Mickey Mantle. That was the last thing I could ever be because I didn't have those types of skills." When Devine and Shepard compared Bosch to star outfielders on a defensive basis, most fans ignored the distinction and expected him to hit like Mays, Flood and Mantle.

The obvious question was why, if Bosch had ability comparable to Flood and Mays, he spent seven years in the minor leagues, and had never even been invited to the Pirates' major league camp. He'd led the Carolina League in hitting in 1963, but that was Class A ball. In 1966 with Columbus, Bosch hit a respectable .283 with 11 home runs, good but not spectacular results.

"I thought going to the Mets was going to be a wonderful opportunity," Bosch said, "because they were struggling, they needed players and I had a chance to make the team. But some of the older players down in the Dominican Republic told me it would be tougher to go to a team like the Mets because there was no supporting cast. I was going to be out there in full view of everybody without people hitting ahead of me or behind me. They said I'd be expected to do too much. That's exactly what happened."

Bosch, playing in the Dominican Republic when he learned of his trade to the Mets, was told he could go home and take the rest of the winter off. He declined, feeling obligated to fulfill his commitment to play the entire season. "It was a mistake," Bosch said, "because I got dysentery and a few other things and lost twenty pounds. By the time I got to spring training, I could barely lift a bat."

Many were taken aback by their first glimpse of the new Met phenom. "They were shocked at his size," wrote Jack Lang. "Bosch is listed on the roster at 5–10, but he doesn't look that big." He seemed a bit small for the next Willie Mays. Joe Durso compared Bosch to another Willie, jockey Willie Shoemaker. "I was a little surprised," said Westrum. "I expected a tall, slim fellow." Not only was Bosch short, he was weak and underweight, and suffering from an ulcer and a sprained wrist. The ulcer had first appeared two years earlier and flared up again in the spring of '67. "It was nerves more than anything else," Bosch said.

Needless to say, Bosch had a poor spring. With the intense pressure on him and his debilitated physical condition, he couldn't even be Don Bosch, let alone Willie Mays or Mickey Mantle. During the exhibition games, he batted .151, the lowest average of any Met regular, and his fielding lacked its reputed spectacular flair. He appeared completely overmatched by big league pitching, at one point going 25 at bats without a hit. "In Triple A," Bosch said, "you get a good pitcher today and then a mediocre pitcher tomorrow. But when you get to the big leagues, they're all good. Some are just better than others. You don't have the opportunity to build your average up against somebody mediocre. Everybody is at the top of their game and they're smarter. They don't give you the pitch over the middle."

In late March, Westrum realized that the youngster was cracking under the pressure and told him to take a couple of days off and go fishing. He needed to relax, Westrum said. But how could Bosch relax when the press was running him down daily? He declined Westrum's offer and continued to play.

Rather than conclude from Bosch's slight stature and underwhelming offensive skills that the Mets' scouting system was deficient, the fans and media decided it was Bosch's fault that he was not what they had been told he was. "If there is an award for the most disappointing player of the spring," wrote Lang, "it goes to center fielder Don Bosch."

"The writers in New York are ruthless," Bosch said. "They build you up to be something you can't be, and then when you don't meet their expectations, they break you back down to an embarrassing nothing." "Naturally," Westrum said, "we're going to go a long way with this boy. We're not giving up on him by any means. But I have to admit that if he was just another outfielder in camp, he would have been gone by this time. All of the people who saw him and raved about him can't be wrong." Westrum said that once Bosch learned to relax, he would be fine. How could he, however, after being called the most disappointing player of the spring, compared to a jockey and told he was the key to the Met season?

Despite his horrendous spring, Bosch was in the opening day lineup as the leadoff batter and center fielder. He started the Met season with a single, stole second and scored the team's first run. That was the high point of Bosch's Met career. By the end of April, he was batting .139, and his fielding was tentative. In early May he was taken out of the lineup, and Cleon Jones was moved back to center field. For a month, Bosch sat on the bench, then played a few more games. He still felt intense pressure and his performance was no better than before, his average hovering around .150.

"I was really struggling," Bosch recalled, "so Wes took me out of the lineup and said, 'I want you to sit here with me for a couple of days and just kind of learn from the bench. It will take some of the pressure off of you. You're not going to go anywhere. I don't want you to be afraid that you're going to go back to the minor leagues.'" Two days later, Westrum decided that Bosch could learn more in Jacksonville, Florida than he could on the New York bench, and dispatched him to the International League. Bosch believed that the front office had ordered the move and Westrum had not resisted. "I think his job status was pretty fragile," he said.

After Bosch was sent to the minors, a writer asked Bud Harrelson about his fellow rookie. "I don't know what it is about Don," Harrelson said, "but I think he tried too hard to impress people. But he couldn't convince himself. He's a worrier even though he tries to give a nonchalant appearance — To me, Don tried to be too explosive. He would go up as a leadoff man expecting to hit doubles and triples when all they want a leadoff man to do is get on with a single or a walk."

When the International League season ended, Bosch was recalled to finish the season in New York. He met Joe Durso, who had recently written a book on Casey Stengel. "Are you the fellow who writes about successful people in baseball?" Bosch asked. He was, Durso replied, and why was Bosch curious? "I thought maybe you'd like to write one about a failure," he responded.

At the end of the season, certain that Bosch was not the answer to their center field problems, the Mets traded their leading hitter, Tommy Davis, and one of their starting pitchers, Jack Fisher, to the White Sox for center fielder Tommie Agee and infielder Al Weis. Unlike Bosch, Agee was a proven major league commodity, the American League Rookie of the Year in 1966. Bing Devine was not about to make the same mistake twice.

In 1968, Agee was the man under the microscope. Bosch was a forgotten man, save for a few references to the disastrous trade. Perhaps center field was cursed, for Agee struggled as desperately as Bosch. After being beaned by Bob Gibson in the opening exhibition, Agee couldn't hit.

Bosch, out of the limelight, played reasonably well in the spring, and earned a spot on the squad. That didn't mean, however, that he played. It was Memorial Day before Bosch got his first hit. As the summer wore on, and Agee remained mired in a deep slump, Bosch got to play more often. On June 14, he started against lefthander Mike McCormick of the Giants, the 1967 Cy Young Award winner. "He threw me a fastball on the outside corner," Bosch recalled, "and I hit it to center. I didn't think I hit it that good. Mays is going back and Mays is going back and going back. He's tapping his glove at the 406 sign and it goes over the center field fence." It was Bosch's first major league home run. "A buddy of mine in California," he said, "told me he was coming home from work listening on the radio. He was pulling into his garage and almost drove into the family room.'

The next day, against Juan Marichal, Bosch hit another home run, plus two singles. Even when he succeeded against the best, however, Bosch was as amazed as his buddy. "You would think that Marichal would make mincemeat out of me," he said recently. "But I always hit him well because he didn't waste a lot of energy on me. He threw the ball in there to let me hit it because I was hitting .165. He didn't have to give me his best stuff."

If this were a fictional account, Bosch would stay in the lineup, become an established star, and make his critics eat their harsh words. It wasn't to be. He hit another home run a few days later, but even after his batting spree, Bosch's average remained under .200 and he returned to the bench. In August, Ken Boswell was activated from the disabled list and the Mets had to cut someone. Hodges called Bosch into his office and said, "Don, you've done everything I've asked you to do. You're not going to the minor leagues for any reason other than I don't have a choice. I've got to make a spot for Ken — he's our second baseman — and you're the odd man out." "Gil, I have one question for you," Bosch replied. "I understand your position and I'm not angry and I'll do whatever I have to do. But the last game I played I got a home run and a double, drove in two runs and scored two runs. That's the last time I saw home plate. Why?" "I can't answer that question," Hodges replied. "I just thought that Tommie Agee could do a better job on a day-to-day basis, so I played him."

"What could I say?" Bosch recalled. "He was honest with me. He gave me his honest appraisal of the situation." Bosch took his .171 average to Jacksonville, where he finished out the season. The Mets recalled him for the final month, but he had family problems and elected to go home to California. In October, he was selected by the Montreal Expos in the expansion draft. "Bosch will go down in Met history," wrote Lang, "as one of the all-time busts."

Bosch had little more success in Canada than he had in New York. His first season with the Expos was his final one in the big leagues. The last New York fans heard of Bosch was a quote in *The Times* while the Mets were in Montreal in April. Commenting on the usherettes in Jarry Park, he said, "How do they expect me to hit .400 if they keep all those pretty girls around home plate." Bosch had finally relaxed a bit, as Westrum had urged him to do two years earlier, but it was too late. In parts of four major league seasons, he played in 146 major league games, and batted .164, with just four home runs.

In 1970, Bosch played with the Astros' Triple A farm club in Oklahoma City. "I just couldn't do it any more," he recalled. "I had bad knees. My eyes were playing tricks on me. I just told Hub Kittle, our manager, one day, 'I'm gonna go home.' I had family problems again. That was the last time I played in a baseball game. I just packed it in. Nobody knew where I went or what I did. Nobody ever contacted me."

After more than 30 years, Bosch put his often-frustrating career in perspective. "I think that what I've said might be helpful to other players who've gone through the same thing," he said. "I never live in the past. I always live for today and hope tomorrow's a nice day. Just to get to the big leagues is very good fortune. It's an opportunity that people would give their entire fortune to get and they can't do it because they don't have the opportunity or the skills. I look at it from that perspective. I saw the whole United States. I saw the Dominican Republic for free.

"I always thought it would be nice at my age to be able to jump in a motor home and travel around the country and find some of the guys that I played poker with, that I drank with, that I roomed with or had dinner with, played next to or sat on the bench with. I think it would be nice just to find some of them. I've always told people that I've been very, very fortunate to have played ball because it's opened doors for me. It's kept my self-esteem up at times when you get kind of down. You know you can achieve, so you're going to come back. If you can achieve once, you can achieve again. How many people even get there? I love to tell stories about the other players—the camaraderie—the experiences I had playing cards with the guys. There's no anger. There's no disappointment. There's just thoughts."

· 15 ·

Tom Terrific and Wild Bill
The 1967 Season

The spring of 1967 was the first time Tom Seaver appeared in a Met training camp. The 22-year-old pitcher had arrived in St. Petersburg by a most unusual route, which began at the University of Southern California, detoured to Alaska, and nearly to Atlanta, before heading north to New York by way of Jacksonville. In the spring of 1966, while preparing for the season with USC's Trojans, Seaver accepted a $50,000 bonus to sign with the Atlanta Braves. Although Seaver had not pitched in a game, Southern Cal had played two exhibitions. The Braves assured Seaver that so long as the Trojan's league schedule hadn't started, he was eligible to sign. They were wrong, however, and Commissioner Eckert declared the contract void. This placed Seaver in a quandary, for he was now ineligible to play for USC.

Seaver wrote to Eckert, telling him he thought the ruling was unfair. His father threatened to sue if Seaver wasn't allowed to play. Eckert, whose intention had been to punish the Braves, not Seaver, arranged for a lottery to auction off the young ex-Trojan. He gave each major league club the opportunity to obtain Seaver's services* by matching the Braves' offer. The name of each team willing to give Seaver a $50,000 bonus would be placed in the hat of Eckert's assistant Joe Reichler, with Eckert to pull the name of the winner. The Mets' reports on Seaver weren't that good, but at the last minute George Weiss decided to join the bidding. The Phillies, Indians and Mets ante-ed up, and Eckert pulled the Mets' name out of Reichler's hat.

Seaver was not just an excellent pitcher; he was a fine all-around athlete who could hit, field his position and even steal a base. He came from an athletic family, with his Walker Cup golfer father, a sister who was a swimmer and volleyball player at Stanford and another sister who was a physical education major at UCLA.

Tom played baseball and basketball at Fresno High, but hadn't matured and didn't throw particularly hard. After six months in the Marines and six more working in his father's factory, he filled out to 6'1" and 190 pounds. Seaver played one season at Fresno City College and received a scholarship to USC. In his second year at USC, Seaver caught the eye of major leagues scouts with a 10–2 record and 100 strikeouts in 106 innings. The Dodgers selected him in June, 1965, but he didn't sign, which made him eligible to be drafted by the Braves in January, 1966.

Seaver spent the entire 1966 season in Jacksonville, the Mets' new Triple A club. He won his first three starts, while posting a 0.68 ERA, and became the talk of the league. Seaver didn't

The pitcher, whose given name is George Thomas Seaver, was referred to as George Feaver in the New York Times *account of Eckert's action.*

155

maintain his torrid pace, but finished with 210 innings pitched, a 12–12 record and a 3.13 ERA. He set a Jacksonville record with 188 strikeouts and another with 14 in one game.

While his overall record was not outstanding, Seaver made an indelible impression on many who saw him that year. "He's the best pitching prospect in the minor leagues. He has a 21-year-old arm and a 35-year-old head," said Jacksonville skipper Solly Hemus, who expressed the common observation that Seaver reminded him of Robin Roberts. "You never have to tell him something twice," said Met minor league pitching coach Frank Lary. "We may be watching one of the great ones of our time," opined Buffalo manager Red Davis. "He'll join the Mets by mid-June," added Buffalo GM Clay Dennis. "I'd never seen anyone use his legs like he used his legs,' said Syracuse pitcher Jack DiLauro. "His fastball just exploded when it reached the plate," added my old friend Tim Harkness, then playing with the Buffalo Bisons.

"He was brilliant," said Jacksonville teammate Larry Miller. "I took batting practice against him and he hit the low outside corner about six times in a row. I mean, this was during batting practice. He was very focused, very intense. I think you had a good idea that if he stayed healthy, he was a Hall of Famer." "You could tell he was going to be a good pitcher," said Jerry Hinsley. "You couldn't say he was going to be a Hall of Famer, but you knew he was going to do something."

Dick Rusteck, who had seen Seaver pitch in an Alaskan summer league, was astounded at his development. "He really didn't do very much up in Alaska," Rusteck recalled. "He didn't pitch very well or very often." The Seaver Rusteck saw at Jacksonville was a different pitcher. "I remember seeing him pitch a game against Buffalo that was just awesome," he said. "He really showed some good stuff." "Seaver threw so hard," said Jim Hickman, "and he had good control. If you can put those two things together, it makes you pretty tough."

When Seaver appeared in St. Petersburg the next spring, Bob Shaw cast a discerning eye on the youngster. "You could tell at that time," Shaw said, "that he was going to be really outstanding. He had maturity. He had concentration. There was only one question mark in my mind. The only thing that worried me was that he threw with a slightly dropped elbow. Both he and Robin Roberts dropped their right knee low to the ground. If you do that, you're not going to get your elbow up high enough to allow you to have a really good curveball. Tom had a very powerful fastball and a great slider. He never had a great curveball and neither did Roberts. But obviously that was not a problem."

"I was standing in the outfield with Shaw," said pitcher Chuck Estrada, "and we were watching Seaver throw batting practice. We said, 'God almighty, look at this young kid! Is that some kind of talent!' And he was just throwing batting practice! I said, 'Look at his delivery. This kid's got a chance.' We wondered what his makeup was. That's what all players and coaches wonder about. What will they do when they cross the white lines?" Estrada laughed. "We found out."

The thing that most impressed the veterans, in addition to Seaver's crackling fastball, was his pitching mechanics. Seaver used his powerful legs to generate power and relieve the strain on his arm. He also had a perfect follow through, which left him in ideal fielding position. "It's funny," said Bill Denehy, "that people talk about his perfect motion. It was a perfect motion for Tom Seaver. He took a long stride — a real long stride — and got very low to the ground. He felt that the long stride took a lot of pressure off his arm. When I came back to the Mets in 1971, Tom had some pretty good seasons under his belt and they were trying to teach everybody in the organization to pitch like Seaver. They had everybody taking long strides, just like Tom. In the spring of '71, there were at least five guys with groin pulls, because the motion was not natural to them. It was to Tom."

Seaver's physical ability and outstanding technique were supplemented by a maturity that was amazing for a 22-year-old. He could remember nearly every pitch he threw, and wrote down his observations after each game. Before the Mets' first World Series appearance, Seaver was asked about Frank Robinson. He'd pitched against Robinson in spring training, Seaver recalled, and Robby had grounded a slider to short and lined a fast ball to left field.

"Seaver was a young guy," said pitcher Jim McAndrew, "but he was mature beyond his years. Hodges communicated with him very well and Tom was secure enough to spend a lot of time with Gil and learn a lot from him. Tom was just a special personality at a very young age. Most guys take five or ten years to mature into what he was at 25. He was the emotional leader of that team. It was almost the opposite of Mantle with the Yankees. Everybody loved Mickey as one of the guys. Tom was almost like a guy in a suit and tie as far as being corporate and professional. He intimidated most of us. We really didn't get to know him that well as a young star because he was so intimidating. All of us wanted to be Tom Seaver and we weren't. Tom was a superstar but nobody worked harder. In addition to being great, he had a fantastically disciplined work ethic at a very early age." "If he wasn't a 300 game winner," said Jack Fisher, "he probably could have been chairman of the board of General Motors. He was born a winner."

"I hit against him in the minor leagues," said Don Bosch, "and you could tell he was something special. He was very confident. He had an arrogance that wasn't a bad thing, it was just confidence. He knew he could get people out. He was always very in tune with his mechanics and knew how to get the most out of his body. He really worked at it and I think that's what made him successful."

Like Roberts and Christy Mathewson, Seaver had the personality to complement his ability. He had an educated, articulate manner, a beautiful wife, and, as a public relations major at USC, was able to relate to the media. Seaver was a voracious reader, preferring books such as *Death of a President*, *Hawaii* and the works of John Steinbeck. Seaver was exactly what the public wanted in a hero. "Tom was a very nice young man," said Ed Bressoud, "and still is. He remembers your name. He remembers your family. He's congenial, he's hospitable, and he's generous. He's a nice, nice man."

Jim Gosger, who played with Seaver in '69 and '73, recently stopped at a flea market near his home town in Michigan. "I wanted to see what my baseball card is worth," he said. "It's up to a buck or a buck and a quarter now. I walk in and who's up on stage signing autographs but Tom Seaver. I hadn't seen Tom in 30 years. I waited until he was done and walked up to him and said, 'I'll bet you ten dollars you can't remember who I am.' He looked at me for a minute and said, 'Jim?'" The two men proceeded to have a pleasant chat about their changed appearance, their pensions and their current activities. "He's such a nice gentleman," said Gosger. "He hasn't changed since I played with him. There's no question he's the greatest pitcher I ever played with. It was his demeanor and the way he went about his job."

Seaver had an excellent spring in '67, but the biggest surprise of the Met camp was Bill Denehy, a strapping 6'3" righthander who didn't turn 21 until the end of March. Denehy had a fabulous prep career in Connecticut, pitching two no-hitters in American Legion ball. In his senior year in high school, he was 10–1 and fanned 151 in just 88 innings. Carl Hubbell, scouting for San Francisco, heard about the young phenom and wanted him to work out for the Giants. Denehy suggested that rather than simply watch him throw, Hubbell go to the next Legion game and see him in action. For some reason, Hubbell couldn't make it, and missed seeing Denehy strike out 24 in a nine inning game. Later that summer, he struck out 27 in a 15-inning 1–0 win.

During his senior season in high school, as major league scouts surrounded the Denehy home, Bill and his father decided they wanted a $75,000 bonus. The Cubs said they would pay that amount, but only if they were unable to sign a shortstop from Mississippi with whom they were negotiating. "As soon as the scout left," recalled Denehy, "I ran two blocks up the street to the Catholic church and prayed the rosary that they didn't sign him. But a day or two later they signed Don Kessinger." Kessinger got Denehy's bonus.

Denehy visited Yankee Stadium to try out with the Yankees. He went to the Yankee locker room, met Mickey Mantle, Ralph Terry, Yogi Berra and some of the other players and took the field wearing manager Berra's pants and Terry's sweatshirt. Under the supervision of coach Whitey Ford, Denehy began pitching to bullpen catcher Jim Hegan, and threw hard enough to get the attention of some of the Yankees lingering nearby.

Mantle decided to pick up a bat and stand in to give Denehy a target. The youngster, who had been so confident, suddenly had a disquieting thought. He was young, he threw hard, and his control wasn't always that good. He could see the headlines in the next day's papers: "Pitching Hopeful Beans Mantle." Then he noticed Mickey wasn't wearing a helmet. "Pitching Hopeful Kills Mantle," the banner might read.

Fortunately, Denehy's control was good, and the workout concluded with Mantle still in one piece. Ford told Denehy that he thought he had a future in New York, and urged him to consider signing with the Yankees. Denehy and his father drove back to Connecticut to think it over.

Met scout Len Zanke, who followed Denehy throughout his high school and Legion career, was persistent. Zanke couldn't offer $75,000, but he kept coming around, and finally convinced Denehy to go to Shea Stadium for a tryout. "Ironically," said Denehy, "I was working out for the Mets when they were playing the Giants. I looked to my right and there were Mays and McCovey watching me throw. I was thinking about what might have happened if Hubbell had shown up at that Rockville game."

After his workout, Denehy went up to talk to Casey Stengel. "I wish I could tell you what he said," Denehy related, "but he talked so fast and with so much gibberish. Basically what I got out of it was that they didn't think they had very good starting pitchers in the major leagues and didn't have a lot of great prospects in the minor leagues. If I was as good as the scouts said I was, I could be pitching in Shea Stadium within three years. I really wanted to sign with the Yankees or the Dodgers, but when he said I could pitch in the big leagues in three years, that turned my head."

Denehy signed for a $20,000 bonus and had an excellent 1965 season (13–9 with a 2.78 ERA) at Auburn of the New York–Penn League. He was promoted all the way to Triple A Jacksonville the following spring, but struggled. Demoted to Williamsport of the Eastern League, Denehy was 9–2 and earned an invitation to the Mets' '67 camp. "When I signed with the Mets," Denehy said, "I was a hard-throwing righthander. Then, in the Instructional League in the Fall of 1964, Johnny Murphy came down and completely changed my pitching motion. I went from being a straight over the top high fastball pitcher to a sinkerball, curveball pitcher. I went to the Instructional League in the Fall of 1966," he said, "and went back to being a power pitcher, coming right over the top and throwing hard again."

When Denehy reported to spring training in 1967, he was called to the manager's office to meet with Wes Westrum and Johnny Murphy. "You've been the talk of spring training," Murphy told him, "and it hasn't even started yet. You'll never guess what we were talking about." Denehy hadn't a clue. "It's those fucking sideburns you've got," Murphy shouted. "I want you to cut them off before the first practice tomorrow."

Virtually no one gave Denehy much of a chance to stick with the Mets. "I really didn't know," he said, "going to spring training, whether I was going to have much of an opportunity. I think they expected me to spend a year in Triple A, so I went down there without any thought of making the team. But one day Jack Fisher's daughter fell off the slide at the hotel pool and cut herself and they had to bring her to the emergency room. It was Jack's day to pitch, so when I got to the ballpark they told me I was going to start the game against Cincinnati."

"When I warmed up," Denehy said, "I knew I had real good stuff." The Reds' leadoff batter was Pete Rose. Denehy threw three fastballs right past him. He pitched three shutout innings, allowing only one hit while striking out four. "I think that game opened a lot of people's eyes," he said. In his next appearance, Denehy was even better. He pitched five innings against the White Sox, allowing only a scratch infield hit. Denehy was wild, and allowed some unearned runs, but major league batters weren't hitting him. He'd thrown eight innings and given up only two hits.

"For the rest of the spring," Denehy said, "I thought I was playing Russian roulette. As long as I continued to do well, I would open some eyes. One bad outing and I was gone. But I thought that even if I went to Triple A and pitched well, if there was a problem with one of the older pitchers early in the season, I might be called up."

On March 25, Seaver started and threw five impressive innings, before being relieved by Denehy, who pitched the last four innings and gave up only two hits. "[T]he 20-year-old Denehy," wrote Joseph Sheehan, "was even more of an eyecatcher [than Seaver]." Seaver or Denehy, Sheehan speculated, had the inside position as the Mets' #4 starter. Dick Young said Denehy threw harder than Seaver. In his final spring appearance, Denehy pitched four hitless innings against the White Sox, giving him a total of 16 innings with only four hits allowed, and just a single earned run. "I don't know what happened," Denehy said. "You talk about being in a zone. Every time I went out, I had a good fastball, a good curve and a good slider."

Unlike many young pitchers, Denehy was not afraid to throw his hard fastball inside. He bore a physical resemblance to Don Drysdale and, like the Dodger righthander, didn't hesitate to move hitters off the plate. Sometimes Denehy did it by accident. He attended the Mets' training camp as a 19-year-old in 1966, the first year Ken Boyer was with the club. As the 1964 National League MVP, Boyer was a big name, and when he stepped into the batting cage for the first time, reporters and photographers gathered around. Denehy was on the mound. "I was nervous," he recalled. "I was wild back then, and if you removed the catcher as a target, I had nothing to throw to. Kenny was supposed to get in the batter's box, bunt a couple of balls and then take batting practice while the photographers snapped away. I think I knocked him down with the first three pitches."

At other times, Denehy was wild on purpose. He recalled a clubhouse meeting that took place before he faced the Giants about a month into his major league career. "Mays was the last hitter we talked about," Denehy said. "Jerry Grote was running the meeting, and he said, 'Fuck Willie Mays. Let's knock his ass down on the first pitch. We'll throw a fastball and I want you to knock him right on his ass.'" Apparently, Grote hadn't compared notes with Jerry Hinsley. "I kind of looked around the room to make eye contact with the other players," Denehy said. "No one looked shocked and the coaches weren't say-

Bill Denehy was the sensation of the 1967 training camp, but he developed a sore arm after the season started and won only one major league game.

ing anything. So I went out and got the first two guys out and here comes Mays. They had a full house that night. All I remember hearing is: 'Now batting for the San Francisco Giants, number 24' and the crowd got so loud I couldn't hear them say his name. I turned around to face him and my first thought was 'What would happen if I killed him? What would that do to my baseball career?'"

Denehy hadn't killed Mantle, and he wouldn't kill Mays. "Grote gave the sign for the knockdown — he just flicked his fingers — and I took a deep breath and let it go. Mays went down and his helmet flew off, and someone said the ball went between his head and the helmet. The interesting thing about that incident is that I heard that during the Giants' next series, Mays and Marichal got into an argument in the dugout, and it was about the fact that when I came to bat, Marichal didn't retaliate."

Later in his career, when his arm was gone, Denehy was Billy Martin's enforcer in Detroit, which was nearly a full-time occupation. Denehy took to the job with zest, sometimes being sent into a game with the express purpose of hitting a certain batter. Years later, in 1981, when he was working as a reporter for Enterprise Radio, Denehy approached Reggie Jackson for an interview. "Denehy, Denehy," Jackson said. "Where do I know you from?" Denehy told him he had pitched against him for the Tigers. "Yeah," said Jackson, "you're the fucking head-hunter. I'm not going to do any interview with you. You used to throw at my teammates and I ain't doing any interview with a fucking head-hunter."

In 1967, with a live arm and a bright future ahead of him, Denehy was more interested in getting people out than taking them out. Both he and Seaver opened the season in the starting rotation. After Don Cardwell pitched the opener, Seaver started the second game, against the Pirates, pitched creditably, and left in the sixth inning with a 2–2 tie.

On April 16, Denehy made his major league debut, against the Phillies in Connie Mack Stadium. "I didn't have the fastball I had in spring training, and my control was so-so," he recalled. "I came out of spring training pitching every four days, and I was in perfect rhythm. Then I didn't pitch for seven days." Still, in the first four innings, Denehy looked sharp, allowing only one hit and two walks, both to Richie Allen.

When Allen came to bat for the third time, Denehy didn't walk him. With two outs and none on in the fifth, Dick Groat stepped up to the plate. "Before the game," Denehy said, "when we went over our scouting report, we said, 'Whatever you do, don't walk Groat, because you don't want to face Richie Allen with a man on base.' But for some reason, I just could not get Groat out that day." He walked Groat and went 3–0 on Allen, bringing Westrum to the mound. "Throw him a slider low and away," Westrum said, "and let's take our chances pitching to Callison." "I threw him a slider," said Denehy, "that was knee high and maybe two or three inches off the plate. The center field fence in Connie Mack Stadium was 440 feet away. There were two decks of seats and then, beyond that, there were three signs on the roof. The farthest one was a Coca-Cola sign. He hit a line drive that hit that Coca-Cola sign and, I swear to God, that ball was still rising when it went out of there. I had never seen a human being hit a ball that far."

Two innings later, Denehy walked Groat again and threw two balls to Allen. Westrum came to the mound a second time. After seeing what Allen had done to Denehy's low, outside slider, Westrum decided to bring in Don Shaw. Shaw held the Phillies in check, but the Mets couldn't score and Denehy was a 2–0 loser.

A week later, Denehy made his second start, also against the Phillies, this time in Shea Stadium. Once more, he pitched well and again, he lost. Again, Richie Allen was the culprit. Allen scored a run in the fourth that broke a 1–1 deadlock, and came to the plate in the seventh with the Phillies still holding a 2–1 lead. "I'd gotten him out earlier with fastballs and sliders away," Denehy recalled, "so when he came up in the seventh, Grote came out to the mound and said, 'He's going to be guessing either fastball or slider so let's start him off with a curveball.' I hung a curve. Allen had a tendency to flick the barrelhead of his bat just before swinging. He would take the barrel from a cocked position and kind of point it at the pitcher before he'd swing. I think out of the corner of my eye I saw him do it twice. He hit the ball completely out of Shea Stadium. He hit it over the home run fence, over the bullpen fence, and over the fence where they kept the bus for the visiting team. It was in the parking lot rolling toward Jamaica Bay. I think he hit it 900 feet." For the record, it was only 480 feet, and resulted in Denehy's second loss.

A few days later, the Mets went to St. Louis. When Denehy put on his uniform, he heard some snickers. As he ran around the outfield shagging flies, there was more laughter. Finally, Tommy Davis sidled up to him and pulled something off his back. It was a picture of Richie Allen. "I didn't know you were such a big fan," Davis said. "Nobody ever admitted to it," Denehy said, "but I think Tommy was the one who did it."

In Denehy's third and fourth starts, the Mets were shut out. In four games, they had scored exactly one run behind him. Finally, on May 28 against the Braves, before a crowd of more than 48,000 at Shea Stadium, the Mets scored. Davis, making amends for the Richie Allen gag, drove in five runs in the Mets' 6–3 win. Denehy earned the first of what he believed would be many big league wins.

In late April, Denehy had slipped on the outfield grass while shagging balls in batting practice and severely sprained his ankle. It was taped up and injected with a painkiller, and he continued to pitch. Denehy didn't feel any pain during his next start, but when he woke up the following day, his ankle was badly swollen. "We just played through pain in those days," Denehy said. "If today's kids get a hangnail, they don't play. Back then, if you weren't bleeding from the heart, you stayed in the game." Pitching with a bad ankle, Denehy soon acquired a sore arm.

"I think it happened in Los Angeles," he said. Denehy was not scheduled to pitch against the Dodgers, so one afternoon, he, Swoboda and Kranepool went to Disneyland. That night, he was getting in some work in the bullpen when Westrum called down and asked if he could come into the game. Denehy pitched four innings, only two days after his start against the Braves. He didn't pitch particularly well and Kranepool made an error. "After the game," Denehy remembered, "we had a team meeting and Disneyland was put off limits. It's kind of funny to think about it today. Now they've got bars with strippers and places that the Mob hangs out and they tell the guys to stay out of them, but to this day we may be the only team ever banned from Disneyland."

By late June, Denehy's record was 1–7, and he had been banished to the bullpen. The next stop was Jacksonville, and by the end of August, he went on the disabled list. Denehy never won another game in the major leagues. The season that began so promisingly on the West Coast Florida city of St. Petersburg ended on the disabled list in the north Florida city of Jacksonville.

In October, 1967, Denehy was sent to the Washington Senators in return for the Mets obtaining the right to sign Gil Hodges as manager. The following spring, the Senators and Mets faced each other in an exhibition game, and a New York writer asked Denehy who he thought got the better end of the deal. "If I make the Washington team and win 12–15 games," Denehy said, "and the Mets stay in last place, then I'd say Washington got the better part of the deal. If I get sent to the minor leagues and Gil moves the team up to fourth place, I'd say the Mets got the better part of the deal."

"The next day," Denehy recalled, "the headline read, 'Denehy Says Washington Gets Better End of Deal.' They brought Gil and I together, and asked us to take a couple of pictures. Gil was a big man who had huge forearms and hands. They asked us to stand together and for Gil to put his arm around me and pretend to be saying something to me. At the time I hadn't seen the article in the paper. Gil put his arm around my shoulder and kind of squeezed it a little bit. He grabbed my other hand like we were shaking hands and said, 'I saw your comments in the paper, kid.' I had no idea what he was talking about."

Denehy reported to Washington with a sore shoulder, and spent most of the 1968 season in Buffalo, pitching just two innings for the Senators. After splitting 1969 between Buffalo and Portland, Denehy returned to the Met organization in 1970 and pitched well in the minors. Thanks to the miracle drug DMSO, Denehy's arm felt better than it had since the spring of 1967. He went to training camp with the Mets and had a chance to make the squad. A couple of days before the Mets broke camp, Denehy found himself, on a day he was to pitch, sharing a cab with manager Hodges. He asked Hodges when he'd know whether he'd made the team. "He put his hand on my left knee," Denehy said, "and told me, 'Young man, today's performance will tell you whether you've made the team.' I pitched four hitless innings against the Dodgers, and went into his office after the game and said, 'I guess I made the team.'" "I guess you did," Hodges replied.

Denehy made plans to have his father come to Florida, get his gear and bring it to New York, since Bill had to serve some reserve duty over the next few days. He picked up his father at the airport, brought him back to his apartment and found a note taped to the door. It instructed him to call GM Bob Scheffing. Scheffing told Denehy he'd been traded to the Tigers.

After a short stint in the minors, Denehy was called up to Detroit and posted an 0–3 record in 31 games. Nineteen seventy-one was Denehy's last season in the major leagues. He pitched in the minors the following year, then left professional baseball, with a major league record of 1–10. The phenom of the 1967 camp, the man some thought threw a little better than Tom Seaver, had won only a single game in the majors.

After he left baseball, Denehy descended into a life dominated by drugs and alcohol. He had been a star athlete and, although he tried a number of different careers, couldn't seem to find one that captivated his interest as much as the challenge of trying to throw a baseball past major league hitters. After hitting bottom, Denehy found sobriety and began lecturing on the evils of addiction. He currently lives in Orlando, Florida and works for Universal Studios.

Seaver's rookie season was much more fruitful. By the middle of the season, it was apparent that he was the best pitcher the Mets had ever had. Seaver won his first major league game in his second start, on April 20 against the Cubs at Shea Stadium. In the eighth inning, with the Mets holding a 2–1 lead, Westrum came to the mound and asked Seaver how he felt. He was done, Seaver told Westrum, who brought in Don Shaw to save the game. How many rookies, everyone wondered, have the confidence to tell their manager that they've lost their stuff?

On April 25, Seaver won his second game, 2–1 in 10 innings, scoring the winning run after leading off the 10th with a single. After the 1969 season, Seaver reflected upon that game. "I felt that," he said, "for the first time maybe, we realized we could achieve something. It was the first time in my experience with the Mets that we believed in each other, the first time I felt I wasn't here to lose."

By the end of June, Seaver, with six wins, was ahead of the pace of Al Jackson, who still held the Met record with 13 wins in 1963. With eight complete games, he was well within reach of Roger Craig's team record of 14. His earned run average of 2.54 was well below Carlton Willey's record 3.10. In July, Seaver became the first Met pitcher ever named to the All Star team. When the game went deep into extra innings, the rookie took the mound in the 15th inning as the National League's seventh pitcher. He preserved a 2–1 lead, ending the game with a strikeout.

The All Star Game was the first time Seaver pitched under the pressure of a big game, but it wouldn't be the last. "He wanted the ball." said infielder Bob Johnson. "If there were two guys I wanted to have pitching in a game you had to win, it would be Seaver and Gibson. With their intestinal fortitude and their desire, nobody was going to beat them." Jack Fisher had always wanted the ball, and no one was a tougher competitor, but Fisher didn't have Seaver's stuff. "I remember one time we were playing Atlanta," said pitcher Joe Grzenda. "Seaver was in a tough situation in the ninth inning and had Aaron, Carty and someone else coming up and, buddy, he just blew the three of them away. He had it."

Having Seaver on the mound seemed to make the rest of the Mets just a little better, for he refused to accept the attitude that the Mets were losers. "I feel I'm telling the other fellows," Seaver related to Arthur Daley, "that they should do their job just as I'm going all out to do mine. It lifts the team. Maybe that's why the Mets have played better behind me than anyone else. I don't like to lose." "Seaver won 25 games in 1969," said Jim McAndrew, "and I think a lot of it had to do with the mental makeup of the eight guys playing behind him. They really believed in Tom and made plays for him and maybe worked a little harder."

Seaver pitched even better in the second half of '67 than he had during the first half. As the year rolled to a close, he began to accumulate records. On August 13th, with his 12th victory, he topped Jack Fisher, Bob Shaw and Dennis Ribant's record for wins by a righthander. On the 27th, he topped Craig's mark for complete games. On September 13th, he passed Jackson to become the winningest Met pitcher in a single season and also knocked Jackson from the record book with his 146th strikeout.

There were a number of outstanding rookie National League pitchers in 1967. Teenager Gary Nolan of the Reds was 14–8 with 206 strikeouts, Dick Hughes of the pennant-winning Cardinals was 16–6, and Don Wilson of the Astros and Rich Nye of the Cubs also made strong showings. Seaver was the best of a good lot, and finished the year with a 16–13 record, a 2.70 ERA, and 170 strikeouts. In November, he was named the National League Rookie of the Year.

The dominant theme of the Mets' 1967 season was change. Only nine men from the 1966 opening day roster appeared for the opener a year later. Seven of the pitchers, including starters Seaver, Denehy and veteran Don Cardwell, had never pitched for the Mets. The turnover continued all season long. When pitcher Les Rohr, the club's first round draft choice of 1965, started against the Dodgers on September 19, he was the 54th Met to appear in a game during the season. It was a new National League record. Rohr was also the 27th New York pitcher, which tied the major league mark held by the 1915 Philadelphia and 1955 Kansas City Athletics. The '55 As finished 33 games out of first, while the '15 version was 58½ games behind, not a strong argument for using 27 pitchers in a single year. The '67 Mets, 40½ lengths behind the pennant winning Cardinals, confirmed the theory.

Of the eleven pitchers on the opening day roster, only four, Seaver, Fisher, Ron Taylor and Cardwell, acquired from the Pirates in the ill-fated Don Bosch trade, spent the entire season in New York, and Cardwell and Taylor both spent time on the disabled list.

Cardwell suffered a freak injury while batting. "I tried to hold up on a pitch," he said, "and it was like I hit my funny bone. I stepped out of the box and kept working it and working it until finally the trainer came out and asked me what was wrong. The pitch was ball four, and I was left on first base when the inning ended." Cardwell went straight to the mound, found he couldn't pitch, and had to leave the game.

Fisher was the only reliable starter, other than Seaver, but the sturdy righthander won just nine games while losing eighteen. The rest of the rotation was patched together on a weekly basis. Denehy ended up back in the minors. Bob Shaw, whose career was essentially over due to chronic knee and back problems, was traded to the Cubs. Cardwell missed seven weeks with his elbow injury and won just five games. Bob Hendley, acquired from the Cubs in June, was suffering from a chronically bad elbow that would put a premature end to his career.

The bullpen was as unstable as the starting rotation. Taylor, who had struggled for two years in Houston with a bad back, came off the disabled list in May and became the Mets' best reliever. He was in 50 games, posted a 2.34 ERA and had eight saves. Rookie left hander Don

Shaw pitched well early in the season, but had to go into the service in August and missed the rest of the year. Westrum, unable to stomach Jack Hamilton's wildness any longer, traded him to the California Angels.

Hal Reniff arrived in a trade with the Yankees in mid-season, won and saved a flurry of games in his first month, and set a club record by throwing 21 consecutive scoreless innings. Reniff was only 29, and had been the Yankees' best reliever just a few years earlier. Perhaps he would be the new Met stopper. Reniff faded after his quick start, however, and was sent home for the final three weeks of the season. Westrum wanted to see his young pitchers, he told Reniff, and there would be no work for him. Major league veterans like Hendley, former Oriole Chuck Estrada, ex–Phillie Dennis Bennett, ex–Dodger Nick Willhite and Joe Grzenda found their way onto and off the Met roster at different times during the season.

Estrada had been one of the Baby Birds, whose live arms had put a severe scare into the Yankees in 1960. "I thought I was going to last a long time," Estrada said, "because I did it so easy. It was so easy on me physically and my arm was so live. By my second year, I said, 'I can play with these guys.' I didn't know what I had, but now I do." He laughed. In 1962, pitching against the Yankees, Estrada felt something pop in his elbow. By 1963, he had a serious elbow problem, and pitched a total of just 86 painful innings in 1963 and 1964.

Estrada had surgery to remove bone chips after the 1964 season, and started on the long road back. Met executive Bob Scheffing saw Estrada pitch for Tacoma in 1966, and couldn't believe what he was seeing. Estrada was pitching well, not as a rehabilitated finesse pitcher, but by throwing nearly as hard as he had in 1960. He recommended that one of the Mets' minor league clubs purchase Estrada's contract and that he be invited to spring training.

Estrada had a very good spring with the Mets in 1967, and made the team, but struggled almost from the start. After nine games and a 9.41 ERA, he was sent to the minor leagues. "The thing that bothered me most about my short career," Estrada said, "is the fact that I was just learning how to pitch when my arm blew out. I used to challenge everybody. If it was three and two, you got a fastball. If I was behind in the count, you got a fastball. But then I got to the stage where I'd throw a 2–2 change or a 3–2 curve ball. I wasn't afraid to do that and I found out how much fun it was. Then I hurt my arm and that was it."

Non-pitchers on the opening day squad included Greg Goossen, Sandy Alomar, Ken Boyer, Chuck Hiller, Bart Shirley and Al Luplow, all of whom were long gone before the season was half over. Players came and players went; one of those who came was the old Yankee utility infielder, Phil Linz. Ever since he had been traded by the Yankees, Linz had been longing to return to New York. "When I went to Philadelphia," he said, "I found out that they had also traded for Dick Groat. I thought when I got traded I'd have a chance to play every day, but it turned out to be even worse in Philadelphia than it was in New York. Gene Mauch was supposed to trade me back to New York, but I guess that deal fell through, so there I was languishing in Philadelphia. I was pretty disgusted with baseball at that time. I really wanted to play. I was sick and tired and bored of sitting."*

Linz had another reason for wanting to return to New York, for by that time he had a thriving bar/restaurant known as Mr. Laffs. Linz lived in an apartment building in Manhattan. "For some reason," he said, "the superintendent would only rent to single people." That was OK with Linz. "Stewardesses were coming in by the busload," he recalled. "We were all under 30 years old. We would have parties every night in my apartment. In those days the apartment building had a switchboard which was connected to a phone in each apartment. In order to make a call, you had to do it through the switchboard. When we wanted to have a party, we would just go

---

*Late in 1968, when Linz was with the Mets, he got two hits in Philadelphia. "This is a great town to play in," he said. "I wish I had."

down to the switchboard operator and say, 'Look, we're having a party in Apartment 7A. Start calling.' He would hook in and call all the apartments and tell the stewardesses there was a party in 7A. There's a party in 7A. There's a party in 7A. He'd call each apartment. A half hour later, we'd have fifty girls up there. Of course, there were a lot of young, single guys that we knew, too, and were friends with. We were partying every single night.

"The area we lived in was really hot. It was a hot singles bar area. The superintendent, who was a friend of ours, knew of a store for rent. He asked us if we wanted to go into the bar business. We said sure, and he said he would arrange the lease and all of that and we would be partners." Linz decided to open the place, just for laughs, and the bar had a name. "We said, 'Let's do it. Let's have some fun,'" Linz said. "We transferred all the people we were partying with in my apartment into the club. The first night we opened, we were packed, and we were packed for about the next seven years."

Linz served as host, greeting, joking, and making everyone happy. "I was there every single night during the off-season," he said, "working people, saying hi and stuff like that." He didn't play the harmonica, which had brought him such fame with the Yankees in 1964. "It's a high class place," Linz explained. "You don't play the harmonica in a joint like that." The Yankees helped business by holding press conferences at Mr. Laffs. Mantle and most of the Yankees appeared at least once, as did many of the Mets and football Giants. The bar was so successful that Linz went into partnership with Art Shamsky of the Mets and opened three other bar/restaurants in the New York area.

Linz longed to be back in New York and, during the 1967 All Star break, got his wish when he was traded to the Mets for infielder Chuck Hiller. "I told Gene Mauch that I was quitting," Linz said. "I was going to go home. I told Mauch, 'I'm not playing here and I've got my club. Business is real good and I'm opening a second place with Art Shamsky.' He said he'd trade me. I told him the only place I'd go was New York. If he traded me back to New York, I'd play. If not, I was quitting. He told me to give him three days. He called me on the second day and told me I was traded to the Mets. That was thanks to Yogi. He was a coach there and Hodges [*sic*] asked him about me." Linz was back in New York, where he wanted to be, and he was happy, although he didn't play any more for the Mets than he had for the Phillies.

A more valuable addition to the 1967 Mets was two time National League batting champion Tommy Davis. To get Davis from the Dodgers, the Mets surrendered Hickman, the last remaining original Met, and Hunt, the only Met ever to start in an All Star game. Hunt's departure came as somewhat of a surprise, since he was one of Mrs. Payson's favorite players. After the 1964 season, Weiss was all set to trade him to the Twins, but Payson vetoed the move. No one, least of all Hunt, thought he would leave New York. In 1966, writer Jack Mann had described Hunt as "the only player the Metropolitan Baseball Club, Inc. can be absolutely sure it would like to have on its payroll in 1969 — which should be first division time."

The scrappy second baseman, who had been voted the most popular Met in 1966, was angered and upset at the prospect of leaving New York. He was angry because he learned of the trade not from Bing Devine, but from writer Dick Young. He was upset because, after suffering through three last place finishes in a row, Hunt thought he could be an integral part of a team that was finally turning the corner toward respectability. He had grown to like New York and his wife, Jackie, was the founder of The Benchwarmers, a group consisting of the wives of Met players and employees. Hunt, a farmer from Missouri, did not appreciate the glitter of Los Angeles, and he expected to miss the Met fans. He departed with a heavy heart. For Hickman, it was an opportunity for a fresh start. He had never been able to meet expectations in New York, and perhaps a new organization, where he was not expected to be the savior, was the answer.

Davis, on the other hand, was delighted to be returning home. He grew up in the Bedford-

Stuyvesant section of Brooklyn and had been an all-city basketball player at Boys' High. His mother still lived in Brooklyn and he had numerous relatives in the area. In 1956, Davis had signed with the Dodgers in order to stay home, only to see the Dodgers pull up stakes for the West Coast a year later, before he ever played a game in Brooklyn. Now, eleven years later, he was back.

Davis had something to prove. After winning back-to-back batting titles in 1962 and 1963, he had an off year in 1964. In April of the following season, while sliding into second base, he suffered a horrible fracture of his right ankle, which finished him for the entire year. As a young player, Davis had fantastic speed, once stealing 68 bases in the minor leagues. When he returned to action in 1966, however, he ran with a limp, and suffered from a series of nagging injuries. Manager Walter Alston platooned him, claiming he wasn't physically able to play regularly. Since there are far more right handed pitchers in the major leagues than left handers, a right handed hitting platooned player is destined to see limited activity. Davis appeared in just 100 games and had only 313 at bats. Although he led a light hitting Dodger club with a .313 average, Davis drove in just 27 runs, exactly 126 fewer than the 153 he plated in 1962. He felt that Alston, who sometimes criticized his defense, lacked confidence in him.

While the addition of Davis added another bat to the Met lineup, the subtraction of Roy McMillan deducted a glove. McMillan tore tendons in his shoulder in 1966, ripping them from the bone, and aggravated the injury late in the season when, walking across the field in Pittsburgh after a game, he accidentally bumped into a fan. He had surgery during the winter, and declared his determination to return to the Mets for a 17th major league season. McMillan was somewhat of a medical marvel, having endured a broken collarbone, floating cartilage and bone chips, and the various gashes, bumps and bruises associated with playing shortstop for sixteen years. In 1965, Met doctor Peter LaMotte said McMillan, then 34, had the ankles of a 60-year-old man.

The rehabilitation process following McMillan's shoulder surgery was long, painful and unsuccessful. When he began to throw in January, he had severe pain, but persevered and came to camp. In the event he couldn't play, the Mets assured him of a coaching job. During an exhibition game, after covering second on a stolen base attempt, McMillan tried to throw the ball back to the pitcher, and felt something pop in his shoulder. The ball floated about ten feet and fell to the ground. While the temporary dislocation was not related to the surgery, it was the final blow. McMillan, hunched over, left the field in obvious pain. His playing career was over, and the shortstop position was in the hands of rookie Derrell (Bud) Harrelson, a 23-year-old rookie who hit just .221 in the International League in 1966.

The other great veteran who had contributed so much to the 1966 Mets, third baseman Ken Boyer, was traded to the White Sox in July. Boyer, 36, was troubled by a bad back and hit just .235 in 56 games, with only three home runs. He drove in just one run in his first 21 games, far too few for a hitter in the middle of the order. Boyer's back trouble had robbed him of mobility in the field, and Westrum often played him at first base.

When the Mets acquired Ed Charles from the Athletics in May, Boyer's days as a regular were over. Charles, 34, was not much younger, and didn't hit much better than Boyer (.238) but he still covered third base reasonably well, and took over the position on a regular basis.

Charles was a throwback to the Met intellectuals of 1962. A high school dropout who left school to pursue a baseball career, Charles earned his diploma after he reached the major leagues with Kansas City in 1962. He didn't stop learning, taking courses at Central Missouri State College and writing massive volumes of poetry in his spare time. Everywhere he went, Charles carried with him an epic, autobiographical poem, for which he continually wrote additional verses. Whenever a fan wrote asking for an autograph, Charles sent along a poem for good measure.

With McMillan and Boyer gone, and Ed Bressoud, who played a key role in 1966, traded to the Cardinals, the revamped Met infield was Kranepool at first, Jerry Buchek, obtained from the Cardinals for Bressoud, replacing Hunt at second, Harrelson at short and Charles at third. Early in the season, the new combination was frightful in the field. In one four game stretch, the Mets made nine errors and scored just three runs, an improbable and alarming combination.

The middle infield was a particular problem area. Buchek, who had received a $65,000 bonus from the Cardinals in 1959, was known for his hitting, not his fielding. He had power, but struck out too often. Buchek hit a few home runs early in the season, then went into a deep slump. Chuck Hiller was another iron-gloved offensive specialist. Sandy Alomar, acquired during the spring to shore up the leaky inner defense, couldn't perform either at bat or in the field, and soon departed. "If Alomar can hit .100," said Eddie Stanky, from the Mets' front office, "it will be a great trade." He couldn't, in fact Alomar didn't get a single hit in 22 Met at bats.

Harrelson was the shortstop, but only by default. He wouldn't have started if McMillan's shoulder had recovered, or if Alomar had shown the fielding ability he was reputed to possess. Harrelson, who had just began switch hitting a year earlier, appeared completely overmatched by big league pitching, and in his first 21 spring at bats, couldn't even get a ball out of the infield. Worse yet, his fielding skill, which had been taken for granted, was, like Bosch's reputed defensive prowess, sadly lacking. "If there is an award for the most disappointing player of the spring," wrote Jack Lang, "it goes to center fielder Don Bosch, but only after a close contest with shortstop Bud Harrelson." "If they don't hit," Westrum said of the two rookies, "there'll be three 'out' men in the lineup, including the pitcher. That is too much of a handicap for any club."

While losing their sixth straight opening game, the Mets committed five errors. One of them was by Harrelson, who had a terrible April. He batted under .200 and during the last four games he played that month, committed seven errors. With Harrelson pressing and his team guilty of 29 errors in its first 17 games, Westrum decided to "rest" his rookie shortstop. After trying Alomar for a couple of games, he went back to Harrelson. At first, the youngster's fielding wasn't much better, and the error total reached 12 in his first 27 games, but the more he played, the more confident he became. McMillan spent time with him and simply tried to get him to relax. He convinced Harrelson he could play shortstop if he just let his natural ability take over and stopped worrying so much. Yogi Berra convinced him to use a heavier bat and just make contact with the ball.

Harrelson's new confidence showed not only in his fielding, but in his batting, and his average began to climb. Before the season, Westrum had said he would be happy if Harrelson hit .220. When he reached .230, the Mets were satisfied. If the youngster could hit better than .230, and field like he did in the minors, he would be a valuable major leaguer.

Harrelson's average kept climbing. By the end of June, he was up to .247, and he was named the Mets' Player of the Month. If Harrelson could hit .247, he would be an All Star. McMillan, an All Star on many occasions, had a lifetime average of just .243. With a great month of July, Harrelson brought his average up to .290. If he could hit .290, he would be a Hall of Famer.

As the season wore on, however, Harrelson wore down. At less than 150 pounds, he was having difficulty keeping up his weight and stamina. "He played every day," said Don Cardwell, "and we couldn't keep him still to take a break. When we were taking batting practice, he'd be out there shagging flies with the pitchers. We'd tell him to go sit down. 'How much do you weigh now?' we'd ask him. 'What are you down to now?'"

By the end of September, Harrelson's average was down to .254, but Westrum was more than happy to carry a young, slick fielding shortstop who could steal bases and bat .254. "I don't think Buddy Harrelson ever gets the credit he's due for what an outstanding defensive player he was," said Jim McAndrew, "for years and years and years. He made the tough plays look easy, and during my tenure, there was no better shortstop in baseball. He's one of the reasons that pitching staff was as good as it was."

A second Met who wore down in the latter stages of the season was Tommy Davis. Davis suffered from a myriad of ailments in the spring, including an achilles tendon injury, an eye infection, a pulled hamstring and a sore shoulder. When the regular season began, however, Davis managed to go to the post almost every day. For the first half of the season, despite some troubles with his ankle and bone bruises in his left foot, he seemed to be proving Alston wrong, appearing in nearly every Met game and leading the team in virtually every offensive category. His ankle was fine, Davis said, and he convinced Westrum not to remove him regularly for a pinch runner or for defensive purposes, as Alston had.

Davis appeared to be a threat to the Met records for RBI (94 by Frank Thomas), doubles (28 by Hunt and Boyer) and hits (163 by Joe Christopher). By September, the long season (he played in 154 games) took its toll. "Tommy's been a weary player the last few weeks," wrote Lang, "and the sting appears to have disappeared from his bat." Davis did lead the Mets in hitting with a .302 mark, and set club records with 174 hits and 32 doubles. He also led the club in home runs, runs scored and RBI, but drove in just 31 runs after the All Star break and sat out the final game of the season to protect his .300 average. Davis hit his last home run of the year on August 11th. His fielding during the second half of the year also left something to be desired.

Davis didn't get a lot of help. Cleon Jones, after a fine rookie season in 1966 and a terrific spring, was a complete mystery in '67. He put on about 20 pounds, wasn't able to get his average above .200 until late July, and it took a strong finish for him to reach .246 for the season. Buchek was second to Davis with 14 home runs, but hit only .236 and struck out more than 100 times.

Jerry Grote, who had won the regular catching job in 1966, slumped to .195, was criticized for a lack of hustle, and had moments where his temper got the better of his judgment. In a game in Los Angeles on July 27, Grote became engaged in a running battle with plate umpire Bill Jackowski over ball and strike calls. Still steaming after the inning ended, Grote threw a towel from the Met dugout, and was immediately ejected. That created a problem, since New York had only 21 available players, and Westrum had already used his other two catchers, John Sullivan and Greg Goossen.

Westrum had no shortage of volunteers to go behind the plate. Swoboda strapped on a pair of shin guards before Westrum told him to take them off. Davis had done some catching on the sandlot, but Westrum wasn't about to put his best hitter behind the bat. First base coach Berra asked one of the umpires if he could be activated on the spot. He couldn't without league permission, which wasn't available on a moment's notice. Finally, Westrum decided upon outfielder Tommy Reynolds, whose catching experience consisted of warming up pitchers in the bullpen.

The Mets were leading when Reynolds entered the game in the eighth inning. Dick Schofield reached base and immediately attempted to steal second. Reynolds' throw bounced in the dirt, and Schofield scored the tying run shortly afterward. Reynolds' and Westrum's agony was prolonged when the game went into extra innings. For a man who had never worn catching gear under fire, Reynolds performed remarkably well. He survived the tenth without incident. In the eleventh, with Nate Oliver on third, Bob Bailey swung at a pitch. Reynolds thought it was a foul tip and made no effort to retrieve it. Bailey stood at home plate, making no motion to wave the runner in from third. Oliver took off and crossed home plate as Jackowski ruled the pitch a swinging strike. The game was over.

Westrum was furious. He was angry at the call and even madder at his starting catcher. After the game, he lectured Grote in front of the entire team and fined him one hundred dollars. The next morning, Grote got a call from Bing Devine, who echoed Westrum's sentiments and told him to stop picking fights with umpires.

The infield defense tightened up after the early season woes, but the outfield play left much to be desired. Swoboda was improving, but still shaky and Jones, playing out of position, was not a major league center fielder. Hitting, however, was the real weak point of the '67 Mets. They were last in the majors in runs scored and first in shutouts. Their 83 home runs were just one more than the Dodgers, who were last in the majors. No Met hit more home runs than Davis's 16, which was the lowest total ever to lead a Met team, and well in arrears of Thomas's club record. "In six years," wrote Lang, "the Mets haven't been able to come up with anyone who could match the top slugger on the worst team that ever played in the major leagues."

With so many of their batters either having off seasons or fading in the stretch, the Mets lost 60 of their last 90 games, falling back to tenth place, with a 61–101 record. In May, the Mets began flying an orange flag over Shea when the team won and a blue flag when they lost. By the end of the season, the blue flag was aloft far too often. In September, Westrum hoisted the white flag and resigned.

After one glorious season in ninth place, the Mets had returned to their familiar spot in the cellar. They no longer, however, had Casey Stengel to distract the fans from the players' ineptitude. They had a good young pitcher in Tom Seaver, but Seaver could only pitch every fifth day. The Mets would need some hitting, some fielding, and another pitcher or two before Seaver could lead them to the promised land, or even out of last place.

· 16 ·

Gil Comes Home

During the early days of spring training in 1962, a matronly Met fan said confidently, "Gil is going to lead this team to a pennant some day." The woman meant, of course, that Gil Hodges' playing skills would take the Mets to the flag, but by the time he was drafted by the Mets, Hodges was no longer the player he'd been when he left Brooklyn in 1957. In Ebbets Field, with its inviting fences, Hodges had been one of the premier power hitters in the National League. Six times during his Brooklyn career, he hit more than 30 home runs in a season and twice he connected for more than 40.

Hodges was not just a great offensive player; he was probably the best fielding first baseman in the National League, and perhaps all of baseball. Gil had enormous hands. Teammate Pee Wee Reese said he didn't really need a glove, and wore one only because it was fashionable. Hodges won the Gold Glove Award at first base in 1957, 1958 and 1959. The only reason he didn't win more often is that the award wasn't instituted until 1957.

What his teammates remember most about Hodges is his character and strength, both physical and emotional. He was a product of the Midwest, son of an Indiana coal miner, and spent his high school summers working in the mines. He began a career in professional baseball in 1943, but left the Dodgers that same year, joined the Marines and served in the Pacific. No one questioned Gil Hodges' toughness or his courage.

On a Dodger team loaded with character, Hodges was the man his teammates looked up to. "Here was this supposedly tough bunch of Brooklyn Dodgers," said reporter Gordon White, "whose emblem was the cartoon character of a bum, yet on that team you had a number of gentlemen who were as far from being the bum as we are from being on the moon. Gil, Carl Erskine and Pee Wee Reese were just excellent men. I covered a number of different sports, and Gil was the nicest, most gentle person I had the pleasure to cover. I never saw a surly or grouchy moment. Gil was a special person."

"Gil Hodges was a guy who made you feel that everything was going to be all right," said Dodger pitcher Danny McDevitt. "He had quiet strength. If I was having a little trouble, he'd come over to the mound and talk to me." "Everybody liked Gil," said Fred Kipp, another Dodger pitcher. "He was probably one of the strongest guys on the Dodgers. Nobody would give him any trouble and everybody liked being around him." "He could probably kick everybody's ass," said McDevitt, "but he wouldn't, because he was just a great guy."

"When I first got to camp as a young rookie," said former Dodger pitcher Nick Willhite, "there were a few reporters standing around Gil. He stepped out of the crowd, shook my hand and welcomed me to the team. He took me back and forth between the hotel and the ballpark. He was just very encouraging."

Even Dodger veterans like Clem Labine looked up to Hodges. "If he went into a slump," Labine remembered, "he never said a word. He never got on anybody, and he could break up any bad conversations that were going on." "For the star that he was," said Met pitcher Larry Foss, "you could sit down and talk to him. He was pretty helpful and just a nice guy."

"Gil was one of the nicest guys you'll ever meet," said Ted Schreiber. "Without a question. Everybody says that. He was a very analytical guy. He didn't go to college, but he just had good, innate common sense."

When the Dodgers moved to Los Angeles for the 1958 season, Hodges went with them, but by then he was 34 years old, a rather advanced age for a 1950s ballplayer. With the short left field Coliseum fence to aim at, Gil managed two more good seasons, helping the Dodgers to the 1959 pennant with a .276 average, 25 home runs and 80 RBI. He won Game Four of the World Series with an eighth inning homer.

During the next two years, however, Hodges was plagued by injuries and played sparingly. He couldn't catch up with a good fast ball any more. Hodges had a terrible season in 1960, batting only .198. He was better in 1961, but the Dodgers had Ron Fairly, Tim Harkness and Frank Howard, all of whom were young and could play first base. With his great popularity in New York, it was a foregone conclusion that Gil would be placed on the list of those eligible for the expansion draft and that the Mets would select him.

Hodges, who owned a bowling alley in Brooklyn, was delighted to return to New York. While playing for the Dodgers, he had married a Brooklyn girl and, after the Dodgers moved to Los Angeles, his family remained behind. Now he could join them full time. At 38, Hodges thought he could still help the Mets. "Of course I'm not the player I was ten years ago," he said during spring training, "but I'm sure I have a couple of years left."

Hodges' return to New York was marred by a series of injuries. In spring training, he disembarked after a bus trip and noticed soreness in his left knee. He didn't recall hurting it during the game, and believed the pain resulted from being cramped in an awkward position on the bus. By opening day, the injury was no better, and, although Hodges played whenever he could, he was not able to run or move well.

Hodges started the Mets' first game in St. Louis, and hit a home run, which gave him 370 for his career, one more than Joe Dimaggio. In mid–May, despite his painful knee, he ran out a 455 foot inside the park home run at the Polo Grounds. Gil saved his best effort of the season for the arrival of his old Dodger teammates. In a Memorial Day doubleheader, Hodges hit three home runs, raising his total for the season to eight and lifting his batting average to .316. Gil wasn't going to lead the Mets to the pennant, but it looked as though he was headed for a pretty good season. In the friendly Polo Grounds, 25–30 home runs were a distinct possibility.

Memorial Day was the high point of Hodges' year. His knee stubbornly refused to heal, and his playing time was limited. On July 14, following the Mets' first Old Timers' Day, Gil was attending a dinner for the returning stars when he collapsed in pain from a kidney stone attack. In 1962, kidney stones required surgery and a lengthy recuperation. If one were a ballplayer, it meant going on the disabled list. On August 24, still disabled, Hodges was honored with a day at the Polo Grounds, and showered with numerous gifts. Despite his extended absence, Gil was also awarded a car as the most popular Met. Reporter Howard Tuckner speculated that Hodges was the most popular Met because he had contributed so little to their dismal season.

Hodges returned to the active roster in mid–September and appeared in a few pinch hitting roles. He had a knee operation in October, and, although he would turn 39 the following spring, resolved to come back in 1963. Hodges' progress was slow. Stengel allowed him to set his own spring schedule, and Gil didn't play until the last few exhibition games. He made the team and appeared in a few early season games. On May 10, after injuring his right knee, Hodges was placed on the disabled list again. His playing career was clearly in jeopardy.

Knowing his active career was nearly over, Hodges had decided he wanted to manage. "I'd sit around with Gil and Don Zimmer and some other guys that had managerial aspirations," said Rod Kanehl, "and we'd rehash the game. Why did someone do this? Should they have done something else?"

On May 22, when the Mets were in Los Angeles, the club announced that Hodges was being released as a player in order to allow him to accept the job as manager of the last place Washington Senators. George Selkirk, the Senator GM, thought Mickey Vernon had been too soft, and wanted someone who would provide discipline.

While the timing of the announcement came as a somewhat of a shock, the ascension of Hodges to a managerial role was no surprise. "Gil was such a steadying force on that Met team," said Craig Anderson. "He was just a class guy. I admired him so much and I can see why he became a good manager. He never lost his cool, and he was always able to say the right thing when things were tough and the pressure was on." "I definitely saw him as a future manager," said Jay Hook, "mostly because of his demeanor. I really thought he was the kind of guy people would respect and look up to. Gil knew a lot about baseball and he had a sense of maturity. He had a real sense of stability."

Duke Snider, Hodges' old Dodger teammate, was also liked and respected, but in a different way. In his early years in the major leagues, Snider had a tendency to pop off. He once said in a magazine article that he only played baseball for the money. In 1959, he hurt his arm foolishly trying to throw a baseball out of the Coliseum. Few saw him as a future manager. "Duke was 38 going on 18," said Don Rowe. "He was a riot."

Nobody ever described Gil Hodges as a "riot." In many ways, Hodges was reminiscent of Stan Musial, another superstar who was more than just a superb player. Al Moran recalled meeting Musial during his first visit to St. Louis with the Mets. "I was standing behind the batting cage watching the Cardinals hit," said Moran, "and a guy tapped me on the shoulder and said, 'My name's Stan Musial, what's yours.'" Choo Choo Coleman couldn't remember anyone else's name, but at that moment, Moran couldn't remember his own name. "I couldn't even speak," he said. "Musial was a great ballplayer and a great personality and very sincere."

Hodges was like Musial in many respects. He was a great player. He was well-liked. He almost never used profanity. And he commanded respect. Hodges was one of the most well-liked men in baseball, but he was not one of the guys. Rod Kanehl recalled the Mets leaving on a road trip in 1962. Among the group of family and friends seeing the club off was Kanehl's young son. "Stengel called Hodges Gilly," said Kanehl, "and some of the fans had picked it up. When we were boarding the plane some of them were saying 'Good luck, Gilly.' My son heard them and said the same thing. When we were airborne, Gil came over to me and said, very seriously, 'Rod, don't you think your son ought to call me Mr. Hodges?'"

Kanehl's son was only allowed in the Met clubhouse after a victory, which meant he was not a frequent visitor. One day, after the team returned home and won a game, young Kanehl walked into the clubhouse, went right up to Hodges' locker, stuck out his hand and said, "Nice game, Mr. Hodges." Hodges looked over at the senior Kanehl and gave him a silent nod of approval. "He was that way," said Rod. "I used to refer to my father as my old man. One time Gil said, 'Rod, you can refer to your father as your old man around other people, but around me, would you call him your father?'"

Hodges never won a pennant in Washington; in fact, his club never finished in the first division. Yet, each year, the Senators were a little better than they had been the year before. Under Vernon, the expansion Senators tied for ninth in 1961, finished tenth in 1962, and were in tenth place when Hodges took over the team the following year. In 1963, they again finished last, with a total of just 56 wins. Hodges had managed to find a team that was nearly as bad as the Mets.

Washington, including the expansion club and the old Senators who moved to Minneapolis, had not finished in the upper half of the standings since 1946.

In 1964, Gil's first full season in Washington, the Senators won 62 games and moved up to ninth. The following year they won 70 games and finished eighth, and in 1966 won one more game, although remaining in eighth place. During 1967, Hodges' final season in Washington, the club was at the .500 mark in mid–August, and late in the season was only six games out of first place in the wild AL pennant scramble. The Senators won 76 times and tied for sixth, the best finish in the new club's brief history.

As the Senators improved, so did Hodges. He learned how to handle a pitching staff, and was one of those rare individuals who admitted to mistakes and profited from them. Hodges never had a plethora of talent in Washington, and didn't expect superhuman feats from his athletes. The two things he demanded of them were mental alertness and proper execution of fundamentals. Gil knew that a team with limited talent could not afford to give the opponent any further advantage. The only times he ever blasted his players was when they botched rundown plays, missed signs, failed to bunt properly or committed similar blunders. "I can't abide errors of omission," he once said. Hodges benched outfielder Chuck Hinton, probably the best player on the team, when Hinton forgot the number of outs and jogged to the bench while a run scored.

During his tenure in the nation's capital, Hodges, as he had done everywhere he'd been, earned the respect of the players, with one notable exception. On June 23, 1966, the Senators acquired first baseman-outfielder Ken (Hawk) Harrelson from Kansas City. Harrelson was an impressive physical specimen, with considerable athletic ability, and had great potential as a power hitter. In addition to his baseball skills, Harrelson was a star high school basketball player who attracted a number of college scholarships. He was a terrific golfer, an accomplished pool hustler and claimed to be baseball's champion arm wrestler.* No one, in fact, was more impressed with his ability than Ken Harrelson. "You have to love talent, baby," he said during his first spring with the Senators, "and I have nothing but talent. Why, I amaze myself."

The Hawk may or may not have been baseball's champion arm wrestler, but he was clearly not baseball's champion defensive first baseman. *Sports Illustrated* described him as "the game's best arm wrestler, pool shooter and golfer as well as being a man who plays defense with all the finesse and surety of Venus de Milo." Moreover, Harrelson didn't seem inclined to mount much of an effort to improve. When he was with Kansas City, he made four errors in a single inning of an exhibition game against the Yankees, then failed to cover first base for a fifth miscue. Finally, Harrelson ended the inning by dropping a line drive, and crawling to first base on his hands and knees to make the putout. "I just lay there for a minute," he wrote, "laughing so hard I couldn't get up. When I went to bat I got a standing ovation. I lifted my cap and bowed half a dozen times, making a complete circle so I wouldn't miss anybody. Then I hit into a double play."

The Hawk said his manager, Eddie Lopat, was laughing so hard that he had to dry his eyes with a towel. One can only imagine how Hodges would have reacted had he been managing the Athletics. It is safe to assume that Harrelson would not have bowed to anyone, for he would have been yanked out of the game before he ever came to bat. Baseball was a very serious affair for Gil Hodges, and one did not smile after making four errors in an inning, let alone laugh so hard as to be unable to get up.

Predictably, Harrelson and Hodges did not see eye-to-eye. "With Gil Hodges and me," Harrelson wrote, "it was a case of dislike at first sight. From the first month on, there wasn't a day that I didn't wish I were somewhere else.... He was unfair, unreasonable, unfeeling, incapable

*He claimed to be the best arm wrestler in all sports until he lost to 270 pound Curt Merz of the Kansas City Chiefs.

of handling men, stubborn, holier-than-thou and ice cold. Joining the Senators was like starting a prison term. Hodges was the warden, expecting the worst from everyone."

Hodges, the best-fielding first baseman of his era, attempted to improve Harrelson's defense.
"While you're here," Hodges told him, "we're going to make you a good first baseman or no
first baseman at all." Harrelson actually showed some improvement in the field, but not enough
to make up for his continuing clashes with Hodges. Gil told him to cut his hair, which the Hawk
claimed he had to wear long to compensate for his big nose. Harrelson suggested that Hodges
let him steal on his own, since he had stolen nine bases for the Athletics in less than half a season. By doing so, The Hawk had unknowingly pressed one of Hodges' hot buttons. Only the
manager decided who would steal and when they would run. In 1970, when the Mets acquired
Joe Foy from the Royals, Hodges indicated that Foy would no longer have carte blanche on the
base paths. "I do not believe in letting a man run on his own," Hodges said. "To me, there can
be only one manager of a ball club. When people start doing things on their own, you are taking the reins away from the manager." Ken Harrelson was not going to tell Gil Hodges how to
manage the Washington Senators.

Late in the 1966 season, Harrelson botched a play which cost the Senators a game. He felt
badly and went up to Hodges' room late at night to apologize for letting the team down. Hodges,
always willing to forgive physical errors, told him not to worry about it, and the two men commenced one of the few civil conversations of their relationship. Things were going well until
Harrelson offered to shake up the team by starting a fight on the field. Hodges was taken aback.
He had never even been ejected from a game as a player, let alone intentionally start a fight. If
hostilities broke out, Hodges was usually a peacemaker. "I don't want you to start a fight," he
told Harrelson. "This shows me something about the kind of person you are."

The kind of person Harrelson was was not the type Gil Hodges wanted on his ballclub,
and the following June, The Hawk was sent back to Kansas City. He did not leave quietly. When
he wrote his autobiography, which was excerpted in *Sports Illustrated*, Harrelson spewed his
venom at Hodges. "[I]n general," he wrote, "he treated his ballplayers like dogs, and I was no
exception — I can tell you without reservation that every Washington player he ever had hated
his guts." Harrelson not only exaggerated, he misjudged Hodges' motives. Gil wasn't looking
for love. "I won't say the Washington players loved him and were ready to lay down their lives
and die for him," wrote a Washington reporter, "but I know they respected him. He demanded
that and he got it." Rod Kanehl's son could attest to that.

During his tenure in Washington, Hodges remained a beloved figure in New York, and
maintained his home in Brooklyn. Before Stengel was engaged, there had been rumors that
Hodges would be the first Met manager. When Casey retired late in the 1965 season, it was no
secret that the Mets would have loved to sign Hodges, if he weren't under contract to the Senators. "His Washington contract had a year to go," wrote Arthur Daley, "and he is too strong a
character to wriggle out of a commitment and to default on an obligation." In July, 1966, Hodges
signed a two year extension which bound him to Washington through the 1968 season. July was
the month Westrum's Mets were setting all manner of team records and looked as though they
might challenge for eighth place. Wes appeared to be a safe bet to hold on to his job for at least
a year or two.

Within fifteen months, the situation changed dramatically. The Mets regressed and
Westrum resigned. Everyone in baseball knew the Mets wanted Hodges as their manager, and
Hodges made it known publicly that he would love to return to New York. Senator GM George
Selkirk knew of the pressure on Hodges to return to New York, for the two men had talked
about it. Just tell them you're under contract, Selkirk told Hodges.

Although the mutual love affair between Hodges and the Mets was an open secret, no one
thought the Senators would release him. Hodges said he had no intention of broaching the sub-

ject, and that it was up to the Mets to approach Selkirk if they wanted him. The odds of persuading Selkirk didn't seem good. Shortly after Hodges had signed his extension, Selkirk was asked about the possibility of Gil being released if he wanted to take another job. "Over my dead body," he replied. Speculation regarding the next Met manager therefore revolved around other candidates. The names of Berra, Billy Martin, Bill Virdon, Harry Walker, Al Lopez and a few others were mentioned, but no one appeared to be a front runner.

There was no front runner because the Mets were pursuing another course. Johnny Murphy said that he had been talking to Selkirk, his old Yankee teammate, about the possibility of swapping pitcher Bill Hepler for Senator pitcher Jim Duckworth, when Selkirk brought up the topic of Westrum's resignation. Murphy asked if anything had changed in the Hodges situation. "Let's talk about it," Murphy reported Selkirk as saying.

That was not exactly true. It was the Mets who initiated the conversations in the late summer of 1967, well before Westrum's resignation. If Westrum believed he had heard footsteps, he was correct. Discussions to replace him were well underway, with Murphy handling the Mets' side of the negotiations. Had GM Bing Devine been seen with Selkirk, it would have elicited suspicion, but Murphy was the perfect cover, for he and Selkirk had been roommates with the Yankees, and it was not unusual for them to socialize.

On October 9, 1967, the Mets announced that the Senators had given them permission to negotiate with Hodges. Once discussions began, the result was almost a foregone conclusion. After Hodges began talking to the Mets, it would have been very awkward to return to Washington. Further, the Mets had plenty of money, and were determined not to let Hodges get away.

Devine, who was attending the World Series in St. Louis, got in touch with Hodges, who was also there, and made arrangements to ride to the airport with him. They spent an hour and a half together. "I'll bet there were twelve managers in the big leagues," Devine said later, "that I'd known better than him. After we drove about six blocks, I said to him, 'Isn't it funny that this is the longest time we've ever spent together.'" Hodges went home to talk things over with his wife, then called Selkirk and Devine to inform them he'd decided to accept the New York offer. The Mets' opening day first baseman of 1962 signed a three year contract to be their manager, commencing in 1968.

Why had Selkirk changed his mind? "I guess he was just trying to be magnanimous," Murphy said at the press conference. Chairman of the Board Don Grant interrupted. "I don't think he was being magnanimous," Grant said. "I think he was just facing reality. Selkirk knew we wanted Gil after Casey retired, but we were turned down then. We had made every attempt to get Hodges, but were refused permission by the Washington owners even to speak to him." Perhaps Selkirk realized that he was going to lose Hodges after the 1968 season, Grant suggested, and might as well give him up when he could get something in return (pitcher Bill Denehy and $100,000).

Hodges said his goal was to improve his new team. "You can finish tenth and still improve," he'd once said. One area in which the Mets would improve, he declared, was discipline. No player was to instruct another without obtaining the manager's permission. The players would be prompt, they would dress in coats and ties, and wouldn't wander around the practice field. No one was to leave the bench before the game was over. Long hair and sideburns were out, as were the radical Nehru jackets.* One day during his first training camp, a number of players wore cowboy hats. "Enjoy the hats tonight," Hodges told them, "because you won't be wearing them tomorrow."

Hodges brought his Washington coaching staff with him. Third base coach Eddie Yost,

---

The first person to wear a Nehru jacket to a baseball game was Jawaharlal Nehru, who attended a World Series game in 1960.

pitching mentor Rube Walker (an old Dodger teammate) and bullpen coach Joe Pignatano replaced Harvey Haddix, Sheriff Robinson and Salty Parker. Berra was the lone holdover.

There was a further implication to the Hodges signing. When asked, Devine replied bluntly that the decision to hire Hodges was not his and had been made before he became GM. This was par for the course for Devine, who had personally selected only one of the six managers he had worked with during his career as a general manager. Johnny Keane had been his choice, while the others had been inherited or chosen by the owner without his input. Devine said he thought Hodges would make a fine manager, but the fact that he stated publicly that Hodges had been chosen by others was widely interpreted as disapproval. Devine was known to have favored Harry Walker, who he knew from his days in St. Louis. Bing made many brilliant decisions over the course of his long career, but hiring Walker over Hodges would not have been one of them.

As Hodges had returned to his former home, Devine decided less than two months later to return to his original roots. After winning the World Series in 1964, the Cardinals had struggled in 1965 and 1966 under GM Bob Howsam. Gussie Busch, who had abruptly jettisoned Devine in 1964, decided he had made a mistake. To his credit, Devine had never burned his bridges in St. Louis. Despite the shabby treatment he'd received from the Cardinal owner, Devine, while accepting the 1964 Executive of the Year award, thanked Busch for having given him the opportunity to be general manager.

In 1967, Busch wanted Devine back and asked the Mets for permission to negotiate. After the Hodges situation, the club could hardly refuse. In early December, Devine resigned his GM post, having served just a year, and rejoined the Cardinals, where he would take over many of the duties of Stan Musial. Musial had served as Cardinal GM for a year, and it wasn't a good fit. He was an icon, not a bureaucrat.

Although Devine insisted he had been happy with the Mets, it had not been a pleasant tenure. Upon his arrival, he had to deal with Weiss, who had been reluctant to step aside. Weiss kept saying he wanted more free time, and longed for leisure, but he kept re-signing rather than resigning. When Weiss's initial five year contract expired in late 1965, it was expected that he would step aside for Devine, who'd spent most of his first year with the Mets on the road scouting. Instead, Weiss's contract was extended for another year.

Finally, in November, 1966, Weiss retired—sort of. He was to remain with the Mets in an advisory capacity through 1971, and pledged to assist Devine in whatever way he could. In a tearful farewell, he praised the Met organization and took a subtle slap at the Yankees, who had cast him aside in 1960. "I am grateful to the owners of the Mets," he said, "who send you out of the game with this kind of taste in your mouth." At his retirement party the following April, Weiss even made an attempt at humor. "Now that I have the time to take a course in public speaking," the reclusive man said, "I'll probably never have another opportunity to speak."

After more than two years of waiting, Devine finally moved into Weiss's place. Now, just a year later, he was leaving. Devine claimed that the most important element of his unhappiness was his wife's reluctance to relocate from St. Louis. When Bing first took the Met job, the family lived briefly in Connecticut, but Mrs. Devine didn't like the East Coast and moved back to St. Louis. Her husband lived at the New York Hilton, became a commuter between St. Louis and New York, and saw his family only occasionally. Devine also appeared uncomfortable with the power play that had brought Hodges to New York, and his Met tenure had been marked by tremendous change and uncertainty. "For 25 years," Devine said, "my life in baseball seemed orderly. Then suddenly everything grew hectic and for the last three years I've been surrounded by nothing by chaos."

In Devine's place, the Mets appointed Murphy interim GM. Murphy, the old Yankee relief star, had been associated with the Met franchise since 1961. In contrast to Devine's ambivalence, the new general manager was delighted that Hodges had been hired. "Gil and I think alike," he said. Dick Williams' toughness and will to win had taken a ninth place Red Sox team to the American League pennant the previous year, and Murphy believed Hodges could do the same for the Mets. "We can instill a winning spirit in New York," he predicted.

Meanwhile, as the Mets board of directors pondered the choice of a permanent general manager, Weiss eagerly indicated his availability to help as needed. At the age of 73, he still wasn't ready for a life of inactivity, and there was no activity he enjoyed so much as operating a major league ballclub. Weiss wasn't needed, however, as Don Grant quickly announced that Murphy would fill the GM post on a permanent basis. Hodges went to Florida to watch Met prospects in action and then returned to New York to view film of his new team. The Gil Hodges era was about to begin.

• 17 •

The Second Wave

The 1968 Season

After finishing last in the majors in runs scored in 1967, the Mets made the obvious move. They traded their best hitter. In December, they sent Tommy Davis and Jack Fisher to the White Sox for center fielder Tommie Agee and infielder Al Weis."* Agee was the man the Mets wanted, for during the past two years, Westrum had employed ten different center fielders without success.

An Alabama native, Agee had been friends with Cleon Jones since grade school, having been born just five days after Cleon. They played football together at Mobile County Training School and became close friends. The Mets weren't just looking for companionship for Jones, however. Agee had been the American League Rookie of the Year in 1966, batting .273 with 22 home runs and 86 RBI, and earned a Gold Glove Award. He stole 44 bases and played center field in a flamboyant manner reminiscent of Willie Mays. As Marv Throneberry had copied the mannerisms of Mickey Mantle, Agee adopted the habits of Mays. He ran out from under his cap, made basket catches, and waved his arms around under fly balls. While Throneberry only acted like Mantle, however, Agee could actually play the outfield with the skill of Mays. Hodges had managed against Agee in the American League and felt that he was the best defensive center fielder in the circuit.

In 1967, Agee fell victim to a severe sophomore slump. His batting average plummeted 40 points, and his home run and RBI production dropped off precipitously. He struck out 129 times. Clearly, the Mets were taking a risk. Which was the real Agee? The Rookie of the Year of 1966 or the sophomore flop of 1967? Since they had given up Davis, virtually the only offensive threat they had in '67, to get him, the Mets dearly hoped it was the former.

A second newcomer, 21-year-old pitcher Nolan Ryan, also arrived in St. Petersburg in the spring of 1968, hoping to win a job in the Mets' starting rotation. Ever since he signed with the Mets, Ryan had been a legend. The story began the first time he worked out with the club. Ryan lived in the Houston area, and during the summer of 1965, when the Mets were playing the Astros, they invited the young pitcher to throw for them. "We brought him to Houston to throw in the bullpen before the game," said Chuck Hiller. "You hear the glove smack and you say, 'Jesus Christ, this guy's something.'" John Stephenson, who was asked to catch Ryan, also said "Jesus Christ!" "Catchers don't get too excited," said Larry Miller, "about the duty of catching rookie

---

*Hodges had to be very smart," said Fisher, "because one of the first things he did was trade me for Agee and Al Weis. That made them a much better ballclub."

178

pitchers who are trying out. They're usually nervous and they don't know where the ball is going."

"He was a skinny little high school kid," recalled Stephenson. "Red Murff [a Met scout] brought him to the Astrodome to throw on the side. I was catching him. Yogi Berra and War-ren Spahn were standing there watching him, and he was throwing hard, with a good curve ball. He was throwing real good curve balls, and then they asked him to throw a fastball. Being a high school kid, he didn't realize he should tell me he was going to throw a fastball. He threw one when I was looking for a curve and it hit me right on the left collarbone. I wasn't wearing a chest protector, a mask or anything. We didn't wear those things at that time down in the bullpen. I didn't even get a glove on the ball and it hit me flush on the shoulder. I was out for a while and didn't think too much about it after that. Then, in 1997, I fell on my shoulder and had to have it x-rayed. The doctor asked me when I broke it. I told him I never broke my shoul-der, but he told me I had an old break in it. That had to be it."

"I didn't know who the kid was," recalled Miller, "and as I walked away after John got hit, I thought, 'Well, they'll never sign him.' A few years ago, I went to dinner with John and said, 'John, you know the only reason they signed him was because he broke your collarbone. If he had just bruised it, they wouldn't have cared. But the fact that he broke it ... have you ever thought about how close you came to making history as the only catcher Nolan Ryan ever killed with a fastball?' If the ball had hit him in the throat, it probably would have killed him. It was that close. I was watching and thought about standing in there as a hitter to give him a target, but the way he was throwing, I thought it might not be a good idea."

The Mets selected Ryan on the 8th round of the 1965 free agent draft, signed him and sent him to Marion of the Appalachian League. His record at Marion was just 3–6, and his ERA wasn't very good, but he struck out 115 batters in just 78 innings. The next season, Ryan put up eye-popping statistics at Greenville of the Western Carolinas League. He was 17–2, allowed just 109 hits in 183 innings, and struck out 272, an average of about one and a half men per inning. In August, Ryan was advanced to the Eastern League, made three starts, and struck out 35 in 19 innings, including 21 in one game, which he lost in ten innings. The Mets called him up to New York when the minor league season was over.

"They brought him up in September," said Ed Bressoud. "One night, we were getting ready for the game and he was supposed to throw batting practice. About five of us opted not to take batting practice that night." Young, fast and wild was a dangerous combination. "It wasn't any fun to hit against him in batting practice," said infielder Joe Moock. "You couldn't get any work done. He was either overpowering you or throwing the ball over your head. His ball would move so much he couldn't keep it in the strike zone. It wasn't that he couldn't control the pitch. His ball was just so live when he was young that he had trouble keeping it in the strike zone. We used to laugh and say, 'If he throws a pitch at your waist, take it, because it will come through at your eyes.'"

On September 11, 1966, Nolan (his name was spelled Nolen in *The New York Times*) Ryan made his major league debut. He pitched two innings in relief, gave up a run and struck out three, including the first two major league batters he faced. Atlanta pitcher Pat Jarvis was Ryan's first victim. A week later, Ryan made his first major league start and lasted just one inning. He struck out the side, giving him six in three innings, but also gave up four runs and suffered his first major league loss. For the season, with the three clubs, Ryan posted a total of 313 strike-outs in 205 innings. The thing that caught everyone's eye, of course, was his tremendous veloc-ity. "They talk about a rising fastball," said Bill Denehy. "Ryan's fastball got there so quickly it didn't have time to rise."

The next season (1967) was a lost one for the young righthander. Ryan was called up by his reserve unit, released in late May, and after one game in the Class A Florida State League, was moved up to Triple A Jacksonville. In his first appearance with Jacksonville, he struck out eight of the ten men he faced, including the last seven. That was the high point of Ryan's season. He suffered from tendinitis in his elbow and pitched only eleven innings all year, logging 23 strikeouts, including an amazing 18 in just seven innings at Jacksonville.

In 1968, Ryan came to the Met camp with a chance to win a varsity job. His minor league statistics were so glowing that, if his arm was sound, he would need to pitch himself out of a spot, rather than work his way onto the squad. During the previous year, Ryan's body had caught up with his arm. Between the time the Mets last saw him in September of 1966 and March, 1968, he had gained 20 pounds, much of it in his legs. "His nickname was Clydesdale," said Jack DiLauro. Dennis Musgraves remembered Ryan at Greenville in 1966. "Nolan threw pretty hard," Musgraves recalled, "but he was a real skinny kid and he didn't really catch your eye at first. He went to boot camp with the reserves and came back a man. He put on good weight and his legs got heavy and muscular."

Despite a few lingering effects of his elbow injury, Ryan pitched very well in the spring of '68. Each time he pitched, even in B games, the media came out in force, and every twinge in his arm was subjected to minute examination and speculation. Ryan was clearly something special. Reporters labeled his fastball "The Ryan Express" after the popular movie *Von Ryan's Express*. "There are about three categories of velocity for pitchers," said Hodges. "Ryan is in the first one with Bob Gibson and Sandy Koufax." "We call him reheat," said fellow rookie Jerry Koosman. "He has heat plus extra heat." An intimidating fastball, however, did not in itself ensure pitching success. Hodges compared Ryan to Koufax, Sam McDowell, Rex Barney and Karl Spooner. His point was that each had achieved vastly different levels of success. Which of them would Ryan emulate?

On April 14, Ryan made his first start. He struck out the side in the first inning, and seven in the first three innings. Ryan didn't give up a hit until the sixth inning. He began to tire, however, and was removed in the seventh, even though he was pitching a shutout. He earned his first major league win, along with eight strikeouts. Ryan lost his next game, despite fanning 11. On May 7, he pitched his first major league complete game, beating St. Louis 4–1, giving him a 3–2 record, a 1.02 ERA and 44 strikeouts in 35 innings. In his next start, Ryan set a club record by fanning 14 Reds, and took over the National League lead with 58 for the season.

While achieving these amazing feats, Ryan was fighting what was to become a chronic problem, one that had troubled him since high school. After a few innings of pitching, he invariably developed a painful blister on the thumb and middle finger of his pitching hand. Trainer Gus Mauch prescribed soaking the finger in pickle brine, which he claimed toughened the skin. Mauch invested ten cents in a quart jar of brine and put it in small bottles for Ryan and Jerry Koosman, who also had a bout with blisters.

Mauch's home remedy garnered a lot of publicity for the pickle industry, but it didn't work.* Blisters continued to plague Ryan, as did military obligations, which caused him to lose ten weekends and two full weeks to reserve duty. He lost five of seven decisions during one stretch, and finally, in late July, when the blisters grew worse, Ryan was placed on the disabled list.

Ryan did not pitch again until September, and finished with a 6–9 record and 133 strikeouts in 134 innings. His last win was on June 23, and he didn't appear to be throwing hard during his rare late-season outings. The legend was tarnished, and there were lingering questions about the soundness of Ryan's arm.

Meanwhile, another rookie, Jerry Koosman, was creating his own legend. Koosman was

---

In 1975, Lou Napoli, who worked in the Shea Stadium press room, said Mauch actually used olive brine, not pickle brine. Napoli, an ex-fighter, said he used olive brine to toughen his hands, and had suggested the remedy to Mauch.

raised on a farm in Minnesota and attended college for two years, studying electrical engineering. Then he joined the Army, and became a Nike-Hercules radar fire-control man. A career as a professional baseball player was not in the future of most radar fire-control men, especially those who hadn't played in high school or college.

The Mets found their two best pitchers in unusual fashion. Seaver's name had been drawn out of a hat. Koosman was "discovered" by a Polo Grounds usher, whose son played service ball at Fort Bliss, Texas, and told his father about a talented pitcher on the team. Father contacted the Mets, who signed Koosman as a free agent in August, 1964 for a $1200 bonus.

Koosman's minor league career was not as spectacular as Ryan's. The year before Ryan was 17–2 at Greenville, Koosman pitched there and was 5–11 with a 4.71 ERA. He also developed a reputation as a happy-go-lucky individual who didn't take the game seriously. Koosman joked around on the bench and missed a couple of planes and buses. He was overweight.

The following two years, however, at Auburn and Jacksonville, Koosman found himself, and led both leagues in earned run average. He wasn't as fast as Ryan, but threw harder than most, and had good natural movement on the ball. "When you played pepper with him," said pitcher Ralph Terry, "you couldn't hit the ball solidly. He had an off-center spin on his fastball. God, he was hard to hit."

"When I played minor league ball with him," said Joe Moock, "he had one pitch, a good fastball that ran. He kept messing with sliders and slurves and finally got a breaking pitch." "He started out with a slider," said Chuck Estrada, "but then they made him throw a curve ball. He had a very good curve ball and he was one of those guys who could keep the ball down."

At 6'3" and 205 pounds, the young lefty was an impressive physical specimen. "Kooz was an unbelievable pitcher," said Estrada, "because he was so damn strong. He was a warrior and he could throw all day long. He was a gamer." "Koosman was a tough guy," added Rod Gaspar, "not just physically but mentally." "I think that in sports," said Ron Taylor, "you've got to have a certain amount of raw talent and a certain amount of discipline and intelligence. Jerry Koosman was a very intelligent man — a very intelligent pitcher."

While Ryan was tabbed a phenom almost from the day he started playing, Koosman was always the underdog. "Jerry didn't think he would ever get past Double A ball," said Moock. "You could tell that just from being around him. Or else he put on a real good act." "Jerry was a hard worker," added Jim Bethke. "I think he made himself a good pitcher. I remember in spring training one year there was talk he was going to be released. He went to Auburn and pitched us into the league championship game. I just remember him as a diligent worker."

Koosman first caught Westrum's eye in the Florida Instructional League in the Fall of 1966, and impressed him again the following spring. Seaver and Denehy were the stars of spring training camp in 1967, however, and although Koosman started the season with the Mets, he was sent down in May. He was recalled in September and pitched well enough to make him a candidate for a starting spot the following spring.

By the time he reached the major leagues to stay in 1968, Koosman had learned how to pitch. "Koosman could throw his curve ball anytime," said catcher J.C. Martin. "I caught another good lefty, Gary Peters, in Chicago, and Gary only threw his curve ball when he was ahead. Koosman could throw it anytime. He was very consistent around the plate and was just a super pitcher." "Koosman was the best lefthander I've ever seen," said Al Jackson, "at throwing inside to right handed hitters. To be able to do that, you have to have some pop on the ball. He had some pop. He would throw the ball up and in to a righthander and they just couldn't get to it. He got away with it time after time after time."

Like Ryan, Koosman got off to an excellent start in 1968. In the second game of the season, he pitched a four hit shutout in Los Angeles, and impressed Hodges by seeming to get stronger in the late innings. When his curve failed him, he reared back and threw his fastball to finish off the Dodgers.

In his next start, the Mets' home opener against the Giants, Koosman found himself in trouble in the very first inning. The bases were loaded with no outs and Willie Mays was up. Koosman struck out Mays, got the next two batters and went on to pitch a second shutout, the first Met ever to achieve two white washings in succession. In his third start, Koosman finally gave up a run, but beat the Astros 3–1 on a four hitter. He had a 3–0 record, three straight complete games and an ERA of 0.33. Another win made him 4–0, giving him four of the six Met victories.

In baseball's least offensive year, it was fitting that the Mets, 1967's lowest scoring team, played in the longest scoreless game in major league history. In the Astrodome, with its still air and distant fences, and hard-throwing Don Wilson pitching against Tom Seaver, one could expect a tight pitching duel. No one expected what actually took place, however, on April 15. Seaver pitched a two hit shutout for ten innings and Wilson shut out the Mets for nine. Then the Met relievers shut out the Astros and the Houston relievers shut out the Mets. One after another, they paraded to the mound—Ron Taylor, Cal Koonce, Billy Short, Dick Selma, Al Jackson, Danny Frisella and Les Rohr for the Mets and John Buzhardt, Danny Coombs, Jim Ray and Wade Blasingame for the Astros.

"I pinch hit in the 13th inning," said Don Bosch, "and in those days after you were out of the game you went in the clubhouse and played cards or whatever. Seaver was already in the clubhouse because he'd been taken out after ten innings. He was drinking a beer, so I grabbed a beer. We think the game's going to be over shortly, but two or three hours later Seaver and I were still drinking beer and playing cards. We weren't drunk, but we had a few beers."

In the 16th inning, the Astros had a runner at first and pitcher Jim Ray at bat. It was an obvious bunting situation, so Hodges had Swoboda, the right fielder, don a first baseman's mitt and come in to play first. Kranepool, the first baseman, moved well in toward the plate, leaving just two outfielders. It didn't matter, because Ray struck out.

Never before had two teams gone more than 20 innings without scoring. The Mets and Astros surpassed that mark and kept going. There were very few threats, as each club was able to get a runner as far as third base on only three occasions through the first 23 frames. The second, third and fourth hitters in the Met lineup, Ken Boswell, Agee and Swoboda, combined for one hit in 30 times at bat. By the end of the 23rd inning, neither team had scored and it seemed as though the game might go on forever. Not only had Met pitchers thrown the equivalent of more than two shutouts in one night, they had not allowed a run in 38 innings, having blanked the Astros the day before and ending the Dodger series with six scoreless innings.

By the time the Astros came to bat in the bottom of the 24th, it was nearly 1:30 A.M. and only about 1,000 of the 14,219 fans who were there at the start were still in the stands. The Mets had used 22 of their 25 players, with only Ryan, Koosman and reserve catcher Greg Goossen still available. The Met pitcher was rookie left hander Les Rohr, who, not expecting to see action, had thrown batting practice before the game. When the Mets ran out of pitchers, he entered the game in the 22nd.

Norm Miller led off the Astro 24th with a single, and Rohr immediately committed a balk which sent him to second. An intentional walk, a groundout and a second intentional pass loaded the bases with one out. Bob Aspromonte hit a hard grounder right at sure-handed shortstop Al Weis. It looked like a certain double play and the gateway to a 25th inning. The ball went right through Weis's legs, however, Miller scored, and the tortuous marathon was finally over.

In 1920, the Boston Braves and Brooklyn Dodgers played a 26 inning 1–1 tie, but the Met-Astro game was the longest National League contest ever played to a decision, and tied the major league mark set in 1906 by the Red Sox and the Athletics.

"Everybody came into the clubhouse pretty dejected," said Bosch, "and Gil wasn't all that happy. But he never showed his emotions, never got angry or made an example out of anybody. There were others besides me and Seaver who had come out of the game and joined the party, and Gil saw that we had sort of jumped the gun as far as the post-game refreshments. He asked Rube Walker whether Seaver had permission to have a beer. Rube said yes, and Gil never said another word."

There were two further ramifications of the long game. The first was that Rohr, having pitched batting practice plus 2⅓ innings, came down with a sore arm. "My arm just swelled up," he said. "I pulled a tendon in my elbow." Just nine days after the game, he was optioned to Jacksonville. "That year," Rohr said, "I went from the big leagues, to Triple A ball, to Double A ball and then to A ball."

The second issue involved the ground ball that had gone through the legs of Weis. It had taken a bad hop, said Johnny Murphy, and the reason it had taken a bad hop was that the infield, after having been manicured following the fifth inning, was not touched for the final nineteen innings. Murphy wrote a letter to Fred Fleig, supervisor of National League umpires, who issued instructions that, during extra inning games, the field was to be dragged every five innings, the "Murphy drag" as it was called.

With Seaver and Koosman, the Mets had two All Star caliber starters, and the team's overall pitching was the best in the club's history. "That was our whole team," said left hander Bill Short, "our pitching. We didn't make too many mistakes in the field and had a good infield and outfield, so we had a lot of close games." Every major league team had an impressive earned run average in 1968, but the Mets' 2.72 mark was fourth in the league, and almost exactly a full run lower than the 3.73 ERA posted by the transient 1967 staff. Starting with the second game of the season, Met pitchers allowed just two earned runs over a 58 inning span. Amazingly, the club managed to win just three of the six games.

Most of the credit for the improved pitching was due to the men throwing the ball, but many of them believed that having Jerry Grote behind the plate made them better pitchers. "I think Grote was a major influence on what happened," said Bob Hendley, "particularly with the young guys as they came up. He was an experienced, take-charge guy and he had some fire about him. I think he took charge of the young pitchers in the beginning and guided them toward what they needed to do to be successful. He came to play every day and he'd let you know it if you weren't ready to play."

As a high school player in San Antonio, Grote had been a pitcher and infielder. One day he was scheduled to pitch the second game of a doubleheader. Grote didn't want to sit idle during the first game, and convinced his coach to let him try catching. He did so well and enjoyed it so much that he forgot about pitching the second game and caught that one, too. After a year of college, Grote signed with the Astros and made it to the major leagues for a few games at the end of 1963, his first year of pro ball.

In mid–1963, the Mets talked to the Colts about trading for one of their catchers. At the last minute, negotiations collapsed, when Houston tried to substitute Grote for John Bateman, the Colt starter. "Hell, Bateman's the guy we wanted," Casey Stengel said. "What would we want with that Grote?"

A little more than two years later, Grote was acquired for pitchers Gary Kroll and Tom Parsons, and surprised many by winning the starting catching job in 1966, his first Met season. The trade turned out to be one of the best the Mets ever made, for neither Parsons nor Kroll lasted long with the Astros. Catching had been a problematic area for New York ever since Weiss made Hobie Landrith his first pick in the expansion draft. Landrith, Choo Choo Coleman, Chris Cannizzaro, Norm Sherry, Hawk Taylor, Jesse Gonder and many others had been tried and found wanting. The biggest problem was that the catchers who could catch, such as Cannizzaro and Sherry, couldn't hit, and those who could hit, such as Gonder, couldn't catch. Those who saw Grote play a full season in Houston in 1964 knew he could catch and throw as well as any catcher in the major leagues. Lou Brock once rated him the most difficult catcher in the National League to steal on. His .181 batting average, however, sent him back to the minors in 1965. Was Grote another Cannizzaro?

"I pitched to a lot of good catchers," said Jack Lamabe, "but I'd say Jerry was just a little cut above them. He understood pitchers. He put himself in your place and he understood the emotions of pitchers. He knew when you were getting tired. He could get you through a game when you didn't have your best stuff, just by his pitch selection." "He knew my style," said Dennis Ribant, "and was very good. He knew when I was on. If for some reason I was just throwing mediocre, we would try to finesse them with sliders and curve balls and just keep the ball down." "A great competitor who had a rocket for an arm," added Jim McAndrew.

Jack Fisher became so comfortable with Grote that Fisher could predict what Grote was going to call for in almost every situation. "Out of 110 pitches," Fisher said, "I could tell you before he even put the sign down what at least 90 of them were going to be. We thought so much alike on how to set the hitters up. I don't know how you can teach that. It's like mental telepathy."

Grote was just irascible enough to make the pitchers a bit afraid of him. "Grote made us work," said Jack DiLauro, "especially the young pitchers. If he wanted it inside, you'd better throw it inside or he'd come running out there. One time he got mad because Ted Sizemore hit a double off me. After the next pitch he threw the ball back at me at about 105 miles an hour. I didn't think it was for me so I dropped to the ground. The ball just missed me, went to Harrelson at second base and Sizemore just got back. I picked myself up and Grote came out to the mound. He said, 'I'm glad you ducked.'"

Like Harrelson, Grote could be a great asset to the Mets if he could just hit a little. In 1966, he was the regular catcher even though he batted just .237. The following season, when his average slipped to .195, Grote became less of an asset, particularly when his attitude tumbled along with his average. Westrum criticized his defense, and by the end of the season, he was being platooned with John Sullivan. When Hodges became the Met manager, he praised Grote and said he considered him an excellent defensive catcher. "How many good defensive catchers are there in the game," he asked, but added that Grote needed to learn to control his explosive temper.

During the winter of 1967, the Mets acquired J.C. Martin, who had been a regular with the White Sox, to platoon with Grote. Martin had a reputation as the best catcher of knuckleballs in the major leagues. Hoyt Wilhelm called him the best catcher he ever had. Martin's skill was not of any particular value to the Mets, who had no knuckleballers on their staff, but it had been highly useful to the White Sox, who had Wilhelm, Eddie Fisher and Wilbur Wood. "The knuckler was a pitch that nobody knew where it was going," Martin said. "It was exciting to sit back there and watch the thing break. It was going everywhere and you're doing everything you can just to keep it in front of you. You have to wait until the ball gets right on top of you and then snatch it. If you put the mitt out, you hide the baseball and it would continue to break at ninety degree angles. If you put your hand out too quick, you hid the ball. You thought it was going to be there, but all of a sudden it would break, hit the side of the glove and you'd have a passed ball. Wilhelm always came in when the game was on the line and a passed ball could do you in, so it was very stressful." Martin knew a lot about passed balls, having set a major league record in 1965.

Martin began his career as an infielder, and played quite a bit at first and third base for Chicago in 1961. "All of a sudden," Martin said, "they realized that Sherm Lollar was 38 years old and they had no one to back him up. In 1962, they asked me if I would go down to the minor leagues and learn how to catch, because I was a left handed hitter and had a good arm. [Chicago manager] Al Lopez said he'd get me an extra thousand dollars if I'd learn how to catch and in those days a thousand dollars was a lot of money. He also told me if I couldn't do it he'd bring me back as an infielder, so it was a no-lose situation for me. They sent me to Savannah, because Les Moss was the manager there and Les had been a catcher in the major leagues. He taught me how to catch in three months, and then I went back to the big leagues and stayed for ten and a half years." "I converted J. C. Martin into a catcher because he could hit," Lopez said in 1963. "Now, he has turned out to be a good catcher, but he has forgotten how to hit!'

During the winter before he joined the Mets, Martin was working on a construction project in Chicago. "I was an ironworker helper," he said, "and we were building Heinz Hospital. We were about fifteen stories up, burning steel. One day when I got back to my car to go home, my arm was locked at the elbow." Martin went to the hospital, where his elbow was x-rayed. He had a bone spur in the front of the elbow and another one in the back. "The doctor told me," Martin recalled, "that the only way to fix the problem was to have surgery. I made the decision not to have the operation, and played the rest of my career with a bad arm. In those days, boy, if you had an operation on your arm, you didn't have a job left."

"From that point on, when I'd get ready to sit behind the plate with a guy on first base, sometimes my arm would lock. I'd have to throw my arm up and pop it over the spurs. When I was with the Mets, I had a terrible arm. After catching for a couple of years like that, my arm started losing strength, and I had to have an operation. When I finally had the operation, in 1973, it was a terrible ordeal, and I couldn't play after that."

For several years, Martin had caught the fluttering knuckleballs of Wilhelm, Wood and Fisher without suffering serious injury. In his first game with the Mets, however, disaster struck. On opening day in San Francisco, Willie Mays fouled a ball off Martin's little finger and broke it. The left handed side of the platoon was gone, leaving Grote and Greg Goossen as the only catchers on the squad.

Goossen, a 22-year-old right handed hitter, had been with the Mets since 1965, when, on Westrum's recommendation, he was drafted from the Dodgers. After showing well at the bat in a few late season games in 1965, Goossen was practically handed the starting catching job the next spring. He managed to lose it by opening day. Westrum called Goossen his biggest disappointment of the spring when he shipped him to Jacksonville.

Goossen was another in the long line of one-dimensional Met catchers. He had power, hitting 24 home runs at Auburn in 1965 and 25 at Jacksonville the following year. His defense, however, was reminiscent of Jesse Gonder. "All he wanted to do was hit," said Jim Bethke. "He wasn't much of a catcher." In an exhibition game in 1967, the White Sox stole six bases against Goossen, who'd been victimized for 11 in three games. "He was there one hundred percent because of his bat," said Bill Denehy. "His brothers are all in the boxing business, and as a catcher he was like a boxer. If you put a pair of Everlast gloves on him, that's the way he would have caught you. A lot of balls got past him."

Goossen, a handsome, strapping blond from Los Angeles, was a unique individual, many of whose quirks were immortalized in Jim Bouton's *Ball Four*. After meeting him, no one forgot Greg Goossen. "Casey Stengel once said of Goossen," Shaun Fitzmaurice recalled, "that he was the only 20-year-old with a 40-year-old body. He definitely burned the candle at both ends." "He was one funny dude," said Martin. "He was a Beach Boys, surfer type of guy from California," said Lou Klimchock. "Greg was Greg," said John Sullivan. "You couldn't help but laugh with him and at him and everything else."

In November, 1966, Goossen applied for unemployment compensation, claiming that from October through February, he was not employed. His claim was denied. "On the plane ride to New York for the start of the '67 season," said Denehy, "the guys started playing cards in the back and they beat Greg out of his first paycheck. The club found out about it and got a little peeved at some of the older ballplayers. He literally had to take his whole paycheck and pay off the guys he had lost bets to on the plane."

"When we were playing for Memphis," said Bethke, "we had quite a brawl in Little Rock. They'd hit several guys and we'd hit several guys. Goose got plunked, and rather than charge the mound, he charged the dugout and went after their manager. I think it was Vern Rapp. Whitey Herzog was in the stands that night, and so were some other old time players, and they all said it was one of the better brawls they had ever seen. We had quite a few injuries."

While Goossen's defense reminded Met fans of Gonder, his batting style reminded the players of Choo Choo Coleman. While Coleman specialized in foul balls to right field, the right handed Goossen hit them to left. "He had a quick bat, but he couldn't hit a fair ball," said Don Bosch. "Everybody in the bleachers had to duck when he got up." "You could take the fastest pitcher in the world," said Denehy, "and Greg could hit his fastball and pull it foul." "They never threw the ball hard enough," said Martin. "He could always hit it thirty yards foul, no matter who was pitching. His longest hits were up over the dugout into the upper deck. He could really pull the fastball, but they were all foul. They never threw it hard enough for Greg."

Goossen had a lot of offensive potential, but in parts of three seasons with the Mets, he had yet to realize it. "He never wanted to make the adjustment with two strikes," said Klimchock. "He still wanted to go for the long ball." "Goose had trouble hitting the breaking ball," said Lamabe, "and that did him in."

Goossen never made it big with the Mets. After starting the 1968 season in New York, he was sent to Jacksonville. In August, during a plane flight, Goossen made up some lyrics and sang them to the tune of "He's Got the Whole World in His Hands." Goossen's lyrics were directed against a number of his teammates, and manager Clyde McCullough took exception. "Greg," he said, "you're through playing for me." "That's fine," Goossen replied. "Just give me my release."

Rather than release him, the Mets sent Goossen to Memphis, but he refused to report. Goossen eventually reported, and was sold to Vancouver the following spring. He played with the Seattle Pilots in 1969 and briefly with the Brewers and Senators the following year. After he retired, Goossen acted in a number of movies, including *The Firm, Get Shorty, Wyatt Earp, Mr. Baseball* and *Enemy of the State,* appearing frequently with Gene Hackman. He also joined his brothers, who were boxing trainers, and worked with a number of professional fighters.

In 1968, with Martin injured and Goossen the only available replacement, Grote caught nearly every game. Over a five week span, he sat out only once. Despite suffering a bruised thigh in the second inning, he caught the entire 24 inning game in Houston, and two other games of 16 and 17 innings. Grote not only caught with the skill he had shown in 1966, he began to hit. By July, he had an average of over .300 and was voted the starting catcher on the National League All Star squad, ahead of a Cincinnati rookie receiver named Johnny Bench. Grote had already equaled his hit total for all of 1967, and his average was more than 100 points higher. "Jerry had been a dead pull hitter," said Jim McAndrew. "Hodges was the one who told him to choke up on the bat, change his swing and hit the ball to right center." Under the calming influence of Hodges, Grote also learned to control his temper.

"It's funny how things happen," said Martin, whose broken finger played a major role in Grote's resurgence. "I went home for a few weeks, Grote caught every game and had one of the best years he ever had in baseball." When Martin returned to the lineup in mid–May, the Mets had the strongest catching corps in the team's history.

Buoyed by the formidable young pitchers, the Mets also had their best team ever. The 1968 Mets were the youngest team in the major leagues. Cardwell was the oldest pitcher at 32, and Charles, 35, was the greybeard among the regulars. Harrelson and Swoboda were the only two players who started the first game of 1967 to repeat on opening day the following year. All of the veterans from the last two years, Shaw, Davis, Boyer, Bressoud, Hiller, McMillan, Fisher and the others, were gone, replaced by promising youngsters like Seaver, Koosman, Agee, and second baseman Ken Boswell.

Seaver pitched as well in his second season as he had in his rookie year, although he suffered from a lack of offensive support. In early May, he was 1–2 with a 1.58 ERA. He continued to have difficulty winning, as the Mets scored just 24 runs in his first 13 starts. Seaver is an intelligent man, and finally realized that the secret to winning with the 1968 Mets was to pitch shutouts. Then the victories began to come. He beat the Dodgers on a ten inning, 1–0 shutout on June 10, shut out the Reds on June 25, and blanked the Astros on June 30.

Seaver pitched in the All Star game for the second straight year, and fanned five in two innings. One of his victims was Mickey Mantle, making his final All Star appearance. Seaver finished the year with a 16–12 record, 205 strikeouts and an outstanding 2.20 ERA. In many years, that would have led the league. In 1968, however, the year of the pitcher, his ERA didn't even place Seaver in the top five. He was more than a full run behind Bob Gibson's 1.12.

Seaver's ERA didn't even lead his own team. Koosman's four early wins were no fluke. He tied the Met record of four shutouts in a season, shared by Al Jackson and Carl Willey, on July 12th, and broke it nine days later. Like Seaver, he was named to the All Star team, and saved the game by striking out Carl Yastrzemski. By the end of the season, Koosman set a Met record with 19 victories, and his 2.08 ERA was fourth in the league. He also set a major league mark for pitchers by striking out 62 times as a batter. Koosman finished second to Bench in the Rookie of the Year balloting.

The Mets now possessed two standout young pitchers around which they could build a team, and several others who were nearly as good. Ryan's season was disappointing, but he had shown flashes of brilliance and, if he could keep the skin from peeling off his fingers, had the potential to be as good as Seaver and Koosman. A fourth pitcher, 24-year-old righty Jim McAndrew, was brought up from Jacksonville in July and made twelve starts. Although his record was only 4–7, his ERA was a sparkling 2.28. This was nothing new for the youngster, who led the Eastern League with a 1.47 ERA in 1967, but had only a 10–8 record. McAndrew didn't throw as hard as Seaver, Koosman or Ryan, but had good movement on his pitches and fine control.

In 1968, McAndrew also had some remarkably bad luck. In his first major league start, he had the misfortune to be matched against Bob Gibson, who was in the midst of arguably the best season of any pitcher in the history of baseball. McAndrew pitched well, but lost 2–0. The only run he gave up was an inside the park home run that was misplayed by Cleon Jones and Larry Stahl. He lost his next three starts, as the Mets failed to get him a single earned run in any of the games. McAndrew had four losses, three by scores of 2–0, 2–0, and 1–0. Finally, the Mets got him a run, which was all McAndrew needed to post his first win, beating Steve Carlton 1–0. Two of his three other wins were two hitters, one of them another 1–0 game.

A fifth pitcher, Dick Selma, was an extremely hard thrower who had long been a Met prospect. "The guy that impressed me," said infielder Bob Johnson, "was Dick Selma. I couldn't believe how hard he threw the ball for a little guy. He could throw the ball in the mid–90s." Selma had a terrible exhibition season in 1968, but was out of options and couldn't be sent to the minors without getting waivers from every team in both leagues. With Selma's live arm, it wasn't likely the other clubs would let him slip through without a claim. Therefore, he made the team and, after sitting idle for nearly a month, got a start and won. By the beginning of June, Selma was 6–0, the best start ever for any Met pitcher. By the middle of June, the Mets had four starters (Seaver, Koosman, Ryan and Selma) with earned run averages of less than 2.00.

As he had been in 1967, Ron Taylor was the Mets' best relief pitcher. His 13 saves don't seem like many by current standards, but they were fifth in the league. Cal Koonce, acquired from the Cubs in 1967, backed up Taylor, with eleven saves and a 2.41 ERA, and tied a Met record with six consecutive wins.

The bullpen lacked an effective left hander. The two lefty relievers were Al Jackson, the original Met, who returned after two seasons in St. Louis, and Billy Short, a former Yankee hopeful who spent the better part of a decade battling elbow problems in the minor leagues. He was in his fourteenth year of professional baseball, and had pitched for the Yankees, Orioles (twice) Red Sox and Pirates, accumulating a total of approximately one year of big league service. Everyone was worried about his elbow. On a couple of occasions, he'd lined up jobs outside baseball and intended to retire, but reconsidered each time. In 1967, Short was 14–9 at Columbus, and the following spring beat out Tug McGraw, Don Shaw and Hal Reniff for the final spot on the staff.

It was fortunate that the Met pitching was good, for their team batting average of .228 was the worst in the National League. Only the Dodgers, with 470, scored fewer runs than the 473 plated by the Mets, which was less than three runs per game. The total number of runs was 144 less than the mark posted by the woeful 1962 club.

Cleon Jones bounced back from a poor 1967 season to bat a team leading .297, hit 14 home runs, and broke his own club record with 23 stolen bases. Ed Charles, who had not even been on the Met roster in spring training, hit .276, with 15 home runs, which led the club. Grote slumped toward the end of the season, but still hit .282, by far the best average of his career. Outfielder Art Shamsky, acquired from the Reds, hit 12 homers.

The rest of the team contributed little. Swoboda, after encouraging everyone with a strong finish in 1967, had a poor 1968. As in 1965, he got off to a terrific start, leading the majors in home runs during the first few weeks of the season. After hitting seven homers in his first 16 games, Swoboda hit just four the rest of the season. He led the club in RBI, but had only 59.

Kranepool, the other perennial hopeful, was even more disappointing. By 1968, it was apparent that Kranepool was not going to be a superstar. During the previous three years, however, he had at least progressed to mediocrity. In 1968, Kranepool regressed, hitting just .231, with three home runs, and drove in only 20 runs in 373 at bats. He didn't drive in his first run until his 94th at bat of the season, and didn't hit his first home run until July 14. Although Kranepool was only 23, he lacked the enthusiasm and fire of the other Met youngsters. "Kranepool is only nine days older than Seaver," wrote Robert Lipsyte, "...yet the tall first baseman's eyes seem middle-aged and he carries himself with somewhat of the spirit of the Ancient Mariner." Mark Mulvoy wrote that Kranepool "looks like an advertisement for Inertia, Inc." "He is ... still the same lethargic player," wrote Jack Lang, "he was when he came up five years ago." Hodges thought he was too defensive at the plate. When Kranepool briefly tried glasses, one reporter said they would allow him to see the game much more clearly from the bench.

Kranepool said people expected too much of him, and kept reminding everyone of his youth. "A lot of guys don't make it in the majors until they're 23 or 25," he said. Seven years into his Met career, however, Kranepool was clearly running out of chances. How could a 210-pound, 23-year-old left handed hitter play an entire season and drive in just 20 runs?*

Agee, acquired to be the starting center fielder, never got off the launching pad. Not only wasn't he the Agee who was Rookie of the Year in 1966, he didn't even come close to duplicating his statistics of 1967. He was beaned by Bob Gibson on the first pitch of the Mets' first exhibition game and never got untracked. Agee went nearly as long as Kranepool without driving in a run, getting his first in his 78th at bat. He lost all concept of the strike zone, began swing-

*In 1967, the Mets held an old timers' game featuring the 1962 club. Kranepool, 22, became probably the youngest player ever to appear in an old timers' event.

ing at bad pitches, and his troubles multiplied. Agee suffered through an 0–34 slump early in the season, tying the mark Don Zimmer set in the Mets' first season, and in early August, was batting just .168. He hit .374 in September, but ended the year with just a .217 average and only 17 RBI. Agee and Kranepool, in a combined 741 at bats, managed somehow to drive in just 37 runs between them.*

Nineteen sixty-eight was the last year of professional baseball for Phil Linz. Linz had been released after the 1967 campaign, and contemplated retirement. He was 28, not old for a ballplayer, but his restaurant business was thriving and he was undecided whether to spend another season on a major league bench or spend all his time at Mr. Laffs. When the Mets offered him an invitation to spring training as a non-roster player, Linz decided to accept. New York was the only place he would play, and he thought he had a good chance to make the club.

In St. Petersburg, two Yankees from the championship years, Linz and Hal Reniff, fought to make the Met roster. "Reniff prepared himself for this ordeal mentally and physically," Linz said during camp. "I did neither, and never felt better." Apparently, lack of preparation was the key, for Linz made the team and Reniff didn't. With second baseman Ken Boswell injured and saddled with reserve duty, Linz played more than he had since his Yankee days, batting 258 times, but hitting just .209. He did manage to get five hits in one game, just the third Met player to do so.

After the season, Linz was released again, and decided it was time to call it a career. "Hodges called me in '69," he recalled, "and said, 'Come to spring training. You'll be our utility guy. We've got Al Weis and you'll be our second utility guy.' I thanked Gil but told him I was tired of sitting on the bench for a ninth place team."

Despite the woeful offense, Gil Hodges brought home the best team in Met history. Before the season began, he predicted his team would win 70 games, which would eclipse the record 66 wins of Westrum's 1966 club. Hodges had the luxury of low expectations. Both beat writers for *The Times* picked the Mets to finish last. Las Vegas oddsmakers made them a 100–1 shot to win the pennant.

After a poor 9–18 record during the exhibition schedule, the worst in club history, the Mets began the season the same way that had begun each of their previous six—with a loss. This year, however, the first win came quickly, as Koosman shut out the Dodgers the next day. With Seaver and Koosman working every fifth day, the Mets avoided the long losing streaks that had plagued them in prior seasons.

As April ended, despite the great pitching, 1968 was shaping up like other Met seasons. On the 26th, the club landed in last place with a 5–8 mark. After climbing out of the cellar for a few weeks, the Mets fell back into it in early June. The Mets were accustomed to last place, but this year there was a noticeable difference. When the Mets hit the bottom rung on June 2, their record was a nearly respectable 20–27, and they were just 6½ games from first in a tightly packed field. Moreover, many of the losses had been by a single run, often in extra innings, for with tight pitching, the Mets were in almost every game. "The difference," wrote Joe Durso, "with the New York Mets this year is that they are losing more respectably." Another difference was the fact that Hodges had put an end to the instability of 1967. By mid-June, the same 25 players who'd started the season were still on the roster.

Like Westrum's '66 squad, the 1968 Mets began to establish positive records. June was a very good month, featuring a 7–2 road trip, the best in Met history. A seventh win against their old nemeses, the Dodgers, set a single season high. On June 21st, the Mets were in sixth place, just one game below .500, a plateau they kept threatening but were never able to surmount.

Fortunately for Johnny Murphy, neither Davis nor Fisher, the two players he sent to the White Sox in exchange, sparkled. Davis got off to a terrible start and finally lifted his average to .268, while Fisher posted a record of 8–13.

They came within a single game of .500 on five occasions, but lost the next game each time. At the All Star break, the Mets were 39–43, by far their best record ever at the halfway mark.

The Mets' last place finish in 1967 had been discouraging, but of even greater concern was the fact that, for the first time, Met home attendance declined. In 1968, the Mets were playing better ball, and fans were packing the ballpark again. A June homestand drew nearly 350,000, and, for the season, the Mets trailed only the St. Louis Cardinals, who won the pennant in a new ballpark. The Mets' total attendance of 1,781,657 represented an increase of more than 200,000 from the previous year. It was 600,000 more than the Yankees attracted with a team that won more games.

The second half of the season brought continued success, at least measured by Met standards. The club wound up winning 11 of the 18 games played with Hodges' old team, the Dodgers, taking the season series for the first time in their history. In late August, another record fell as the club won its 31st road game. On September 13th, Koosman threw his seventh shutout of the season, tying the National League rookie record of Grover Cleveland Alexander and Irving (not Cy) Young. Koosman's win was the Mets' 67th, making the 1968 club the best in franchise history, with more than two weeks left in the season. On September 20, the Mets beat the Phillies for their 70th victory, matching Hodges' pre-season prediction.

The final won-lost record was 73–89 but, despite the great improvement, the Mets nearly finished in the cellar again. It wasn't until the final game of the season that a Houston loss gave the Mets sole possession of ninth place. Still, the 24 games by which the Mets trailed the pennant-winning Cardinals was by far the closest they had ever been to first place. The previous record had been 40 games. The high number of close losses also provided hope for 1969. The Mets lost many one run and extra inning games, and were involved in a major league record 47 shutouts. A hitter who could drive in a few runs could have a tremendous impact in 1969.

There was a significant difference between the '66 and '68 squads. Westrum had accomplished the "miracle" of bringing the Mets out of the cellar with fading veterans. Hodges was winning with youngsters like Seaver, Koosman, Ryan, Harrelson, Grote, Swoboda and others who figured to be around for a few years and might get better. As he'd done in Washington, Hodges made his young players concentrate on fundamentals. No longer did the Mets kick games away with sloppy play. They hit the cutoff man. They threw to the proper base.

Hodges also instilled the team concept for the first time on a Met squad. During the Stengel years, the club had no prospect of success, and Casey's main task was to distract the public from the ineptitude of his team. The combination of Westrum's weak personality and the high turnover that marked his tenure created an environment that fostered a focus on individual performance and survival. Hodges' strong persona molded the Mets into a team. "Gil had the same type of patience as Wes," said Lou Klimchock, "but he was just a little more disciplined." "Charming bumblers under Casey Stengel in 1962–65," wrote George Vecsey, "dreary bumblers under Wes Westrum in 1966–67, the Mets have become spirited performers under Hodges." "He didn't care much for guys who loafed or dragged around and didn't have a good attitude," said Joe Moock. "He didn't put up with any nonsense. Some of the guys had their own personalities. They wanted attention. They had childish ways of getting it by pouting. Swoboda put on a pouting act and Hodges just jumped his case about not being professional."

"I went 0 for 25 once," said Linz. "When I finally got a single, Gil ordered a case of champagne so that everybody could celebrate." There was a message behind the champagne. Linz wasn't Seaver or Koosman, and he wasn't Cleon Jones. But on Hodges' team, everyone was important.

Hodges was a key to the development of the young players, but there was a second individual who played an integral role in selecting talent and nurturing it through the minor leagues. Dorrel (Whitey) Herzog had a mediocre career as an American League outfielder from 1956 through 1963. After retiring as an active player, he scouted for the Athletics for a year and in 1965 served as a Kansas City coach. In 1966, he joined the Mets as their third base coach.

Herzog, only 34, was an animated coach. He raced down the baseline, threw himself to the ground to indicate that a player should slide, and windmilled runners around third with frantic enthusiasm. The writers loved Herzog who, in contrast to the drab Westrum, always had a colorful quote. More importantly, like Billy Martin was doing as a coach in Minnesota, Herzog instilled an aggressive spirit in what had been a somewhat timid Met club. He took chances on the base paths, forcing the opposition to make a play. What did the last place Mets have to lose? With stronger pitching and bigger ballparks, Herzog realized that aggressive base running would be more effective than waiting for a three run homer. It was a strategy that would win for him in spacious Busch Stadium in the 1980s.

In the fall of 1966, Herzog was moved to a scouting position, responsible for observing minor league players and potential signees. Many felt it was a mistake to remove the popular coach from the major league scene, but in 1967, the Mets' future stars would not be rounding third base; they would be playing in places like Jacksonville and Williamsport.

"Whitey was the man responsible for me being in the big leagues," said Jim McAndrew. "I was playing in Jacksonville in 1968 and Clyde McCullough who was—pardon my French—an old piss and vinegar manager, did not like me. I was buried in the bullpen and hadn't pitched in 21 days. Whitey came into town. He used to catch batting practice and get out on the field and talk to the guys. He was really outstanding that way with the young players. He asked me if I was hurt, and I said no, my number just hadn't been called. He told me I was going to throw batting practice that day and in two days I was going to start. Then he left town.

"Clyde scratched me, and Whitey came back the next day and asked what the hell happened. I told him my number wasn't called and I found out about 25 years later that that was the only time he came close to firing somebody for insubordination. Clyde scratched me again and Whitey almost fired him. Whitey stayed and watched me throw and five starts later I was in the big leagues—because he believed in me."

Herzog was a remarkable judge of talent. "He'd go out on a minor league field," said McAndrew, "and watch a group of six or eight guys play catch and just run around. He'd say, 'He's a year away,' or 'He's two years away.' It was mind boggling, because he didn't know a lot about them or their background. He just had a honed, inherent gift when it came to assessing talent. He was also very honest, and there weren't too many baseball people back then who were honest. Whitey would tell you what he thought you could do, what he thought you couldn't do, and what you had to do to be successful. If you listened to him, you were in the big leagues. If you didn't, you were a guy with a lot of ability who never got to that level."

Herzog also had a knack for relating to people. "He was a real people person," recalled infielder Bobby Pfeil. "When our wives would join us in Jacksonville—he'd met them maybe a year earlier—he'd always know their names. He made you feel as though you were important to him. I always respected him."

"I give Whitey credit for the eight years I had in the major leagues," said Bob Heise. "I think he looked for people who could do the little things, add a little talent, and who wanted to win. If you knew him and played for him, you didn't want to let him down. He just loved his ballplayers and you felt so bad if you let him down. He got the best out of you."

Herzog took a special interest in Bud Harrelson. "Whitey worked with him religiously every day," recalled Ed Bressoud, "primarily on bunting and what he should do as a leadoff hitter." Herzog showed Rod Gaspar how to get rid of the ball quickly from the outfield. He convinced the Mets to give up a minor league catcher for pitcher Jack DiLauro, who he'd liked after watching him pitch in the International League.

While Herzog was on the farm, nurturing the Mets of tomorrow, Hodges was on the bench, leading the Mets of today to the best record in their history. Gil was not on the bench, however, when the Mets clinched ninth place. Hodges was an intense man, who kept his emotions to himself and constantly smoked cigarettes. He'd acquired the habit while serving in Okinawa, in order to escape the boredom of patrol duty. In 1962, Hodges did a series of ads for a cigarette company. "If Hodges smokes our cigarette," said one of the marketing men, "it might do something for you, too."

Hopefully, their cigarette wouldn't do to others what it did to Hodges in 1968. As the pressure of managing mounted, Gil smoked even more. In August, he felt some discomfort in his chest, but ignored it and it went away. A month later, the pain returned, with more intensity. Hodges ignored it again, but this time it didn't go away. For five days, he suffered with what he described as "pain like a drill boring into my chest." It was so intense Hodges couldn't sleep, but he told no one and kept managing. "He had those pains for several days," said a Met coach a few days later, "but he wouldn't admit it. He was smoking like crazy. Two, three packs a day. He was keeping it all inside."

On the evening of September 24, the Mets were in Atlanta. It was a very hot, humid night but Hodges, despite his discomfort, pitched batting practice. During the second inning, he told Rube Walker he wasn't feeling well and was going to the clubhouse to lie down for a while. "I was on the bench," said Phil Linz, "and went up to the clubhouse to get myself a soda and a hot dog. Gil was laying on the trainers' table. It was the fourth or fifth inning and I was thinking, 'Geez, that's unusual for him to be taking a nap in the middle of the game.'"

Gus Mauch, the Met trainer, had suffered a heart attack in 1960, and recognized the symptoms immediately. He summoned Dr. Harry Rogers, the Braves' team physician, who insisted that Hodges be taken to the hospital. Hodges wasn't sure he should go. Finally, during the eighth inning, Mauch and Rogers convinced Hodges to get into a taxicab with Mauch, who accompanied him to Crawford W. Long Hospital in Atlanta. Cardiologist Linton Bishop examined Hodges' electrocardiogram and discovered a "small coronary thrombosis" or a mild heart attack. After a hospital stay and prolonged rest, Bishop said, Hodges should be capable of resuming his managerial duties in the spring.

Many Met players, some who remember ballgames and at bats in great detail, do not recall that Hodges suffered a heart attack in 1968. "I don't remember him having a heart attack in Atlanta," said Don Cardwell. "Maybe they didn't tell us he had a heart attack." "I guess I was like the others at that time," said McAndrew, "self-absorbed. For young men at that time there's no such thing as death. You don't even think about it. He was strong and masculine, so it was one of those things that was surreal and wasn't really happening. We didn't take it seriously. That's all there is to it."

Joan Hodges flew to Atlanta, and stayed with her husband as he slowly regained his strength. Just a day after he was hospitalized, Hodges received a call from Casey Stengel. By all medical knowledge, it should have been Stengel, after a life of smoking and drinking, who was in Long Hospital, not the much younger Hodges. Gil also received a call from Hubert Humphrey, whom he'd met while managing the Senators.

On October 21st, nearly a month after his attack, Hodges was released from the hospital. He stopped smoking, started walking, lost 25 pounds, and spent some time in the warmth of Florida, catching a few instructional league games with Mauch and Herzog. Hodges talked to Birdie Tebbetts, like Hodges a three pack a day smoker for 25 years, and Danny Murtaugh, both of whom had returned to managing after suffering heart attacks. He couldn't consult with his former manager Chuck Dressen, who died within two years of his first attack.*

---

*Ironically, Hodges' doctors wanted him to play golf, and play until he tired. It was on a golf course that Hodges suffered his second, and fatal, heart attack in 1972.

Hodges' physical condition was the great uncertainty that confronted the Mets after the best season in their history. Not only did he have to deal with the physical symptoms, he had to grapple with the knowledge of mortality that strong men like Hodges find difficult to accept. At first, he wouldn't accept the fact he was having a heart attack and, even after he was hospitalized, it was several days before he would admit what had happened to him.

Would Hodges return to the club in 1969? Would he be the same Gil Hodges he had been in 1968? Would the Mets continue to rise in the National League standings? Would Tommie Agee recapture his 1966 form? Would Nolan Ryan realize his vast potential? Those were questions that would be not be answered until 1969.

• 18 •

The Answer Is Pitching

"In baseball," said long-time infielder Bob Johnson, "no matter what the question is, the answer is pitching. It always has been and always will be. No pitching equals no chance." "If you've got pitching," Gene Mauch once said, "you've got a chance, because the middle of that diamond is the most important place." Veteran executive Paul Richards once called pitching the most uncertain commodity in baseball. It also may be the most discussed topic in baseball. Hitting, on the other hand, may be one of the least discussed topics. Conversations with retired position players about hitting tend to follow two threads. Were they guess hitters or did they simply react to the pitch? Did they try to pull the ball or did they hit to all fields? "You don't make hitters," said light hitting infielder Joe DeMaestri. "Those guys are just born, I think. I had some pretty good teachers. They can teach you all they want but nothing seemed to click for me at the bat."

For some hitters, knowledge came too late. "I wish I knew then what I know now," said John Stephenson. "I know a lot more about hitting now than when I played. Things like how to prepare, what happens in your swing — I had no idea at the time. I was just out there playing without thinking about it. If I could do it all again, I would really know how to prepare, know what to look for and what your swing does." "I think I'd have paid more attention to watching pitchers and how they pitched me," added outfielder Bobbie Gene Smith. "I still think about the way some of them got me out all the time and wondered how they did it. Now I know."

"Hitters just don't watch pitchers enough," Jim Frey once said while coaching for the Orioles. "If a hitter would keep a book on pitchers, on who threw what and where, he'd rate a picture and a three page story in *The Sporting News*. But pitchers do that all the time and spread the news. If Max Alvis singles on a low outside slider on the West Coast Tuesday night, they know it in Boston the next morning." "Curt Flood was a great, great fastball hitter," said pitcher Don Nottebart, "but when he first came up, he couldn't hit a curve ball. The second time around the league, he was a curve ball hitter. He was looking for the curve ball all the time." Nottebart therefore revised the Flood entry in his book. "I had a black book on every hitter in National League," he said. "Del Crandall had his book and he taught me to do it."

While batters rarely spoke of the science of hitting, pitchers and catchers seemed to possess the ability and willingness to speak endlessly on the philosophy and strategy of pitching. If the amount of thought given to the respective disciplines of hitting and pitching determined their relative success, every game would be a no hitter. My first interview for this book was with Clem Labine, the old Brooklyn relief ace who pitched briefly for the Mets in their first season. "Oh, my god," Labine said apologetically after delivering a lengthy primer on different types of pitches and their movement, "I'm really getting into pitching here." After another half hour of pitching theory, he asked facetiously, "Aren't you glad you called me?" I was, in fact, very glad I called, for Labine was the first of a series of tutors who provided a thorough education in the art of pitching.

The Met pitchers of 1962 were not terribly successful in retiring enemy batters, posting the worst ERA in the major leagues, but they proved to be among the best students of pitching of their era. Roger Craig became the guru of the split finger fastball, the miracle pitch of the 1980s. Al Jackson was a long time pitching coach, as were Galen Cisco and Bob (Righty) Miller. Craig Anderson and Ken MacKenzie were college coaches for many years. Labine was minister without portfolio, a great student of the art of pitching who undoubtedly could have been a fine coach had he not been so successful in business.

Nearly every former pitcher and every old catcher has strong opinions on the science of pitching, beginning with elementary questions. How does a pitcher get a batter out? "The whole idea," said Paul Richards, "is to try to get hitters who won't swing at bad pitches and pitchers who can make them bite at them." "Yogi was always hollering at me to be patient," said former Met Bobby Pfeil, "and here Yogi was one of the all-time bad ball hitters. But if you're going to swing at bad pitches, that's what you're going to get to hit. If you're going to swing at a ball, why would they throw you a strike?"

"If you can throw hard and keep it low," Labine said, "they're going to have a hard time hitting against you. High pitching is the bane of the game. It's like golf. If you can't extend your arms, you can't hit the ball very far because you're not getting all your strength into the ball."

"The concept of hitting is timing," said pitcher Skinny Brown. "You've got to learn to change your speed a little bit on your pitches. You couldn't constantly throw the ball by good hitters like Williams and Mantle. You had to change speeds and move the ball up and down or in and out to throw the hitter off stride."

Is speed the key to success? "I still think the best pitch in baseball is the fastball," said Jack Fisher. "There's no way they can stand up there and look for off-speed pitches if you can get the fastball by them. They've got to gear up to get your fastball and that sets up all your other pitches. When I first came to the big leagues, Paul Richards said, 'Just rare back and throw the damn thing down the middle of the plate.' At that time our stuff was good enough so that we could do that. Then it gets to the point where you don't have that good stuff and you have to learn how to pitch. That just comes with experience. I think the difference between a mediocre pitcher and a guy who's a winner is mental toughness. You have to be mentally ready for when the situation gets tough and just hike it up another notch and get through it."

Galen Cisco, pitching coach for the Toronto Blue Jay team that won World Championships in 1991 and 1992, said, "I think the key is preparation and knowing what you can do and what you can't do and learning how not to let certain people on opposing teams beat you, especially in the late innings. Walks are a very important part of the game and there are times when a walk is the best thing for a certain hitter in a certain situation."

"Warren Spahn used to say that ninety percent of pitching is confidence," said Larry Miller. "You've got to believe that if God Almighty himself steps into the batter's box, you can get him out. The hitters know when you're not confident. It's like a sixth sense. They can tell by your body language whether you're confident or not."

"You can pitch in the big leagues," coach Al Widmar told Gary Kroll, "if you can throw three pitches consistently. This year [Kroll was 17 at the time] if you can get your fastball over, you're doing good. Next year, if you can get your curve ball over any time you want, you've had a good year. If you can get another pitch over, then you're ready to pitch."

The beauty of pitching theory is that for every opinion, someone equally as knowledgeable will advocate the opposite. Is keeping the ball low, as Labine contends, the pre-eminent goal of the pitcher? Labine pitched in Ebbets Field, in an era when most National League parks were small. Keeping the ball down was the secret to keeping it out of the seats.

Not everyone, however, believed in keeping the ball low. In spacious Yankee Stadium, pitchers threw high and let hitters pound fly balls into left center and center field all game long. "The hardest adjustment for a hitter to make in the way you have to adjust your hands and adjust your swing," said Hawk Taylor, "is in and out. The second toughest adjustment to make is a change of speeds. The easiest adjustment for a hitter to make is up and down." "Jack Fisher convinced me," said Dennis Ribant, "that in and out was more important than up and down."

"When I came up to the Mets in '67," said Bill Denehy, "Harvey Haddix was our pitching coach. He said that if you could throw hard, you moved the ball in and out and didn't worry about keeping the ball down. You let your stuff dictate the way you were going to pitch that day. If you could throw your fastball inside, you threw inside, not up and down. I found it very easy to pitch that way. Take your time, cock and just let it fly and let your stuff take care of things. Whether I pitched up or down didn't seem too meaningful to me. Every time my uncle saw me that year, he'd pat me on the back and say, 'Just remember one thing, Bill. Keep the ball down.' I actually pitched better when I threw the ball high."

While everyone has his own theory, deciding to throw low, high, inside or outside is much easier than doing it. "All I knew when I signed," said Dave Hillman, "was to throw hard, hard and harder. The first spring training I went to, the manager took me off to the side and said, 'Dave, it isn't how hard you throw. It isn't how big a curve you've got, or how good a change. It's where you throw it. Location, location, location.'" Throwing it where one wants, however, is one of the problems that has vexed pitchers, mangers and pitching coaches since Harry Wright captained the Cincinnati Red Stockings in the 1860s. "I remember Rube Walker saying," recalled left hander Fred Kipp, "that most pitching slumps are caused by a lack of control. It's not just walking people. You can be wild in the strike zone."

What is the secret to control? Why do some pitchers have it and others don't? Is it mental or physical? "I think once you get the mechanics of your delivery down," said Bob Hendley, "you train the muscles. They call it muscle memory. During the 30 years I coached baseball, I pitched batting practice almost every day. I could pick up a baseball the first day of practice, throw two or three hundred pitches and throw one strike behind the other. I've done it so long that the muscle memory is there and you just react. But if you struggle and begin to think about it, then it becomes mental."

"First of all," said Jack Fisher, "you have to have confidence that you can throw the ball where you want to throw it. Then you have to develop a good, mechanically-sound delivery which allows you to do it."

As a pitching coach, Al Jackson has worked with many hurlers who just couldn't seem to throw the ball where they wanted to throw it. His approach is primarily mechanical. "First," Jackson said, "you've got to understand why things happen. If a guy is throwing the ball upstairs all the time, there's a reason for it. You have to make him understand why he's throwing the ball up there. If he's throwing it in the dirt, there's a reason for that. You straighten out your control through mechanics. The most important thing is the point of release. Each person has to find out where the best point of release is for him and be able to get to that point a majority of the time. When you find your release point and get there a majority of the time, you throw strikes. I'm talking about quality strikes. Anybody can throw the ball in the strike zone."

"Roger Craig taught me how to become a control pitcher," said Don Rowe. "The key thing he taught me was not to look at the ball. That may sound stupid, but it's so simple. Guys don't have the discipline to do that. Wherever you pick up the ball, that's where your concentration point is. That's where your best stuff is. If you pick up the ball halfway to home plate, your best control is halfway to home plate. You focus on home plate."

Two former Met pitchers, Chuck Estrada and Tracy Stallard, had control problems early in their career. "Oh, gosh," said Stallard, "I couldn't even throw batting practice. The guys wouldn't hit against me. I had to go throw against a wall. It's just something you don't work on when you're young. When you throw hard, they're all swinging at everything, so you don't want to ever work on your control." When he was with the Mets, Casey Stengel told Stallard, "Aim the ball right at the middle of the plate, because you won't hit anything you aim at and maybe you will catch a corner." Stallard worked with Johnny Murphy and the coaches in the Boston organization, and while he never acquired pinpoint control, it improved enough to allow him to become a decent major league pitcher.

Estrada, on the other hand, never found the answer. "I had terrible trouble," he said recently. "I think mechanics create control. Your delivery has a lot to do with how wild you are. Timing and co-ordination are factors, but the key is the delivery. It's like golf, where you have to repeat the same motion, the same swing, over and over. I wasn't one of those guys. I'd release the ball from different places and never get in a groove. It was hard for me to do that consistently, but I was blessed with such a live arm that I'd get away with a lot of mistakes. That's why I was pretty successful for a couple of years."

Pitching is more than just control and mechanics. It also involves a pitcher and catcher matching wits against a batter. What does a pitcher throw when the chips are down? "I nibbled too much when I got to the big leagues," said former Yankee hurler Johnny James. "In pre-game meetings they'd say, 'You can't throw so-and-so a fastball in a certain area. You can't throw Al Smith a curveball because he'll hit every curveball.' That's a bunch of malarkey. You have to pitch to whatever your strength is. I got away from pitching from my strength and tried to pitch to the hitter's weakness all the time. You get behind a lot when you do that."

That's an interesting question. Do you go to the pitcher's strength or against the batter's weakness? In other words, if you are a fastball pitcher and the hitter is a fastball hitter, does the catcher call for the fastball, or the curve that the hitter can't hit very well but the pitcher can't throw well? Opinion was virtually unanimous. "If we're going to get beat," said Joe Ginsberg, a major league catcher for 13 seasons, "we'll go with his best pitch." "If a pitcher gets beat throwing his second or third best pitch," added catcher Bill Bryan, "he can only blame himself. You have to go with your pitcher's strength."

"You always go with the pitcher's strength," said former Yankee catcher Jake Gibbs. "If you try to throw something different, you're going to mess him up. Whitey Ford was a low ball pitcher. If we came across a low ball hitter, hell, we would match strength against strength." "I tried to never let the pitcher get beat on anything worse than his second best pitch," added Doc Edwards. "If he got beat on his third or fourth best pitch, I wouldn't sleep all night thinking that I had two better pitches to get the job done with. If I got beat with number one or two, I'd go home and sleep."

"You don't try to fool hitters," said J.C. Martin. "When you've got one good pitch and you're in a tough situation, that's what you've got to go with." "In 1967," said Denehy, "our five starters were Bob Shaw, Jack Fisher, Tom Seaver, Don Cardwell and me. The only guys who threw fastballs to Hank Aaron were Tom and me. When the others threw him a fastball, it was off the plate. Tom and I would throw the fastball on the outside of the plate, because at this point in his career, Aaron was trying to pull the ball and hit home runs. We would go strength against strength and try to make him hit the ball to center field."*

Who are the toughest hitters to face? "I wouldn't mind pitching against a guy like Mark McGwire," said former Yankee Tom Metcalf, "or Jeremy Burnitz, who has a mile-long swing. I'd much rather pitch against a guy like that than somebody who's always going to get wood on the

---

*Denehy should have consulted with Jay Hook concerning the wisdom of getting Aaron to hit fly balls to center field.

ball, because they wear you out. Now if you get a guy who can get wood on the ball and also has power, then you've got a problem. That would be Henry Aaron." Metcalf's former teammate Bud Daley agreed. "I didn't like guys like Nellie Fox and Luis Aparicio," he said. "I would much rather face power hitters, because power hitters look for pitches. You can change speeds with them, fool them and keep them off balance. Jim Gentile couldn't hit me with a paddle. Boog Powell couldn't hit me. Fox hit me really good until my last three years. I finally realized that if I threw him fastballs right down the middle and let him go for the fences, he'd hit nice fly balls."

"I had more trouble with the Richardsons and Kubeks," said Fisher, "than I did the Berras, Mantles or Skowrons. The big hitters didn't really hurt me that much. It was the single, the double, the little bloop hit." One must remember, of course, that during the 1960s, there were only a few sluggers in each team's lineup. In the 21st century, there are shortstops that hit 20 or 30 home runs, and precious few slap hitters.

The psychological aspects of pitching can be as important as the strategic and physical. "I remember pitching a game against Cincinnati at Crosley Field one night," said Hendley. "I pitched a shutout and I think there were about eight rockets hit off me that were right at somebody. On the other hand, I've had games where I had great stuff and I couldn't get anybody out. That's probably why this game is so frustrating. You can't figure it out. You go out and get lit up and then you wait four days to pitch again. If you get lit up again you've got to wait another four days. If it becomes a mental thing, the game is over. I coached high school baseball for 30 years and that is something I always tried to make my players understand. The game is a mental game and what's gone is gone. You can't bring it back. You have to take what's in front of you. Be positive and aggressive. The mental part of the game will whip you and it will whip you a whole lot faster than the physical part."

Joe Grzenda was a journeyman left handed relief pitcher who found himself, at the age of 34, with the Washington Senators. Sid Hudson, the Senators' pitching coach, gave Grzenda some advice. "I'm going to tell you something, son," Hudson said. "If you go out there and you're afraid to lose, you're going to lose." "That turned my career around," Grzenda said. "That was what my whole career had been. I was always fighting for a job and I was afraid of losing my job. When I went out there, I was afraid to lose."

The hitter is on his own at the plate. The pitcher has a catcher, who in the 1960s called the pitches and location with little input from the manager and pitching coach. The catcher had to anticipate a pitcher's thought process and, further, instill the pitcher with confidence that he could handle a pitch in the dirt or off the plate. "The catcher's job is to make the pitcher comfortable," said Craig Anderson. "Then the pitcher gains confidence. If you've got a good catcher, he'll call 95 percent of the pitches you want to throw without even blinking an eye. But if I'm shaking him off half the time, there's a big problem because there's no communication or feeling between us." "If you put down the same number of fingers they're thinking of," said Edwards, "they'll usually throw a better pitch. If you're not on the same page, if they wind up with doubt on their face, they're probably going to hang one or throw it up in the strike zone.

"We were the quarterbacks of the ballclub," Edwards said. "Our number one job was getting everything we could out of ten pitchers. We felt that if you got everything out of the ten pitchers, they're going to contribute more than one ballplayer. So any hitting we do is just icing on the cake. I tried to figure out each pitcher individually, because two pitchers might have to pitch the same hitter differently. If you say that you should pitch a hitter high and tight, that might be great if you throw 95 miles per hour. But if you're Whitey Ford, and you don't throw that hard, you might have to go about it another way. Whitey might have to throw sliders down and in."

"You have to learn the pitches that each pitcher throws," said Bill Bryan, "and then you have to learn what the ball does. Is he a sinker ball pitcher? If he throws across the seams, the ball will rise. Some pitchers don't want to pitch inside. Some want to keep everything away."

One of the catcher's jobs was to calm nervous young pitchers. Larry Miller recalled his first major league start, which took place for the Dodgers against the Reds in the second game of a doubleheader. Veteran John Roseboro was the catcher. "My adrenaline was pumping so hard I didn't even know what town I was in," Miller recalled. "Koufax had pitched the first game and I had to run my act out there after him." Miller retired the first two Reds, but then Vada Pinson blooped a double, which brought Frank Robinson to the plate. "Frank had a stance where his head was out over the strike zone," Miller said, "so I decided I'd just bust him high and inside with a fastball. He had me set up for it and stepped toward third base and hit the most vicious line drive right through the box about four feet over my head. It hit the center field wall on the fly and it was hit so hard you could almost hear it rattling around the hills. I was so shook up.

"Roseboro called time, walked out to the mound and put his hand on my shoulder. He was a very quiet guy, in fact his nickname was Gabby because he hardly ever said a word. He said, 'Miller, I think you're playing Robinson a little too close.'" Miller laughed, calmed down, and stopped trying to throw the ball through the side of a battleship. "He had confidence in me that I probably didn't have," Miller recalled, "and I remember that as a defining moment of my major league career."

"I think a catcher needs a good memory," said J.C. Martin, whose accurate recall of detail astonished me during our interview.* "You have to remember all the hitters. I didn't remember the pitchers too well. My batting average shows that. But I remembered the hitters and the way you were supposed to pitch them. I never missed batting practice. I'd watch and see what guys liked to hit and how they handled the ball and when I was in a game I pitched them accordingly."

While he played an important role, and many pitchers swore by certain catchers, the backstop's duties were purely advisory. "Paul Richards pulled me aside once," said Skinny Brown, "and said, 'Brownie, if you have a good year, that catcher is not going to get any of your pay increase and if you have a bad year he's not going to take any of your salary cut. So you pitch your own ball game.'" Legendary pitching coach Johnny Sain had the same theory. "Sain always told me," said Bud Daley, "shake off the catcher as much as you want because if you get beat by one pitch the catcher called and you didn't want to throw, that loss goes on your record, not the catcher's record."

"Most catchers know an awful lot about pitching," said Don Nottebart, "except they've never been on the mound. Until the day they get on the mound and pitch an inning or two, they can say all they want. When you walk out there and you're facing the hitter and it's you and him, that's a feeling I'll never forget."

Each catcher had his theory about calling pitches. Tom Shopay, an outfielder who caught a couple of games for the Orioles in the '70s, had a very simple philosophy. "I was calling every pitch that I wouldn't want to hit in that situation," he said. "You study your pitching staff," said Joe Ginsberg. "You find out what each guy's best pitch is. You call a ballgame with that in mind. You say, 'OK if we get in a jam, what are we going to do?' Sometimes a pitcher's curve ball isn't breaking early in the game, but in the later innings, he'll pick that curve ball up, so you don't discard it. Maybe he was doing something wrong and he corrected it."

Jake Gibbs caught for many years and spent a great deal of time analyzing the game. "I studied pitching," said Gibbs, "and I knew what each pitcher had and what he could throw for a strike. We were always taught not to call something a pitcher couldn't throw for a strike.

---

*I mentioned the name Ron Taylor to Martin, who stated that he had first hit against Taylor when the latter pitched for the Minot, South Dakota, club in 1957. I quickly flipped through The Baseball Register I keep next to the phone during interviews and, sure enough, Ron Taylor pitched for Minot, South Dakota, in 1957. Every other detail Martin mentioned during the interview was absolutely correct.

Always get ahead of the hitter. But nobody can really teach you how to call a game. You have to experience that yourself, by studying the pitchers and studying the hitters. Who's hitting? What's his power zone? What's his weakness? Where are his feet in the batter's box? It ain't that hard."

"Back then," said former catcher Johnny Ellis, "it was pretty easy, because you were catching pitchers who had good stuff. You could call a slider when maybe you should have called a fastball and still get by, because the pitcher's slider was as good as his fastball."

Sometimes it wasn't easy. "One time in Boston," recalled Bryan, "Joe Coleman was pitching and Reggie Smith hit a gigantic home run off him. The next time he was up, I called the same pitch and he hit another one. I know Joe was cussing me." J. C. Martin had a story with a happier ending. He was catching Joe Horlen of the White Sox, who had a 1–0 lead and a no hitter against the Senators with two out in the ninth and a runner on second base.* Martin called for a curve ball. Horlen hung one and Don Lock hit it out of the park for a 2–1 Washington victory. "He lost his no hitter, his shutout and the game on one pitch," Martin said, "but he never said a word to me."

Three years later, in 1967, Horlen was again pitching a no hitter, this time against the Tigers, with two out in the ninth. "I remembered the game in Washington," Martin said, "so I called time out and went to the mound. Dick McAuliffe was the batter and I said, 'Joe, how do you want to pitch this guy?' He said, 'Jay, you've called 'em for 8⅔ innings, you might as well finish.' I don't think anyone can get a better compliment than that." Martin told Horlen he wanted to keep the ball away from McAuliffe. They did, McAuliffe hit an easy grounder to short and Horlen, the second time around, got his no hitter.

"One night I was pitching in Chicago," said Bud Daley, "and they had the bases loaded in the tenth inning with Aparicio up. Yogi was catching and Blanchard was playing right field. Yogi called for a knuckleball and I shook him off. I shook him off three times and he finally came to the mound. I said the last two or three times I threw the knuckler it didn't do anything. He said, 'Throw the knuckleball and you'll get him out.' I said OK, threw it, and it didn't do anything. Aparicio hit a line drive to right. Blanchard came in, fell down, but as he fell, he happened to hold his glove up and the ball stuck in the web. When we went back to the dugout, Yogi said, 'See, I told you you'd get him out.'"

Another way Berra helped his pitcher was by distracting the hitter. "Yogi would try to get your mind off hitting," said Joe Hicks. "He'd say, 'Hey, Hicksie, how's the family?' I'd say, 'C'mon, Yogi, I'm tryin' to hit here.' Then he'd say, 'Hey, Hicksie, where are you going to eat tonight?' He was always trying to distract you when you came up to bat."

Catchers called the pitches, pitchers shook them off, catchers talked to the hitters and infielders gave advice to the pitchers, although it wasn't always the best. Nottebart recalled pitching for the Braves against the Dodgers in the Coliseum, with its 250 foot fence in left field. Don Drysdale, probably the best-hitting pitcher in baseball, was up with the bases loaded. After Drysdale fouled off a number of pitches, third baseman Eddie Mathews came to the mound. "Throw him a curveball, Nottie," he said. Nottebart said he didn't have a curveball. "Then throw him a slow slider," Mathews advised. "He'll be way out in front." Nottebart let up on a slider and Drysdale, out in front as Mathews had promised, hit a pop fly over the left field screen for a grand slam. When the Braves came off the field, Mathews went up to Nottebart. "Don't ever listen to me again," he said.

Nottebart was a slow learner, however, and a few years later, while pitching for Houston against the Giants, took some advice from first baseman Pete Runnells. "We were ahead 5–1 in

*Horlen had an interesting habit. He tried chewing tobacco, but it made him sick. Gum made his mouth sore, and gauze didn't work, so he chewed Kleenex when he pitched.

the tenth," Nottebart recalled, "and there were two out. I had a 3–1 count on McCovey. Run-nells came over and said, 'Why don't you just throw one right down the middle and see how far he can hit it?' Well, I did and he did. It went in the bay [sic]. But we still won 5–2."

Sometimes the Runnells strategy worked. "Roberto Clemente was such an awesome hit-ter," said Hawk Taylor. "I never knew how to pitch him. You could throw the ball a foot inside and he'd hit a line drive down the left field line. Throw it a foot outside and he'd hit a home run over the right field fence." "One time in spring training," said Darrell Sutherland, "I was pitching against Clemente and Wes Westrum came out and said, 'He can't hit the fastball inside off the plate.' I threw a fastball about a foot inside and he hit it on a dead line. It was still going up as it went over the center field fence."

"Dick Selma was pitching in Forbes Field one time," said Taylor, "and it was a tight spot late in the game. Roberto was up with a chance to beat us, and Westrum came out to the mound. He knew that if you threw the ball inside or outside, Roberto could still hurt you. So he said, 'Throw one right down the middle of the plate letter high. He won't be looking for it there.' Sure enough, Roberto hit it 400 feet, but he hit it to dead center field for an out."

Each old time pitcher has his views on the modern game and how today's pitching differs from that of 40 years ago. "One of the things I really don't understand about the game today," said Bill Monbouquette, "is why it's so tough to throw strikes. Working with kids today, the only thing I can come up with is that they don't trust their stuff, they give the hitter too much credit, or they're intimidated by the hitters. That's a bad combination. They're constantly in a 'hitter's delight' situation. They're 2–0 and 3–1. On 0–2 and 1–2 the batters hit .190. I keep telling these kids, 'Why do you always want to pitch from behind?' I know of no hitter who likes to hit 0–2 or 1–2. You don't have to have a 100 mph fastball, but you'd better be able to locate and pitch ahead in the count and then learn to put the hitter away. Make him hit your pitch. Don't let the hitter hit his pitch, which is what happens when you pitch from behind all the time. We go over the charts and they're surprised at how many 2–0 and 3–1 counts they had. At the rookie league level, the pitch count jumps up so fast. They can pitch three innings and throw 90 pitches."

Jim McAndrew agreed with Monbouquette about one, getting ahead in the count and, two, his opinion that today's pitchers don't challenge hitters enough. "I don't know if it comes from the strike zone being pinched by the umpires," he said, "or if pitchers don't have enough confidence in their stuff to challenge hitters on the first pitch, but today there's too many 2–0 and 3–1 counts. You make .300 hitters out of .150 hitters if you pitch 2–0 and you make .150 hitters out of .300 hitters if you pitch 0–2. The Mets were in [Phoenix] the other night and I watched Glavine pitch. He's throwing 82–86 mph and pitches a three hitter and wins a 1–0 ball-game. I thought I was back in the '60s or '70s watching Glavine and Randy Johnson pitch because they threw strikes and got ahead of guys. The game was played in less than two and a half hours. That's the way I remember it being played. It's not nibbling. It's challenging, but not challenging down the middle of the plate."

One of the principal differences in pitching today is the rarity of the complete game. Forty years ago, a pitcher felt emasculated if he couldn't go the full nine innings. In the 1950s, Robin Roberts pitched 28 complete games in a row. In both 1965 and 1966, Sandy Koufax completed 27 of 41 starts. From 1964 through 1969, Juan Marichal finished what he started 146 times in 206 attempts, including 14 of his first 15 starts against the Mets. In his first year of professional baseball, Dennis Ribant started 19 games and completed 17.

"That's what you were supposed to do at that time," said Clem Labine. "When the man-ager came out to take the ball, you didn't want to give it to him. I can't believe what goes on today. They've taken pitching and put it into another sense that never existed in the old days. How did all these things come to exist and how did all those pitchers pitch so many more innings than a lot of pitchers pitch today?"

"I remember pitching against the Yankees in the first game of a doubleheader," said Bob (Lefty) Miller. "Back then we had those heavy woolen uniforms and by the seventh inning I was wiped out, dehydrated. About the eighth or ninth inning, I kind of glanced over my shoulder to see if anybody was warming up. My third baseman, Ray Boone, caught me looking, and said, 'Get some hair on your balls. You're going nine.' After that I never looked."

"My attitude," said Monbouquette, "was that I'm starting this and I don't want anybody in my game. That's not going to happen all the time but that should be your attitude. When I was in Boston we had Dick Radatz, the greatest relief pitcher I ever saw. But still I hated giving the ball to the manager. I hated that. One time down in the Instructional League I said to Sparky Anderson, 'I wouldn't have given you the ball.' He went bananas. When Radatz used to come in I'd say to him, 'If you don't get 'em, I'm gonna kick your ass.' He'd say, 'Just go up in the clubhouse and crack me a Bud. I'll be right there.'"

"There's no way in hell," said Chuck Estrada, "I would want to leave a game just because I had a four or five run lead — or even if it was 1–0. It would kill me. I didn't give a damn how many pitches I threw. I took great pride in that, because I wanted the respect of my teammates. I wanted them to know I wasn't going to bail. They knew I was going to be there. I wasn't going to say I was tired. I had many a coach come out and ask if I was tired and I would never tell them, even if I was exhausted, because I would never want the players to think, 'He bailed on us.' I would not allow that."

Not only did pitchers stay in the game longer, they generally started every fourth day. The result was that they pitched many more innings than today's pitchers. As late as 1969, the Yankees' top four starters threw 304 of the club's first 399 innings. The Mets were one of the first teams to switch to a five man rotation, to protect the fine young arms in their organization.

No one worried too much about the pitch count. During a game in 1966, Denny McLain threw 229 pitches while beating the Orioles. In 1963, Juan Marichal and Warren Spahn hooked up in a 16 inning masterpiece in which both pitched complete games. Marichal threw 237 pitches. "I had no idea how many pitches I'd thrown," said former Yankee Pete Mikkelsen. "When you couldn't get them out, you'd thrown too many pitches." "Steve Barber and I would throw 150 or 160 pitches in a game." Estrada said. "Now they throw 120 and they're tired. I've thrown almost 200 pitches in a game and they didn't take me out because nobody in the bullpen had better stuff than I did." "As long as the starting pitcher was going good," said Dennis Bennett, "they left him in there. There was no pitch count. Now it's 'Oh, jeez, he's thrown 110 pitches, we better get him out of there.' That's ridiculous."

"One spring," Al Jackson related, "I was talking to Al Leiter and a few of the Met pitchers. I told them that in June of 1962 I pitched three extra inning games, ten, eleven and fifteen innings. Leiter said, 'Didn't they have any other pitchers?' Guys today just don't do that. In the fifteen inning game, they were trying to take me out for the last five innings, but I wouldn't come out. I didn't want to come out until I won. I think I threw 168 pitches. We were prepared to do that. As long as you were getting them out, you stayed."

"I had a real strong arm," said Bill Denehy. "How many pitches would you think I threw when I pitched a 15 inning game in Legion ball where I struck out 27? After the game, my arm was throbbing from throwing so many pitches, but my shoulder wasn't sore; my elbow wasn't sore. I went swimming for an hour, and two days later I was throwing again."

As the number of complete games began to dwindle, the relief pitcher emerged. Before the 1960s, not too many players wanted to be relievers, since all the money went to the starters. "The relief pitcher," said Bob Miller, "was the guy who didn't make the starting rotation." In the '40s and '50s, most relievers were older pitchers who didn't have the stamina to go nine innings, kids looking for a chance to be a starter, or former starters who had failed. Johnny Murphy, the great Yankee reliever of the '30s, landed in the bullpen after getting a sore arm.

"I'm sending him to the bullpen so he can straighten himself out," many a manager said of a struggling starter. "The long reliever, the guy who came in early in the game," said Craig Anderson, "was usually in the doghouse with the manager. Long reliever was a bad word [note: actually two bad words]. You were the 'in case' man, in case the starter didn't make it through the fifth inning."

All in all, the bullpen was a place most pitchers were looking to get out of. "We didn't have specialists," said Bill Wakefield. "They hadn't invented the long man, the setup man, the short man, or the closer. You either started a game or you relieved. I was just a pitcher who pitched in any situation I could."

What did the pitchers prefer? "Why, starting," said Bud Daley, as if stating the obvious. "I preferred starting," said Ryne Duren, the most dominant reliever of the late '50s. "I think most pitchers do." "To make a lot of money relieving," Tracy Stallard once said, "you have to give up about two runs a season." "Being a relief pitcher is great for 11 months of the year," Hal Reniff said one winter. "But the other month is when you negotiate your contract and that month isn't so nice."

That began to change in the 1960s. For the first time, organizations started grooming minor leaguers to become "short men" as the late inning relievers were known. The most dominant relief pitcher in the early 1960s was Dick Radatz of the Red Sox, an intimidating 6'6" 230 pound righthander who threw a sidearm fastball with such velocity that Red Sox fans sometimes rooted for the starting pitcher to get knocked out of the game. When he began pitching in the minor leagues, Radatz was a starter. In 1961, Seattle manager Johnny Pesky had too many starting pitchers, and told Radatz he was going to the bullpen. Radatz considered himself demoted, and asked to be sent to a lower classification where he could start regularly. How could he get to the big leagues if he couldn't even make the starting rotation at Seattle?

Radatz needn't have worried. He reached the major leagues the following season, and made an immediate impression. "He was the most unhittable pitcher I ever played with or against," said Jack Lamabe. "He threw the ball so hard it would rise. He threw it by the Yankees. He could throw it by Maris, by Mantle and by all those dead-red fastball hitters. That's how good he was."

From 1962 through 1964, Radatz posted 24, 25 and 29 saves in an era where 15 was considered a good season. He also won 40 games in those three seasons. At a time when strikeouts were far less common than they are today, he fanned 487 in 414 innings. In 1963, despite pitching in relief, he led the Red Sox pitchers in strikeouts. The fact that Radatz pitched 414 relief innings in three seasons was perhaps the most remarkably statistic of all. Once, he pitched 12 innings in two days, including 8⅔ on the second day.

Tom Metcalf was a young pitcher in the Yankee organization, who had good success in his first year in the minors. The next season, he was promoted from Class D to Class A, but when his team played the first four games of the year and went through the rotation, Metcalf hadn't pitched. He went to Ernie White, his manager, and asked why. "He said," Metcalf recalled, "'You're a designated short man.' In those days, the relievers were the guys who were on their way down, couldn't go the distance, or were having arm problems. But he convinced me that they were breeding a new position in baseball and that was going to be my role. He said I had good control and a good curve ball, which was good for getting double plays, which you need late in the game. I didn't know if they were blowing smoke at me, but it was obvious I didn't have a choice."

Metcalf had a great year for Augusta, winning 14 games while losing just six. "I started liking it," he said. "I liked the thrill of it. I liked the idea of coming in under fire. It's like going out and taking the putter away from some guy on the 18th green and saying, 'You've got a four foot putt for the championship. I'll take it for you.' Some guys want to do that and some guys don't. I wanted to be in there in the ninth inning. Also, it was a quick way to the big leagues."

Labine was one of the great relievers of the '50s. "I would rather have been an infielder or outfielder playing every day," he said. "I enjoyed playing. How can you become anything in baseball if you don't take part in most of the games? Who wants to sit on the bench or in the bullpen and not do anything? Relief pitching was great because when you come in, the game is usually on the line. I would rather pitch as a late man than anything in the world. Can you imagine being involved in a game all the time when it means something."

"I always thrived on coming in tough spots," said Craig Anderson, who found more than his share of them with the '62 Mets. "I was a reliever all the way. I never thought of becoming a starter. You don't want to think too much in relief, you've just got to throw strikes. I'd just block out everything and concentrate on the hitter. When you're going good, you feel like you can come in there and get anybody out."

"The thing you had to learn about relief pitching," said Metcalf, "was that you don't get a second chance. It's not the first inning, where you can give up a couple of runs and still win the ballgame. In relief, two runs and you're dead. You have to do it now, with this pitch. When you come into a game, somebody's usually telling you the situation as you're reaching for your jacket. I would not ride in because I wanted the opportunity to walk to the mound, get oriented and develop a hatred, a meanness. You talk to yourself and get yourself juiced up."

Bob Shaw began his career as a reliever, then was a starter from 1959 to 1962. He moved back to the bullpen for two years and then finished his career as a starting pitcher. "The night before you start," he said, "you don't sleep too well. You're getting ready to go into battle and you get yourself all keyed up. Even when I was 35, I still had that nervous tension. In relief, I never had that feeling. Yet you're coming on in the last two or three innings and the pressure's on, but since you don't know you're going to pitch, you don't get nervous. I found that being in short relief was almost less pressure than starting, because you don't know if you're going in that night. Therefore, you're relaxed."

Perhaps the most difficult adjustment for a starting pitcher who turned to relieving was learning to warm up in a hurry. "I learned from Ed Roebuck [the Dodger reliever]," said Don Nottebart. "He told me that when you warm up, just throw breaking balls. It loosens your arm up faster. Just four or five breaking balls and your arm is loose."

Warming up was a science unto itself. Some managers liked to get pitchers up frequently, just in case they might need them. In addition to the number of games pitched, say the old firemen, the times they warmed up but never got in the game should almost count as a statistic, for it took a toll on their arms. "You learn to pace yourself," said Metcalf. "You don't want to get real warm, because if you don't get into the game, you don't get credit for it, but your arm still hurts, so you learn to fake it. You have somebody watching the game, telling you what's going on and whether it looks like you might be going in. If it does, you step up the pace and start throwing a little harder."

Another adjustment for the reliever was learning about life in the bullpen. With three hours to kill, and often little to do until the late innings, there was plenty of time for conversation. What did bullpen inhabitants talk about? "I've been in bullpens where we played bridge," said Labine. "I've been in bullpens where nobody paid attention to anything. Bullpens are very strange. If you have a good bullpen, it's a great place to be, but if you've got a bad bullpen, you watch a guy throw and say, 'Oh, boy, I hope he doesn't get into the game.'"

"We'd mix it up," said Don Rowe. "You can only talk baseball for so long. Relief pitchers are psychos, because you go to the ballpark and don't know if you're going to be in the game or not. When they call your number you get an adrenaline rush you wouldn't believe."

"Willard Hunter invented a game in the bullpen," said Bill Wakefield. "We tried to see how long we could go without talking. We would all put a couple of dollars in the pot and whoever talked was out. We were playing in Cincinnati one time, where the bullpen is right along the stands. There was a high pop to right that fell one or two rows into the seats. The right fielder came running over and we didn't say anything. Instead of yelling, 'Look out,' or 'You've got room,' we just sat there. He looked at us and said, 'What the hell's wrong with you guys. Can't you talk.' We just looked at him."

By the middle of the decade, the relief pitcher's role was firmly established, but remained very different from the role of his 21st century counterpart. In 1966, *The Sporting News* published some interesting statistics. American League pitchers completed 334 starts, while those in the National League finished 402. Each league averaged 1.63 relief appearances per game, and it rarely took more than four pitchers to finish off a contest. The Yankees, even though they finished last, employed only 1.40 relievers in an average game. While starters pitched fewer innings than in previous years, relievers pitched far longer than they do now, which resulted in fewer appearances per pitcher. Larry Sherry of the Tigers set a club record by pitching in 55 games. Few relievers pitched more than 60 games. Managers employed lefty-righty switches, but far less frequently than today, and typically only in close games. The nature of pitching had changed from the 1930s and '40s, and was destined to change even more drastically over the next 40 years.

There is one issue on which virtually every ex-player is in agreement. In order to be effective, they said, pitchers need to throw inside and move hitters away from the plate. "When I first started playing, I didn't understand what pitching inside meant," said Galen Cisco. "I'm not talking about hitting guys, but you have to pitch inside. I think that's one thing that pitchers lack today — the art of pitching inside — making good pitches out of the strike zone." "It's an old adage," said John Sullivan. "You put them on a rocking chair. You throw up and in and down and away — up and in and down and away. It makes it a little tougher when the hitter knows the pitcher is going to come up under his chin and then throw a slider down and away. That's the way you pitch and that's the way you get people out." "I'm an advocate of establishing the inner half of the plate," said Estrada, like Cisco and Sullivan a long time major league coach. "If you don't do that, the hitter gets too damn aggressive. You have to establish early in the game that you pitch inside, and then you can pitch away."

Jim Lonborg joined the Red Sox in 1965 and, despite his strong arm and good stuff, was a losing pitcher for two years. In 1967, tutored by Sal (the Barber) Maglie, one of the great all-time proponents of the knockdown pitch, Lonborg began moving hitters off the plate. He led the American League by hitting 19 batters and won the Cy Young Award with a 22–9 record.

"Most hitters today are looking for the ball away," said Al Jackson. "If you're looking for the ball away, it's going to be tough to hit the ball inside. Today, you see a lot of guys being called out on strikes with their hands stretched up over their heads, trying to get out of the way of the ball."

Why don't today's pitchers throw inside more often? For one thing, they might get ejected. "How ridiculous can it get?" said Sullivan. "If you want to go home and play with your dollies, then go ahead. I can't understand all this garbage about somebody throwing a ball inside and [getting thrown out] just because it's under their chin."

"I remember one instance," said Bobby Klaus, "when Drysdale knocked Frank Robinson down four times in the same at bat. He went to first base and didn't say anything. He came up the next time and hit the first pitch out onto the highway. No umpire stepped in. You just handled it. And Frank wouldn't move an inch, either."

"Hitters do not move at all," said Fred Kipp. "If you throw the ball inside, you have a very good chance of hitting someone. They dive into the ball. If you throw it a few inches inside, they want to fight. When I started playing ball, they had those inserts for the cap. They didn't have helmets. Now they have helmets, chest protectors, shin guards and elbow guards. They do not move out of the way. Somebody's going to get hurt really bad."

"If you had first base open and a good hitter up," said Joe Grzenda, "you'd hit him in the leg, where there was some meat. You didn't cripple the guy. But today, you're thrown out of the game. I've been hit with pitches and it hurts, but they've taken too much away from the pitchers."

Monbouquette works with Tiger minor leaguers today, and often talks to them about the importance of throwing inside. "They say, 'Well, they won't let you throw inside.' I see the hitters really intimidating the pitchers today. Years ago, if the hitter jumped out over the plate, you'd say, 'Hey, don't do that again.' They wouldn't because they knew you might plunk them. But the umpires have a lot of power today. I remember knocking somebody down and the hitter would be lying there taking their time getting up and the umpire would say, 'Hey, let's go, pal. Get up. It's part of the game.' Do you think Drysdale would be intimidated today? I don't think so. Do you think Sal Maglie would be intimidated today? I don't think so. Clemens throws inside. Martinez throws inside. These guys today don't know how to get out of the way. They all turn into the ball, whereas we turned the other way, so that if you got hit, you got hit in the back. Piazza gets hit because he turns into the ball."

"Can you imagine Gibson and Drysdale today?" asked Bobby Pfeil. Those were the two names that always seemed to come up when knockdowns were mentioned. "If they hit Canseco," Pfeil said, "and he glared out at them, they'd hit him five more times!" Drysdale, who learned his craft from Maglie when the latter was finishing his career with Brooklyn, often kept throwing at a hitter until he finally got him. "Sal says sometimes you have to throw at them twice," he innocently told a reporter after he dusted Willie Mays off a couple of times. In his heyday, Drysdale plunked 62 batters over a four year period. His battles with Frank Robinson, who leaned well over the plate, were legendary. Some of the Giants claimed Drysdale practiced shouting "Oops," in preparation for pitching against them.

"When I was working for the White Sox," Estrada said, "Larry Himes asked me why pitchers don't throw inside. My opinion is that they're afraid of hitting somebody or hurting somebody. Or they might hit somebody and they'll charge the mound."

Hitting a batter in the head was many pitchers' greatest fear. Jack Fisher recalled an incident that occurred while he was pitching against the Cubs in 1966. In the first inning, he surrendered a leadoff home run to Adolfo Phillips. "I threw him a really good slider low and away," Fisher said. "As soon as I let it go, he dove across the plate, pulled it and hit a home run. That's just a no-no. You don't let guys do that." The next time Phillips came to bat, Fisher hit him on the elbow with a fastball.

The Cubs were managed by Leo Durocher, who was not about to let the incident pass unnoticed. He ordered his pitcher, Curt Simmons, to retaliate. Simmons threw a pitch over Ron Swoboda's head, then hit Ron Hunt, always a willing target, and the teams were even. The umpires told both managers that was it. There was to be no more retaliation. "Everybody'd had their shot," Fisher said. "I'd settled the score with the guy I wanted to settle a score with."

Later in the game, Ron Santo of the Cubs came to bat. "Santo was leaning over the plate," Fisher recalled. "I just wanted to come inside and shove him off the plate a little. As soon as I threw the ball, I knew it was going to be trouble. It was about halfway to the plate and I hollered, 'Look out!' He didn't move and it hit him right on the jaw. He went down and started screaming, 'I'm blind! I'm blind!' I came running down to home plate. Durocher was talking to him. Leo said, 'You can't see because your eye's swollen shut. That's why you can't see. You're all right.' I walked over to Leo and said, 'Leo, I wasn't trying to do that. I wasn't throwing at him.' He turned around while he was kneeling on the ground and said, 'I know you didn't, son,' and patted my knee."

"I couldn't wait to get back to New York. I had the number of the hospital and as soon as we got home I called Santo and talked to him on the phone. He said, 'It's just one of those things. I didn't pick the ball up until it was about fifteen feet away from me.' I really felt bad."

"When I first signed with the Red Sox," said Cisco, "we were having an intrasquad game in spring training. The guy's name was Bob Findler. He was a kid the Red Sox really thought a lot of. I was pitching that day and hit him square in the left eyeball. He just didn't read the ball and moved right into it. It broke the bone around his eye socket and ended his career. He was never the same after that. That really bothered me. It bothered me a lot. It took me several months to get over it."

The purpose of throwing inside was to intimidate, not to maim. Don Cardwell, who was always among the league leaders in plunking batters, said, "It took me three years before I learned how to pitch inside without hitting somebody in the head. You just had to hold the ball a certain way. If you hold it one way, the ball tails in. If you grip it across the seams and throw it over the top more, it's straighter." "I'd throw at Mantle's knees," said Bob Shaw. "It would snap him back and he'd be in pain. We were in a lounge having a drink after a golf tournament, and he said, 'I'm going to pinch your head off if you hit me.' I said, 'Don't get all excited, Mickey. I haven't hit you yet.'"

Players yapped, but being dusted off was an accepted part of the game of the 1960s. "If I didn't get knocked down at least once or twice a game," said Hawk Taylor, "I didn't think the pitcher was showing me very much respect." "When Maris and Mantle hit home runs, and you were up next," I asked Yankee outfielder Hector Lopez, "did you expect to go down?" "Oh, yes. Oh, yes. Oh, yes," he replied. "I'd get mad at times. I'd say, 'Why are you throwing at me?' But I'd be ready for them. They didn't throw at your head, but they'd make you move your feet." "I never understood it," said Bobby Pfeil. "You're hitting .220 and the guy in front of you hits a home run and you've got to walk up there and get hit." He laughed. "Why did I have to get hit? But that was part of the game."

"You knocked guys down for a reason," said Grzenda. "When a guy was hit, he probably knew he was going to be hit. It was expected. I'm on the mound, and that's my living. If you hit me, I'm going to hit you back. You have to fear me, have a fear that I can throw it by you and a fear that I can knock you on your ass."

"If you knocked somebody down," said outfielder Jim Gosger, "you were going to get knocked down. One night in Montreal we were playing against the Cubs, and Gene Mauch [the Montreal manager] came right out and said, 'I want Santo knocked down.' Santo came up the next inning and got drilled. Durocher was on the other side and he told Ferguson Jenkins that somebody had to go down. We went through the lineup and I was the only one to get a hit. The next time up, Fergie drilled me in the leg. When the third out was made, I passed him on his way to the dugout, and he asked me if I was all right. 'Yeah,' I told him, 'but Christ, I'm only hitting .200, why did you hit me?' He said, 'Orders from Durocher. If I don't hit you it costs me five hundred. That's why I hit you in the leg.'"

"If someone knocked one of our guys down," said Dennis Ribant, "I'm going to retaliate. Otherwise, your players aren't going to respect you." Alvin Dark once said he would risk a lifetime suspension from the game rather than not order retaliatory knockdowns after one of his players had been hit.

In 1960, Vada Pinson of the Reds collided with Roger Craig on the basepaths and broke Craig's collarbone. The next night, the Dodger pitchers used him for target practice, before Stan Williams finally connected in the seventh. That wasn't the end of things, for when the Dodgers went to Cincinnati two months later, Drysdale hit Pinson in the head.

In 1966, Wes Westrum admitted telling Fisher to hit Phillie pitcher Bob Buhl after Buhl hit Dick Selma on the right elbow and knocked him out of the game. Buhl had hit Selma in retaliation for Selma hitting Richie Allen. "I have a standing order," Westrum said after the game, "to get the pitcher who threw the ball ... I believe in an eye for an eye. You've got to protect your ball players."

When he was pitching for the Braves, Carl Willey was given the sign to knock down Orlando Cepeda after Mays homered. Willey ignored the order and struck out Cepeda instead. He was removed from the game and didn't pitch again for three weeks.

Jim McAndrew is one of the few dissenters to the theory of pitching inside. "I just don't think a lot of guys know how to plain, old-fashioned, pitch, or they don't have enough confidence in their stuff," he said. "I watch Tom Glavine and Greg Maddux, and I firmly believe that if you have good stuff, you can pitch away almost all the time. Catfish Hunter didn't really pitch inside. He just had good stuff, kept the ball down, changed speeds and challenged people."

Since the purpose of knocking hitters down and moving them off the plate was to intimidate them, it was interesting to hear hitters tell of the effect of knockdown pitches on them. "The good hitters," said Taylor, "it just steeled their resolve. I saw Henry Aaron get knocked down, maybe twice in a row, and then they'd make a perfect pitch, a low outside slider, and he'd hit the most awesome line drive home run over the right center field fence. Same thing for Willie Mays. Knock him down and you just made him a tougher hitter. Same for Roberto Clemente."

Far less talented hitters than Aaron, Mays and Clemente were unaffected by the brushback pitch, or so they said. "When a guy knocked me down," said former Yankee utility man Len Boehmer, "it just made me more intense." Was Gosger intimidated? "Not at all," he said, "not at all. If they want to pitch you inside, you've got to prove you can hit the ball inside." Given the imperviousness of hitters to the knockdown pitch, why is it so critically important that the pitcher be able to throw at them? Pitcher Ken Johnson laughed. "They're liars," he said. "I guarantee you they're intimidated."

How did hitters cope with this wealth of pitching knowledge and the fear implanted by the knockdown? With such brainpower and strategy aligned against them, how did they ever get a hit? What did they think about hitting? "I played three years with Henry Aaron," said Nottebart, "and I talked to him about hitting. Henry never guessed. He just hit what he saw. He told me there was an imaginary box over the pitcher's pitching shoulder. He looked at that box. He never looked at the pitcher's face or anything but this box, because the ball was going to come out of that box." Even Henry Aaron couldn't outsmart a pitcher, however. "I remembered that," said Nottebart, "and when I got traded to the Colt 45s, I never threw from the same angle to Henry. I'd come overhand, three quarters, sidearm. That bothered him."

Perhaps the best hitting theorist of all time was Ted Williams. Williams had a forceful, aggressive personality that was indelibly imprinted on the mind of anyone who knew him. The media created an image for the shy Joe Dimaggio, but despite the best efforts of the press to crush Williams, the excitement and dynamism of his huge personality shone through. He had charisma. "I don't know if there's anyone in baseball today like Ted," said former teammate Monbouquette. "If we were getting beat 10–1 or 15–3, and it was the ninth inning and Ted was scheduled to hit, people stayed in the park to watch him hit."

"When I first came up to the Tigers," recalled Bob Shaw, "the Yankees came in and I saw Mantle hit a ball into the upper deck in left center field at Briggs Stadium. I said, 'Holy cow!' Then the Red Sox came to town and I watched Williams hit 11 out of 12 balls into the stands in batting practice. I thought, 'What am I doing here?' The thing I remember about Williams is that if you were warming up in the bullpen, you'd glance over and see him looking at you. He always had his eyes on the guy who was warming up. He'd study him and watch every move, really concentrating on every detail. If I was warming up alongside the dugout before the game, he'd be standing on the dugout step watching me. He would study the pitchers endlessly to try to get an edge. What's his release point? Is the ball moving? Does he have a changeup? He concentrated on hitting more than anybody I know."

As a keen student of hitting, Williams wanted to know everything about pitching. When Dave Hillman joined the Red Sox in 1960, the first person he met was Williams, who asked all about Hillman's style and his theories on pitching. He did the same thing to Herb Moford when he joined the Boston club. "How did you pitch me last year?" he asked. Rosters were fluid, and Williams might have to face Moford on some future date. After hearing Hillman's theories of pitching, Williams gave his own opinion. "Over here, Dave," he bellowed, "all they believe in is jamming, jamming, jamming, jamming. That's OK, but you'd better keep the ball away from them, too. If you make a mistake outside, most hitters won't pull it. If they hit it out of the park to the opposite field, just think how far they would have hit it if they pulled it."

One day when Ralph Terry was pitching for the Athletics, he had a long conversation with Williams about how to pitch to certain hitters. Terry told Williams he couldn't get Harvey Kuenn out. Williams said that the Red Sox pitchers had their best success with sliders. "But you don't have a slider," he told Terry. Terry, a renowned experimenter, had every pitch ever invented, but realized he had never thrown his slider to Williams. He said nothing, and stored the information away. The next time he faced Williams in a crucial situation, he threw him a slider, the last pitch he thought Williams would be expecting. Ted hit it for a triple, and Terry realized he had been conned.

Despite his encompassing knowledge, Williams was not always the greatest instructor. "Ted couldn't teach hitting to anyone," said Joe Ginsberg. "He was the greatest hitter in the world, but he wasn't a good hitting instructor because he thought everybody had to hit like him. If guys could do that, they'd all hit .400." "When Ted talked about hitting," said Grzenda, "he compared the break of the ball with the wing of a jet. After that, I was lost."

"He was a great believer in the four degree upstroke," said Shaw. "All power hitters have a slight upswing, but the trouble is, when you're dealing with the average college, high school or Little League player, they don't have the strength to hit the ball out of the ballpark, so I'm not sure you want to teach them the four degree upstroke."

The most loquacious hitter I encountered during my interviews was former Met Joe Christopher, who has some unique theories about the art. "To me," Christopher said, "baseball is 72 percent spiritual, 27 percent mental and 1 percent physical. If you do not change a man psychologically, you cannot change him physically." His predominant theory is to attack the ball. "The pitchers never get anybody out," he said. "The hitters get themselves out by not being quick enough to strike the ball at a certain point. In the same way you throw the ball, you have to throw the bat. You cannot swing a bat at a baseball, you have to throw the bat. To me, throwing the head of the bat is the way to swing. Wally Moses [one of the best hitting coaches of the 1960s] used to take a bat and literally throw it against the fence."

Christopher continued. "Most hitters want their body to work with their feet. It's got to be the other way around. The feet are the base of the house and the base of the foundation so that the top half, which is the least important of the three, will move off the same principle. Your legs are your arms on the ground."

Sometimes Christopher's instruction is hard to follow. "All these players today," he said, "believe that the hand that is closest to the pitcher is the one that you move. If you understand the laws of oscillation, you have to go beyond the same principle. You have to go from left to right, from left to west to east to north to south and come back. You have to go through two different dimensions of time. And that's the reason many of these guys today are not hitting. All the hitters today are going counterclockwise to motion." Hitting sure sounded complicated. I understood the concept of throwing the bat, but got lost somewhere between east and south and the different dimensions of time.

Regardless of the value of the four degree upstroke and the laws of oscillation, an old baseball adage says that good pitching will always stop good hitting. All pitching stopped all hitting in 1968, the year offense nearly disappeared from the game. In 1969, Met pitching would take them to the top of the baseball world.

• 19 •

Assembling the Cast

The returnees from the best Met team ever arrived in St. Petersburg in late February, 1969, poised to participate in the first four division pennant race in major league history. Well, the Mets probably wouldn't participate, but they didn't expect to be as far from the summit as they had been in their first seven seasons. Unlike previous years, when almost every position was wide open, the Mets entered the spring of 1969 with a relatively set roster, and just a few openings. Hodges hoped for improvement not by the wholesale addition of new players but by adding a few members to the supporting cast and getting better performances from some veterans who had not played up to expectations in 1968.

Tommie Agee had looked more like Don Bosch than Willie Mays during his first year in New York. He played good defense, but no team could win with a centerfielder who drove in seventeen runs. Despite his poor season, the Mets protected Agee in the expansion draft. He went to the Florida Instructional League for a short while to work on his hitting, then went back home to Mobile and talked hitting with Cleon Jones and Hank Aaron's brother, Tommie. Agee reported to spring training mentally ready and eight pounds lighter. Eight pounds might not seem like a lot, Hodges said, but they had all disappeared from Agee's mid-section.

A second disappointment of the '68 season had been shortstop Bud Harrelson. After a horrible start in '67, Harrelson came on strong and was probably the Mets best player from June through August, before he wore down in September. In 1968, Harrelson's average dropped from .254 to .219, and he drove in only 14 runs. With Agee, Harrelson and Kranepool driving in a combined total of 51 runs, it is easy to see why the Mets averaged less than three runs a game in 1968.

Agee and Kranepool were expected to drive in runs, but Harrelson was on the field mainly for his defense. In 1968, however, he played poorly in the field. Although he was still sure-handed, Harrelson's mobility had been limited and he didn't come close to equaling his spectacular performance of mid–1967. Hodges had been told of Harrelson's great play of '67, and couldn't believe he was seeing the same player they were describing.

There was a reason for Harrelson's alarming decline. Since the latter stages of the 1966 season, the little shortstop had been playing with a troublesome knee. "It just started to give me trouble," he said late in 1967. "Sometimes it would feel like it needed oil. Other times it felt like a motor wearing down. Sometimes it felt like a meat grinder making hamburger." During the winter of 1968, Bud finally had surgery. While lifting weights as part of his rehabilitation, Harrelson not only rebuilt his knee, he added pounds and strength.

Harrelson had reported to spring training in 1968 weighing just 146 pounds, the lightest player in the major leagues. Mike Kiner, 14-year-old son of the Met broadcaster, who served as the Met batboy in spring training, outweighed Harrelson by nearly 40 pounds. Harrelson's slight stature was the subject of many jokes, some of them his own. One day an elusive balloon floated around the infield. Seaver swiped at it and missed, then decided to give up the chase before he looked foolish. Harrelson managed to puncture the balloon with his spikes, stuffed it in his pocket and turned to signal two outs to the outfielders. "He wouldn't dare grab it," Seaver said. "He was afraid the balloon would carry him away."

Near the end of Harrelson's poor 1968 season, he said he wasn't worried about going to an expansion club. Mrs. Payson wouldn't allow it, he said. "She figures if I can't play ball," Harrelson said, "she can always use me to ride one of her horses."

Harrelson's lack of stamina was no laughing matter to the Mets. He had run down in '67 and broken down in '68. By mid–December, 1968, after two months of weightlifting, and quitting smoking, he was up to 156 pounds. Harrelson continued working out for the rest of the winter and reported to camp looking like a different man. He would never be mistaken for Frank Howard, but he was no longer the frail will o' the wisp he had been in 1968. Typically, discussions about weight in the spring concern players who report overweight and need to slim down. The most exciting news in the Met camp of 1969 was that Bud Harrelson now weighed a whopping 165 pounds. He proudly pointed out that he was no longer the lightest player on the Met squad, having ceded the honor to 157-pound Amos Otis.

Agee was eight pounds lighter, Harrelson nineteen heavier, and Ron Swoboda weighed about the same as he did in 1968. During his rookie year, writers had speculated that Swoboda might break Maris's home run record some day. When Eddie Stanky left the Met organization after the 1965 season, he predicted that Swoboda would hit 25–40 home runs a year. "[O]f all the men on the Met roster," Stanky said, "he would be the last one I would trade."

The tremendous power he had shown during the first half of the 1965 season, however, represented the peak production of Swoboda's career. There would be flashes of brilliance, then a relapse. The second half of 1965 was a dry spell, as was all of '66, when he hit just .222 with eight home runs. Swoboda said he was working so hard to improve his fielding that his hitting suffered. Following his disappointing 1966 season, the player Stanky said he wouldn't trade was offered to the Athletics for utility man Ted Kubiak. The Athletics declined.

The following year, with the acquisition of Tommy Davis, there were rumors that Swoboda would be sent to the minors, where he could obtain the polish he badly needed. "He has all the potential," said Wes Westrum, "but I just don't know how long it will be before he arrives." Swoboda wound up staying in New York, and had his best season, batting .281 in 134 games. After wallowing in the .220s through mid–June, Swoboda had a terrific second half and re-kindled the hope that he had finally arrived. The following year, however, he was handed a regular job and lost it. Swoboda got off to a fabulous start, but faded badly and ended the 1968 season as another Met question mark. Although he drove in a career-high 59 runs, Swoboda continued to have inexplicable mental lapses that drove Hodges crazy.

There were innocent incidents, such as the time during a spring training exhibition when Swoboda was hitting in the batting cage behind the stands. Hodges summoned him to pinch hit, but Ron had accidentally locked himself into the cage and couldn't get out. Hodges had to use another pinch hitter.

Sometimes, Swoboda just didn't seem to have his attention on the game. In 1967, playing first base in an infield drill, he started daydreaming and was almost decapitated when Jerry Grote fired a throw past his head. A few weeks into Hodges' first spring as manager, he pulled Swoboda from a game when Ron, not realizing it was his turn at bat, wasn't in the on deck circle. Swoboda belatedly emerged from the clubhouse to find Cleon Jones on deck in his place. He did some running in the outfield, then went back into the clubhouse. Hodges sent Yogi Berra to retrieve Swoboda and made him spend the rest of the game sitting on the bench, pondering his mistake.

In June, 1968, Swoboda was involved in a sequence of events on the West Coast that was reminiscent of the 1962 Mets. In San Francisco, he walked back to the bench after a called second strike, thinking it was strike three. For Hodges, who deplored mental mistakes, not knowing the count was inexcusable.

A few days later, in Los Angeles, there was an even more bizarre episode. Swoboda was on first base in the tenth inning of a tie game, and became, as correspondent Jack Lang pointed out, "the first man in history to ever try for the same base three times before making it." Kevin Collins lined a ball up the right field alley and Swoboda took off, speeding past second. Halfway to third, he realized he had missed the bag and reversed his field. He was racing to second from one direction as Collins approached at top speed from the other. Collins turned around and headed back to first as Swoboda re-touched the bag and started again for third. The throw would have beaten him had it not hit him on the leg and bounded away. As Dodger pitcher Don Sutton chased the ball, Swoboda rounded third and headed for home. He saw Sutton retrieve the ball and realized he wasn't going to make it. Again, he reversed course and headed for third, barely beating the throw with a headlong dive. Eventually, he scored the winning run on Al Weis' single.

What was Hodges' response? "I just said to him, 'Nice eye, Ron,'" Hodges told reporters. "He did walk to start the inning, didn't he?" In private, Hodges was more frank with his young outfielder. After an episode later in the season where Swoboda forgot the number of outs, Hodges called him into his office for a lecture on the need to concentrate. When the Mets opened camp in 1969, Hodges expressed the hope that Swoboda, in addition to Agee and Harrelson, would discover maturity and be the third Met whose improvement would be a key to the team's success.

Swoboda vowed that he was going to act more maturely and responsibly. "Gil wants me to be more of a pro," he said. On the day Swoboda made that remark, however, he bungled a fly ball that cost the Mets an exhibition loss. Would Swoboda be any different in 1969 than he had been in 1968?

Hodges didn't mention a fourth player who was capable of contributing more to the Mets in 1969. Art Shamsky was a left-handed slugger acquired from the Reds during the winter preceding the 1968 campaign. Shamsky hit 25 homers for the Reds in 1965 and 21 in just 234 at bats the next year. In 1967, however, he rarely played, batting just .197, with only three homers in 76 games. His trade value, which had been considerable, plummeted, and the Mets were able to obtain Shamsky during the winter for utility man Bob Johnson.

On the surface, it appeared to be a lopsided trade, for Johnson had batted .348 for the Mets, more than 150 points higher than Shamsky's minuscule average. The Mets desperately needed power, however, particularly of the left handed variety, and if Shamsky could hit like he did in 1965 and 1966, he could be the answer to their prayers. In his first year with the Mets, Shamsky wasn't as bad as he'd been in 1967, but wasn't as good as he'd been the previous two years, batting .238 with 12 home runs. The Mets hit only 81 homers as a team, so 12 for a platoon player wasn't bad, but Shamsky, only 27, had shown during his days with the Reds that he could do better. He made news by saying that, like Sandy Koufax, he would miss a World Series game rather than play on a Jewish holiday. Everyone laughed. Since when did the Mets have to worry about World Series games?

There was, of course, one more question mark in the Met camp, the manager himself. Hodges received a clean bill of health after his physical on the first day of camp, and insisted he felt fine. He walked part of the way from the hotel to Huggins-Stengel Field each morning, but no longer pitched batting practice. In order to preserve Hodges' strength, the Mets planned fewer overnight flights, but otherwise it would be business as usual.

In addition to the returnees from 1968, a few new faces dotted the Mets' opening day roster. One was switch hitting rookie Rod Gaspar, a cocky 23-year-old Californian who hit .309

at Memphis and led the Texas League in base hits in 1968. Like Harrelson, Gaspar had an unusual weight problem. He weighed only about 155 pounds when he signed, and the humid Memphis weather knocked a few more pounds off him. "When you're young and have a high metabolism and are running around all the time," he said, "it's hard to keep weight on.' Gaspar began to drink a supplement called Nutriment to gain weight.

The following spring, Gaspar received his first invitation to the major league camp, but no one except the confident rookie thought he had a chance to make the team. "I realized after a few days," he recalled, "that they didn't know who the heck I was, because I wasn't playing at all and I was really upset about it. I saw the outfielders they had — Cleon, Tommie, Swoboda and Shamsky — and I thought I was the best guy out there. I was so stupid at that time. I didn't realize that these guys were excellent ballplayers and had major league experience. I wasn't impressed. I thought you didn't need experience. All you needed was the ability to play the game." One day Gaspar was sitting in the stands with Wes Stock, the Mets' minor league pitching coach. "I was telling Wes that I was better than all those guys out there. Here I was, 23 years old, and I'm telling him I'm better than all the outfielders they have. At that time, I had a nickel brain. I just wasn't that smart. I thought that I was the best out there, and you've got to think that way if you're a professional athlete. Of course, there's a right way to show it. I didn't have the maturity of Tom Seaver, but physically I thought I could play with any of them."

Finally, Gaspar got a chance to play and made good on his boasts. He didn't have any power, and possessed only an average throwing arm, but he was always hustling, and never seemed to strike out (only twice in 42 spring at bats). Still, with all the veteran outfielders in camp, Gaspar figured to start the season in Tidewater. Suddenly, opportunity knocked. One day, Shamsky bent over to field a ground ball and couldn't straighten up. He developed back spasms and had to go on the disabled list, which opened up a spot for Gaspar. "We were about to make a trip," Gaspar said, "and Art couldn't go." Gaspar went in his place, fashioned a 14 game hitting streak, and virtually forced his way onto the squad.

"I didn't hit home runs," Gaspar said, "but in the minor leagues, I averaged around .300. I had a good eye, I could get on base and I didn't strike out. I ran the bases well. I wasn't fast like Jones and Agee, but I was quick. I loved playing the outfield. I got a good jump on the ball and could get rid of it quickly." Gaspar began the season as a platoon starter and eventually settled into a role as the club's fourth outfielder.

Four other rookies made the opening day roster. Catcher Duffy Dyer would back up Grote and Martin. Infielder Wayne Garrett, although he batted only .239 as a second baseman in the Texas League, was selected in the minor league draft from the Braves' organization. They had to keep Garrett the roster or offer him back to the Braves. Hodges decided to keep him.

Amos Otis and pitcher Gary Gentry also went north with the Mets. Otis was a skinny youngster, not yet 22, who attended a Met tryout in 1964, but wasn't signed, and wound up with the Boston organization. He had been drafted from the Red Sox in 1965. Otis had tremendous speed, some power, and had always hit for a good average in the minor leagues. Like Jones and Agee, he was a native of Mobile, Alabama, and offered the Mets' the possibility of an all–Mobile outfield.

One of the biggest questions concerning Otis was where he would play. He had been a third baseman in the Boston chain, and had played first base, third base and the outfield for the Mets. In the fall of '68, the Mets sent him to the Florida Instructional League to play third base and shortstop, two positions expected to be soft spots in 1969.

Whitey Herzog was a tremendous booster of the young prospect. Otis was ready to play in the major leagues, Herzog declared, and within four years had the potential to become a $50,000 a year player. The Mets declared him an untouchable, and refused to include him in potential trades for the slugger they desperately needed.

A second question about Otis was his attitude. The father of three children by the time he was 20, Otis should have been a hungry ballplayer, but he wasn't. Otis had to be pushed at times, Herzog admitted, and sometimes the youngster's grace and ease of movement appeared to be merely indifference. "Lackadaisical is the word people in our organization use," Hodges said in spring training. "I will have to see for myself before I will say he's lackadaisical." Otis admitted that he sometimes needed to be prodded to play his best, and Hodges promised to provide inspiration, if that was what was needed. Although Otis had a disappointing spring, both at bat and in the field, Hodges maintained that he would get the majority of playing time at third base.

Gentry was a 22-year-old flame throwing right hander from Arizona State University. In 1967, the Mets added Seaver, and in 1968 he was joined by Koosman. If Hodges could find a third young hurler with anywhere near the ability of the first two, the Mets might have the best starting rotation in the major leagues. Gentry appeared to have that kind of ability. He was 17–1 in 1967, his final college season, led Arizona State to the College World Series title, and was the Mets' first draft choice. Previously, he had been drafted by the Orioles, Astros and Giants, but had elected to stay in school. Gentry signed with the Mets and, in 1968, at Jacksonville, stamped himself as a bona fide major league prospect, with 12–8 record and a 2.91 ERA, striking out 15 in one game. Jacksonville manager Clyde McCullough said his fastball was comparable to Nolan Ryan's. That may have been an exaggeration, but Gentry wasn't far behind Seaver, Koosman and Ryan.

Gentry thought he might need another year in Triple A ball, but Johnny Murphy thought otherwise. "Let's make another Koosman out of him," he told Herzog. In February, Gentry packed his wife, six-month old baby and 150-pound St. Bernard into his small car and headed for St. Petersburg. During the exhibition season, he convinced Hodges that he had the ability to pitch in the major leagues, and became the third rookie to join the Met rotation in as many years.

One player on the opening day roster wasn't a rookie, and he wasn't new to the Mets. Tug McGraw, who spent the entire 1968 season at Jacksonville, was added to the bullpen crew. McGraw was not just a pitcher, he was a good all around athlete. "We had an apartment in Jacksonville," said Shaun Fitzmaurice, "that surrounded a swimming pool. Tug would dive off the second story roof and do flips and everything." McGraw was also immature. "I remember saving McGraw's win once," said Bob Friend. "He was like a 14-year-old kid, jumping up and down." "Sometimes when he got a big out," said Jim Bethke, "he might do a backflip on the mound. He wouldn't think about it. That was just his natural reaction." McGraw was so excitable that, during one game, trainer Gus Mauch gave him a tranquilizer to calm him down.

"He was from left field," said Gordon Richardson. "I mean he was really way out in left field. During batting practice, he'd walk around the outfield on his hands." "He was always trying to experiment throwing right handed," said Bill Hepler. "He would do pushups with his right hand, trying to make his right arm stronger."

"Tug and I were roommates," said Larry Miller. "I'd say he was pretty immature for a 20-year-old. We were in San Francisco. I'm fighting for a job. I'm sleeping and it's after curfew. The next thing I know, the lights come on and he brings two or three of his buddies in. The music went on and the TV went on like there was nobody else there. I sat up and said, 'Hey, I've got to get some sleep. Maybe you've got the club made, but I don't and I've got to get some sleep.'"

McGraw, who had pitched well as a 20-year-old rookie in 1965, had yet to realize the potential he showed that season. As a first year player who was only on the roster because he had to be protected from the draft, McGraw saw little action early in the year. When Westrum took over as manager, he pitched McGraw more frequently. By September, McGraw was starting games and was probably the Mets' best pitcher. With little more than a week to go in the season, he reported for six months of active duty in the Marine Corps.

McGraw claimed he learned maturity in the Marines. "They've taught me concentration and self-control," he said. "I used to go out there and jump around and wave my arms. I was pretty Little League-ish. You've got to go out there with a big league attitude." Tug reported to the Met camp in the spring of '66 with a stated goal of 15 wins. "You've got to aim high," he said. "McGraw has got the earmarks of a splendid big league pitcher," said camp visitor Charles Dillon Stengel.

McGraw fell 13 wins short of his goal, equaling his 1965 total of two victories. When he was released by the Marines, he tried to rush himself into playing condition, hurt his elbow, went on the disabled list, and was sent to Jacksonville. McGraw returned to New York in August and pitched some good games, but didn't get many wins. He pitched a two hitter against the Phillies and threw his glove high in the air after the final out. So much for his Marine training.

In the fall of 1966, McGraw went the Florida Instructional League, where he met former Yankee pitcher Ralph Terry, who was in Florida working on a knuckleball. One day McGraw said to Terry, "The big right-handed hitters are giving me fits. I've got a big curveball and a so-so fastball. I get behind with the curve ball and then I've got to come in with the fastball. Sooner or later, they get hold of one and I've got trouble. Do you have any ideas?"

Terry did. "I'll show you how to throw the scroogie that Spud Chandler showed me a long time ago," he said. The next morning, Terry got a catcher and worked with McGraw on a screwball. "It was just like throwing a duck in the water," Terry recalled, "with that beautiful overhand delivery." It looked just like Warren Spahn's, Terry thought. McGraw had picked up the screwball so quickly that he was ready to use the new pitch in a game. "They couldn't touch him," Ralph said. "They'd hit it right off the end of the bat."

There was one problem. Sheriff Robinson was the Mets' pitching coach, and Robinson thought the screwball was a pitch for veterans trying to hang on. Young pitchers should stick to the fastball, curve and change. Robinson sent McGraw to the minors with instructions not to use the screwball, orders that qualify him for the Prognosticators' Hall of Shame, with fellow mystics like Bobby Bragan, the old Milwaukee manager who told a young Phil Niekro to stick his knuckleball "you-know-where" because he would never win in the big leagues with it.

McGraw went to Jacksonville and followed orders. He wasn't pitching well and decided that, if he was going to fail, he might as well fail his way. Using the screwball, he began pitching better and wound up leading the International League in ERA. In September, he was called up to the Mets. Pitching against the Astros, McGraw had the bases loaded, and was facing Bob Aspromonte. McGraw decided to throw the screwball, Sheriff Robinson be damned. Aspromonte hit it off the end of the bat. It spun about five feet in front of the plate for an easy out. The next batter struck out on two scroogies and a fastball and the inning was over. McGraw came off the field, slapping his glove against his leg. Robinson met him at the top of the stairs. "Are you using that pitch?" he asked. "I thought I told you to stick that screwball up your ass." McGraw told Robinson he had tried doing things his way and had gotten killed. He was going to do things his way. He wound up striking out 10 Astros.

The arrival of Hodges in 1968 did not bode well for a free spirit like McGraw. Not only did McGraw's antics annoy Hodges, his dog caused even more trouble than he did. The canine, who was as immature as its owner, tore up John Murphy's flowers, and did what dogs do in front of coach Joe Pignatano's doorway. When Pignatano stepped in it, McGraw was one step closer to Jacksonville.

McGraw was hit hard in exhibition games and sent to the International League, where he was just 9–9 with a 3.42 ERA, in a year when any ERA above 3.00 wasn't that good. One day, Jacksonville manager Clyde McCullough found McGraw dropping paper bags full of water from his hotel window, aiming at passersby below. Tug needed to pitch better if he wanted his antics to be tolerated. No one was more eccentric than Denny McLain, but Denny was in the process of winning 31 games for the Tigers. There was less tolerance for pitchers who win nine games in the International League. McGraw either needed to calm down or pitch better.

When he reported to the Mets in 1969, McGraw was 24 years old, and looking to salvage a career that had looked so promising in 1965. He was just one of several candidates for a bullpen job, one who hadn't won a big league game since 1966. The Tug McGraw fan club, formed in 1965, remained intact, and was still sending newsletters. Their hero hoped the letters sent in 1969 would contain news of him pitching for the Mets rather than the Jacksonville Suns. McGraw made the team and announced his intention to drive his trailer to New York, plug it into the scoreboard and live there. Shea Stadium may have been the home of the Mets but it wasn't zoned for residential use, and McGraw wound up living in an apartment like everyone else.

As the 1969 season progressed, others found their way onto the Met roster. On June 24, Harrelson left the Mets to join his reserve unit for active duty, and was not scheduled to return until July 13. Al Weis would play shortstop while Harrelson ran a motor pool at Fort Drum, but someone would have to fill Weis's shoes as the utility infielder. Bob Heise was the shortstop at Tidewater and the logical man to be called up. Heise, 22, could play second short, and third, and had been with the Mets each of the past two Septembers. When Jacksonville manager Clyde McCullough told Heise he would join the Mets when Harrelson went into the service, Heise informed him that he had active duty the same two weeks.

The next choice was third baseman Bobby Pfeil, who was leading the International League in hits. Pfeil was three years older than Heise, and had been bouncing around the minor leagues since 1962, mostly in the Cubs organization. He was not considered much of a prospect and had never even received an invitation to a major league training camp. Pfeil had always hit for a good average, but was no more than an adequate fielder, having twice led his league in errors, and he had little power.

In 1968, his first year in the Mets' organization, Pfeil paced the International League with 157 hits and led the league's third basemen in fielding percentage but, despite the Mets' legendary third base problems, was left unprotected in the expansion draft. Pfeil considered expansion his best chance to make it to the major leagues, and was disappointed when he was passed over by the Padres and Expos. "That was getting a little scary," Pfeil admitted. "I was thinking of getting out of baseball. They came pretty close to convincing me that I didn't belong there, but Whitey Herzog was the farm director and he treated me just super." Pfeil decided to report to Jacksonville for spring training and began his eighth season of professional ball at Tidewater.

By mid–June, Pfeil was batting .316 and, when Heise was unable to go to New York, the Mets summoned the veteran minor leaguer instead. "When I reported," he said, "I went to Johnny Murphy's office and he said, 'You're here to replace Harrelson for two weeks. Whether you play depends on how you do.' It was that cold."

Hodges asked Pfeil if he could play second base. "I said 'sure,' "Pfeil recalled. "I don't think I played five games at second in my life, but I was not going to say no." He would pitch if Hodges asked him to. Just two days after he arrived in New York, Pfeil started against the Phillies. "I was a little bit in awe of the situation," he recalled, "but fortunately I had played against [Phillie starter] Grant Jackson for several years in the minors." Pfeil got a hit in his first game, and played well in his early opportunities. Soon, however, the two week period was up, and Harrelson was due to return. "I'd just gotten a big base hit to win a game in Montreal," Pfeil recalled, "and we were in the Montreal airport getting ready to leave town. I finally got up enough courage to go up to Hodges and say, 'Gil, my wife's in Virginia. Should I bring her to New York?'" That was Pfeil's roundabout way of asking whether he was going to be sent back.

Hodges looked at Pfeil. "She's your wife," he replied. Then he continued. "They want to send you down," Hodges said, "but I want you here. You'll be here the rest of the year."

"Hodges liked me because I understood baseball," Pfeil said. "I liked the game and believe I understood how the game is supposed to be played, even though I don't know if I had as much ability as some other people. Gil would walk up and down the bench and ask questions. I always had my head in the game and gave him the right answer and knew what he was talking about. I think he liked me for that."

Hodges had told Pfeil he would stay with the Mets for the rest of season, and he did. He saw quite a bit of playing time at third, alternating in an irregular platoon with Ed Charles and Wayne Garrett. Pfeil hit well at first, then leveled off, but played steady, reliable defense. He was ready and willing to play anywhere at any time, and fit beautifully into the Met scheme, although he batted just .232 in 62 games.

When Jack DiLauro was a teenager, he used to play catch with his father in front of their house in Akron, Ohio. Everybody called Charles Emilio DiLauro "Mims" and knew him as a pretty fair right handed industrial league pitcher who once threw two consecutive no hitters. There was a big tree near the sidewalk in front of the DiLauro residence, and the roots of the tree had pushed up the concrete of the sidewalk to make a hump that young Jack used as a mound. Mims measured out sixty feet and six inches and set down a home plate made of rubber. He painted black edges to make it look official and squatted behind it while Jack stood on the hump in the sidewalk and threw.

One evening, when Jack was throwing to his dad, Mrs. DiLauro stuck her head out the front door and hollered, "Hey, Mimmie!" Mims looked over to see what she wanted. "I was right in the middle of my delivery," Jack recalled. "I threw and it smacked him right in the forehead, and he sat down, right there on the sidewalk. I ran up to him and said, 'Dad! Dad! Are you OK?' He just looked at me and said, 'Yeah, why?' From that day on, I figured I'd better be a control pitcher. I'd just hit my father in the head and didn't even hurt him."

As he grew older, DiLauro threw harder, but never hard enough to impress a major league manager. Signed by the Tigers in 1963, he won consistently in the minor leagues. DiLauro was 14–10 in '63, 14–8 in '64 and 12–7 in '65, which earned him a promotion to the International League. From 1966 through 1968, he pitched at the Triple A level with reasonable success, but never got a call to spring training. During the season, Tiger pitchers would be called away for two week reserve stints, and someone else would get the summons to Detroit. In 1968, as the Tigers won the World Series, DiLauro got off to a 10–1 start at Toledo. "I didn't even get a smell," he recalled, "so I made up my mind that that was probably going to be my last year. It was time to get a real job because nobody was interested in a lefthander who didn't walk anybody and just won ballgames."

It turned out that someone was interested. On December 4, 1968, at the suggestion of Whitey Herzog, the Mets' Tidewater farm club traded catcher Hector Valle for DiLauro. With an opportunity in a new organization, DiLauro decided to give it another try, and got his first invitation to a major league camp. "I was throwing a little harder by then," DiLauro said. "When I got to the Mets I got hooked up with [minor league coach] Wes Stock, who noticed that my shoulders were too parallel when I was going to home plate. He had me work on a more diagonal release. I worked with him night and day, and eventually I could throw harder and snap the ball off better. My ball was moving so much faster and breaking so much better."

DiLauro was sent to the minors at the end of camp and began the season with Tidewater. In his first four starts, he was excellent, and when Nolan Ryan was placed on the disabled list with a pulled groin muscle in mid–May, DiLauro was called up to the major leagues. "It was about 6:15 A.M. and I was in bed," DiLauro recalled, "and the phone rang. Someone said, 'Jack, it's Clyde [McCullough, the Tidewater manager]. Get your butt down here to the coffee shop right now. You're going to the big leagues.' I said, 'Yeah, OK, right,' and hung up. I thought it was a joke. I thought someone was pulling my leg. About fifteen minutes later I got another call."

"Goddamn it, DiLauro," McCullough shouted, "get your ass down here now or I'm going to send somebody else!" This time DiLauro leapt out of bed, threw on some clothes, and ran downstairs to the coffee shop. After more than six years in the minors, Jack was finally going to get his chance to see if he could get big league hitters out.

After missing one flight, DiLauro caught a second plane and arrived at Shea while the game with the Braves was already in progress. He went to the clubhouse, signed a major league contract and was taken to the bullpen. Phil Niekro of the Braves was pitching a no hitter, but just as DiLauro arrived, Ken Boswell cracked out a base hit. "I'd just walked out from under the overhang and into the lights," DiLauro recalled. "I got about four or five feet into the lights and the crowd roared. It scared me. I looked up to see that someone had just broken up the no hitter. I took my hat off, bowed to everybody, waved and went back under cover. I thought, 'This is awesome. I show up and I've got 35,000 people giving me a standing ovation.'"

Hodges quickly sent DiLauro into action, and he performed admirably. After some strong relief outings, he started against the Dodgers at Shea. "I was ready," he said. "I was strong. I'd always been a starter, so I knew what the hell to do. It was just a matter of doing it without being a nervous wreck."

It was a big game for the Mets, who had won six in a row, only one short of the team record, and DiLauro was up to the task. For nine innings, he matched Dodger star Bill Singer pitch for pitch. Singer threw blazing fastballs, while DiLauro tantalized the Dodgers with curve balls. He gave up a double to Bill Russell in the first and another to Ted Sizemore in the second, but escaped without a run each time. When he departed for a pinch hitter in the last of the ninth, having retired the last 19 Dodgers, he received a standing ovation from the more than 30,000 fans. This time it was really intended for him. The Mets finally scored a run in the 15th for a 1–0 win and their seventh straight victory. In his first four major league games, DiLauro had pitched 16⅔ scoreless innings.

On a typical pitching staff, such a performance would rate an immediate promotion to the starting rotation. But on a team with Seaver, Koosman, Ryan and Gentry, DiLauro's nine shutout innings gained him no more than a solid hold on his role as a reliever and spot starter. "Hell, what was I going to say," he pointed out, "that I can pitch better than Seaver or Ryan or Koosman or Gentry?" DiLauro pitched in 23 games and, while he posted a record of only 1–4, his ERA was a splendid 2.39. When the World Series began, Jack DiLauro, who a year earlier had decided he was quitting baseball, was in the Met bullpen.

Perhaps the most important addition to the 1969 Met roster arrived on June 15, the trading deadline. Donn Clendenon grew up in Atlanta, in an African-American family with a tradition of outstanding academic achievement. His father, Claude, earned a PhD and was chairman of the math department at Langston University. His mother, a librarian, was also a college graduate. "Claude Wendell Clendenon," Donn wrote in his autobiography, "began an academic tradition in our family that my mother, my sister, my two sons, my daughter and I have worked to live up to." Clendenon was inspired by his father's example, but he never knew Claude Clendenon, who died when Donn was just six months old.

Six years after Claude's death, Clendenon's mother, Helen, remarried, bringing a second influence into young Donn's life. Her new husband, the only father Clendenon ever knew, was Nish Williams. Although he was also an educated man, a graduate of Morehouse College, Nish was renowned not for his academic ability, but for his prowess as a baseball player. From 1929 through 1938, Williams was a star catcher for a number of clubs in the Negro Leagues. Nish helped develop young Roy Campanella and, according to Satchel Paige, was the only hitter who could consistently pull his legendary fast ball. Had he been born twenty years later, Nish Williams would have played in the major leagues, but by the time he married Helen Clendenon in 1941, he had been retired for three years.

If the memory of Claude Clendenon drove Donn to academic excellence, the presence of burly, 265-pound Nish Williams encouraged him to play sports. Nish had not been able to play in the big leagues, but the rules had changed and he wanted to see his stepson achieve his dream. His mother wanted Clendenon to become a doctor, but around the family dinner table the talk was about baseball. Nish encouraged Donn to play baseball, football and basketball, but mostly baseball. "I knew that if I didn't play baseball," Clendenon recalled, "then I just might not get my allowance." Nish owned Williams' Restaurant and Tavern, and whenever the old Negro League stars passed through Atlanta, they stopped in to eat, drink and reminisce. Clendenon met Campanella, Paige, Jackie Robinson, Joe Black, and all the big stars. When he was ten years old, he hit against Paige on a high school field. "I remember the day and the time," Donn wrote, "because my mother and stepfather had a big argument because he had me miss my Tuesday violin lessons."

Clendenon graduated from Booker T. Washington High School at the age of 15, and matriculated to Morehouse College, his father's and stepfather's alma mater, on a full academic scholarship. At Morehouse, an all-black institution, Clendenon earned a remarkable twelve varsity letters, four each in football, basketball and baseball. He also ran one hundred yards in 9.6 seconds.

In the mid–1950s, the South was an adventurous place for an African-American family to live. Nish once bought a boarding house from a white man, only to see it blown to bits by the Ku Klux Klan. In case he failed to get the message, they burned a cross on the Williams' front lawn. Nish rebuilt the boarding house and let it be known that, should the Klan coming calling at his home again, they would get a lively reception. There were no further problems.

During his college days, Clendenon made some interesting friends. Each Morehouse freshman was assigned a "big brother" to help them adjust to college life. Clendenon, who was only 16, was assigned a 1948 Morehouse grad named Reverend Martin Luther King, Jr. "To me," Clendenon wrote, "Martin, Jr. was the third best orator in Atlanta. It was Daddy King first; William Holmes Borders, who was pastor of Wheat Street Baptist Church second; and Martin, Jr. third." Clendenon often visited King in search of advice, and if Martin, Jr. wasn't at home to dispense it, he talked with Martin, Sr. or Coretta King. Clendenon also formed a lasting friendship with a precocious 15-year-old classmate named Maynard Jackson, who later became mayor of Atlanta.*

After graduating from Morehouse in 1956, Clendenon rejected an offer from the Cleveland Browns and took a job as a fourth grade teacher in Atlanta. In the spring of 1957, he took a 10-day leave of absence to attend a Pittsburgh Pirate tryout camp in Jacksonville, Florida. There were 500 hopefuls in the camp, and after a few days of batting, running and fielding, Clendenon returned to Atlanta. No one had told him anything in Jacksonville. "Did the Pirates want to sign you?" Nish asked. He didn't know, Clendenon replied. Nish wanted to hear more, but Clendenon, exhausted by the trip, went to sleep.

The next day, Branch Rickey, Jr., the Pirate farm director and Joe Brown, the general manager, appeared in Clendenon's classroom. The Pirates had wanted to sign him on the last day of camp, but he'd left so quickly they couldn't find him. Now that they had, they offered Clendenon a $500 bonus and a bus ticket to Jamestown, New York. Clendenon gave the Board of Education two weeks notice and embarked upon a career in professional baseball.

Later in his life, Clendenon became friends with Vernon Jordan, a confidante of President Clinton, and black radical Stokely Carmichael.

Clendenon progressed steadily through the Pirate farm system. Like any black player in professional baseball, he was forced to endure the indignity of segregation whenever he played in the South. In 1959, he began the year at Wilson, of the Carolina League. It was only the second year that blacks had been allowed to play in the Carolina League, and there were nine on the Wilson club. One Jackie Robinson on the Dodgers had been enough to instigate riots, and Wilson, North Carolina was not ready for a team composed of so many black athletes. Some of them would have to go, and they weren't going to be promoted. Although Clendenon was batting .370, he was told to report to the Class C Idaho Falls club.

He refused to go. Clendenon, about to turn 24, was not going to take a step backward, particularly when he didn't deserve it. He went home and called the Cleveland Browns to see if they were still interested, but the Browns told him he would have to obtain a release from the Pirates before they would sign him. He either went to Idaho Falls or found another career. Rickey, Jr. came to Atlanta and met with Clendenon and his stepfather. Report to Idaho Falls and play well, he told Clendenon, and he would give him a bonus. What was the difference between C and B ball anyway, he asked rhetorically. If Donn had a good year he'd move up, regardless of where he played. Nish agreed and told him to report.

Clendenon swallowed his pride and left for Idaho Falls. He was too good for Class C ball, and showed it by hitting .356 with 15 home runs and 96 RBI in just 105 games. The next year, he led the Sally League in home runs, and by 1962 was in Pittsburgh to stay. From 1963 through 1968, Clendenon was the Pirate first baseman, enjoying his best season in 1966, when he batted .299 with 28 homers and 98 RBI.

Meanwhile, Clendenon built a second career outside of baseball. Following the 1961 season, he was hired as a management trainee by Mellon Bank in Pittsburgh. Throughout the winters, and during the season when the Pirates played at home, he worked for Mellon and learned the banking business. During his baseball career, he also worked for U.S. Steel and the District Attorney's Office. While at the latter position, he developed a deep interest in the legal system and decided to go to law school. He attended Harvard for a while, but found the commuting impossible, and transferred to Duquesne, which was located in Pittsburgh.

In the fall of 1968, Nish Williams died of cancer, but not before he experienced one of the proudest moments of his life. Just a few months before his death, Nish was honored by the Atlanta Braves during their Old Timers' Day festivities. The old Negro Leaguer, who had never been permitted to wear a major league uniform in his prime, stepped on the field in a Braves' jersey. Williams' excruciatingly painful death was a heavy blow to Clendenon, and also impacted his business career. During

Donn Clendenon was acquired from the Expos in June 1969, and provided power and leadership to a young Mets team. He was named the Most Valuable Player in the 1969 World Series.

his stepfather's illness, he returned to Atlanta and, in 1967, took a job with Scripto Pen Company as Assistant Personnel Director. The job with Scripto would affect the Mets' 1969 season in a way they couldn't imagine.

Clendenon was shocked when the Pirates didn't protect him in the 1968 expansion draft. He was 33 years old and the Pirates had a youngster named Al Oliver ready to play first base. The Pirates chose to protect Oliver and the Montreal Expos grabbed Clendenon. Knowing he was near the end of his career, Clendenon had one remaining goal in baseball. He wanted to play in a World Series. The Pirates were consistent pennant contenders. The Expos, like the Mets and Colts before them, were destined for a long struggle.

Eventually, Clendenon reconciled himself to the idea of playing in Montreal. Then came another shock. On January 22, 1969, he was traded to the Houston Astros for outfielder Rusty Staub. Houston had a better team than Montreal, but there was a complicating factor. Harry (the Hat) Walker, who had managed Clendenon at Pittsburgh, was the Astro manager. Clendenon didn't like Walker at Pittsburgh and didn't want to play for him in Houston. Harry's older brother, former Brooklyn Dodger star Dixie, was a blatant racist, and Harry was not far behind. In 1966, Walker had a much-publicized shouting match on the bench with catcher Jesse Gonder, and was despised by many of the black players.

That was not to say, however, that African-Americans were the only players who disliked Walker. Harry was Leo Durocher without the quick wit, the smart clothes and the pennants. While managing in the minors in the '50s, he got into four major fistfights in as many years. He was proud of his pugilistic prowess, and was generally the instigator.

"I don't have any enemies in baseball," said Bob Friend, "and I want to keep it that way. But I've got one story to tell you." Friend was in the last year of his career, mopping up a 10–1 game for the Mets against Walker's Pirates. "I got along with Harry," Friend said, "but sometimes he could get to you." In this instance, Walker called for a squeeze play. "This is unheard of with a 10–1 lead," Friend said. "I threw the runner out and go back to the dugout. Westrum said, 'Bob, you don't have to take that shit. That's bush league. That SOB!' Meanwhile Harry was over there saying, 'C'mon over! C'mon over!' Wes said, 'Let's go get him!' So I charge out of the dugout and go after Walker. I look around and Wes is nowhere in sight."

Friend was stopped before he got to Walker, and the two men eventually got over it. "The next year," said Friend, "Harry and I talked about it and laughed about it. He said 'I try to get all the runs I can, Bob.' I said, 'I guess you do.' But there's an unwritten rule about squeezing with a nine run lead. You just don't do it."

But Harry did. Once, with an eleven run lead, Walker gave Clendenon the sign for a delayed steal. Clendenon ignored him, and received a blast from Walker when he returned to the bench. On another occasion, Walker ordered Clendenon to drop a sacrifice bunt against Bob Gibson. When Gibson saw Clendenon square around, he threw the ball at his head. Clendenon hit the dirt and the ball went to the backstop, which got the runner to second base anyway. Harry, apoplectic over Clendenon's failure to sacrifice, called a full-team bunting practice for 8:30 the next morning, which is to a baseball player what 4:30 a.m is to the nine to five worker.

Walker stood beside the plate and lectured on the art of bunting while Bob Veale, the Pirates' ace starter, stood on the mound, fuming at the early practice. Veale, who wasn't known as an "early to bed, early to rise" type, didn't want to be there, and he wasn't any happier when he had to wait interminably for Walker to finish his oration. Finally, when Harry stepped to the plate for his expert demonstration, Veale fired the ball over his head, sending the Hat sprawling into the dirt. Shortly after the incident, Walker was replaced by Danny Murtaugh, much to the relief of the Pittsburgh players.

Jack DiLauro played for Walker at Houston in 1970. In late August, DiLauro wasn't pitching at all, and Walker didn't explain why. DiLauro just never pitched. After several games of inactivity, the bullpen phone finally rang for him. DiLauro jumped up, grabbed a ball and prepared to warm up. Wait a minute, coach Jim Owens told him, Harry wants you to pinch run. DiLauro was no Maury Wills, and couldn't imagine why Walker wanted to use him as a runner, but he went into the game. After a difficult time on the bases, he came to the dugout and thought he saw Walker laughing at him. DiLauro is a self-admitted excitable Italian, and after not pitching for weeks, and feeling that Walker had tried to humiliate him, was in no mood for The Hat's little games. He started to go after him, but was intercepted by pitcher Don Wilson, who lifted him off the ground and said, "You don't want to go there."

A few days later, DiLauro went to Walker's office to ask him why he wasn't pitching. A shouting match ensued, peppered with profanity and shouting. When he left the manager's office, DiLauro said, the players gave him a standing ovation, an indication of Walker's popularity with the rest of the squad. The incident probably sealed DiLauro's fate, but there was one more episode before the season ended. DiLauro never wore a hat in batting practice, or at any time before the game, and one night while he was sitting bareheaded on the bench, some of the other players began to tease him, telling him to put his hat on. "Ah," he said to them, "Fuck the hat." Walker, standing at the end of the dugout, spun around. DiLauro might have told him he was referring to *his* hat, not *The* Hat, but by that time, he didn't care. He let Walker draw his own conclusions.

Dilauro never pitched in the big leagues again. He went from a key member of a world championship team to a minor leaguer in just over a year. Soon, he couldn't even get a job in the minors. There would be expressions of interest, for he was a solid lefthander still in his 20s, but the offers were mysteriously withdrawn. Walker, DiLauro was certain, had blackballed him. "Thirty-five years later," he said, "the way I left baseball still bugs me. I still wake up at night thinking about it." Harry Walker had made another friend.

Clendenon talked to Jim Wynn and Joe Morgan of the Astros, who told him Walker had mellowed a bit and wasn't that bad. Clendenon decided he could play for Walker, or at least ignore his baser tendencies. He visited Houston and was given the VIP treatment, until it came time to talk salary. Astro general manager Spec Richardson told Clendenon he expected him to take a significant cut in pay. Why had they traded All Star outfielder Staub to get him, Clendenon wondered, if they valued his ability so little? He went back to Atlanta and talked to Arthur Harris, the CEO of Scripto, who told him his salary would be doubled if he came to work for Scripto full time. Clendenon accepted the offer and told the Astros on March 1 that he was retiring from baseball.

Clendenon's retirement presented a troubling situation for major league baseball, for the first baseman had spent years building a business career and had a viable option to baseball. Too many incidents like that and the lords of baseball were concerned that they might lose their stranglehold on the players. "Donn was a bright guy," said Jim McAndrew, "who got in trouble sometimes because he didn't accept things. You've got to realize that 45 years ago, when he was breaking in, things were a lot different from a social standpoint. He said it like it was and a lot of people didn't like to hear it like it was."

Montreal claimed they had made the trade in good faith and were entitled to keep Staub whether or not Clendenon ever reported to Houston. Staub said he was playing in Montreal or he was not playing at all. On March 7, new commissioner Bowie Kuhn said he believed Clendenon would play for the Astros and ordered Staub and Jesus Alou, who had been sent to Houston with Clendenon, to report to their new clubs. Ten days later, the Astros announced that the trade would probably be rescinded and said the players would return to their old clubs. Kuhn ordered the two clubs to work out an agreement. If they couldn't, the commissioner said, he would impose one.

The clubs were unable to reach an accord, and, convinced that Clendenon was not going to play, Kuhn asked the two clubs to agree upon a replacement. On March 24, the Houston club sued the Expos in federal court, demanding the return of Staub. The Astros cited Rule 12F, which specifically dealt with the situation where a traded player retired prior to reporting. They asked Kuhn why he didn't insist on the application of the rule, but the commissioner declined to answer. Although Kuhn was not a party to Hofheinz's lawsuit, the Astro owner blasted him, and accused him of trying to destroy baseball.

Clendenon was invited to meet with Kuhn on April 1 in West Palm Beach. Although he insisted he had no intention of changing his mind, Clendenon agreed to attend. He arrived with Arthur Harris, to find not just Kuhn, but a number of general managers and owners of other major league clubs, including Roy Hofheinz and GM Spec Richardson of the Astros. Hofheinz began by asking Clendenon who had paid him to retire. Harris, assuming he was being accused of some nefarious role in the drama, started to reply. "Shut up and sit your ass down," Richardson told the 5'3" Harris. "We didn't come to talk to you and we don't want to hear from you." Harris sat down.

Hofheinz again asked Clendenon who had paid him to retire and told him he was threatening the structure of baseball. Clendenon couldn't imagine why his presence on the field was so essential to the survival of a game that was celebrating its 100th year as a professional sport. He decided that the entire episode was merely a battle of two gigantic egos, those of Hofheinz and Charles Bronfman, the owner of the Expos. Clendenon reiterated his intention to retire and the meeting eventually came to an end without resolution. During the ride to the airport, Harris told Clendenon that Richardson had told him Hofheinz was going to buy Scripto and fire both him and Clendenon.

Within 24 hours, Clendenon changed his mind. The following day, he announced that an agreement had been reached that would allow him to join the Expos, one that reportedly gave him a $14,000 increase in salary. Houston received pitchers Jack Billingham and Skip Guinn as compensation. Hofheinz apologized to Kuhn and Clendenon prepared to get ready to play baseball.*

During the winter following the 1968 season, the Mets had set their sights on two right handed sluggers, Richie Allen and Joe Torre. Ken Harrelson was available, but, needless to say, Hodges wasn't interested. He wanted Allen or Torre. If nothing else, getting Allen would prevent him from wreaking havoc against the Mets. In his five years in the majors, Richie had hit 25 home runs against the New Yorkers.

Despite his great ability, Allen appeared to have reached the end of the line in Philadelphia. Richie had one basic problem. He didn't think that rules applied to him. Allen showed up for games when he felt like it, sometimes after they had started. He battled constantly with manager Gene Mauch, and was benched for two weeks in June, 1968 for insubordination. Mauch's battles with Allen led to the manager's dismissal, and the appointment of Bob Skinner in his place. Skinner vowed to get along with Allen, and tried very hard, displaying remarkable patience, but Allen was every bit as divisive an influence under Skinner as he had been under the previous regime. When pitcher Larry Jackson retired after the 1968 season, he said the Phillies had a lack of unity on the team and that Allen's immaturity was the major cause.

During the off-season, the Phillies attempted to move Allen, and the Mets, despite his troubled history, were interested. One complicating factor, however, was the potential relationship with Hodges, whose philosophy was that there was only one decision-maker on a team, and it was not Richie Allen. Hodges was not flexible. With Richie Allen, one needed to be not only flexible, but oblivious. Mauch, as strong-willed as Hodges, had battled constantly with his petu-

---

*After the season, a new rule was enacted stating that all trades were final when made. The acquiring team was at risk if a player didn't report.

lant star and failed to change him. Why entrust the care of Richie Allen to a man recovering from heart trouble?

The trade discussions continued throughout the winter, but the Mets would only take Allen if they could steal him for surplus players. The Phillies wanted to get rid of Allen, but they weren't desperate. When they mentioned Seaver and Koosman, the talks ended. The Mets pursued Vada Pinson of the Reds, but their offer of Selma, Larry Stahl and a choice of McAndrew, Gentry or minor league pitcher Steve Renko was rejected.

The discussions for Torre were much more serious, and continued well into the spring. Joe had an off season in 1968, as did so many hitters, but just two years earlier he'd hit .315 with 36 homers. At 27, he was an All Star in his prime, and a New Yorker who would be a fan favorite at Shea. Torre was at odds with Atlanta GM Paul Richards, and thus available. He had angered Richards, the most reactionary of the management group, by playing an active role in the recent player strike. Torre also refused to sign the contract offered by the Braves, who wanted to cut his salary by $5,000.

Johnny Murphy complained that Richards could not decide who he wanted in return for Torre. First, Richards asked for Grote, Ryan and Otis. Then he didn't want Grote. He wanted Otis and a couple of pitchers. Everyone knew the Mets wouldn't part with Seaver or Koosman, which left McAndrew, Ryan, Gentry or top pitching prospect Jon Matlack. When Murphy balked at including Otis, Richards retorted that he had never seen a ninth place club with so many "untouchables." "I'm surprised they didn't win the pennant," he said.* The Mets wanted Torre as a gift, Richards claimed. Eventually, Torre was traded to the Cardinals for Orlando Cepeda.

The Mets resumed talking about Allen, but to no avail. They weren't willing to give up their young players for one established hitter. Veteran writer Dick Young insisted that the Mets should swap a pitcher for a basher. "If I were the Mets," he wrote, "I'd give up a Tom Seaver or Jerry Koosman for a Frank Robinson.... Who knew Jerry Koosman a year ago? Who knew Tom Seaver two years ago? Pitchers pop up overnight. You can take your chances on a replacement. Pitchers are everywhere. Hitters are nowhere. That's why I would give a 24-year-old pitcher for a 35-year-old slugger."

The favorite strategy of Murphy's predecessor, Bing Devine, was to trade a good pitcher for a good everyday player. Devine believed that an established pitcher had great market value, while an everyday player had more actual value. Devine used his theory to build the Cardinals with regulars like Lou Brock, Bill White, Curt Flood, Julian Javier and Dick Groat. Each had been obtained for a well-regarded pitcher. Had Devine stayed with the Mets, it's very possible that Seaver or Koosman might have been traded for a Joe Torre or a Richie Allen. But Murphy was not going to follow the Devine theory. He held on to his young pitchers, and therefore landed neither Allen nor Torre.

Prior to the expansion draft, the Mets had expressed interest in Clendenon. They continued to ask about his availability after the Expos acquired him. The Expos, however, wanted two starting pitchers. "Not for two young pitchers and not at his age," Hodges replied. Throughout the spring, there were rumors that Clendenon was coming to the Mets and in June, Murphy renewed his efforts. Finally, on the trading deadline, June 15, the Mets obtained Clendenon in exchange for four minor leaguers, far less than they had been offering for Allen and Torre. Hodges had the slugger he needed without depleting his pitching staff.

Clendenon, a month from his 34th birthday, was not a marquee name in the class of Allen and Torre, but he was still a feared hitter. "As far as I'm concerned," said McAndrew, "the big difference in the club was Clendenon. He was the one guy who could strap you on his back and

---

*At the end of the season, Murphy couldn't resist letting Richards know that the Mets had won the pennant, and taken it from Richards' Braves.

carry you for a week or two if he got hot. That's what he did. Instead of losing 1–0 or 2–1 we were winning 2–1 and 3–2."

With his intelligence and maturity, Clendenon also blended in well with the Met youngsters and provided leadership in the clubhouse. He kept the atmosphere relaxed and provided a good example with his hustle on the field. It was not easy to come to a new club and become a leader, but most of the Mets were young, and Clendenon made an immediate impression with his hitting and strong personality. "The thing that was so unique about Clendenon," McAndrew remembered, "was how supportive he was. Donn was a pretty bright guy, and maybe realized that I was the kind of guy who needed stroking, who needed positive feedback. Donn was really supportive of me off the field, as well as driving in runs, which we usually didn't do much of."

By the middle of June, the Met club was complete. It was apparent that this would be the best team in franchise history, and now that a big bat had been added to complement the outstanding pitching, who knew how high they might go.

• 20 •

Team of Destiny
The 1969 Season

Baseball's centennial season was remarkable in many respects. It was first to have the start of spring training delayed by a work stoppage. It was the first time the two major leagues had been divided into four divisions. It was the first season of Bowie Kuhn's lengthy reign as commissioner and the first year in which there was a round of playoff games prior to the World Series.

Nineteen sixty-nine was also a momentous year for America. In January, Richard Nixon was inaugurated as the 37th President. In July, a man landed on the moon. That same month, a music festival in Woodstock, New York was the climax of an era of free love, peace and hallucinogens and represented the symbol of a new generation. Race riots, peace riots and disturbances of every kind raged in the streets, and the country was rapidly becoming polarized between the "establishment" and the forces of revolutionary change. "My goodness," said Rod Gaspar, "1969 is probably the most famous year because of all the things that happened. There was Woodstock and a man landing on the moon. The world was starting to go wooly in 1969. And the Mets were winning. Geez!"

The Met victory in the World Series was perhaps the most astounding event in that remarkable year. Man had been getting close to a moon landing since the late '50s. There had been large festivals and concerts prior to Woodstock. But the Mets? Bob Johnson played with the last place club of '67. "If somebody had said they were going to win the World Series two years later," he said, "I would've said, 'You've got to be kidding!'" Pitcher Bill Graham joined the team late in 1967. What if someone had told him the Mets would win in '69? "I would have thought they were crazy," Graham replied. "No chance," said Bob Hendley, laughing.

In the spring of 1969, beat writer Jack Lang stated confidently that the Mets were far from a pennant contender and expressed his astonishment that the ninth place team had made no significant moves during the off season. A few months earlier, Leonard Koppett had written, "The Mets ... have really turned the corner toward respectability — but they remain a woefully weak team ... for [the Yankees and Mets], pennant contention is still years away." In an article about Jerry Koosman, written in 1968, Lang wrote of his aspirations, and added, "Jerry doesn't dream about pitching in the World Series these days. With the Mets? Are you kidding?"

While no one expected a world championship, the situation in Flushing was clearly improving. After winning 73 games in 1968, by far the best performance in the hapless history of the club, better things were expected in '69. For the first time, fans dared speak of the possibility of a .500 record. Manager Hodges predicted 85 wins. No matter how the Mets played,

226

under the new divisional setup, they were assured their best finish ever. No longer could they finish tenth, or even ninth. With only six clubs in each division, the Mets were guaranteed to end the season at least three notches higher than their previous best finish, and with the expansion Montreal Expos in the National League East, they seemed assured of no less than fifth place.

First place was out of the question, for the Cardinals had won the National League pennant two years in a row. Not only that, they had added Vada Pinson, Joe Torre and some solid backup players during the winter. "The Cardinals should lead the East," predicted the *Times* prior to the season, "... without too much difficulty." "[T]he Cardinals could be the king of the hill in the new Eastern Division of the league," added Joe Durso, "for a long time." "[T]he East is the personal property of the St. Louis Cardinals," wrote Arthur Daley, "perhaps the best and deepest ballclub to be seen in the preseason tournament. It's impossible to pick against them"

"How the Mets do," Koppett wrote in his pre-season prediction, "depends on how many runs they can score to cash in on their pitching." The Mets indeed had many talented young pitchers, but aside from Koosman and Seaver, none had shown they could win in the big leagues. Ryan, McAndrew, Gentry and McGraw were great prospects, but none had ever won more than six games in a major league season.

The players thought third place was a realistic goal, and Daley agreed. He picked New York to finish ahead of the Expos, Pirates and Phillies. Durso picked the club for fourth, ahead of the Expos and Pirates. New York mayor John Lindsay made an even bolder prediction. "Every candidate is entitled to make one whopping promise," Lindsay said at the Yankees' welcome home luncheon in mid–April, "and mine is that we will have a subway World Series this fall. I've already obtained agreement from the Mets, and I'm sure the Yankees will go along." Lindsay was a liberal visionary, and in this case was 31 years ahead of his time, but he was at least half right, which is better than most campaign promises.

A more knowledgeable and credible observer had similar feelings. Al Jackson, after two seasons in St. Louis, rejoined the Mets in '68. "I think we were in Philadelphia," Jackson recalled, "the first time we reached .500 [in 1969]. All the writers came to me and asked what I thought of this team." Having suffered through the cellar-dwelling years, Jackson thought the team was great. "I said, 'This team is far better than .500.' I could see it coming. It was just a matter of getting a couple more players to plug in and it was going to be a good ballclub because those young pitchers were really starting to throw the ball well."

One little-noticed good omen had occurred the previous fall, when the Mets captured the Florida Instructional League championship. In the fall of 1965, Baltimore won. In 1966, it was Boston, and in 1967 the Tigers. Each of those clubs had gone to the World Series the following year and the Orioles and Tigers had won. Well, everyone thought when the Mets took the title, there was the end of that streak.

For the eighth straight year, the Mets lost their opening game, even though they were pitted against the fledgling Expos. The supposedly dominant pitching was weak in April, and the club had only one complete game in their first nine. They dropped seven of their first ten games, and then began to lose pieces of the sterling staff. On April 29, Koosman, who'd had arm trouble all spring, was forced to leave a game in Montreal when he felt something snap in his shoulder while delivering a pitch. On the 3rd of May, Ryan, who had pitched brilliantly in relief of Koosman in Montreal, made his first start and had to retire with a pulled groin muscle in the seventh inning. He re-injured himself a week later, was placed on the disabled list and missed a month.

Fortunately, pitching depth was the strength of the Met team. "We had six quality starters," said Jim McAndrew, who was one of them. "Baseball people talk about a number one starter or a number two or number three starter. We had three or four number one starters, with

Seaver, Koosman, Ryan and maybe Gentry." "These guys could throw," said Bob Hendley. "I mean could *throw*. Every one was an attacker. They weren't finesse guys. They were power guys who go right at hitters and attack them. With pitching and defense, you're going to win."

By early May, however, the Mets were struggling to find four healthy starters. McAndrew was pitching in St. Louis when Tim McCarver hit a sharp grounder up the middle. "I made the mistake of trying to field it with my bare hand," said McAndrew, "and it went between my middle finger and my index finger, bruising the middle finger badly. So that I wouldn't miss a start, Gus Mauch stuck my hand in a whirlpool for three days, which did nothing but soften up the tissue in my hand. In my next start, in Chicago, it was a 0–0 ballgame in the fifth inning when I threw the end of my finger off. The blister was so deep because of the soft skin that I literally threw off three or four layers of skin. They just flew off with the pitch. I felt the pain and looked down and saw the blood." With McAndrew out for a month, Murphy asked Hodges if he wanted him to get a pitcher. Hodges, not wanting to disrupt what he believed was a winning combination, said no, he would get by.

Fortunately, Seaver remained healthy and was pitching well, although, as in 1968, his efforts did not always result in victories. By May 3, he had an ERA of 2.35, but his record was only 2–2. Don Cardwell was getting even less support. On May 1, Cardwell lost 3–2 to the Expos when Montreal scored a run in the bottom of the ninth, dropping his record to 0–4, despite a 2.93 ERA. The Mets had scored just two runs for him in his first 28 innings. "You can't do anything about it," Cardwell said recently. "You can't go up to someone, look 'em in the eye and slap them in the face. We just ran into some very good pitchers."* In his next start, Cardwell, one of the best hitting pitchers in baseball, took matters into his own hands and hit a three run homer to win the game.

Gentry, the hard-throwing rookie right hander, turned out to be a gem. He started and won the third game of the season, and remained in the rotation for the entire season. Gentry was 13–12, and pitched 234 innings in a season when, other than Seaver, virtually every Met starter was disabled at least once.

The Met offense wasn't formidable, but it wasn't all that bad. The team batting average hovered in the .240s, about the middle of the league rankings, but the problem in the early season was that the production was concentrated in a very few players. On May 7, for example, the team average was .237, but if one excluded the statistics of Cleon Jones, the average of the remaining 24 players dropped to .216. Jones led the league in batting average for a good part of the early season, and was tearing the cover off the ball, but aside from Boswell and Kranepool, the rest of the hitters were not. Six of the Mets (excluding pitchers) had averages below .200. Grote, who had hit so well in 1968, was one of them.†

The best news of the early season was the resurgence of Tommie Agee. In the third game of the season, Agee hit two home runs against the Expos, but then went into a slump that dropped his average below .200. With the Mets losing, Hodges tried Gaspar, then Otis, in center field. When neither set the world on fire, Agee found himself back in the lineup. Otis ended up in Jacksonville and Gaspar became the fourth outfielder. On May 11, Agee hit three homers in a doubleheader, in the midst of an 11 game hitting streak. By the middle of May, he was in the lineup to stay, and had already surpassed his 1968 home run and RBI totals. His batting average hovered around .300 and his fielding was as good as ever.

By mid–May, the Mets were where they thought they would be before the season started —

---

*Cardwell hadn't been as calm or reflective in 1968, when he was 1–8, despite pitching well. After one particularly tough loss, he drop kicked his glove all the way to the dugout.

†Theoretically, the Met offense might have been formidable, for the 1969 club could have fielded an outfield of Jones, Paul Blair and Reggie Jackson. Blair was a Met farmhand who was exposed to the minor league draft in 1962. The Mets had the opportunity to draft Jackson in 1966, but opted for catcher Steve Chilcott.

third place. With a 15–17 record, they trailed the first place Cubs by seven games. In his fourth year as Chicago's manager, Leo Durocher had gotten the Cubs off to a flying start, winning 10 of their first 11 games.

When he was signed prior to the 1966 season, Durocher immediately stuck his foot in his mouth by declaring that the Cubs were not a ninth place team (they'd finished ninth in 1965). He said the Cubs' personnel were better than either of his Giant pennant winners. Durocher's enemies, who were legion, gleefully pointed out after the season that the Lip had been absolutely correct. In his first year at the helm, Durocher brought Chicago home tenth, behind even the Mets. "Leo Durocher of the Chicago Cubs," wrote Mark Mulvoy, "who last year managed two pennant winners from a television booth but this year is managing a last-place team on the field...." A sign at Shea Stadium read, "Bad Guys Finish Last."

During the next two seasons, however, the Cubs were neither a ninth nor tenth place team. In 1967, Leo got his Cubs to play exciting ball, running, taking chances, and always, in the Durocher fashion, looking to take the extra base. They challenged the Cardinals for first place, held the top position as late as July, and wound up third with an 87–74 mark, an improvement of 28 games from 1966. It was the first time the Cubs had finished in the first division in 21 years. In 1968, the Cubs finished third again, with 84 wins, thirteen games behind the Cardinals. It seemed as though Durocher had worked his magic again, transforming the doormat Cubs into contenders.

One of the reasons owner Phil Wrigley brought Leo to Chicago was to revive the Cubs' sagging attendance, which was just 641,000 in 1965. Durocher, through his personal magnetism and the success he produced on the field, increased attendance to over a million by 1968.

Since the early '60s, Chicago had possessed a strong nucleus of third baseman Ron Santo, first baseman Ernie Banks and outfielder Billy Williams. All three had been perennial all-stars and, during the 1950s, Banks twice won the National League MVP award as a shortstop. Unfortunately, during the early '60s, the Cubs had holes at nearly every other position, and lacked quality pitching. When he became manager, Durocher wanted to trade one of his three stars to acquire pitching, but Wrigley wouldn't let him.

Leo particularly didn't like Banks, who was immensely popular both with Wrigley and the Cub fans. "He didn't like Banks," said former Cub Lee Thomas. "How could you not like Ernie Banks?" It is possible that there were not two more disparate human beings on the face of the earth than Ernie Banks and Leo Durocher. Banks had as many friends as Durocher had enemies and vice versa. About the only people who had a bad word to say about Banks were militant blacks, who felt he was too much of an Uncle Tom. "I'm not black or white," Ernie once said. "I'm just a human being trying to survive the only way I know how." Banks' almost psychotic cheerfulness seemed at first to be an act, but if so, he hadn't slipped out of character for 17 years. "When Ernie dies," said one Cub player, "and the undertaker is finished, he'll rise up and say, 'Nice job, buddy.'"

Like Casey Stengel, Durocher wanted to be the center of attention, and resented any player who threatened to steal the limelight. In Chicago, that player was Ernie Banks. In 1967, after a mediocre 1966 season, Durocher made the 36-year-old Banks a player-coach and said the future Hall of Famer would have to compete for a starting job with journeyman John Boccabella. At the end of the exhibition season, Durocher declared Boccabella the starter. Shortly thereafter, however, Durocher re-installed Banks at first, and Ernie drove in nearly 100 runs. What aggravated Durocher the most was that no matter how much he tried to humiliate his aging star, Banks responded with sweetness. He called Durocher the best manager he'd ever seen.

When Durocher was unable to convince Wrigley to build the team by trading a superstar, he brought up young players from the minor leagues, including second baseman Glenn Beckert and shortstop Don Kessinger. He also managed to acquire some key players in trades without yielding a starter, swapping reliever Lindy McDaniel and reserve outfielder Don Landrum to the Giants for two minor leaguers, pitcher Bill Hands and catcher Randy Hundley. Hands became a 20 game winner, while Hundley became the best Cub catcher since Gabby Hartnett left in 1940. He was the rarest of breeds, an iron man catcher, playing 149 games in 1966, 152 in 1967 and an unbelievable 160 the following year, the latter mark easily eclipsing the major league record for games caught in a season. The Cubs now had six all star caliber players, their principal shortcoming being in center field.

The Chicago pitching staff, which *Sports Illustrated* called the worst in baseball in 1966, had also been completely rebuilt through trades and from the farm system. Ferguson Jenkins, a 6'5" Canadian righthander, won 20 games in 1967 and 1968. Twenty-three-year-old lefty Ken Holtzman was another solid young starter. Phil Regan, the former Dodger relief ace, was acquired in mid–1968 to anchor the bullpen.

Seven years earlier, Banks had said, "The Cubs are due in '62." They were due to finish ninth. He said, "The Cubs arrive in '65," but they arrived ninth again. When Banks proclaimed, "The Cubs will shine in '69," however, it appeared as though he might finally be right. On May 15, Chicago had a 23–11 record and a five game lead over the Pirates. The Mets were third and the disappointing Cardinals were fourth with a 14–18 mark. The Expos were about as good as could be expected from an expansion team and the Phillies, with Richie Allen perplexing manager Bob Skinner as much as he had Gene Mauch, were floundering.

The first sign that 1969 might be a good one for the Mets was a sweep of a doubleheader against the Cubs on the 4th of May. Seaver pitched a complete game win in the opener and, with Koosman, Ryan and McAndrew injured, Tug McGraw came out of the bullpen to hurl a complete game 3–2 victory in the nightcap. On May 21, Seaver pitched a three hit shutout against the Braves which lifted the Mets up to .500 (18–18) at the latest point in their history. Jones got two hits, and led the league with a .391 average. Perhaps most important of all, Koosman had pitched well the previous day in an exhibition game against the Mets' Memphis farm club, and appeared ready to return to action.

The Mets soon fell back below .500, losing five straight games, but Koosman, in a losing effort, pitched seven strong innings in his return. In his second appearance, Koosman looked better than strong. He struck out 14 Padres in the first eight innings, and 15 in 11 innings, while allowing only four hits and no runs. Although he was just off the injury list, Hodges let Koosman throw 146 pitches. He didn't get the win, but the Mets did.

The victory started the Mets on an 11 game winning streak, by far the longest in their history. It gave them a record of 29–23, the first time the Mets had been over .500 later than the third game the season. When McGraw saved the win that put the Mets over .500, he leaped up in his old fashion, the one he said he had outgrown. "The wind lifted me into the air," he explained.

During the Mets' winning streak, nearly every one of the eleven victories came in dramatic fashion, perhaps the most exciting of all a win over the Dodgers. In the top of the 15th, with a 0–0 score, Dodger runners on first and third and only one out, Willie Davis hit a line drive off pitcher Ron Taylor's glove. Al Weis, playing second, backhanded the ball and threw home. Grote caught the ball and made a sweeping tag on the sliding Jim Lefebrve to preserve the tie. In the bottom half of the inning, with Agee on first, Wayne Garrett hit a line single to center. Davis let the ball get by him and Agee scored all the way from first for a 1–0 win. In 15 innings, the Mets had gotten only four hits, but found a way to win the game.

In previous years, the Mets had discovered many unusual ways to lose games, but now the breaks were going their way. It was the other teams who faltered in the late innings, or fumbled the key grounder, or walked in the winning run. "I remember back in 1966," Harrelson said late in the 1969 season, "we'd get to the seventh inning and I was scared, scared they'd hit the ball to me, scared we'd lose, and everyone else felt the same way and that's why we lost a lot of games." Now Harrelson wanted the ball hit to him in the late innings, he said, and so did everyone else.

The winning streak also ended the dominance of the West Coast teams against the Mets, who swept three game sets from both the Dodgers and Giants. In their early years, the two former New York clubs had clobbered the Mets. In 1962, the Giants were 14–4 against the Mets and the Dodgers did even better at 16–2. The following year, the pennant-winning Dodgers were again 16–2 while the Giants were 12–6. In their first three years, the Mets lost 43 of 48 games to the Dodgers. They had never won more than one game per season in Los Angeles. Now, in the last year of the decade, the Mets had apparently laid their West Coast demons to rest. A second indication that the times were changing was a 20 game losing steak by the Expos that broke the record for first year clubs set by the '62 Mets. There was a new doormat in the National League, and it was not the Mets.

A third aspect of the Mets winning streak was perhaps the most telling. No one player carried the team. The pitching was terrific, and the hitting was spotty, but the heroics were provided by a different player nearly every game. That was to be the trademark of the 1969 Mets. Jones and Agee played regularly, but the other thirteen players shuttled in and out of the lineup and the most unlikely candidate often struck the decisive blow. The first game of the streak, a 15 inning victory over the Padres, was decided on a single by the light-hitting Harrelson. The next night, third string catcher Duffy Dyer won the game with an eighth inning single. The third victory was sparked by veteran Ed Charles, who hit his first homer of the season and drove in all four Met runs. Then Swoboda plated the winning run with a bases-loaded walk. In the next game, fate intervened, as a pop fly by Grote dropped safely behind third base to beat the Dodgers. The following night Kranepool hit two home runs. Then Jack DiLauro, in his first major league start, pitched nine innings of two hit shutout ball before Weis' defense and Garrett's offense beat the Dodgers in 15. The eighth win came on a pinch hit single by Art Shamsky. In the tenth game of the streak, Garrett again provided the heroics. The next night Agee hit two home runs and Jones one. Finally, when the Mets ran out of heroes, the streak came to an end.

Shamsky had returned from the disabled list red-hot. Art was thin and wiry, ran flat-footed and slowly, and didn't look like a ballplayer, until he whipped the bat with his quick wrists. Two days after he joined the Mets, Shamsky appeared as a pinch hitter and singled in a run. He began platooning in the outfield and by the beginning of August was hitting nearly .350, with power, and finished the season with a .300 average and 14 home runs in 100 games.

The fine performance of the Met reserves was not an accident. In its pre-season issue, *Sports Illustrated* opined, "New York's Mets, for example, lack many things, among them reserves. The best thing that can be said of the bench is that it is made of wood; the worst thing, that it is made of deadwood." *Sports Illustrated* was in for a big surprise. Even good bench players have difficulty in key situations if they haven't played much. That wasn't the case with the Met reserves, for Hodges made sure that everyone got to play. The club was the first ever to win a World Series with only two players (Jones and Agee) having more than 400 official at bats. "Everybody was given an opportunity," said Bobby Pfeil. "When I played in Philadelphia, if you were a second tier player, you were lucky to get an at bat every two weeks. In New York, everybody got a couple of starts and eight or ten at bats a week, no matter who you were."

"Some guys had great years in '69," said J.C. Martin. "Agee hit 26 home runs and Cleon hit .340, but there were a lot of other guys who really contributed. I have to give Gil credit because he had all of his people ready to play at any time during a game. He used Al Weis in the World Series like he'd been playing every day and Al performed like he'd been playing every day. Everybody was ready to play. Some of those guys were pretty young but, by gosh, Hodges just instilled so much confidence in those young guys. He would put people in the lineup at crucial times and they performed. He used all 25 men. When you get into serious trouble and you need some-one to come off the bench, you want them to have confidence. Gil knew how to do that."

"I don't think anybody felt they had to do more than they were capable of doing," said Pfeil. "Look at Al Weis and other guys who were such great contributors." Hodges didn't have a lot of complete ballplayers, so he combined talent. Second baseman Ken Boswell was a good hitter, but not much of a fielder. Weis was a great fielder, but didn't hit much. Together, how-ever, they made an adequate second baseman. When Boswell went into the service for two weeks, Wayne Garrett played second. When Ed Charles came to the Mets in 1967, Westrum had played him every day. Charles hit well at first, but at 34, wasn't capable of playing regularly. By the end of the season, he was tired and his play showed it. When Hodges arrived, he used Charles less frequently, and the veteran responded with one of the best seasons of his career in 1968. In 1969, at the age of 36, Charles alternated at third with Pfeil and Garrett.

"We were winning ballgames 2–1, 3–1 and 4–1," said DiLauro, "and if someone got three runs off us, it was 'OK, Clendenon hit a homer and get this shit over with,' or 'Shamsky, pull one out of your butt and hit it 450,' and Kranepool, he was unbelievable. He was an average major leaguer, sometimes below average, but you put him at the plate and the son-of-a-gun came through."

On June 15, the Mets found themselves in the lofty world of second place, with a 29–25 record, eight and one half games behind the Cubs, who had a 39–18 mark, by far the best record in the National League. Seaver said he was shooting for 25 wins and the division championship. "We were in San Francisco," said Don Cardwell, "and I was sitting down to dinner with trainer Joe Deere and somebody else. It might have been Yogi. I told them, 'We're going to win this thing.' They looked at me kind of funny and said, 'What have you been drinking?' I said I really felt we could win this thing." An old Met chimed in with his opinion. "When we started," said Casey Stengel, "I just couldn't get home from third base and that's just 90 feet, as you know. It's still hard, but the pitching is better, and the manager has done a splendid job improving them."

Unlike the old Mets, who generally collapsed after a hot streak, the new Mets were resilient. They finished June with a 19–9 record, the best month in their history. On July 1, the club was solidly entrenched in second place, poised to make a run at the Cubs. They already had as many wins at the '62 Mets had all season.

On July 6, Joe Durso wrote, "One year ago today [the Mets] stood eighth in a 10-team league

	W	L	Pct.	GB
Chicago	49	27	.645	—
New York	40	32	.556	7
Pittsburgh	38	38	.500	11
St. Louis	35	41	.461	14
Philadelphia	33	39	.458	14
Montreal	21	52	.288	26½

and were being called 'amazing.' Their most critical games usually involved them with the Hous-ton Astros and 'the battle for ninth place.'" In July of 1969 the battle would not be for ninth place, but for first, when the Mets played two three-game series against the Cubs. Hodges said he wanted to win two games in each series but stressed that it was too early to call the games "crucial."

The first series began on July 8 at Shea Stadium. "It has taken them 7½ years," wrote George Vecsey, "439 victories and 771 defeats, but today the Mets finally begin an important series." "I don't think the World Series was as intense as those series against the Cubs," said DiLauro. "Striv-ing to get to the playoffs is more intense than being there. Nobody liked Chicago. Hate is the wrong word. You just respect them so much you want to kick the living crap out of them. Those series against the Cubs were so intense. It's pretty hard to play harder than you normally play, but in those games...."

Before the first game of the series, Clendenon went into the Cub locker room to visit with his friends Banks, Williams and Jenkins. "I saw right away that the Cubs' locker room was filled with tension," he wrote. "Our guys were laughing, playing cards, and kidding around in the Mets' clubhouse — most of the Mets were too young to feel much pressure at that time of the season."

Met fans had come out in droves when the team was losing, and throughout the Mets' first few years, many questioned whether the fans would abandon them if they began to win. They did not, and the prospect of a pennant race brought 55,000 to Shea for the first game of the Cubs series.

The onset of divisional play had not been welcomed by the Mets. Instead of playing the Dodgers and Giants nine times each in New York, they would be reduced to six dates with each team. The timing of the switch was fortuitous, for by 1969, Met fans weren't interested in seeing the Dodgers and Giants. When Koufax retired after the 1966 season, the Dodger crowds had declined. In 1967, when the Dodgers came to New York for the first time without him, attendance at the first game was just 15,000. By July, 1969, the fans came to watch the Mets in their first pennant race. By the time the season was over, the club had broken the two million mark for the first time, with attendance of 2,175,373.

Both the series at Shea and the one the following week at Wrigley Field took place in a World Series–like atmosphere. Seventeen writers accompanied the Mets to Chicago. The Cubs began the first game in New York as if they intended to teach the upstart Mets a lesson, as Jenkins, their ace, began the ninth inning with a 3–1 lead. Boswell opened the inning with a pop fly to short center. Center field had been the Cubs' weakness ever since the season started. In 1967, Durocher thought he had a budding superstar in Adolfo Phillips, a young Panamanian acquired from the Phillies with Jenkins. Phillips was a great defensive player, had good speed and could hit with power. But he struck out too much and didn't always play as hard as Durocher thought he should. In June, 1969, he was traded to the Expos. Jim Hickman, the former Met, played center for a while, but he was better in right.

With Phillips gone and Hickman in right, it was bespectacled, 23-year-old rookie Don Young who, after taking a couple of steps back, came charging in after Boswell's popup. Young dove for the ball, but it fell safely and Boswell had a double. With one out, Clendenon, pinch hitting for Pfeil, lashed a long drive to left center. Young raced after the ball and had it in his glove, but when he hit the fence, it popped loose. Clendenon made it to second and Boswell, who waited to see if the ball would be caught, held at third. Jones doubled to tie the game, and an intentional walk and ground out brought Kranepool, for years the favorite whipping boy of Met fans, to the plate.

Every year, the Mets had attempted to find someone to replace Kranepool. In 1966, it was Dick Stuart. The next year, Westrum tried Swoboda at first. In 1969, Hodges gave Jones a first baseman's glove. Each Met manager tried to provide Kranepool with some competition, hoping to light a fire under the placid first baseman. Once the great hope of the organization, Kranepool had been unprotected in the expansion draft, and neither Montreal nor San Diego wanted him. The Met fans didn't want him either, and referred to him as Super Stiff. Yet, in the most important game in the history of the New York Mets, it was Kranepool who stepped to the plate with the game on the line. Ed had accounted for the Mets' first run with a homer, and now had a chance to win the game. He reached out for a 1–2 pitch and looped it over shortstop to bring home the winning run and send the New York fans into paroxysms of delight. "It's the first time they've cheered me since I signed," Kranepool said happily after the game.*

In August, Kranepool set a Met career record with his 61st home run. He'd tied Maris, although it took him seven years.

The Cub locker room was not as gleeful. Santo fingered Young as the goat. "[Young] took us down to defeat because he was brooding about his hitting," Santo said. "I don't know who Leo has in mind to play center field, but I hope to sell him on Hickman; any ball Jim reaches, you can bet your money he'll hold onto." "I'll never forgive Ron for that," said a Cub veteran recently. "He was all over the poor kid." Joe Torre said after the season that other teams were more motivated when they played the Cubs because of the way Santo and the other Cubs treated Young.

Durocher piled on as well. "That kid in center field," Leo said in disgust. "Two little fly balls. He just stands there watching one and gives up on the other. It's a disgrace." Banks defended Young, saying that he was just a kid, he was nervous, and who could blame him.

Winning had smoothed over the divisions in the Chicago clubhouse, but a single loss was bringing them to the surface. While Santo and Durocher agreed that Young was to blame for losing to the Mets, they had begun their relationship seeing eye-to-eye on precious little. When Leo took over as manager of the Cubs, Santo looked forward to the change. "He'll bring back confidence and the winning spirit to the Cubs," he said. Durocher was less enamored with Santo. He wanted to trade Santo or Banks, claiming he couldn't win with them in the middle of the lineup because neither could run. Wrigley wouldn't let Leo trade Banks, so he tried to get rid of Santo, claiming that many knowledgeable baseball people told him he couldn't win a pennant with Santo at third. "Five runs ahead," Durocher wrote, "and he'll drive in all the runs I could ask for. One run behind and he was going to kill me." Saying that a player couldn't come through in the clutch was one of the most stinging insults a manager could deliver. The reason Santo couldn't deliver in tough situations, Leo said, was because he couldn't control his temper. Durocher, of course, was an authority on not being able to control one's temper. The only reason the Cubs hadn't traded Santo, Leo said, was that no one was willing to offer anything in return. The Astros had rejected an offer of Santo for young Doug Rader, the Houston third baseman. Over the next three years, however, Durocher saw bits of himself in the fiery Santo, and Leo could never resist anyone like himself. Santo was hard-nosed and irascible, and tough as nails. When he had one good season after another, Leo finally became a convert.

The next evening, another rookie, switch-hitting Jimmy Qualls, replaced Young in center field. Qualls started the season playing second base for Tacoma, but the Cubs' center field situation had become so desperate that he found himself starting against the Mets in the middle of a pennant race. It was his 18th major league game.

Seaver started the ninth inning with a 4–0 lead, having retired the first 24 batters to face him. Hundley tried to beat out a bunt to start the ninth, but Seaver threw him out easily. Qualls was the 26th Cub to face Seaver. Tom tried to keep the ball away, but got a fastball right over the plate, and Qualls lined it to left center field for a solid single. Seaver retired the last two men and wrapped up his 14th win, his eighth in a row.

The Mets had won seven straight and the Cubs had lost five in a row. Their lead was down to three games. "Wasn't that a magnificent game Tom Seaver pitched?" Banks asked. "And he's such a nice young man as well as being a great pitcher." One could almost hear Durocher's teeth grinding in the background.

The next day, Qualls was booed when his name was announced in the starting lineup. He hit a key double as Chicago salvaged the final game of the series and limped home to Chicago. Were these the real Cubs, someone asked Durocher after Chicago's win in the final game. "No," he replied, "those were the real Mets." "Wait'll we get 'em in Wrigley Field next week," said Santo.

The following Monday, July 14, the rivalry resumed at Wrigley, the home of 25 Cubs and about 75 rowdies who populated the left field stands and called themselves the "Bleacher Bums."

The Bums, mostly college students and night shift workers, first appeared in 1968. They wore yellow construction helmets, and their main occupation was making life miserable for the opposing team, especially the left fielder. "They made us play awfully hard when we went in to play the Cubs," said J.C. Martin. "We didn't like the Cubs and we didn't like the Bleacher Bums. We were watching the Cub highlights and they showed the Bleacher Bums going crazy and Santo jumping up clicking his heels. We just had enough of that kind of reaction. It made us stay focused and we played as hard as we could when we went in there." During the Mets' final series in Chicago at the end of the year, one of the despairing Bums threw their helmet at Jack DiLauro, who kept it. Someone asked DiLauro if he was going to wear the helmet on the field. "Hell, no," he replied. "I'm going to take it home and throw rocks at it."

In New York, Santo had earned the enmity of Don Young and a few of his teammates. In Chicago, he managed to tick off all 25 New York Mets. In the opening game of the series, Bill Hands pitched a beautiful game and won 1–0. After the final out, Santo, heading for the clubhouse, leaped high in the air and clicked his heels. He was kicking the losing habit, he explained. "It's my salute to the Bleacher Bums," Santo said. "I'm practicing a double kick for the World Series." The Bums liked Santo's antics so much that he repeated the heel click several times.* Met coach Joe Pignatano didn't share the Bums' delight. He called Santo's leap "bush" and exchanged a few words with the Cub third baseman the following day. "Nobody liked to be shown up," said DiLauro. "That was not a good thing for him to do to any club, but to us especially. There were a couple of pitchers who didn't like it, Koosman being one of them."

The Mets were not the only team that was upset with Santo. When the Cardinals' Lou Brock hit a key home run against the Cubs late in the season, he jumped up and clicked his heels at home plate.

Hodges dealt with Santo in his own understated fashion. When the Cub captain brought the lineup card to home plate the following day, he told Hodges he had only clicked his heels because the fans expected it and would be disappointed if he didn't do it. Hodges listened patiently, then said, "You remind me of Tug McGraw. When he was young and immature and nervous, he used to jump up and down. He doesn't do it anymore." Hodges then turned and walked back to the Met dugout.

While Santo's histrionics were confined to the post-game, former Met pitcher Dick Selma played the role of cheerleader throughout the entire nine innings. After the 1968 season, Selma, who had been such a hot prospect, had fallen out of favor and been left unprotected in the expansion draft. Jack Lang described him as a "hard-throwing, light-thinking" pitcher. John Murphy said he didn't know how to pitch.

Selma did some strange things. One winter, he decided to have shoulder surgery, but neglected to tell the Mets, who discovered it when trainer Gus Mauch noticed the scar during a spring physical. Eventually, the Mets wrote Selma off as an eccentric. The Padres selected him in the expansion draft and traded him to the Cubs early in the season.

In the left field bullpen, Selma jumped up and down, waving a towel, whenever the Cubs did something worthy of a cheer. Between the Bleacher Bums, Santo and Selma, the Mets had plenty of reasons for wanting to show the Cubs they were not the best club in the National League Eastern Division.

During the second game of the series, Santo's feet remained firmly anchored to the ground. With the game tied 1–1 in the fourth, Al Weis, of all people, hit the fifth home run of his eight year major league career, just his second since 1965. To the great delight of the Mets, Selma was the victim. Ron Taylor preserved Gentry's eighth win.

In a supreme and sad irony, Santo, who so infuriated the Mets with his heel clicking, has no heels today. Plagued by diabetes, he has had both feet amputated.

The Mets also won the final game of the series, as yet another hero emerged. Cal Koonce, who had been terrible early in the season, pitched five shutout relief innings for the win. Weis hit his second home run in two days. "Now don't try to make me out a home run hitter," he said after the game. "In fact, I'm not even a hitter." Following the final out, Seaver raced from the dugout, did a jig, jumped up and clicked his heels.

Again, the locker rooms of the two clubs presented a stark contrast. In the Cub enclave, Durocher criticized Selma's pitch selection to Weis. He should have thrown Weis a curve ball, Leo said, rather than the waist-high fastball Weis hit over the fence. In the Met quarters, Joe Pignatano imitated Santo's heel click. "Let's hear it for Leo!" said Seaver. Kranepool led a cheer for "Cheerleader Selma" and Shamsky initiated one for the Bleacher Bums.

The Cubs weren't ready to fold, and for the next two weeks, their lead remained about the same. Hodges downplayed the race, stating repeatedly that it was too early to get excited and he was quite happy to be in second place. "It's still a long way to go," he said, "and this is a young ballclub."

On July 30, the Mets lost a disastrous doubleheader to the Astros, New York's nemesis ever since the two clubs had entered the league. It was Casey Stengel's birthday, and the Mets celebrated by showing him the kind of baseball he had been accustomed to. Houston won the first game 16–3, scoring 11 runs in the ninth inning while hitting two grand slam home runs, the first time that had ever been accomplished in the National League.

In the third inning of the second game, nine Astros reached base consecutively in the midst of a ten run rally. After Jones made a half-hearted pursuit of a Houston double, and tossed a soft lob back to the infield, Hodges walked slowly out to left field, held a brief conversation with Cleon, and led him back to the dugout. Jones was suffering from a strained left hamstring, the Mets announced after the game. Hodges said he didn't know the specific nature of Jones' injury, but had seen him grab his leg earlier. "It put out a message," said Martin, "that this guy was serious, he wanted to win and he wouldn't tolerate any loafing." Jones got the message, the players knew what was going on, and so did the fans but, unlike Durocher, Hodges never criticized his players publicly. "I don't like to embarrass a man," he once said, "because I know how it feels." Hodges allowed the charade of the hamstring injury to stand, although everyone knew the real reason for Jones' departure.

Following the doubleheader loss, Hodges closed the clubhouse door and blasted his team for twenty minutes. When Gil Hodges talked, everybody listened. "He never chewed out his players unless it was absolutely necessary," said Cardwell. "If somebody didn't do what he was supposed to do, Gil would come out the next day, hit ground balls to the infielders and then walk around. I'd stand out there with the young pitchers and say, 'Watch, Gil's going to go over and talk to so-and-so. He'll come behind him and talk to him.' Sure enough," Cardwell laughed, "he'd walk up to him and have a little conversation—just a little chew time on somebody's rear end. He was just schooling the young guys, and it helped the player. It woke him up. If the situation came up again—boom—you know what you're supposed to do." If a player was to be fined, Hodges generally left a note on their stool, rather than announcing it in front of the team.

Hodges' young Mets listened. They had great pitching, but one of the keys to the Met success was the way they executed fundamentals. "They make the cutoff play," Stengel observed. The Mets did all the little things Hodges insisted his teams do, and it showed in the fine defense they played all season. An old baseball saying is that a team must be strong up the middle. The Mets, with their fine pitching staff, Grote behind the plate, Harrelson at short and Agee in center, were the defensive equal of any team in the major leagues.

They also may have had the best manager in baseball. Rod Gaspar recalled a time he had been mouthing off to clubhouse man Nick Torman. "I was running my mouth off as a young punk back then," said Gaspar, "and Gil found out about it. He brought me into his office and just chewed on my butt big time. That was fine. I looked him in the eye, just took it and walked out of his office."

Hodges kept high-spirited players like Gaspar in check, but took the opposite approach with those whose ego needed a boost from time to time. Jim McAndrew was an introspective sort with a degree in psychology from the University of Iowa. "I came from a very sheltered background," McAndrew said. "I wasn't very worldly. I had parents who I loved and respected, who taught me the right kinds of things as far as values were concerned. But sometimes the values you're taught are not necessarily the things that make you successful in New York. At that stage of my life, I was still trying to figure out who I was and what I wanted to be." With a divisive war going on and deep schisms in American society, was throwing a baseball really a worthwhile occupation? "I was one of those lost young souls," he said, "who enjoyed the competition but just couldn't figure out how I contributed to the whole scheme of things by throwing a ball." While commuting to New York from Connecticut on the train with his uncle, a Pfizer executive, McAndrew posed the question of his value to society. His uncle explained that McAndrew was an entertainer, and convinced him of the contribution of entertainment to the happiness of the average person. McAndrew laughed. "I became self-absorbed after that."

Yet, there was something else bothering McAndrew. "Between Ryan, Seaver and Koosman," he said, "we probably had three of the hardest throwers in the game. I wouldn't go so far as to say I felt emasculated, but some of my teammates weren't shy about letting me know I didn't throw as hard as the other three."

Johnny Murphy didn't help McAndrew's confidence. "I know a lot of people in baseball," he said in the fall of 1968, "who didn't think much of Jim McAndrew's minor league record. He was eligible for the draft last year and no one took him. Now he comes up and pitches several strong games in the majors and you assume he's a proven major leaguer. Let's not forget his record was 4–7." And let's not forget the Mets were shut out practically every time McAndrew pitched.*

"The one who helped me get back to reality," McAndrew said, "was Hodges. He heard the conversations that were going on and called me in and told me he believed in me. He said Whitey Ford was the best pitcher he ever saw, and compared to me, Ford didn't throw hard at all. He knew how to pitch and get guys out. Gil told me that what he looked for was results. I really needed that bolstering. Hodges was a true psychologist without the formal education. When it came to handling men, he was the best. He had the same set of rules but interpreted them differently for each player. He understood their social backgrounds. I was fortunate to have played for him because he was a small town boy from Indiana and I was a small town boy from Iowa. I think we had similar backgrounds and similar outlooks on life."

DiLauro joined the Mets in mid–May. The club had been playing sloppily for a few days, culminating in a game against the Braves where Cardwell messed up a double play ball and Shamsky was thrown out trying to stretch a double into a triple with none out. "It was my second day in the big leagues," DiLauro recalled. "We must've played really bad, because that was the only time Gil came out into the clubhouse in front of everyone and started talking. Everybody stopped what the hell they were doing. Gil started talking and he was talking with authority. He was talking about running balls out and chasing balls down, and said we were never going to play baseball like that again. You could hear a pin drop in that clubhouse. Yogi was sitting directly across from me. We were undressing and had thrown our T-shirts and jocks in the basket. Gil finished talking, turned to walk away and said something. Gil didn't cuss, but he said something. When he said it, he kicked one of the laundry baskets. It went up in the air like he was kicking a football. The dirty clothing — all the underwear — flew out. Yogi was sitting on

*In 1969, Roger Angell wrote that many thought McAndrew might turn out to be a better pitcher than Ryan.

his stool and a jockstrap landed on his head. Gil just looked at him and smirked. Yogi dropped his head and started to laugh. The whole place broke up."

The day following the doubleheader debacle against the Astros, the pitching, with Seaver on the mound, was much better, but the Met ace was out-dueled by Houston's star righthander Larry Dierker and lost 2–0. The Mets were six games behind the Cubs. "A little dry spell," Hodges said after the game. "They'll be all right tomorrow." While Met fans rode the roller coaster with the club, Hodges never got too high or too low. He had a young team and wanted them to focus on each game, not the next two months. "There are certain times," said J.C. Martin, "that you cannot show fear. That's one thing that Gil Hodges never portrayed to his players. If he was nervous, you could never tell it by looking at him. With Durocher and Stanky [Martin played for both] you could see fear. You could see them thinking 'We could lose this game.' The players got so nervous and uptight that they couldn't make a play."

During the first half of August, it appeared that the two series against the Cubs might be the high point of the Mets' year, for they began to slowly but steadily lose contact with Chicago. They could beat the Cubs, but they couldn't beat the Astros, who after a miserable start had become contenders in the Western Division. On August 12, the Mets lost their eighth straight game to Houston when Koosman couldn't hold a 5–1 lead. His record dropped to 9–8.

The following day brought another loss, as Gentry lasted only one inning. Mercifully, that ended the season series with the Astros, with Houston having won 10 of the 12 games. The two teams had started together in 1962, and since that time the Colts/Astros had won 87 times against only 49 for the Mets. With the final defeat in Houston, the Mets dropped to third behind the defending champion Cardinals who, after a dismal start, had come to life. New York was 9½ games behind the Cubs, with a record of 62–51. At about this point, writer Roger Angell asked himself, "Are the Mets real pennant contenders?" "The answer," he told himself, "is probably no." The Mets were losing games with the kind of mistakes everyone expected from young players. Perhaps the magic had ended.

Returning home from Houston, the Mets were rained out of a scheduled doubleheader against the Padres, then swept a doubleheader the following day. Seaver set a career high by winning his 17th game in the opener and McAndrew, who had pitched so poorly earlier in the season that he was on the verge of being sent to the minors, hurled seven terrific innings in the nightcap.

Seaver was having an outstanding season. He set a club record by winning eight straight games in June and July, and another with his 44th career victory, breaking the mark held by Al Jackson. Amidst the milestones, however, there was cause for anxiety. While pitching against the Pirates on July 4, Seaver felt some pain in his shoulder, but stayed in the game. He'd had problems with the air conditioning in his hotel room the night before, and didn't sleep well. Because of the holiday, the game started at 10:30 in the morning, giving Seaver little time to loosen up. After his near-perfect game against the Cubs, his shoulder hurt even more. It was the first time in Seaver's life he had ever had a sore arm. He took medication, adjusted his motion, and kept pitching, although he was not as effective as usual. He used more off-speed pitches, nibbled at the corners, and managed to pitch effectively. Eventually, the shoulder healed and he became Tom Seaver again.

Koosman and Cardwell won another doubleheader on August 17, but the Mets were still well in arrears of the Cubs. Koppett opined that they would be hard-pressed to hold off the Cardinals and Pirates and finish third.

Third place was not what the Mets had in mind, however. The following day, they beat their old nemesis Juan Marichal 1–0 on a 14th inning home run by Agee. Gentry threw 157 pitches in the first ten innings, and McGraw finished for the win. The following day McAndrew pitched a two hit shutout that brought New York to within 6½ games of the Cubs.

At the end of August, the Mets traveled to the West Coast, the site of so many catastrophes during the team's first seven seasons, for a ten game road trip. Seaver began the trip with his 18th win, which was followed by McAndrew's second straight shutout. The next night, Koosman pitched a two hitter to give the Mets their 12th win in 13 games. Gentry, winless in nine starts, beat the Dodgers. Night after night, the pitching was phenomenal.

One of the nights the Mets were in San Diego, the phone rang in the press box. New York writer Jack Lang answered and heard a familiar voice on the other end. "It's a great day for a game in Chicago." Ernie Banks couldn't get the Met-Padre score and decided to call San Diego. He had reason to worry. At the end of August, the Chicago lead was down to 3½ games.

After the club returned home, Seaver became the first Met pitcher to win 20 games by beating the Phillies on September 5. Pennant fever was rampant in New York, where Met

	W	L	Pct.	GB
Chicago	81	52	.609	—
New York	75	53	.586	3½
St. Louis	71	61	.538	9½
Pittsburgh	69	60	.535	10
Philadelphia	52	77	.403	27
Montreal	40	92	.303	40½

announcers relayed play-by-play accounts of the Cub games to their listeners. On the 8th, the Mets and Cubs began a key series at Shea Stadium, the first meeting between the two clubs since the dramatic encounters at Wrigley in July. It was the first September series between pennant contenders New York had seen since the Yankees met the Tigers in 1961. Since August 13, when the Mets had been 9½ games behind, the Cubs were just 11–13, while the Mets had won 18 and lost just five. The Chicago lead was 2½ games.

Signs of both physical and mental fatigue were beginning to show on the Cubs. While Hodges rotated his troops, Durocher wrote the same names on the lineup card virtually every day. "The Cubs are in one way much like a football team," wrote Mark Mulvoy. "They have 11 men who do most of the work." The Chicago infield of Banks, Beckert, Kessinger and Santo played nearly every game, and catcher Hundley strapped on his gear under the torrid Chicago sun every afternoon.

Banks, as always, professed his love of doubleheaders, but at 38, was having trouble playing them. Cardwell laughed at the memory of Banks' enthusiasm. "Ernie'd say, 'It's a great day for two,'" he said. "It'd be 98 degrees, and the other guys would say, 'Ernie if you go out there and play two, we'll have to carry you off the field on a stretcher.'" Even at his advanced age, however, Ernie played 155 games. Hundley caught 151 games, Kessinger played 158, Williams 163, and Santo 160. The core of the pitching staff worked equally hard. The big three of Jenkins, Hands and Holtzman worked 311, 300 and 261 innings, respectively. Bullpen ace Regan pitched 112 innings in 71 games.

By September, the long summer of iron man performances was starting to catch up with the Cubs. "[I]f I had known what was going to happen," Durocher wrote in his autobiography, "I'd have given everybody a rest and played nine pitchers. The way we were getting beat," he added, "it wouldn't have made any difference if I'd played nine girls."

"We were eight games ahead," said Cub pitcher Don Nottebart, "and everybody was counting their money." After the season, Phil Wrigley said that the team's collapse was directly attributable to the players' obsession with earning money from outside interests. The Cubs had agreed to pool all of their endorsement income and split it equally. They were selling Cub Power T-shirts, a Cub Power record and similar novelty items. Songs like "Hey, Hey, Holy Mackerel," the

"Cubs Are on Their Way" and "Pennant Fever" filled the Chicago airwaves. Two Cub executives visited Boston to learn how the city had handled World Series logistics in 1967.

"First thing the Mets did when they got to Chicago September 30," wrote Dick Young, "was to go over to the 100-story John Hancock Building and look for spots on the sidewalk. Coach Gene Oliver said a month ago he would jump off the top if the Cubs blew the pennant." "Gene was our bullpen catcher," Nottebart said, "and he was saying, 'We're going to win it all, Nottie. We'll just sit here and watch them.' Well, we sat there and watched them, all right."

The problem was that all of the reserves had been sitting and watching, and when they were called on, couldn't perform. "Leo tried to go with seven pitchers," Nottebart explained, "and for the last three months of the season Hank Aguirre, Rich Nye and I didn't pitch. When all was said and done, Regan and Selma were out of gas, Billy Hands and Fergy were just pitched out and Holtzie ran out of gas, too." "At the time," said McAndrew, "we weren't aware of it, but the Cubs were real thin. Leo was old school as far as the way he used his team."

Leo was not always old school, however, when it came to attendance. On July 26, during a game against the Dodgers, Durocher left the Cub bench and, shortly thereafter, the ballpark, complaining of an upset stomach, and left the team in the care of coach Pete Reiser. The following day, while his Cubs lost to the Dodgers, Durocher was seen at a boys' camp in Eagle River, Wisconsin.

Earlier in the year, the 63-year-old manager married Lynne Walker Goldblatt, an attractive television personality several years younger than Durocher. Lynn had three children, including a 12-year-old son named Joel. Joel was spending the summer at Camp Ojibwa in Eagle River, and wanted Durocher to attend the parents' day weekend festivities. Leo explained that he was busy fending off the Mets, which seemed like a poor excuse to the 12-year-old. At the last minute, Durocher decided to play hooky, and caught a charter flight to Eagle River. "And I felt great about it," he wrote later. "Free as a bird."

Young Joel was delighted to see his stepfather. So were the camp counselors and other campers' parents, who hung a banner across the street which read, "Welcome Leo Durocher." Durocher thought he would be able to fly back to Chicago in time for the game the next day, but bad weather prevented his plane from leaving, and he missed a second game. It was almost impossible for the manager of the Chicago Cubs, particularly when he was the flamboyant Leo Durocher, to remain incognito for long, especially when his fellow parents hung signs of welcome. When he finally arrived back in Chicago, the news was all over the papers. Leo had gone AWOL in the midst of the first pennant race the Cubs had been in for over 20 years.

Phil Wrigley was one of the most benevolent owners in baseball. Why, he asked Durocher, hadn't he simply asked for time off? He had embarrassed Wrigley, who didn't know where he was, and caused his players to question his commitment to the team. What if a player had pulled a similar stunt? Wrigley felt that Leo owed his team an apology.

Durocher, as usual, blamed the press for picking on him and blowing the incident out of proportion. He felt badly about having embarrassed Wrigley, but dismissed the bad publicity by claiming that the press had a vendetta against him. In his autobiography, Leo described his glee after Wrigley failed to discipline him. He wrote, "[N]ow I'd have all those jackals who thought they had me on the run grinding their teeth. Especially the Unholy Six led by big Jack Brickhouse [you can speak plainer than that, Leo] who had got together to run me out of Chicago. Up yours, too, Brickhouse. Screw you, [beat writer Bob] Enright."

No wonder the press had a vendetta against Leo. He seemed to go out of his way to offend them. Durocher once asked reporters to put out their cigars because he was sensitive to smoke, and flushed a reporter's pipe down the toilet for the same reason. He threatened to punch an editor. He petulantly excluded Chicago's most important media personalities from the invitation list to his wedding. "Flaunting his independence," wrote Melvin Durslag in *The Sporting*

News, "he gave [the press] trouble gratuitously, and they responded by knocking his brains out.... The commotion between Leo and the media grew to staggering dimensions. A bitter undertone pervaded the atmosphere. It couldn't help but have a distracting influence on the team."

During the season, Durocher filmed a commercial for Schlitz beer in which he sat around discussing baseball with a group of reporters. "Of course," Dick Young noted sarcastically, "they're make-believe newspapermen."*

Durocher tried to use his feud as a tool to bring his players together against the common enemy, the media. Like Billy Martin, he loved the fortress mentality — us against the world. "When I played against him," said Nottebart, "I hated his guts. But if you had a Cubs' uniform on, you were part of the ballclub, whether you were an old hanger-on or a rookie [note: unless you were Don Young]." The fortress ploy didn't work, for while the writers couldn't stand the manager, they liked the players and wrote favorably about them. This infuriated Durocher, particularly when the reporters wrote nice things, as they invariably did, about Banks.

Durocher felt that a team required a siege atmosphere in order to play well, and did his best to manufacture tension when none was present. There were few laughs when Leo was around. "The Cubs had a super club," said J. C. Martin, who was traded to Chicago in 1970, "but Durocher was nothing but pressure. He put so much pressure on his players that they could not perform. The club that I was with could not play in the seventh, eighth and ninth innings. He put so much pressure on them that they couldn't make the plays."

Lee Thomas played for Durocher in 1967. Thomas had been an All Star with the Angels, and a regular for most of his big league career. In Chicago, however, he rarely left the bench. "In his day, I'm sure Leo was a good manager," Thomas said, "but Leo and I didn't get along and I don't think a lot of the guys got along with him. He just kept sitting me down and sitting me down, so one day I went in and, as nice as I could, asked him why he wasn't giving me a chance to play. He screamed at me. The door was wide open and all the players were there, and I said to myself, 'Well, I can walk out of here with my tail between my legs, or I can do what I eventually did.' So I let him have it back and then walked out and never played anymore."

"I saw the nose-to-nose thing [between Thomas and Durocher]," said Bob Hendley, "and I was hoping [a fight] would happen. But it didn't. Leo was always a showman. I personally didn't like him, and I don't think he liked me either. He was not my kind of guy, and obviously I was not his kind of guy."

Things were different on the Mets, where practically everybody was Gil Hodges' type of guy, as long as he respected Hodges' authority. As McAndrew observed, Hodges was a non-degreed psychologist who understood his players and their needs. McAndrew needed a pat on the back. McGraw needed a calming influence. Swoboda sometimes needed to be reminded to pay attention. Gaspar needed a strong lecture once in a while. Seaver just needed to be left alone; he was his own manager. The reserves needed to play and to feel wanted.

In 1968, the Mets had an incident on a flight to Houston. Swoboda had been given some love beads by his young fans in Los Angeles and was wearing them on the plane. Cardwell, a conservative North Carolinian, took offense. "We were on the plane," said Cardwell, "and we had gotten beat the game before. I walked to the back of the plane and saw these love beads and snatched them off and almost got into a fight. I didn't believe in the love beads and all the parades they were having and two of our ballplayers were supporting this. That wasn't me. That just rubbed me the wrong way."

In 1967, when the Cubs started winning, Durocher contemplated writing a book, principally for the purpose of lashing out at those who had criticized him in their books. The subject matter might have been entertaining, but the absolute treat of the process would have been watching Durocher work with his ghostwriter, who was rumored to be Truman Capote.

Cardwell and Swoboda were quickly separated before any further trouble ensued, and Hodges dealt with the issue the next day, before the game in Houston. Gil made it clear that he had done most of the talking. He was upset because the incident had occurred on a commercial flight, and had been observed by the other passengers. Hodges also had a private conversation with Swoboda about love beads and other things. "I don't want to reveal what our discussion was about," Hodges said, "but I think if you've been watching Swoboda play lately, you have a pretty good idea." The matter was closed, Hodges said, and nothing like that would ever happen again.

Unlike Durocher, Hodges had a terrific relationship with the media, many of whom still idolized him from his playing days. Gil shunned the spotlight, and always talked about his players, not himself. He accepted blame for things that went wrong and praised the players and coaches when things went well. Hodges was as gracious and accommodating as Durocher was combative and petty.

Needless to say, the Cubs were tight when they arrived at Shea to open the two game series with the Mets on September 8. Koosman, with a 12–9 record, started against Bill Hands (16–12). There had been fireworks earlier in the season when Hands pitched against the Mets. After Seaver knocked Santo down, Hands hit Seaver in the back. Later, Seaver hit Hands in the stomach, Hodges and Durocher rushed onto the diamond and a shower of oranges rained down from the Wrigley Field stands.

Four months later, Hands was still looking for revenge. Agee, the Mets' leadoff batter, had always hit him well, and the Cub righthander announced that he would deck Agee with his first pitch. After Koosman retired the Cubs in order, Agee stepped to the plate. Hands' first pitch sent him diving to the ground. So did his third.

The previous year, the Mets had been involved in a knockdown battle with Juan Marichal. If Marichal hit another Met batter, Hodges told reporters, his pitchers would get him. They'd already hit Marichal, Hodges was reminded. "We'll get him twice," Hodges replied. Pitching coach Rube Walker had also made it clear that, if any Met hitters were thrown at, there would be retaliation. "Rube was from the old school," said Bobby Pfeil, "and somewhere during the year it became known that you better not throw at our guys because we had too many good arms and nobody was going to sit back and not get even in that situation."

The Mets went out without a run, and when Santo led off the top of the second, Koosman drilled him. "I tell you what," said Pfeil, "Santo's never been my favorite. I remember him saying the Mets infield couldn't play at Tacoma. But Koosman nailed him. The ball hit and just dropped straight down. Santo stayed down for about a minute and then got up and ran to first base. He showed me a lot there."

In the third inning, with Harrelson on base, Agee came up for the second time. This time Hands threw the ball over the plate, and Agee drove his 26th home run over the 396 foot sign for a 2–0 Met lead. No Met, other than Frank Thomas in 1962, had ever hit more home runs in a season. "If I had to pick out one reason for our rise," Hodges had said a month earlier, "I'd have to say Agee. He makes the ballclub move." In he Mets' biggest game of the season, when they needed it the most, Agee was putting the team on his shoulders.

The Cubs tied the game in the sixth, but in the bottom half of the inning, Agee hit a shot between Kessinger and Santo. On any other day, it was a single, but the wet grass slowed the ball in the outfield and, Agee, never hesitating, slid into second with a double. Wayne Garrett singled to right and Agee took off for the plate. In right field was Jim Hickman, now 32, but still the possessor of a powerful arm. As Agee rounded third and streaked for the plate, Hickman cut loose a strong, accurate throw to Randy Hundley. Hundley had the ball in his mitt before Agee reached the plate, and tagged him on his left side as Agee slid in through the right hand batter's box. Umpire Satch Davidson's view was obscured by Agee's body as it crossed in front of him. Davidson spread his hands in the safe sign and Hundley leapt high in the air in disbelief. Durocher charged from the Cub dugout. Hundley and Durocher carried on for some time, but to no avail, and the Mets had a 3–2 lead, which Koosman, throwing harder than he had in weeks, held for the last three innings. The only excitement after Agee's slide was when Hands delivered a pitch over Koosman's head in the eighth. With the tying run on base in the eighth, Koosman fanned Banks, his 10th strikeout of the game. He struck out the side in the ninth. The pathetic state of Durocher's bench was exposed when his two last inning pinch hitters were catchers Ken Rudolph, who'd batted just 30 times all season, and Randy Bobb, just recalled from the minors. The Cub lead was down to one and one half games, and the two teams were even in the loss column.

The following night was anticlimactic. The Mets scored early and often and Seaver pitched a five hitter for his 21st win and a 7–1 Met victory. It was the Cubs' sixth straight loss. Chicago was still in first place, but at this point even they didn't seem to think they could win. The Met fans, not to be outdone by the Bleacher Bums, got into the act. In the first inning they turned loose a black cat that ran in front of the Chicago bench. They struck again in the seventh. "We got to the ballpark a bit early," recalled Cub infielder Nate Oliver. "When we drove through the gate, we noticed that people going through the turnstiles were getting this white thing, like a handkerchief or a cloth. We had no idea what that was all about."

In the seventh, the Cubs found out what it was about. "When they stood up for the seventh inning stretch," Oliver said, "the lights went out and fifty thousand people stood up and starting swinging these white handkerchiefs and singing, 'Bye, bye, Leo. Bye, bye, Leo. We hate to see you go.'"

Leo and the Cubs went to Philadelphia, while the Mets stayed in New York to face the last place Expos in a twi-night doubleheader. In the first game, McAndrew, who was pitching tremendous ball, dueled Montreal rookie Mike Wegener through eleven innings of a 2–2 tie. "Just before that start," recalled McAndrew, "I had set the club record for consecutive scoreless innings [23] and lost my spot in the starting rotation. That's how good the pitching was. I spent the second half of September on my duff. It's like being an outfielder and all three outfielders in front of you are hitting .400. There's nothing to complain about because the team's doing what it's supposed to do and that's win. I would never complain about it." Pitching on a staff as good as the Mets' had given McAndrew confidence. "When you see your fellow pitchers go out there and shut people out, or give up just a run or two," he said, "you expected to do the same thing."

Ron Taylor pitched the twelfth for the Mets as Wegener, who had struck out 15 Mets, left for a pinch hitter. In the bottom of the inning, Ken Boswell drove in the winning run, and the Mets waited for the score of the Chicago-Philadelphia game. At 10:13 P.M. on September 10, 1969, the scoreboard flashed a final score: Philadelphia 6 — Chicago 2. After the game, Durocher met reporters at the door of the clubhouse. "No comment," he said. "Out. Close the door." The Mets, who had been 9½ games behind on August 14, were in first place. The Cubs, who had been in first for 156 days, were in second. The nightcap of the Met doubleheader was an easy 7–1 win for Ryan, who struck out eleven.

The lead grew day by day, for the Mets continued to win and the Cubs kept losing. They blew late inning leads. They committed key errors. Selma lost a game on a bizarre play. With a runner on second, and a 3–2 count on Richie Allen, Selma wheeled and fired the ball to third, apparently trying to cut off the runner he expected to be breaking from second. Santo was as surprised as everyone else, the ball flew past him and the winning run scored. Selma said later he was attempting a trick play that would result in a balk being called, because he didn't want to pitch to Allen. It would have seemed easier to throw the fourth ball intentionally, but Selma was light on explanation after the game. "Get the hell out of here," he told a reporter who asked him about the play in the locker room. "I have no comment on that," added Santo. "It just happened, that's all." Durocher, who hadn't smoked in seven months, barged into the clubhouse and asked for a cigarette. The Phillies were delighted that the Cubs were staging a collapse that would dim the memory of their own swan dive in 1964. "I say the hell with the Cubs," said Philadelphia's Johnny Briggs. "I don't think they felt sorry for us then."

The Cubs were clearly coming apart at the seams. Coach Pete Reiser conducted a surprise bed check in Montreal and discovered thirteen Cubs missing. Durocher was disgusted. When Chicago lost to the lowly Expos, Bleacher Bum president Ron Grousl asked if anyone wanted to buy 20 yellow helmets. Another Bum said she was trying to organize a bus trip to watch the Cubs play in Pittsburgh, but couldn't get anyone to go. "We just completely blew it," said Cub pitcher Ken Johnson. "We couldn't field a ground ball. We couldn't make a good throw. We couldn't get the hitter out with a runner in scoring position. It was just everybody."

"What a bunch of athletes," said Oliver. "It was probably one of the best baseball teams assembled in the '60s, and that includes the great Dodger teams [on which Oliver played]. We just happened to have that one cold spell at the wrong time. We couldn't do anything right and the Mets couldn't do anything wrong and they knew it and we knew it."

On September 12, the Mets swept a doubleheader from the Pirates. In the first game, Koosman pitched a three hitter and drove in the game's only run with a sixth inning single. Cardwell repeated in the nightcap, driving in the lone run with a single and pitching a four hit shutout for his seventh victory.

"Pittsburgh had a super team," said J.C. Martin. "Everybody but Stargell chopped down on the ball and the infield was so hard that the ball would bounce fifteen or twenty feet in the air. Everybody hit .300 with Pittsburgh.* Koosman and Cardwell both pitched shutouts, which was unheard of in Forbes Field. On top of that, they each drove in the winning run. That was unbelievable. Cardwell could hit, but Koosman couldn't hit a wall with a brick."

Cardwell, as Martin noted, was one of the best hitting pitchers in baseball. "I got my rips," he said recently. "I wasn't just an easy out." Koosman, on the other hand, had 4 hits in 84 at bats in 1969, and had recently broken a 0 for 48 slump. The run he drove in against the Pirates was his first RBI of the year. Cardwell, who was waiting to pitch the second game, had not seen Koosman's hit. "Kooz kept telling me he hit a line drive," Cardwell recalled. "I checked with the other guys and they said, 'Cardy, he hit it off the end of the bat, it was a blooper.'" Cardwell laughed. "Kooz said, 'No, Cardy, I hit a line shot.' He still swears he hit a line shot."

Two days later, Steve Carlton struck out 19 Mets but lost on a pair of two run homers by Swoboda. "I said right then," recalled Martin, "God is a Mets' fan living in New York, because we are going to win this thing. When you see a team win after 19 of your guys strike out, you think something big is going to happen."

Swoboda, the hero of the evening, had lost his starting job and been booed earlier in the season. "I'm the only 25-year-old has-been in baseball," he joked. By September, Swoboda was playing regularly because Jones was out with a hand injury, and had driven in 24 runs in 26 games. He won a game with a grand slam. He even made some spectacular fielding plays. Swoboda had always had a love-hate relationship with the Met fans, and now they loved him. Grote and Boswell were also red-hot. Grote had boosted his average from .218 on August 1 to over .250, and Boswell had 35 hits in a stretch of 80 at bats.

A few days later, Rod Gaspar believed. On Saturday, Bob Moose of the Pirates pitched a no hitter against the Mets. The following day, New York bounced back to sweep a doubleheader. "I'm thinking," said Gaspar, "that when a guy no hits a team, they're going to be down, but we just bounced back and kept winning. My goodness, we had a young team. I don't know if any

*In 1969, the Pirates led the League with a .277 average, led by regulars Clemente (.345), Matty Alou (.331), Stargell (.307), Manny Sanguillen (.303) and substitute Carl Taylor (.348).

of us, especially me, thought about winning a championship or a World Series, but when we got on that roll, I think we all felt that we could beat anybody."

After Seaver's 23rd win, a 2–0 shutout of the Expos on the 18th, the Mets had a five game lead with just thirteen games left. Since August 13, they had won 29 of 36 games. A five game lead, as the Phillies had proven in 1964, is not insurmountable, but the reeling Cubs showed no indication of being able to mount even the slightest surge. With the Cubs not yet eliminated, only 3,000 fans showed up at Wrigley to see them play the Expos. They were dead. What had happened to the juggernaut of April, May and June?

Durocher had set himself up, and when the walls came crashing in, there was no shortage of enemies to jump on Leo when he was down. "Leo was never, ever a good loser," said Nate Oliver. "He was never a gracious loser." "Leo Durocher's pugnacity," wrote J. Anthony Lukas, "seen two weeks ago as a winner's spunk, is now regarded as a filthy temper that makes umpires into enemies." "A man with a knowledge of baseball history," wrote Tom Fitzpatrick, "would be hard put to recall a time when a major league manager in this town was more feared and more disliked." A letter writer to *The Sporting News* gleefully reminded Durocher of a remark he made as a Los Angeles coach after the '62 Dodgers had blown the final playoff game to the Giants. "I would have liked my chances with a 4–2 lead going into the ninth inning," Leo had said. "Well," wrote John Janetski of Tranquility, California, "old Big Mouth had his chance to make the first guess lately and he has taken the Cubs from a seemingly untouchable lead right into second place. It couldn't happen to a nicer guy."

Durocher wasn't about to take the fall alone. On his pre-game radio show, in late September, he said the players had quit on him. Leo quickly corrected himself, saying he didn't like to use the word "quit," but he had used it. "Did Durocher quit on his players," asked noted Chicago writer Jerome Holtzman, "or did they quit on him?" It was neither, Leo claimed on the final day of the season. Nobody quit, he declared, "but we played lousy. Like a lot of girls.... We played the worst baseball in that stretch that I've seen in years." Holtzman noted his admiration for longtime White Sox skipper Al Lopez "because his teams, though almost always inferior, didn't collapse in the stretch." The Cubs, who had been counting their money in July and August, received $574 each for their second place finish.

With the Cubs out of the way, there was nothing left but the formalities. On September 18, a telegram arrived from Yankee Stadium. "Congratulations on being No. 1," it read. "Am rooting for you to hang in there and take all the marbles. As a New Yorker, I am ecstatic, as a baseball person I am immensely pleased and as a Yankee I consider suicide the only option." It was signed by Michael Burke, President. "I think it's great," Yankee manager Ralph Houk added a few days later. "When we win again, we'll have a great rivalry going — and I don't think we're that far away."

On the 24th of September, exactly one year after Hodges suffered his heart attack in Atlanta, the Mets clinched the first title in their history, the first time they had finished higher than ninth place. Although there were still six games remaining in the Met season, only the game of September 24 was at Shea Stadium, the last chance the club would have to win their title in front of their own fans.

There was little drama, at least during the game. Carlton, who had struck out 19 Mets earlier in the month, didn't survive the first inning. Fittingly, the two Met veteran leaders, Clendenon and Charles, led the way. Clendenon homered with two men on base in the first and Charles followed with a two run shot two batters later. Clendenon hit another in the fifth. Gentry entered the ninth inning with a three hitter and a 6–0 lead. With one out and Lou Brock at first, Joe Torre stepped to the plate. Throughout the winter, the Mets had lusted after Torre, believing that the Brooklyn native could make great things happen in New York. At 9:06 P.M. on September 24, Torre indeed made great things happen at Shea Stadium. He hit a ground ball near second base. Harrelson caught it and threw to Weis, who relayed to Clendenon for the double play that brought Met fans, who had waited eight long and sometimes agonizing years, pouring onto the field. They tore holes in the outfield and ripped up home plate and two bases. One teenager tried to scale the scoreboard, fell 25 feet and broke both his legs. Six others suffered broken bones as the 300 policemen at the scene proved totally inadequate to control 54,000 rampaging fans.

After nine years, the Mets were the first expansion team to win a championship. Who would have believed it just a couple of years earlier? In the locker room, rivers of champagne cascaded over heads and shoulders. "Our team finally caught up with our fans," said Don Grant. Seaver grabbed the first champagne bottle and went after Hodges, showering him during the manager's interview with Ralph Kiner. Craig Anderson, Rod Kanehl and Joe Christopher, veterans of the 1962 Mets, joined the party. George Weiss fought his way to Hodges' office. The celebration continued beyond the locker room. "We ended up walking the halls of our hotel," said outfielder Jim Gosger. "I was hanging with Rod Gaspar and he was beating on doors telling everyone that we won the championship. He was excited as heck. It was a great feeling."

Joan Payson's husband came down to the Met locker room, but his wife was absent. She admitted that the last thing she'd expected was for the Mets to be involved in a pennant race in September. Therefore, Mrs. Payson had booked a trip to visit her daughter in Europe. When the Mets began winning, she said she was too superstitious to change her plans, and followed her team from afar. After attending so many games, and watching so many painful losses, she had missed the ultimate moment of triumph.

Across the river in New Jersey, a New York hero from another era, 45-year-old Bobby Thomson, sat in front of his television set. The former Giant was now a Met fan. "I don't see how you can live around here and not be a Met fan," he said. Mayor Lindsay proclaimed the following week New York Mets Week.

The last series of the year, in Wrigley Field, was supposed to have been the climactic battle of the season. It was an anti-climax. "Happy Wednesday, everybody," chirped Banks before the final game. "Welcome to beautiful Wrigley Field. What a day. Why, you couldn't have asked for a better day to play if we made it ourselves." The Cubs finally beat the Mets, but it was far too late. The Bleacher Bums made their last stand, waving Confederate flags in their left field post. They shot off a flare from the stands that sent a crimson glare across the infield. In the eighth inning, the Bums moved to the grandstand, then the dugout roof, and after the game, sat on the infield and sang. To their credit, they weren't singing "Goodbye, Leo."

The Mets had staged a remarkable run. They won 38 of their last 49 games, and made up 17½ games in the standings while, after August 13, the Cubs had been 20–27. "Oh, my gosh," said Pfeil, "Somebody stepped up all the time. Clendenon was huge and we got great pitching. I just think we really started believing in ourselves and saw that we were good. Once it started to snowball, things sure went our way."

Jones nearly won the batting title, leading the league late in September before being overtaken by Pete Rose. Rose won the crown with a .348 mark, while Jones finished third, behind Clemente, at .340. Harrelson, Agee and Kranepool, who had combined for just 51 RBI in 1968, plated 149 in 1969. Seaver and Koosman won 18 of 19 decisions down the stretch, Seaver finishing with ten victories in a row. "That year," said DiLauro, "there was no one better than Seaver and Koosman as a 1–2 punch. Nobody had better control. Nobody had better stuff. Nobody, not even Gibson, was as competitive as those two. And both of them would drill your ass if they thought you were moving up on the plate."

Seaver had been an outstanding pitcher as a rookie, but now he had become the best in the game, surprising even himself. "A couple of years after he got really good," recalled Chuck Estrada, "he told me, 'Chuck, I never in my wildest dreams thought I'd be this good. I knew I could play, but I never thought I was going to get to this level.'"

The pitching staff threw 28 shutouts, by far the best in baseball, and, during the stretch run, went 221 innings without surrendering a home run. For good measure, the pitchers ripped off a scoreless streak of 42 innings after the Mets clinched the pennant.

Would things go the Mets' way in the playoffs and World Series? Would they be drained by the emotion of the long season? Would the magic continue in October? The answer would come in just eight more games.

· 21 ·

The Impossible Dream
Comes True

The first year of divisional play produced just one tight pennant race. The Baltimore Orioles won the Eastern Division of the American League by 19 games, while the Minnesota Twins took the much-weaker Western Division by nine games. Had there been one, 12-team American League, the race would have been no more exciting, as Baltimore would have beaten the Twins by 12 games. The Mets' run to the pennant was certainly exciting for Met fans, and a bitter disappointment to those in Chicago, but it was essentially over by mid-September, and New York's final margin was a comfortable eight games.

The only race that went down to the wire was that in the National League West Division. The Giants, who had finished second four years in a row, had Juan Marichal and Gaylord Perry on the mound and Willie McCovey, the 1969 MVP and the most feared hitter in baseball, at first base. Willie Mays, soon to be 38, was still a serviceable player, but no longer one of the game's superstars. During 1967 and 1968, Willie hit .263 and .289, respectively, with 22 and 23 home runs. He was rested much more frequently in 1969, and hit just 13 homers and drove in only 58 runs.

Cincinnati had an awesome batting attack, with Johnny Bench, Tony Perez, Lee May and Pete Rose, but little pitching. After praising the Red offense, William Leggett wrote, "One had to wonder how high the Reds might hit if they ever got a chance to bat against their own pitching staff." To make matters worse, Jim Maloney, Cincinnati's top starter, was plagued by arm trouble for much of the season.

"Atlanta has Hank Aaron and Felipe Alou," wrote Leonard Koppett before the season, "and little else to make it frightening." The Braves didn't have a very good defense and their pitching, after Phil Niekro, was shaky.

The Dodgers, after losing Sandy Koufax to retirement after the 1966 season, had struggled for two years. In 1969, their other ace, Don Drysdale, would be forced, like Koufax, to retire at the relatively young age of 33 with a damaged shoulder. Without pitching, the Dodgers were in deep trouble for, as always, they had little hitting. They hit just 67 homers in 1968, only 25 at Dodger Stadium. By 1969, however, Los Angeles had Claude Osteen, Don Sutton and Bill Singer in their starting rotation. Although none was a Koufax or Drysdale, they were better than most National League starters. The two other teams in the Western Division, the Astros and newborn San Diego Padres, appeared to have little chance for the title.

As expected, the Astros and Padres sank to the bottom of the standings during the first month of the campaign. The Astros lost 20 of their first 24 games and fell behind the expansion Padres, before getting as hot as they had been cold and vaulting into the pennant race.

The Braves surprised Koppett and many others by spending much of the early season in first place. The Dodgers, buoyed by youngsters Bill Sudakis, Ted Sizemore, and Bill Russell, remained in contention all year, as did the Giants and Reds. By mid-September, the National League West had the hottest race in baseball, with only the Padres out of contention. For a month, not more than 4½ games separated the top four teams, and the lead changed hands 30 times. During the course of one day in September, three teams held the lead at different times. On September 14, the standings were as follows:

	W	L	Pct.	GB
Atlanta	81	65	.555	—
Cincinnati	78	64	.549	1
Los Angeles	78	65	.545	1½
San Francisco	79	66	.545	1½
Houston	75	68	.524	4½
San Diego	45	100	.310	35½

The Giants began a surge, as Mays suddenly came to life. He won a game with a late inning single, and another the following day with a home run. On September 16, Marichal pitched the Giants into first place, San Francisco having jumped over three clubs in just two days. Houston and Los Angeles fell off the pace, leaving the Giants, Braves and Reds fighting for the pennant. On the 23rd, Mays won a game with his 600th home run, a pinch hit blast off rookie Mike Corkins of the Padres. For his feat, Willie picked up a sports car and 391 shares of stock in the Adirondack Bat Company, one share for each foot the homer traveled. Only 4,779 Padre fans were present to witness the historic blast, which kept the Giants in first place.

The schedule favored the Giants, who played six of their final nine games against the last place Padres. Uncertainty, however, is a cornerstone of baseball. San Diego, light years away from first place, beat San Francisco twice in a row, knocking them out of first. Atlanta, in the midst of 17 wins in 20 games, overtook the Giants, and kept winning. On September 30, the Braves, who had been in fifth place in mid-August, clinched their first title in Atlanta by beating the Reds. Knuckleballer Phil Niekro got his 23rd win, saved by two perfect innings of relief by the dean of flutterballers, 46-year-old Hoyt Wilhelm, acquired by the Braves in early September. The Giants, unfazed by the move to divisional play, finished second for the fifth year in a row.

In April, no one would have imagined that the Mets and Braves would meet in the first Championship Series, for the Mets had been 100 to 1 underdogs and the Braves 50 to 1. "Everybody was talking about the Giants, Los Angeles and Cincinnati," said Aaron. "No one was giving us a chance. We never heard anyone talking about us or writing about us. I think when the Mets were 7½ games out, there was more talk about them than about us when we were a game and a half in first."

Atlanta had surprised the experts with their title, but the Braves had a strong team and, like the Mets, finished the season red-hot. Aaron, who had pondered retirement before the season, had one of his finest years, with 44 home runs and a .300 average. He was ably assisted by first baseman Orlando Cepeda (22 homers and 88 RBI) and outfielder Rico Carty (.342).

The Braves' weakness was pitching. Niekro was the ace of the staff, and posted 21 of the club's 38 complete games. Niekro had only two fewer wins than Seaver, but the Braves' other starters (Ron Reed, Pat Jarvis and Milt Pappas) were not even close in ability to Koosman, Gentry, or any other starter the Mets might use after Seaver. The Braves bullpen was thin, as Wilhelm, acquired after September 1, was ineligible for the Championship Series.*

*The first round of postseason competition was not, under any circumstances, to be referred to as "playoffs," a term ascribed to football, basketball and hockey. Any American League owner who used the "P" word was to be fined one dollar, to be collected by Royal owner Ewing Kaufman.

"We're going to win," said Johnny Murphy on the eve of the Championship Series. "Good pitching stops good hitting and we've got good pitching." "No matter who pitches," wrote Leonard Koppett, "the general pattern is expected to be Met pitching versus Atlanta hitting." Not only were the Met pitchers good, the early clinching had given Hodges a chance to rest his staff and align the rotation for the postseason.

Many of the Mets felt the Braves presented them with the most favorable matchup. They had a terrible time with the Astros, and didn't want to play the first two games in the Astrodome, where they almost never won. They didn't like the prospect of having to face Giant ace Juan Marichal twice in five games, and would rather not encounter Cincinnati's lineup of sluggers. The Mets had beaten the Braves 8 times in 12 games during the season, including six of the last seven, and were sanguine about their chances. Koosman predicted a sweep. When someone asked if he would be prepared to pitch Game Five on two days rest, he said he wouldn't have to because the whole affair would be over by then. Despite Koosman's bold optimism, the Braves were 13–10 favorites.

Joan Payson had returned from Europe and went to Atlanta for the first game. She hadn't been to the Georgia city since attending the opening of *Gone with the Wind* in 1938. Many people had seen *Gone with the Wind*, but few, like Joan and her brother John, had owned part of the rights to the film.

So much for the experts. Seaver, who had a career record of 10–2 against the Braves, gave up five runs in the opening game and Koosman surrendered six before being knocked out in the fifth inning the following day. Yet the Mets won both games. If one had been told that the Braves would score five runs off Seaver with Niekro, their ace, pitching against him, one would think the Braves would win handily. But Niekro looked no more like an ace that Saturday afternoon than did Seaver.

Seaver was nervous. The Braves had been his favorite team as a youngster, and Aaron was his favorite player. He had tried to sign with them when he was at USC. Seaver said he always had the jitters before a game, but they usually disappeared once threw his first pitch. In Atlanta, however, Tom couldn't lose the tenseness, and it showed in his pitching, which was hesitant and not sharp. Seaver rushed his motion and, while he had good stuff, he couldn't control it. He couldn't get his slider over the plate. Grote went to the mound on several occasions to tell his pitcher his mechanics were faulty, but Seaver wasn't able to correct the problem. He gave up eight hits, three walks, one hit batsman and five runs, and managed just two strikeouts. In the seventh inning, with the score tied 4–4, he surrendered a home run to Aaron which gave the Braves a one run advantage.*

Meanwhile, Niekro, who was 23–13 with a 2.57 ERA during the regular season, wasn't pitching any better. He had given up a number of hits, walked a few, and had a run score when one of his knucklers evaded rookie catcher Bob Didier. Wayne Garrett led off the Met eighth with a double, and scored the tying run on Jones' single. Then the Met magic showed it was not limited to the regular season. Shamsky singled, putting Mets on first and second. Boswell, the next batter, missed a sacrifice bunt attempt and Jones was trapped. Didier threw to second and Jones, with no chance of getting back, lit out for third and slid in safely.

Boswell hit a soft grounder back to Niekro, who held Jones at third and forced Shamsky at second for the first out. Kranepool then hit a high bouncer to Cepeda. The Brave first baseman, with plenty of time to get Jones coming home, bounced his throw twelve feet in front of the plate. The Mets had a 6–5 lead. An infield out and an intentional walk to Harrelson loaded

*A home run in Atlanta touched off a celebration, during which a man known as Chief Noc-a-Homa, dressed in full Indian regalia, danced and sent up smoke signals. In May, after Clete Boyer knocked one over the fence, the chief accidentally lit his tepee on fire and had to beat out the blaze with a broom.

the bases, with Seaver the scheduled hitter. Hodges knew Seaver, who'd thrown 123 pitches in seven innings, was done. He'd told Clendenon to loosen up, but when Harrelson was walked, he told Clendenon, "I want to save you for later," and sent J.C. Martin up as a pinch hitter.

"Talk about a coincidence," said Martin. "I caught knuckleballers all my life and then get into the playoffs and I hit against one." On Niekro's first pitch, Martin lined a single to center. The ball went past centerfielder Tony Gonzalez, clearing the bases and giving the Mets a 9–5 lead. "It was just one more time," said Martin, "that Gil called a guy off the bench and he performed and executed and got it done." Ron Taylor came out of the bullpen to shut down the Braves in the last two innings, and the Mets were one game up in the best of five series.

On Sunday, the Mets gave Koosman something he had rarely seen in his two seasons in New York: an 8–0 lead after three and a half innings. Koosman nearly lost it, giving up a run in the fourth and five more in the fifth, a rally powered by Aaron's second home run of the series, a three run blast that made the score 9–6 and ended Koosman's day. Taylor, who had saved the first game, came in and won the second, backed up by three shutout innings from McGraw. "Personally," said Taylor, "that was my biggest thrill of the season. It was a really good feeling to get a win and a save down in Atlanta because we went back to New York with a 2–0 lead." "Suddenly," wrote Phil Pepe, "the Mets are hitting fools and the pre-playoff evaluation has been changed. Can the Braves' pitching stop Met hitting?"

The most exciting event of the day took place in the seventh inning, with Agee on third and Jones at the plate. As pitcher Cecil Upshaw started his delivery, Agee took off for home plate. He was running on his own, and hoped that Jones would see him coming. "Usually," said Agee, "I'll yell 'Look out!' as I head into the plate." Agee didn't yell and Cleon only caught a glimpse of him when Agee was just a couple of steps away. He swung the bat to protect Agee, not intending to hit the ball. The Mets were so hot, however, that Jones couldn't miss even when he tried. He sent a foul liner into the left field stands. His follow through nearly decapitated Agee, who went back to third a wiser man than when he departed. Jones stepped back into the batter's box and hit a home run. It had been that kind of year. The Mets' 13 hits included home runs by Agee and Boswell, in addition to the one by Jones. Agee hadn't hit a home run since September 8, Jones hadn't hit one since August and Boswell since July.

There were no off days in the 1969 Championship Series, and the Mets and Braves flew to New York Sunday night to prepare for Game Three on Monday. Just to let everyone know that he was not overly impressed by the Mets' accomplishments, Hodges fined Agee for being five minutes late getting out on the field before the game. Gary Gentry made it three poor starting performances in a row for the pitching-rich Mets, giving up a two run homer to Aaron in the first, Henry's third home run of the series. Seaver had said he didn't pitch well because he was too nervous. Gentry, pitching on his 23rd birthday, said that, with a two game lead, he was too relaxed. In the third, with the Braves still leading 2–0, Gonzalez singled and Aaron doubled with none out. When Rico Carty hit a vicious foul ball of the left field fence, Hodges decided that Gentry did not have it, and the Met rookie became the first pitcher knocked out of a Championship Series game by a foul ball.

Hodges summoned Ryan from the bullpen. Ryan's season had been fragmented by a series of leg injuries, and at one time he was in danger of being sent to the minors. He pitched well in September and now had a chance to redeem what had been a lost season. McAndrew had been warming up along with Ryan, but with two runners in scoring position and none out, Hodges wanted a strikeout. That's exactly what Ryan gave him. Two strikeouts and a fly ball later, the inning was over without a run crossing the plate.

It was only a matter of time before the Mets got to Atlanta starter Pat Jarvis, who had an unusual outing. Jarvis faced 21 batters in 4⅓ innings, struck out six and gave up 13 wicked shots. He was saved by a few line drives that were caught and a double play he started after catching a liner that nearly took his head off. Eventually, it caught up with him. Agee homered in the third, and Boswell, who hit just three homers all year, hit his second of the series, a two run shot in the fourth, into the hands of bullpen coach Joe Pignatano, which put the Mets in front 3–2.

Cepeda's two run homer in the fifth put Atlanta back on top 4–3. The Met magic surfaced again in the bottom of the inning. Ryan, who had just three hits all season, singled. With one out, Wayne Garrett stepped to the plate. Garrett had started the season hitting well, with an average of .271 in mid-July, only to fall into a deep slump, hitting .156 during the second half to finish the season at .218. His only home run had come on May 6, exactly five months earlier. Garrett stroked the ball off the right field loge, near the foul line, to give the Mets a lead Ryan would not relinquish. Throwing his fastball almost exclusively, he mowed down the Braves over the last seven innings, and even got a second single. The final score was 7–4, and the Mets had won a most improbable National League pennant. In three games, their vaunted pitching staff posted an ERA of 5.00, and their three starters lasted a combined total of 13⅔ innings. Their batters, who were expected to play a supporting role, averaged .327 and hit six home runs in the three games.

As they had done all year, the Mets got key performances from improbable sources. A big pinch hit by Martin, home runs by Boswell and Garrett, who hardly ever hit home runs, a near-death experience by Agee followed by a home run by Jones, and a phenomenal relief outing from Ryan, who rarely pitched in relief. "They are amazing," said Aaron. "They beat the hell out of us," added Brave manager Luman Harris. "You could send the Mets to Viet Nam," said Paul Richards, "and they'd end it in three days. How can we shell their three starting pitchers the way we did, and hardly be in any of the three games? I can't figure it out. I can't."

On the same day the Mets finished off the Braves, the Orioles eliminated Billy Martin's Twins 11–2. There were 13,000 empty seats in Minnesota's Metropolitan Stadium when the game began, and by the fourth inning, when the score was 5–1, many more were vacated. The Minnesota starting pitcher, knocked out in the second inning, was Bob (Righty) Miller, who would not be pitching against his old team in the World Series.

"Ron [sic] Gaspar just said on television," shouted Oriole star Frank Robinson after the game, "that the Mets will sweep the Birds in four games. Bring on Ron Gaspar, whoever the hell he is!" It was Rod, someone told Robinson. "Bring on Rod Gaspar," Robinson said, "whoever the hell *he* is."

Gaspar was the blithe spirit of a very spirited Met club, who wasn't fazed a bit by post-season pressure. Before the first game in Atlanta, an NBC technician was driving a golf cart on the field. When he left the cart unattended near third base, Gaspar jumped in and starting driving through the outfield. He yelled for Yogi Berra to hit him a fungo. Berra hit a fly ball, and Gaspar sped over and caught it.

Both championship series had been decided in the minimum of three games, leaving four days before the beginning of the World Series on Saturday, October 11. The interlude gave the media plenty of time to analyze the respective merit of the two clubs. The consensus was that the miracle run of the Mets was about to come to an end. They had overtaken the Cubs with a furious sprint. They had demolished the Braves in three straight games. Still, the odds were long against them beating the Orioles, the best team the American League had seen since the end of the Yankee dynasty. Baltimore won 109 games, and had the division locked up by mid-season. New York writer Red Foley called them the best team since the '61 Yanks. Most of the Orioles also had World Series experience, having beaten the Dodgers in 1966. The only Met with post-season experience was Taylor, who played for the Cardinals in 1964. Koppett called it a classic confrontation between logic and mysticism.

The Oriole pitchers led the major leagues in ERA, which meant they had a lower earned run average than the vaunted Met staff. "I hear the Mets have six good pitchers," Oriole manager Earl Weaver said. "Well, we've got ten." Lefty Dave McNally won his first 15 decisions, and finished 20–7. McNally had received an $80,000 bonus to sign with the Orioles in 1960, but had never been much more than a mediocre pitcher until midway through the 1968 season. Suddenly, McNally's shoulder, which had given him trouble, got better, and he rediscovered a slider he had inexplicably lost a few seasons earlier. From the middle of 1968 through July of 1969, he won a remarkable 29 of 31 decisions.

Screwballing Cuban lefty Mike Cuellar, a former National Leaguer, was 23–11 in his first American League season and shared the Cy Young Award with Detroit's Denny McLain. The third Oriole starter was 23-year-old Jim Palmer. In 1966, Palmer became the youngest pitcher ever to throw a shutout in the World Series, but after two years of arm miseries, was left unprotected in the expansion draft. Neither Seattle nor Kansas City selected him. In 1969, Palmer's arm healed and he was 16–4, including a no-hitter. McNally, Cuellar and Palmer were the equal of Seaver, Koosman and Gentry, and the Met pitching, their strength for the entire season, appeared to be stalemated.

The Orioles had pitchers as good as the Mets,' but the Mets didn't have hitters the equal of Frank Robinson, Brooks Robinson, Paul Blair and Boog Powell, each of whom hit 23 or more home runs. The Orioles outhomered the Mets 175 to 109 during the regular season, with Powell and the Robinsons accounting for 95 by themselves. Even shortstop Mark Belanger, who'd been an automatic out his first few years in the majors, raised his average from .218 to .287. The Baltimore fielding average was the best in the major leagues, and the left side of the Baltimore infield, with Brooks Robinson and Belanger, was the defensive equal of any twosome in baseball. Four Orioles, second baseman Dave Johnson, Brooks Robinson, Belanger and Blair, won Gold Glove Awards. With the best ERA and the best fielding average in the major leagues, the less than formidable Met offense figured to be in for a challenge. The Orioles had strikeout pitchers, and Met hitters were prone to the strikeout, having the led the National League in that category. Agee set a Met record with 137 and Clendenon had established the NL record with 163 in 1968. If the Met pitching wasn't any better than it was against Atlanta, the series would be over in short order.

"Compared to our team, on paper," said Gaspar, "it was no contest. They had an all star team. You look at our team and who'd we have? Cleon hit .340 that year but that was about it." The Orioles were 8–5 favorites. "I don't believe in that team of destiny business," said Frank Robinson. "Dick Hall and Clay Dalrymple just came over to us from the other league and they both say we're better than the Mets." The Orioles had beaten Drysdale and Koufax in 1966, Robinson said, and Seaver and Koosman couldn't possibly be better than them. "I think Baltimore's attitude toward the Mets," said reporter Gordon White, "had as much to do with the Mets winning as the Mets taking hold of the games and winning the series. The Orioles had the same attitude toward the Mets that the Baltimore Colts had toward the Jets."

The manager of the Orioles was a 5'7" 39-year-old pepper pot named Earl Weaver, who had replaced Hank Bauer in the middle of the 1968 season. Weaver had stayed in the background as an Oriole coach, but when he assumed the managerial reins, his personality burst to the forefront. Weaver was the youngest manager in the major leagues, although after a long career spent mostly in the low minors, he didn't look it. "Out of uniform," wrote William Leggett, "he looks like the guy who comes every Tuesday to read the gas meter." A second baseman of limited ability, Weaver took his first managing job in 1956 at the age of 25, and served in six minor leagues and the Puerto Rican Winter League before finally getting a big league opportunity as a coach in 1968. He was brash, colorful, and smart, and had led the Orioles to the best record in their history.

On Friday, October 10, the day before the opener, Baltimore held a parade for their

Orioles. The players rode in convertibles with attractive young women sitting beside them in a procession that ended with a ceremony at City Hall. The Mets worked out at Memorial Stadium and waited until after the Series to hold their parade.

In Mobile, Alabama, home of Agee and Jones, R.A. Holt, principal of Mobile County Training School, announced that once the World Series games began, classes would be cancelled for the rest of the day. Everyone would head for their television sets to watch the hometown heroes in action. A huge banner honoring the two Mets was hung from the front of the school.

Before the first Series game, Clendenon decided to introduce Frank Robinson to Rod Gaspar. He also told Robinson the Mets were going to beat the Orioles and might do it in four games. Robinson told Clendenon and Gaspar their charmed existence was about to come to an end. "Art Shamsky called me the other day," Gaspar related recently, "and said he'd talked to Robinson about the incident and he said he didn't remember it. I told Art he didn't remember it because those guys are still ticked off that we won. A few years ago I flipped on the TV and Robinson was announcing a game. The Oakland As were playing and Walt Weiss was their shortstop. Frank kept calling him Al Weis. He still couldn't get the Mets out of his head. I mouthed off and said we'd win four straight, and we did. We just lost one in Baltimore first."

The first game went pretty much as everyone expected. After Cuellar retired the Mets in the top of the first, Baltimore left fielder Don Buford led off against Seaver. Buford hit Seaver's second pitch, a fastball, to deep right field. Swoboda backpedaled rather than retreating immediately to the wall, and arrived at the fence just as the ball was clearing it. Ron was still a step away from the barrier, so that when he leaped, he was falling backward and didn't get full elevation. The ball went over his uplifted glove and over the fence as Swoboda sagged awkwardly against it. "I thought Ronnie should have had that ball," said Gaspar, who saw his prediction going down the drain. "Instead of going right back to the fence, he sort of drifted back. If he had gotten to the fence, I believe he would've caught it, but that's history." Swoboda agreed after the game that he should have caught the ball, but admitted that he, like Seaver in Atlanta, was suffering from a case of nerves.

For the second game in a row, Seaver wasn't himself. After pitching in Atlanta, he had strained a calf muscle shagging fly balls in batting practice, and for four days had been unable to run. In the fourth inning, he said, his legs got tired and he ran out of gas. Baltimore scored three runs in the fourth, and with Cuellar mowing the Mets down inning after inning, the game was essentially gone.

Seaver pitched one more inning, then was removed for a pinch hitter. Hodges sent Don Cardwell out to pitch the sixth. Before the Series began, Hodges had called Cardwell to his office. Rube Walker was waiting when the pitcher arrived. "I said, 'Oh, man,'" Cardwell recalled, "'What have I done now?' Gil said, 'Cardy, don't feel hurt because you did a great job all year for us and got us into the playoffs and this Series, but here's what we're gonna do. Rube and I agreed that we're going to start Seaver, Koosman and Gentry in the first three games, and then we're gonna come back with them. But you're our seventh game pitcher if it goes seven games. In the meantime, you're our long reliever. If any of the kids get in trouble, I'm bringing you in.'

"So we went to Baltimore for the first game," Cardwell said. "I warmed up in the first inning. I warmed up in the second inning, the third inning and the fourth inning. Finally, in the sixth inning, I went in to pitch." Cardwell's first two pitches to Elrod Hendricks were balls. "I stepped off the mound and said to myself, 'Don, you've been pitching all your life and here you are pitching in front of several million people on television and you're really messin' up. My knees were just shaking and I was all keyed up. I'd never been there before and I was just keyed up. It's different in football, where you see those guys all worked up and butting helmets. You can't do that in baseball. You just say to yourself, 'Listen, dummy, you've been doing this for how many years? Now is no time to screw up (pardon the expression).'"

Cardwell pulled himself together and got through the inning without any damage. The Mets mounted their only threat in the seventh. Weis brought home Clendenon with a sacrifice fly for the first run in Met World Series history. In the 1966 Series, Baltimore had shut out the Dodgers in the final three games, and Weis's RBI drove in the first run scored against Oriole pitchers in 39 innings of Series play. With two outs and two on, and the Mets trailing 4–1, Gaspar batted for Cardwell. Frank Robinson, in right field, moved in three steps.

"Elrod Hendricks was the catcher," Gaspar recalled, "and he said, 'You nervous, Rod?' I said I wasn't nervous and he said, 'Then how come your legs are shaking?'" Cuellar threw Gaspar his best pitch, a screwball that dipped down and away from right handers, and Gaspar hit it off the end of the bat. The ball dribbled toward third base. With Gaspar's speed, it looked like a sure hit, one that would load the bases again and put Cuellar in deep trouble. With an ordinary third baseman, it would have been a hit, but Brooks Robinson was no ordinary third baseman. He charged the ball, scooped it up with his bare hand and fired to first in the same motion. The play at first wasn't even close. Gaspar was out easily and the inning was over. The Mets never threatened again, and the Orioles had their eighth win in eight post-season games. They'd swept the Dodgers in the 1966 Series, won three straight from the Twins, and had one win over the Mets. Cuellar, the former Cardinal and Astro, pitched a complete game. "The Mets can't beat the Houston Astros," wrote Dick Young, "even after they get traded to the Baltimore Orioles."

The first game had confirmed what many felt would happen all along. These were the Mets, for God's sake, the team that had never finished better than ninth. They won the division because Durocher's Cubs self-destructed. They beat Atlanta, but the Braves were hardly a powerhouse. The Orioles, who were a powerhouse, would restore order and the better team would win.

"This is one of the finest baseball teams I ever saw," former Yankee player and then Kansas City Royals manager Joe Gordon said of the Orioles. Everyone agreed they had no weaknesses, and were about to put an end to the Met magic. "Team of destiny," roared veteran baseball executive Frank Lane, then scouting for Baltimore. "I think they're destined to be beaten by the Orioles." "They're about what we expected," Weaver said of the Mets. Brooks Robinson said the Mets were overrated, which he attributed to New York media hype. The other Robinson, Frank, made an even more biting remark. He said the Mets lost heart after Buford's homer and had no life or spirit for the rest of the game. "It was as if they knew they were beaten and it didn't make any difference," he said. Neither of the Mets' star pitchers, Seaver or Koosman, made him "jump up and down," Robinson added. He said Koosman reminded him a little of Mickey Lolich of the Tigers, but wasn't quite as good.

After the game, Clendenon asked Hodges if the players could have a meeting without the manager and coaches. Hodges gave his permission, and Clendenon told his teammates they could beat the Orioles. They had all been nervous, he said, including him. Yet, even though Seaver had not pitched well, the game had been far from a rout. The Met pitching, Clendenon said, was better than Baltimore's, the defense was just as good [that was wishful thinking] and the hitting would come around. "Gentlemen, trust me," he said. "We are going to kick their asses the rest of this series." Clendenon also had some practical advice. "I'm not hitting the ball to Robinson," he said.

Hodges, who had never been boosted too high by victory, was calm in defeat. He announced he would go with his right-handed lineup the next day against McNally, the same lineup that had been helpless against Cuellar. Left handers like Shamsky, Garrett, Boswell and Kranepool, who had led the assault on the Braves, would remain on the bench until Jim Palmer pitched in Game Three. That was the way Hodges had played it all year, and he wasn't about to panic.

"You guys are in way over your head," Blair told Clendenon before the second game began. Blair hadn't seen the real Mets, however, and hadn't witnessed Met pitching at its best. Finally, for the first time in five games, the Mets got a good performance from their starting pitcher. Koosman, pitching on his son's second birthday, did not allow a hit for the first six innings, holding onto a 1–0 lead forged on Clendenon's fourth inning home run. Imagine what Mickey Lolich might have done. Baltimore tied the score in the seventh, and the two teams went to the ninth inning deadlocked 1–1. The pressure, however, was all on the Mets. If they lost the first two games, while pitching their two aces, they would be in very difficult straits. The Mets had to pull this game out.

They did. With two outs in the ninth, and no one on base, Ed Charles, the right handed half of the third base platoon, singled. On a 2–2 pitch to Grote, the 36-year-old Charles took off for second. Grote lined a single to left and Charles steamed into third. The next batter was Weis, half of the second base tandem. On a team of notable personalities, Weis was notorious for his silence. He was one of Eddie Stanky's favorite players when he played in Chicago, for Stanky thought he saw a lot of himself in the scrappy young infielder. Weis didn't have a lot of talent, but he had good baseball sense and always hustled. He filled in capably at short when Harrelson was in the service, and played second when Boswell was hurt.

The last time Weis faced the Orioles, he was a member of the White Sox. On June 29, 1967, he was trying to make the pivot on a double play when Frank Robinson, always a tough customer on the basepaths, hit him with a rolling block. Weis's knee hit Robinson's head. Robinson suffered a concussion and Weis's knee was torn up badly. The ligaments were ripped and required surgery, which ended Weis's season. Since he was traded to the Mets during the winter, he did not face the Orioles and Robinson again until the World Series.

Weis, a .215 hitter during the regular season, hit McNally's slow curve for a single and the Mets led 2–1. Hodges always seemed to know which button to push, and sometimes he knew when not to push the button. With Shamsky, Kranepool and Martin on the bench, many managers would have hit for Weis, who said after the game that he would have understood. He'd been hit for many times. But Hodges once again made the correct choice.

Weaver hadn't made the right choice. With Koosman on deck, he could have walked Weis intentionally. Weaver said later that he thought Koosman *was* tiring and wanted to keep him in the game; therefore, he pitched to Weis. Koosman was tiring, and the Orioles threatened in the bottom of the ninth. Koosman got the first two batters, and had to retire Frank Robinson to finish the game. Hodges moved Weis into the outfield, and played with only three infielders, hoping to keep Robinson from getting the extra base hit that would put him in scoring position. Gil, who'd learned the strategy from Branch Rickey, had done the same thing during the season against sluggers like Dick Allen and Willie McCovey. The defensive alignment didn't matter, as Koosman walked Robinson. He also walked Powell. Jerry was clearly laboring, and Hodges decided he had gone as far as he could go. He called for Ron Taylor.

Mrs. Payson couldn't bear to watch, and pulled her scarf in front of her eyes. Taylor threw a sinker and got Brooks Robinson to hit a soft grounder to third. Charles scooped it up and started to race Frank Robinson to the bag, but saw he wasn't going to make it. He also saw it was too late to get the force at second, then threw the ball in the dirt in front of first base. Clendenon made a clean scoop and the Series was even. "Imagine that!" Weis said after the game. "I thought I might help win a Series game with my glove. I never thought I would win one with my bat."

It was the first World Series game Baltimore had ever lost, and the win revived the old Met spirit. Bobby Pfeil, although not on the active roster, was on the Met bench. "I remember that after the first game," he related, "Frank Robinson said he looked over into our dugout and we were scared to death. I always thought that was ironic. After a couple of games, you should have looked over at the other side and seen them." After the second game, Koosman was asked about Robinson's comment. He grinned. "We weren't scoring very much," he said, "and we don't often cheer when the other team is scoring." Did Robinson notice any difference in the Met attitude in the second game, he was asked. "Other than the two times they scored," he scoffed, "and when the game was over, it was no different ... [Koosman] didn't exactly dazzle us with his stuff.... If the ball fell in, we could have scored three or four runs."

After an off day on Monday, the teams traveled to New York for the next three games. Unless one of the teams won all three, they would return to Baltimore for a game on Saturday. In Baltimore, one had been able to get all the tickets they wanted, for the first game was not even sold out. During the regular season, the Orioles had posted the lowest attendance (1,212,070) for a pennant winner since the 1945 Tigers. "In this town," Dick Young wrote, "a scalper could starve to death." Quipped another reporter, "This could be the first town to stage a bat day to sell out a World Series game."

There was no such problem in New York, where the Orioles got their first wholesale glimpse of the New Breed. They'd gotten a preview during the first two games, as a few Met fans had journeyed to Baltimore and set up shop in the left field bleachers with their "Let's Go Mets" banners. The wives of Mets Pfeil, Ryan, Dyer and Seaver unfurled their own banner, fashioned from a Sheraton Hotel bed sheet. Now the Orioles were about to get the New Breed at full force. When told the Met fans chanted even when their club was seven runs behind, Weaver responded, "Good, I hope they get the chance."

In New York, unlike in Baltimore, tickets were at a premium. The third game was a sell-out, and celebrities came out in force, including Aristotle Onassis, Jacqueline Onassis and her children, Mayor Lindsay, Governor Rockefeller and his wife, Jerry Lewis and Pearl Bailey, who was starring on Broadway in *Hello Dolly*. Also in the stands was a 23-year-old Met fan who had come all the way from England. Alan Orpin didn't expect to see any of the games in person, but flew to New York just to watch the first two games on television. On Monday, he was given a ticket to Game Three by the Mets, and a vacation by his employer. Hawk Harrelson called Hodges to see if he could get him some tickets.

Game Three belonged to Tommie Agee, who led off the first inning with a home run. In the second, the Mets scored two more times, with both runs driven in by Gentry, a most improbable slugger. Gentry had driven in just one run all year, and had not had a hit in 28 at bats until he hit a double over the head of center fielder Blair to drive home Grote and Harrelson. Gentry didn't need any more runs, but the Mets got him two more, anyway, one on a home run by Kranepool.

Meanwhile, Agee was stealing the show with his defense. *Sports Illustrated* called his performance "probably the most spectacular World Series game that any centerfielder has ever enjoyed ... Agee made a difference of five runs on defense with his fielding and one on offense with his homer." In the fourth inning, with two Orioles on base and two out, Elrod Hendricks hit a high drive to deep left center field. Agee was shading Hendricks toward right center, but got a great jump on the ball. After a long run, he found himself just two steps from the fence. "Plenty of room," yelled Jones, and Agee made a fabulous backhanded catch just before hitting the wall. For Agee, Cleon explained after the game, two steps *was* plenty of room. Press box observers compared the play to the great World Series catches of Willie Mays in 1954, Sandy Amoros in 1955 and Al Gionfriddo in 1947. Mays, Amoros and Gionfriddo, however, made only one great catch. Agee had another one left.

In the seventh, with the Mets leading 4–0, Gentry lost control and walked three straight Orioles, causing Hodges to summon Ryan from the bullpen to pitch to Blair, who represented the potential tying run. Blair hit a fly ball to deep right center. "I actually thought Tommie misjudged the ball," said Gaspar, "which is easy to do the way the winds blow in Shea. That's why he had to dive to catch the ball. But it was a great play." It was a fabulous play. As Agee tracked the ball, he thought he would catch it easily. He had copied Willie Mays' habit of tapping his glove when he was sure he'd catch a ball. Agee tapped his glove, but when the wind blew the ball away from him, he had to put on a burst of speed and dive full-length on the warning track to catch it. "He did the same thing to me in 1963, when he was playing at Charleston," Weaver said ruefully after the game. This time it was a bit more important. The catch broke the back of the Baltimore rally, and ended their hope of winning the game. Ryan set the Orioles down in the last two innings, fanning Blair for the final out with a knee-buckling curve with the bases loaded. As Clendenon put it, Ryan's curve "locked Paul Blair's bowels."

In fact, all of the Orioles' bowels were locked. After three games, they had a team batting average of .133. The Mets, their vaunted staff pitching as it had all season, were now 3–2 favorites to win the Series. According to Hodges, they had the Orioles exactly where they wanted them — one game down and Seaver and Koosman coming up in rotation.

October 15, the day of the fourth game, was also Moratorium Day, a day set aside to protest the United States' continuing and escalating involvement in Vietnam. Mayor Lindsay ordered flags in the city, including that at Shea Stadium, to be flown at half staff. Bowie Kuhn, after the U.S. Merchant Marine Academy band and the New York City police, scheduled to take part in the pre-game ceremonies, refused to do so with the flags at half staff, ordered that the flags at Shea fly at the top of the pole. Veterans who would be attending the game, many in wheelchairs, said they would have protested had Kuhn adhered to Lindsay's original decision.

Many protesters stood outside the stadium holding placards, wearing black armbands, and chanting anti-war slogans. Some were concerned with both baseball and war, such as the young man who carried a sign that read "Bomb the Orioles— not the peasants," and others who distributed a leaflet which read "Met fans for Peace." The leaflet contained a reprint of a newspaper article in which Seaver said that if the Mets won the Series, he would pay for an ad stating that if it were possible for the Mets to win, it was also possible to get out of Vietnam. Nearly two years earlier, Seaver had explained his stance on the war. "I took the view," he said while discussing an editorial he had drafted for a college course, "that it's the wrong war. It's basically a civil war and a guerilla war, but now we are committed too deeply and at an ungodly cost." He said the protesters had not asked his permission to use his statement and that he resented the fact that they had.

On this day, however, Seaver was more concerned about making up for his sub-par performance in the first game than he was about solving the dilemma of Vietnam. His mound opponent was Cuellar, who had completely stymied the Mets in Baltimore. Seaver pitched like he had all season, holding the Orioles to three hits through eight innings. Clendenon's home run, his second of the Series, had given New York a 1–0 lead in the second, and Seaver tenaciously clung to the one run margin until the ninth. He had retired 19 of 20 batters before Frank Robinson got a one out single. Powell singled him to third, bringing up Brooks. Brooks hit a line drive to right field that appeared to be dropping in for a game-tying single.

Ron Swoboda raced in after Robinson's liner. When he came to the Mets in 1965, Swoboda was a comical fielder. Unlike Dick Stuart and Joe Christopher, however, who weren't interested in defense, Swoboda wanted to get better. "When he came up," said Al Jackson, "he was really raw. He probably came up too soon. But he worked at it. Everybody got down on the guy, but he worked at it and became a decent outfielder." Still, even though Swoboda was much improved, Stengel said before the Series, "The right fielder frightens me all the time."

No one worked harder than Swoboda on his defense, and, Stengel's warning to the contrary, the results showed. Maybe Casey remembered Swoboda as he had been when he managed him, for Swoboda not only became an adequate outfielder, he became a good outfielder. "He'll tell you," said Gaspar, "that it was because of me that he became a good outfielder. I played a lot of defense in '69. Ronnie started to work his tail off to make himself a better outfielder because he got sick and tired of me coming in and replacing him."

Swoboda's hard work on defense was the reason he, not Gaspar, was in right field in the ninth inning with the Mets clinging to a one run lead. The sensible play on Robinson's liner would have been to take the ball on the first bounce. The score would be tied, but the slow-footed Powell, carrying the go-ahead run, would be held at second. If Swoboda tried to catch the ball on the fly and it got past him, not only would Powell score, Robinson might round the bases as well. Nevertheless, Ron came sliding in to try for a shoestring catch. "That's Swoboda," said Gaspar. "That's his personality. I don't think anyone else would have tried to make that catch, but that's just Swoboda."

Swoboda did make the catch, skidding in and snatching the ball with a backhand stab just before it hit the ground. He rolled over and fired to second to hold Powell at first. Although Frank Robinson scored the tying run, the Orioles now had just a runner on first and two out. It was the first run the Orioles had scored in 20 innings. After Hendricks hit a ball into the right field seats that barely missed the foul pole, Seaver got him out to end the inning. The Mets got two men on in the ninth, but Oriole reliever Eddie Watt retired them without a run, and Seaver did the same to the Orioles with two on in the top of the tenth.

Enter Met magic in the bottom of the tenth. Grote led off with a broken bat fly ball to left that Don Buford should have caught. Buford lost the ball, broke back, and by the time he recovered, it was too late. Shortstop Belanger raced out from short and nearly made the catch, but the ball dropped safely, and Grote pulled into second with a double.

Oriole strategy was being communicated from afar for, in the third inning, while arguing a strike call on Belanger, Weaver became the first manager ejected from a World Series game since the Cubs' Charlie Grimm in 1935. From that point, Oriole coach Billy Hunter ran the Oriole club, with assistance from a barrel-chested, cigarette-puffing little man in the tunnel between the Baltimore clubhouse and the dugout. On Sunday, the Orioles had decided to pitch to Al Weis, who delivered the game-winning hit. This time, they elected to walk Weis to pitch to Seaver.

Hodges countered with pinch hitter J.C. Martin. Seaver had pitched ten innings and was out of gas, and Hodges wanted to win the game then and there. McGraw was ready to pitch the eleventh, if necessary. When Martin, a left handed hitter, was announced in the game, Hunter removed right hander Dick Hall and replaced him with lefty Pete Richert. Would Hodges counter with a pinch hitter for Martin? "Gil came out of the dugout and walked up to the on deck circle," Martin related. "He said, 'Let's change the strategy. I want you to bunt the ball. Let's get him over to third and then we've got two chances to win the game. What do you think?' I said, 'Gil, you're the manager.' He just grinned and told me to bunt toward first base to keep it away from Brooks Robinson. All I wanted to do was just get the ball down."

Martin bunted Richert's first pitch exactly where Hodges had told him to put it. Richert and Hendricks converged on the ball and hesitated, unsure as to who should field it. Hendricks yelled that he would take it, but Richert couldn't hear him over the crowd noise. Finally, Richert picked the ball up and threw to first. He was virtually on the first base line, and had to throw around Martin, who was running on the inside part of the path. Richert's throw hit him on the left wrist and skittered away toward second base.

Gaspar, who had run for Grote, came steaming into third base. "When you're in Shea Stadium and there are 55,000 people yelling," he said, "you can't hear anything. Nothing. Eddie Yost was our coach, and when I rounded third, he told me later he was yelling, 'Go! Go! Go!' He was two or three feet away from me yelling and I couldn't hear him. It wasn't until I turned around and looked over my shoulder that I saw the ball rolling toward second base and took off. I think Tom [Seaver] was the first person to greet me at the plate." It was Seaver's first and only World Series victory. Frank Robinson now knew who Rod (or was it Ron?) Gaspar was. In 1962, Rod Kanehl had been Stengel's lucky charm as a pinch runner. Now Hodges had Rod Gaspar. "What a beautiful bunt," said Joan Payson.

Another series of improbable occurrences had propelled the Mets to a 3–1 series lead. A remarkable, almost foolhardy, catch by a player who four years earlier had been ridiculed as a clown in the outfield. A long drive by the Orioles in the ninth that barely missed the foul pole. A bloop double that was misjudged by the left fielder. A throwing error on a bunt laid down by the Mets' second string catcher, who ran out of the baseline. "[T]hey let J.C. Martin swerve so far out of the basepath," wrote columnist Jim Murray, "that two cars out on Queens Boulevard ran into a pole to avoid hitting him." The banished Weaver could not come out to argue, and none of the Orioles raised much of a protest. A still picture showed Martin clearly running illegally when he was hit by Richert's throw, but the game was over and the Mets had won. "That play," said Martin, "got me back to New York a whole lot of times for Old Timers' Games. People have done such spectacular things in the World Series and here I am because I bunted that lousy ball in 1969."

The Mets could finish the Series with one more win, and no one seemed to doubt they would do it. After the fourth game, Frank Robinson and Don Buford attended *Hello Dolly* and were invited backstage by star Pearl Bailey. "What are you fellows doing here?" she asked. "The way you're going, you should be home, rehearsing." Even the Orioles' brave statements seemed filled with doubt. "We're gonna break out of it today," said Brooks Robinson without much conviction. Powell promised Oriole starter McNally "two whole runs." McNally said he hoped he'd be around in the 15th inning when it happened. In four games, the Orioles had just two extra base hits, Buford's home run and double in the first game.

Going into the Series, the pressure was on Baltimore. If they won, it was expected. Even if the Mets lost, they'd still had a remarkable year. "When you're expected to do things and you don't," theorized scholarly Oriole second baseman Dave Johnson, "it messes you up. But when you aren't expected to do things and you do, it picks you up." After four games, the Orioles were messed up and the Mets were clearly picked up. "I know they're not a better team than we are," Blair said.

When Baltimore scored three runs off Koosman in the third, it seemed as though they were merely delaying the inevitable. The Baltimore rally included a home run by McNally, Baltimore's first extra base hit in 35 innings. In the sixth, with Baltimore still holding a 3–0 lead, there were two incidents in which batters claimed to be hit by pitches. Naturally, the Mets came out ahead. In the top of the inning, Frank Robinson was clearly hit on the right thigh by one of Koosman's pitches. Plate umpire Lou DiMuro ruled, however, that the ball hit Robinson's bat first and was a strike. While Robinson was in the dugout having his leg treated, DiMuro told Weaver Robinson had better get out in a hurry or Weaver would have to use a pinch hitter. Robinson limped out of the dugout and struck out, which made his thigh bruise even more painful.

In the bottom half of the sixth, Jones claimed to have been struck by a sweeping McNally curve ball. DiMuro said no. Swoboda, standing in the on deck circle, picked up the ball and flipped it his manager. Hodges strode from the Met dugout, holding a ball, which had a smudge of black shoe polish on it. "You always keep a few baseballs with shoe polish on them in the dugout," Stengel said after the game. DiMuro waved Jones to first base, bringing Weaver out of the Baltimore dugout on the fly. Clendenon, the next batter, hit a McNally slider for his third home run of the Series to narrow the margin to 3–2.

The next inning, Weis, the unlikely slugger, hit a drive to deep left center, and took off for first base. He rounded first and sped toward second. Halfway between first and second, he heard a tremendous roar erupt from the crowd and looked up to see what had happened. The ball had gone over the fence at the 371 foot sign and the game was tied. It was the infielder's first home run at Shea and only his fourth in two years as a Met. Two had been hit during the key July series in Chicago, and this one tied the fifth game of the World Series. The Orioles were now behind, 3–3. The winning runs scored in the eighth when Jones and Swoboda doubled and Powell committed an error which allowed a second run to score. At 3:17 P.M. on October 16, 1969, Jones retreated into deep left field, hauled in Dave Johnson's fly ball, and dropped to one knee in silent thanks. The World Series was over and the Mets had won.

Before the ball even settled in Jones' glove, fans, who had been making their way down the aisles throughout the final half inning, began pouring out of the stands and onto the field. There were plenty of police on hand, but they would have needed 57,397 officers, one for each fan, to keep people off the Shea Stadium turf. "I'm looking at a picture I have framed on my wall," Cardwell told me. "It's the last out of the World Series. Here come the cops. Here are the Orioles trying to get to their clubhouse, and here are the fans. There's a guy about to jump off a twenty foot walkway. I don't know if he broke his ankle or what he did, but all of 'em were heading for the field, trying to get a base or home plate or whatever." The unidentified leaper may have been one of two were treated at Booth Memorial Hospital for possible heel fractures. In all, 31 people were given first aid at the stadium and five were sent to the hospital. A number of photographers were attacked by Shea security after they photographed the guards shoving fans around on the field, and had to be rescued by the police. An usher was thrown off the roof of one of the dugouts. Dick Young, who witnessed the riots that followed the clinching of the division title, the win over Atlanta and the World Series finale, ranked the Series rumble above the Championship Series affair but not up to the standards of the mayhem that ensued after the Mets clinched the Eastern Division crown.

The fans scribbled on the outfield walls. They tore up the bases. They ripped up the turf, and one youngster ran over to Mrs. Payson's box and gave the owner a clump of Shea Stadium sod. If the players hadn't fought their way to the clubhouse, the fans would have carted them off as well. "I was in the right field bullpen," said Cardwell, "and as I soon as I saw Cleon make the catch, I ran underneath the stands to the clubhouse and grabbed two bottles of champagne, one to drink and one to pour."

Cardwell, who would not be pitching Game Seven, was a happy man. "I hate to think about what it would have been like," he said recently, "if it had gotten down to one final game. You never know. You might go out there and not be able to hit the screen behind home plate. You get so keyed up." Swoboda did a quick jump and clicked his heels à la Ron Santo, then sprinted to the safety of the Met dugout. Jones and Agee had no chance of running the gauntlet of fans to reach the dugout. They employed the broken field running skills they'd learned as high school halfbacks in Mobile and lit out for the Met bullpen.

Jack DiLauro was in the bullpen with Cardwell, and also ran under the stands to get to the clubhouse. "I had a white Ban-lon T-shirt with the orange and blue Met logo on it in my locker and one of the goddamn reporters stole it," he said. "I'll never forget that. I had to wear my baseball undershirt home. After the interviews and the champagne and all the hoopla, me, Bobby Pfeil, Duffy Dyer and I think Cal Koonce were sitting around one of the rectangular tables. There were four of five of us sitting at the table when Joe Garagiola came over with a bottle of champagne and sat down. He said, 'I'm here to sit with the rest of the rinky-dinks.' He sat there bullshitting with us for a half an hour, just talking. It was kind of neat. I wrote him a letter afterward thanking him for sitting down and talking with us. They were interviewing the Swobodas, the Seavers and the Ryans, but the four of five of us were just happy to be there."

President Nixon placed a call to the clubhouse to give his congratulations to Payson and Hodges, whom he'd met when Gil managed the Senators. Pearl Bailey held up a clump of Shea Stadium sod which she said she was going to use as a powder puff. She told Hodges he was a "cool cat." Take that, Ken Harrelson! Gaspar poured champagne over the honorable head of John Lindsay. "Nothing else will ever be as good as this," gushed Swoboda. "The only thing left for us to do is to go to the moon." It was a win, Swoboda said, that "will give heart to every loser in America." J.C. Martin held a glass of champagne with his bandaged left wrist. Judge Sam Liebowitz stood in the middle of the clubhouse and said, "In this moment, I will even forgive Walter O'Malley for leaving Brooklyn."

The Met heroes were feted. Clendenon, who didn't think he'd be playing at all in 1969, let alone performing in a World Series, and who wasn't sure he could play in the Series because of an injured shoulder, was named Most Valuable Player. His three home runs set a record for a five game Series, and he played in just four of them. He planned to use his winning Series share to expand his Atlanta restaurant. Weis, with 5 hits in 11 times up, including a game winning single in the second game and a tying home run in the finale, was the most unlikely hero. His father was in the clubhouse after the final game, and even dad seem astonished at the feats of his light-hitting offspring. Swoboda batted .400, in addition to making his game-saving catch in the fourth game. Seaver noted that he was the only Met pitcher in history to lose a World Series game.

As he had done all year, Hodges had used his entire team in the five games. Twenty-one of the 25 Mets saw action, including third string catcher Duffy Dyer. The only Mets who didn't play were pitchers McAndrew, DiLauro, Koonce and McGraw. "We had 26 players get us there," Hodges wrote the next day in his ghosted *Daily News* column, "and that includes Bobby Pfeil." Pfeil, who played 62 games for the Mets, had been inactive for the Series, but Hodges hadn't forgotten him. Obviously, Pfeil wanted to be on the World Series roster, but one player had to be dropped. "I don't remember being that hurt," he said recently. "Gil and I always used to talk a lot. He told me he would rather have another pitcher. He wanted me to stay with the team and said that if there was an injury, he would activate me. It didn't upset me as much as you'd think it might. To have spent as many years in the minors as I did, and to be a part of something so special ... everything was fantastic." Although he didn't join the club until June, and wasn't eligible for the postseason, Pfeil was voted a full series share. "I wear my ring daily," he said, "and I'm proud of it." Another Met who had not been active for the Series, Casey Stengel, also received a ring.

Things were a bit more somber in the Baltimore clubhouse. Commissioner Kuhn told Weaver, "I've just congratulated the Mets and told them they beat the best damn ballclub in sight." "It was like trying to stop an avalanche," said Oriole executive Frank Cashen. "They're not a lucky ballclub," added Weaver. "They're good."

It had been a tough sports year in Baltimore. In January, Joe Namath and the Jets had sprung a stunning upset on the heavily-favored Colts in the Super Bowl. In April, the underdog Knicks swept the Bullets in the NBA playoffs. Now the Mets! On the trip home, Connie Robinson, Brooks' wife, said, "Now we know how the Dodgers felt in 1966." The Met pitching had shackled the Orioles as tightly as the 1966 Orioles had throttled the Dodger attack. The Orioles scored just nine runs in five games, only five in the last four, and batted a miserable .146. They had only two extra base hits in the last four games. Three of their nine runs were driven in by Cuellar and McNally. Baltimore started just four innings with hits, just three after Buford's home run in the opening game. The two Robinsons had four hits in a combined 35 at bats. During one game, Oriole coach Billy Hunter, a light hitting infielder in his playing days, passed the box of American League President Cronin. "Billy," Cronin said, "your guys are hitting like you used to."

Eventually, the Mets' clubhouse celebration came to an end and the rinky-dinks and everyone else got dressed and went to the post-game party in the Diamond Club, in the upper level of Shea Stadium. Music was provided by Al Madison's Metcats, and there was plenty of inartistic dancing. "We had a ball," said DiLauro. "My father and mother were there, and so was my older brother, who was a baseball freak. My dad got drunk with Weeb Ewbank. Weeb was blitzed and my father got blitzed with him and they were yelling at each other about football. My dad was in heaven." Casey Stengel was also there. "It's amazin'" he said. Bill Shea, without whom the Mets might never have existed, was there. So were Bowie Kuhn and Warren Giles, who was retiring as President of the National League. The party went to the small hours of the morning. Then it was over. "It was like having an empty stomach," said DiLauro. "It was over. We weren't going to play tomorrow. What the hell were we going to do?"

First, the Mets were going to appear on *The Ed Sullivan Show*. Then, a number of them were going to Las Vegas. Their musical careers had begun the day after the Mets clinched the division title when they recorded a song titled *The Amazin' Mets*. "Half the guys were still drunk from the night before," Clendenon wrote, "and it sounded like it ... amazingly enough, the album sold over 50,000 copies." Many Mets were going to off season jobs that were more lucrative than those they'd held in the past. Art Shamsky was opening up another restaurant with Phil Linz.

A number of players were going on the banquet circuit. Mattgo Enterprises placed an ad which read: "Now available, Tom Seaver, America's top athlete and personality plus Nancy Seaver, Tom's lovely wife, for those situations that call for young Mrs. America or husband-and-wife sales appeal." Seaver's off season income potential was projected at $75,000, well in excess of his $35,000 salary for playing baseball. *Sports Illustrated* named Seaver its Sportsman of the Year. Finally, in addition to any endorsements they might attract, each Met would collect $18,338.18 for winning the World Series, the richest payout in major league history. "After we won the World Series," said Les Rohr, who pitched in just one game in 1969, "if you played for the Mets, they were offering you anything—furniture, refrigerators, houses. It was amazing. People were saying, 'Take this, take that.' You could have walked into a bank and they would have given you the money. It was just amazing."

The city reacted predictably to the Mets' win. It was like V-J Day in New York. Confetti rained down from office windows. Strangers hugged each other on the street. Church bells rang. There was a mayoral election in 1969, and all three candidates strove mightily to identify themselves with the Mets.

The main celebration took place on October 20, when the city held a ticker tape parade for its heroes. Mayor Lindsay gave a speech in prose, and Ed Charles one in verse. Pearl Bailey and Robert Merrill sang a duet. The crowd was believed to be as big as the seven and half million who welcomed General Douglas MacArthur home from Korea in 1951. Every Met was present except Boswell, Jones and Shamsky. "It was 35 years ago," said Ron Taylor, "but I can recall it like it was yesterday. It was intoxicating. That's the only way you can describe the continual roar — the paper coming down on you — the fans on the street running along beside the car. It was just overwhelming." The Yankees had won 20 World Series titles, but not once had they been given a ticker tape parade.

The parade and reception at City Hall were followed by a luncheon at the Four Seasons and another audience with the mayor at five o'clock. Then came a bus ride to Flushing Meadow Park for yet another celebration and fireworks. By then, the New York sanitation department was clearing the debris from the morning parade. By six o'clock, 350 workers had removed 578 tons of paper that had been thrown along the parade route. This was in addition to the 1,254 tons already disposed of from the celebrations of the previous two days.

Nearly all the Mets thought that, even if there weren't ticker tape parades every year, they would be going to the World Series several times in the next few years. At the victory party, Koosman echoed the sentiments of Mrs. Payson, who predicted the Mets would win five championships in a row. Even 35 years later, devoid of the intoxication of victory, others felt the same as Koosman. "I thought we were going to be legitimate long-term contenders," said Taylor, "because of the players we had and their youth, particularly the pitching strength." "I was

25," said Jim McAndrew, "and it was my first full season in the big leagues. I can't say that it was surreal. It just seemed like that was what you were supposed to do. I just accepted it and expected to do the same thing the next year, the next year and the next year." No less an authority than Ted Williams said he saw the makings of a dynasty.

The Mets were a young team. They had four starting pitchers who were the equal of any in baseball. They had Jones and Agee in the outfield. They had the best manager in baseball in Gil Hodges, who was just 45 years old. They had one of the richest owners in the game, who was willing to spend money to keep her players happy. Their top two farm clubs won league championships in 1969. Why wouldn't the Mets establish a dynasty like the Yankees had done? "In a couple of years," Koosman said after the Mets took over first place, "when all the new men find themselves, we'll have a better team than the Yankees ever had — you know, the Yankees of my time, I mean the 1950s and 1960s."

"After the Mets won in 1969," said Rod Kanehl, "I wrote a letter to Dick Young. I pointed out that the reason the Mets won was because of Hodges and his attitude and the way he handled the players. I said that for the same reason, they wouldn't win the next year. This was a bunch of guys who had never won anything and he made them winners. He commanded their respect. Now they're different. They're champions now. But Gil is going to treat them the same way he did the year before. You have to change when you deal with champions. But Hodges is not going to change. He's going to be the same Hodges and what won for him in 1969 is not going to win for him in 1970."

A day after the final Series game, Young wrote a column cautioning against talk of a Met dynasty. "This is your old killjoy, Dickie Baby," he wrote, "reminding you that the Mets are merely amazin,' not invincible." One year did not make a dynasty, he warned, and the odds of all of the fortuitous events of 1969 being repeated were slim. Yes, he knew the Mets had a lot of talented youngsters in their farm system, but could they get repeat performances from Seaver, Koosman, Jones and Agee, and the occasional miracle from Clendenon, Weis and Swoboda? Would throws hit Martin in the wrist and black stained balls emerge from the Met dugout after striking in the vicinity of Jones' shoe? Johnny Murphy also recommended restraint. "The Cardinals thought they were building a dynasty a year ago," he said, "and look what happened to them."

Did it matter? After the Series, Melvin Durslag wrote that even if Hodges never won another pennant, it wouldn't diminish what he had accomplished. "This is like saying that Dr. Jonas Salk had a big year with polio, but couldn't put it back-to-back with cancer."

The original Met fan died after the 1969 season, the rooter who started his odyssey at the Polo Grounds in 1962 chanting "Let's Go Mets," and moved to Shea in '64. The New Breed had loved their Mets when they lost, and they loved them when they won, but they would not love them again when they lost. "The fans loved the team as bunglers for years," said Gordon White. "Then when they started winning, they could never bungle again and make the fans happy. Once you win, never again are you allowed to bungle."

The Mets were entitled to enjoy their triumph, whether it was the first of many or the one and only. As it turned out, there would be no dynasty. Hodges suffered a second heart attack and died just before the start of the 1972 season. Berra took his place. The Mets won one more pennant, in 1973, and lost the World Series to Oakland in seven games. Nineteen seventy-three, however, bore no resemblance to 1969. In 1973, the National East race went down to the wire, but it was a battle of mediocre clubs. The Mets won the championship with a record of 82–79, beating the Cardinals by a game and a half. The fifth place Cubs were just five games out of first.

What was the difference between the '69 and '73 teams. "Night and day," said McAndrew. "Shoot, in 1973 we were only two or three games over .500 while in '69 we won 100 games. There's just no contest. We weren't the defensive team in '73 that we were in '69 and we didn't have what I would call timely hitting. Yogi went back to Yankee ball and we didn't utilize the team at all. We had a lot of injuries in '73, and you had guys coming up and starting. It was managed much like a Durocher team would be managed." Jim Gosger came to the Mets in the latter stages of both pennant races. "The first time you win anything that big," he said, "the thrill is overwhelming. In 1973, we were just trying to get back to where we were in 1969. It was different."

By the time the Mets won their next championship in 1986, the '69 team was long gone. The only one still in the major leagues was Seaver, who had just completed his final major league campaign with, ironically, the Red Sox, the Mets' opponent in the '86 Classic. The excitement of 1969 would never be repeated, and by the mid-1970s, rather than looking back at a dominant era, the few remaining members of the '69 club were just part of a bad team. Seaver was traded in 1977, Koosman departed a year later, and the rest of the team was lost to retirement, bad trades or oblivion. Everyone knew that 1969 was a fabulous occurrence, made even more magical by the fact that it was never to be repeated. The Miracle Mets were one of a kind.

Appendix:
In Their Own Words

Gary Kroll pitched in the major leagues for four seasons, starting in 1964, for the Phillies, Mets, Astros and Indians, accumulating a record of 6-7 in 71 games, mostly in relief. As a young pitcher, he threw extremely hard, but then suffered from arm problems. Now in his early 60s, Kroll owns and operates a very successful marketing firm in Oklahoma City. "Since I was eight years old," he said, "all I wanted to do was play baseball. I used to go down to the ballpark at eight o'clock in the morning and stay until dark. My high school coach said, 'Don't waste your time. You're not going to do anything with it.' But I didn't care. I would go and watch the [PCL] Hollywood Stars and look at the field. I'd have given anything just to walk on it. I'm a fan who got to play. It was fantastic. I wouldn't trade it for anything. When I go to the park now and see someone throw, I can feel the ball coming off my fingers. I remember how it felt. When I see someone push off the mound, I can feel it in my hip. It's like I'm doing the throwing."

Dennis Ribant pitched in the major leagues from 1964 through 1969 and was the Mets' top pitcher in 1966. Ribant is currently the owner and operator of a successful insurance business in Newport Beach, California. "I wish I would have cherished it more," Ribant said of his time in the big leagues. "It was the best time of my life. I've certainly been happy and I've been very successful in my business, but when people ask me what was the best time of my life, I'd certainly say my 20s and my early 30s."

Joe Grzenda was a hard-throwing left-handed reliever who pitched 219 games in eight major league seasons. He pitched 11 games for the Mets in 1967, then played for the Western Division champion Twins in 1969. For two years, he pitched for Ted Williams on the Washington Senators. "I look back," he said, "and can say that I was there. I never smoked in front of kids and I am so proud of my whole 20 years in baseball. There were only 1600 [sic] professional baseball players in the world and I was one of them. I was one of them and I never forgot that."

Rick Herrscher played 35 games with the 1962 Mets, and never played in the majors again. After a few years with the Met farm club at Buffalo, he retired and went to dental school. "All things work out for the best," Herrscher said. "Maybe that was the way for me to get into a profession where I'm able to help a lot of kids with their personalities and their smiles. I've enjoyed that tremendously, but I wouldn't give up my time playing professional baseball. It was one of the great times of my life."

Ron Taylor pitched in the major leagues from 1962–1972, saving a key game in the 1964 World Series and another in the 1969 Series. After retiring from baseball, he became a doctor and is currently the team physician for the Toronto Blue Jays. "One thing I became aware of," he said, "while working in the hospital as an intern and as a resident, was how much baseball meant to people who were ill. I saw how much they looked forward to the games and how it gave them something to do at night. It took their minds off their health problems. It was kind of fun to watch a game with them and see how they really enjoyed it. That made a big impression on me."

Bill Denehy was a Met spring training phenom in 1967, who encountered arm trouble and wound up with just one major league win and ten losses. "I loved pitching," Denehy said. "There was no doubt that I loved being on that mound pitching to the hitters. I really didn't love baseball, though, because when I didn't pitch, there was nothing to do. When you play basketball, you're practicing offensive plays or you're working on your defense. In baseball, when you didn't pitch, you shag balls in the outfield before the game, you do your exercises and your sprints, and then you just sat around and watched the game."

"If I only knew then what I know now." This classic lament is heard time and again from all of us, who wish we could combine the wisdom of age with the vitality of youth. The youth of athletes fades quickly, and many, particularly those who remained active as coaches or managers, learned later in life things they could no longer use in their playing careers. What would former players have done differently during their careers?

Jack Lamabe pitched for seven major league teams between 1962 and 1968, and appeared in three games in the 1967 World Series. Starting and relieving, he finished his career with a 33-41 record in 285 games. Following his retirement, he coached at LSU for ten years, then returned to professional ball as a coach. "I think I would have learned to relax more," Lamabe said. "If you can relax and not let it interfere with your performance — if you can give 100 percent physically and 100 percent mentally, if you just let your body perform at the speed it's supposed to and not let a base hit, a walk, the umpire, the mound, the temperature, errors upset you."

Joe Moock's major league career consisted of a one month trial with the Mets in September, 1967, when he played 13 games at third base. His debut took place on September 1st. "It was one of those cold days in Chicago," he recalled, "with the wind whipping in off the lake. I was sitting on the bench freezing my butt off when Westrum said, 'Go out there and play third.' Of course, the first guy hit the ball down the line. I made the play and turned around and threw the ball to Kranepool. Kranepool wasn't there to catch the ball, so I didn't start out with a bang. On my first at bat, I was a strikeout victim of Ferguson Jenkins when he set the all-time Cubs' season record.

Would he do things differently if he could do it all over again? "I'd have a different perspective," Moock said. "I was a grinder. I fought all aspects of the game because I had to achieve. I had to stretch my talent as far as I could. I think if I'd learned to relax and just play I might have done things a little better."

Norm Sherry was a Dodger backup catcher for three full seasons before joining the Mets for his final year in the big leagues in 1963. He was the brother of Dodger pitcher Larry Sherry, the hero of the 1959 World Series, and the two often formed a battery. "It was exciting to get back there," Norm said. "We used to play catch in the alley or on the playground and here we are playing in the major leagues. You put a lot of pressure on yourself when you're playing, and if you don't do well, it gets to you. Then you compound it because you think about it the next day and put yourself in a deep slump. After I quit playing, I learned to take it one day at a time. That's all you have to worry about. If you can't do it today, you do it tomorrow. I used to preach that to my kids when I managed. Don't worry today about what you did yesterday."

Many former players recalled moments of notoriety that escaped the general public.

- *Larry Miller*: "I was the last pitcher Casey Stengel came out to the mound and removed from a game. Not many people remember that. I wasn't sure myself if there were other people who came out after me, so I found a book on Casey that talked about his last game. If you check the box score of that game, which we lost to the Phillies 5–1, you'll see that I pitched to three batters in the seventh. Casey came out and replaced me with Dennis Musgraves. Dennis pitched the seventh and eighth and went out for a pinch hitter. Tug McGraw pitched the ninth, but I was the last one he came out to the mound to take out of a game. It's a dubious honor, but if somebody had told me when I was ten years old playing catch in the backyard with my father that someday I would make history as the last pitcher Casey Stengel took out of a game, I would have grabbed it in a second. When you think about all the Hall of Fame pitchers who played for him, to have the distinction of being the final one was fantastic."
- *Gary Kroll*: "I was the last starting pitcher in Shea Stadium before the Beatles appeared there in 1965."
- *Shaun Fitzmaurice*: "Yogi Berra and I signed with the Mets the same day. I also introduced bridge to a lot of guys who went up to the big leagues and introduced it up there. It's a fascinating game and I feel I can take some credit for bringing it to the major leagues."
- *Wayne Graham*, who played with the Mets in 1964, coached Roger Clemens and Andy Pettitte at San Jacinto Junior College. Graham later won the College World Series title with Rice University in 2003.
- *Bill Denehy*: "Tom Seaver and I shared the same rookie trading card." Denehy still carries the card in his wallet. Denehy also coached Clemens with the New Britain Red Sox and Jeff Bagwell at the University of Hartford.
- *Bob (Lefty) Miller* beat the Yankees in his rookie year of 1953, just eleven days after his eighteenth birthday. "I was the youngest pitcher ever to beat the Yankees. Remember, they were world champions that year. It was one of the most exciting things in my life at that time."
- *Jack DiLauro*: "When I was drafted by the Astros, I was the first player ever pulled out of a computer. They put every available left hander in professional baseball, about three hundred of them, into the computer. My name popped out first, so they drafted me." He laughed. "And then at the end of the year they blew the computer up." DiLauro also faced Steve Garvey in the latter's first major league at bat and struck him out.
- *Don Zimmer* was the last Cincinnati Red to wear number 14 before it was given to Pete Rose.
- *Norm Sherry* was the last major leaguer to hit a home run in the Los Angeles Coliseum. He connected on September 20, 1961 against the Cubs.
- After Harvey Haddix pitched 12 perfect innings against the Milwaukee Braves on May 26, 1959, former Met *Felix Mantilla* broke the string, reaching on an error by third baseman Don Hoak. It was also the first major league game for *Joe Christopher*.
- In 1962, the Telstar satellite, which allowed television images to be transmitted between continents, was placed in orbit. On July 23, during the first exchange of live programming between the United States and Europe, a game between the Phillies and the Cubs was broadcast overseas. The first pitch seen in Europe was delivered by *Cal Koonce*.
- *Rob Gardner* surrendered one of Bob Uecker's 14 major league home runs.
- *Don Shaw* was the first Met pitcher to be driven the Shea Stadium mound in a golf cart.

- *Clem Labine* was one of the worst hitting pitchers of his era, with a career average of .075. In 1955, Labine had only three hits in 31 at bats. All three were home runs.
- *Larry Miller*: "During my career, I was close to greatness. My locker was right next to Sandy Koufax's when I was with the Dodgers. When I was with the Mets, it was right next to Nolan Ryan and Tom Seaver. I was always close to greatness."

In his personal life, Miller has also been close to greatness. After appearing in 28 Met games, with a 1-4 record, in 1965, Miller pitched only four games in 1966, then began a long sojourn in the minor leagues. He spent a number of years in Phoenix, where he eventually settled. During his minor league career, Miller worked with another veteran minor leaguer, Pete Jernigan, to attempt to set up a medical insurance plan for minor leaguers.

The defining episode of Miller's life involved his daughter, Kathy, who was an Honor Society Student and an excellent runner and swimmer. When Kathy was 13, she was hit by a car. "She was in a coma for three months," Miller said, "and when she came out, she was an absolute vegetable. She couldn't walk, she couldn't talk, and she weighed 50 pounds, which was half her normal weight." When Kathy emerged from her coma, the doctors recommended that she be placed in an institution, but Miller was determined to do whatever he could to bring his daughter back.

"We went to the pool every day," Miller said. "We would walk around and I would hold her, and then finally, she took her first steps. Then she said her first word — mama. Every time we rejoiced in her recovery, the doctors would say, 'She might level off at any place. Don't get too excited.'" Against all odds, Kathy continued to make progress, until one day, her father asked her what she wanted to do. Kathy said she wanted to run again.

Miller took Kathy to the track, and the first time she ran, she covered about sixty feet. "She didn't run," Miller said. "She just took a step and dragged her right leg, which had been broken, and took another step and dragged her leg. After a week or two we were up to 100 feet, then 200 feet." As the distance increased, the Millers decided that Kathy would aim toward a ten kilometer run.

"We were among several thousand runners," Miller said, "and we were one of the last to finish, but we finished the whole damn thing, running and walking." The story was covered by *The Arizona Republican* and picked up by the wire services. It found its way into an English newspaper, where it was spotted by an organization called The Victorian Sporting Club. Each year, The Sporting Club presented an award to the most courageous athlete in the world, and suggested to Miller that Kathy be nominated. "We found out," said Miller, "that she was one of 820 nominees from 120 different countries. Many were internationally renowned professional and amateur athletes. We thought we'd never hear from them, but we got a call saying she was one of twelve finalists. We were flown to London for the presentation, but the winner's name was kept secret until that night. The ceremony was held at the Royal Guild Hall, and Prince Michael of Kent was the master of ceremonies. Elton John was there." Kathy Miller won. "The award goes back to 1936," Miller said, "and some of the past winners were Dizzy Dean, Mickey Mantle, Monty Stratton and Babe Zaharias."

Kathy now lives in Santa Fe, New Mexico. "Her functional IQ has been reduced because of the nature of the accident," her father said, "but the creative part hasn't suffered." She takes art classes and does flower arrangements. Miller collaborated on a book about the experience, which was turned into a television movie called *The Miracle of Kathy Miller*, starring a 17-year-old actress named Helen Hunt. "It was her first starring role," Miller said, "and everybody said she was going to be the next Meryl Streep. She didn't turn out bad."

The inspirational story of Kathy Miller is a good way to end a chapter of Met memories. Like Kathy Miller, the Mets provided inspiration to those who thought they faced a hopeless task. They went from laughingstocks to word champions in a tale too improbable for fiction. In eight years, the Mets went from rags to riches.

Bibliography

Allen, Maury. *You Could Look It Up: The Life of Casey Stengel*. New York: Times Books, 1979.

Angell, Roger. *The Summer Game*. New York: Viking, 1972.

Clendenon, Donn. *Miracle in New York*. Sioux Falls, SD: Pennmarch, 1999.

Durocher, Leo, with Ed Linn. *Nice Guys Finish Last*. New York: Simon and Schuster, 1975.

Kahn, Roger. *The Boys of Summer*. New York: Harper and Row, 1971.

Koppett, Leonard. *The New York Mets: The Whole Story*. New York: Macmillan, 1970.

Lang, Jack, and Simon, Peter. *The New York Mets: 25 Years of Baseball Magic*. New York: Henry Holt, 1986.

Mitchell, Jerry. *The Amazing Mets*. New York: Grossett and Dunlap, 1964.

Piersall, Jimmy, with Richard Whittingham. *The Truth Hurts*. Chicago: Contemporary Books, 1984.

Schecter, Leonard. *Once Upon the Polo Grounds*. New York: Dial, 1970.

Newspapers

Meriden Record Journal 1965
New York Daily News, 1960–1969
New York Newsday 1960–1969
New York Post, 1960–1969
New York Times, 1959–1969

Periodicals

The Sporting News
Sports Illustrated

Index